I0729677

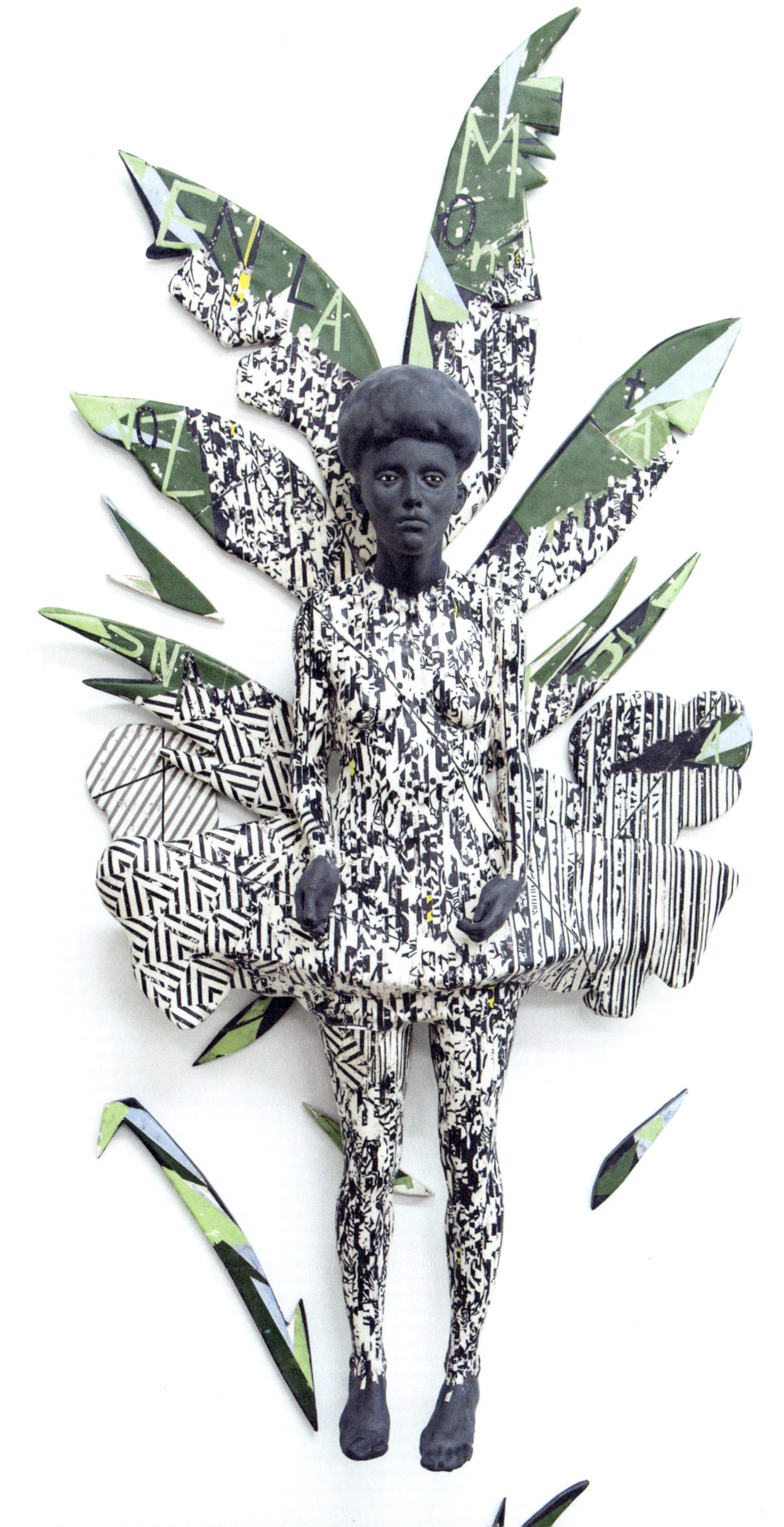
ME
ON
EN LA
VOZ
A
EN
N

(*previous page*) **Cristina Córdova,** *A la montaña.* Courtesy of the artist.

(*opposite*) **Cristina Córdova,** *Que mamen.* Courtesy of the artist.

Quarto.com

© 2022 Quarto Publishing Group USA Inc.
Text and Illustrations © 2022 Cristina Córdova
Photography © Quarto Publishing Group USA Inc.

First Published in 2022 by Quarry Books,
an imprint of The Quarto Group,
100 Cummings Center, Suite 265-D, Beverly, MA 01915, USA.
T (978) 282-9590 F (978) 283-2742

EEA Representation, WTS Tax d.o.o.,
Žanova ulica 3, 4000 Kranj, Slovenia.
www.wts-tax.si

All rights reserved. No part of this book may be reproduced in any form without written permission of the copyright owners. All images in this book have been reproduced with the knowledge and prior consent of the artists concerned, and no responsibility is accepted by producer, publisher, or printer for any infringement of copyright or otherwise, arising from the contents of this publication. Every effort has been made to ensure that credits accurately comply with information supplied. We apologize for any inaccuracies that may have occurred and will resolve inaccurate or missing information in a subsequent reprinting of the book.

Quarry Books titles are also available at discount for retail, wholesale, promotional, and bulk purchase. For details, contact the Special Sales Manager by email at specialsales@quarto.com or by mail at The Quarto Group, Attn: Special Sales Manager, 100 Cummings Center, Suite 265-D, Beverly, MA 01915, USA.

10 9 8 7 6

ISBN: 978-0-7603-7309-5

Digital edition published in 2022
eISBN: 978-0-7603-7310-1

Library of Congress Cataloging-in-Publication Data

Córdova, Cristina, 1976- author.
Mastering sculpture : the figure in clay : a guide to capturing the human form for ceramic artists
ISBN 9780760373095 (board) | ISBN 9780760373101 (ebook)
1. Modelling—Technique. 2. Figure sculpture—Technique.
LCC NB1180 .C67 2022 | DDC 730.28--dc23

LCCN 2021046561

Design and page layout: Laura Shaw Design
Front Cover Images: Jack Sorokin Photography (top, bottom left, and bottom right) and Paloma Soto (bottom middle).
Back Cover Image: Lydia Bittner-Baird
Photography: Except when noted in the image captions, photos are courtesy of:
Alfred Ceramic Art Museum: 8
Audrey Bell: 175, 179
Cristina Córdova: 31, 32, 36, 88, 89, 112, 115, 140, 161, 181-187
Jack Sorokin: 4, 16, 19, 21, 22, 29, 40, 42, 59, 62, 114, 138, 143-145, 154
Lucy Plato: 96, 189
Noah Zeck: 27, 46-47, 88
Palomo Soto: 33, 35, 55-57, 60, 61, 63, 64-70, 76, 77, 78, 80, 81, 82-84, 87, 90, 91, 98-109, 111, 113, 116, 127-130, 131, 132, 133, 141, 151
Penland School of Craft: 50, 124
Robin Dreyer: 74
Shutterstock: 10-12, 44, 147, 148, 150
Steve Mann: 152

Printed in Guangdong, China TT052025

MASTERING SCULPTURE

THE FIGURE IN CLAY

A Guide to Capturing the Human Form for Ceramic Artists

Cristina Córdova

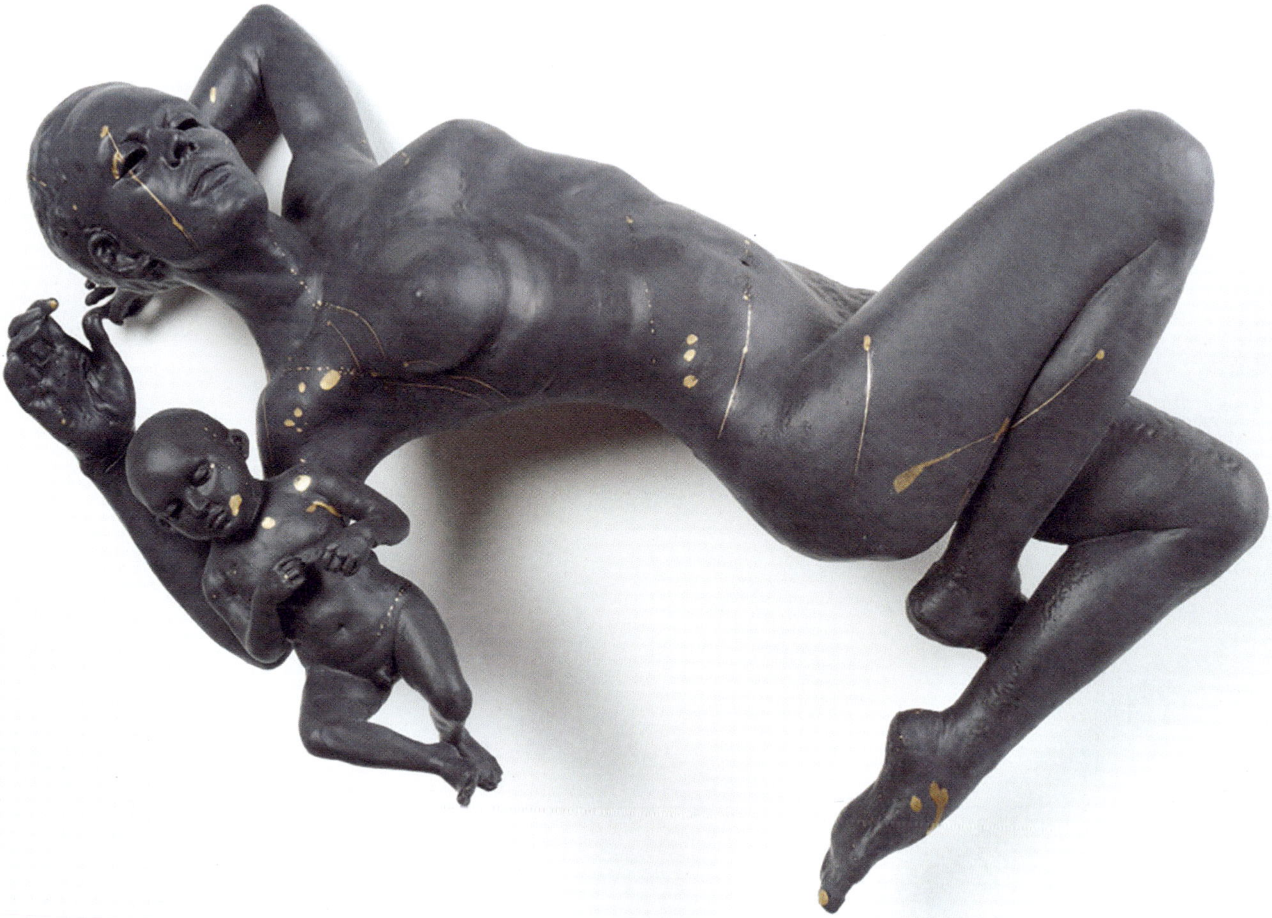

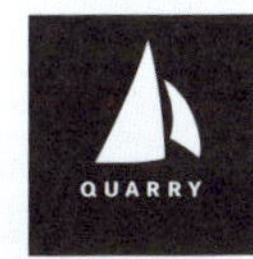

QUARRY

CONTENTS

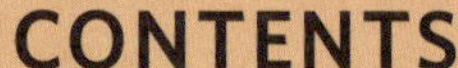

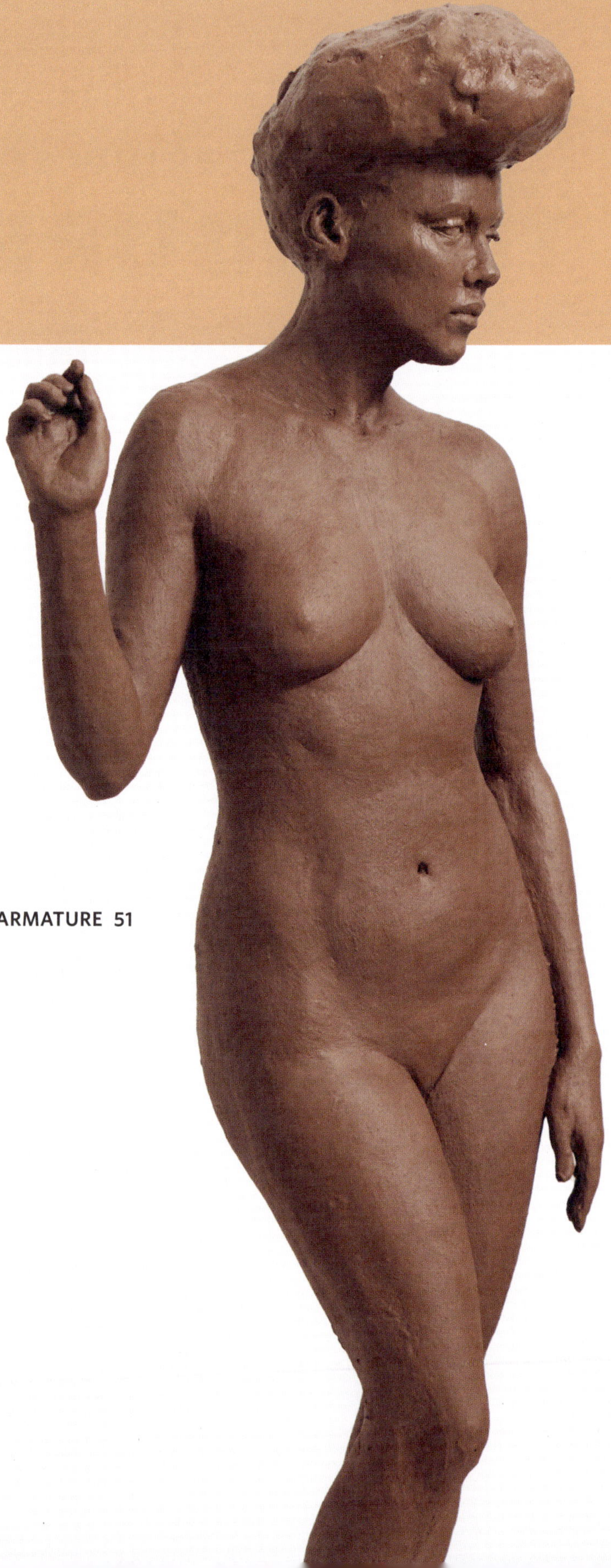

FOREWORD
On Mastery and Leadership

I BEGAN MY CAREER as a young artist working in clay in the seventies. The field was nascent even though the history of the medium was ancient. Contemporary ceramics was dominated by the vessel on the East Coast whereas figural ceramics was prominent on the West Coast. Studio craft provided an entry for Post-War artists and the Baby Boomer generation through independent, entrepreneurial models for their creative practices. I founded my first studio and gallery in partnership with other women artists, all of us working from a place of personal devotion to the medium of clay.

Opportunities to learn were based only in traditional academic settings or community workshops, while inspiration came from print. Books and magazines featured images of seminal works by young artists who later became renowned masters, and these images became burned into our minds, alongside groundbreaking photos of civil rights protests and space exploration.

In and out of ceramics, feminism and identity became both subject and content for artists whose figural and narrative works provided a platform for self-expression. The Guerilla Girls called out gender-based disparities with politically charged posters that began, and continue, to fuel institutional change. Linda Nochlin's pivotal 1971 *ARTnews* essay "Why Have There Been No Great Women Artists?" questioned the exclusion of women from art history and pointed the finger at the authorship of the canon. Through this period, leading ceramic artists Betty Woodman and Ruth Duckworth pushed past the vessel into sculpture and Viola Frey produced monumental figures. Beatrice Wood and Coille Hooven used the figure to both poke fun at gendered norms and deliver social commentary. Judy Chicago's epic multimedia *The Dinner Party* involved 129 people in a collaborative production that celebrated and commemorated 1,038 women throughout history via an installation of thirty-nine ceramic place settings, textiles, and site activations.

By the end of the nineties, when Cristina Córdova began her career, young artists were freer to explore and move between established categories and produce work without many of the restrictions imposed on their predecessors. Women were gaining positions of leadership as educators and artists; likewise, they were offered more exhibition opportunities in galleries and museums. Popular movements rise and fade, and by the 2000s, figural work began its rise again, delivering personal narratives from diverse perspectives to expanding audiences. From Woodman's 2006 solo show at the Metropolitan Museum of Art through to Simone Leigh's historic representation of the United States at the 2022 Venice Biennale, there are still many firsts happening in ceramics and many gender and race-based barriers being broken.

Of course, the changing history of clay and ceramics, and the contemporary social impact of figuration is larger than what we've touched on here. However, a good cross-section of this history is highlighted throughout *The Figure in Clay*, as Cristina has filled these pages with a beautiful combination of instruction and inspiration. Throughout her career, I've had the privilege to work with Cristina and so many other artists featured in this book. I've watched them individually and collectively raise the bar and push beyond the status quo. I've seen their works inspire one another, feed exploration through teaching, join forces to celebrate triumphs of technical challenge, and collaborate in a community known for mutual support. Cristina is widely recognized through major grants and exhibitions and, now at mid-career, her work is seen in context with other sculptors who are current leaders in the art field.

Mastery and leadership are not always synonymous, but Cristina possesses both. What makes an artist both a master of her medium and a leader in her field? Dedication to the studio, of course, but also a spirit of generosity. Cristina is so influential today because of her powerful sculptures, certainly, but also because she has given very deeply as an educator. The result is a strengthening of the figure in clay that is felt throughout the field. By dedicating the time to document her process, share it through teaching, and now through this book, she provides a path for others to follow, to learn from, and to be inspired by.

The Figure in Clay is both a summary of many years of dedication and hard work and a detailed step-by-step guide to aligning thought, eye, and hand. It is very clear why her teaching methods continue to be so influential in the lives and careers of a new generation of figurative sculptors. This book, like the volumes that influenced a generation forty years ago, will continue to influence the field for generations to come.

—LESLIE FERRIN
Founder and Director, Ferrin Contemporary,
North Adams, Massachusetts
www.ferrincontemporary.com

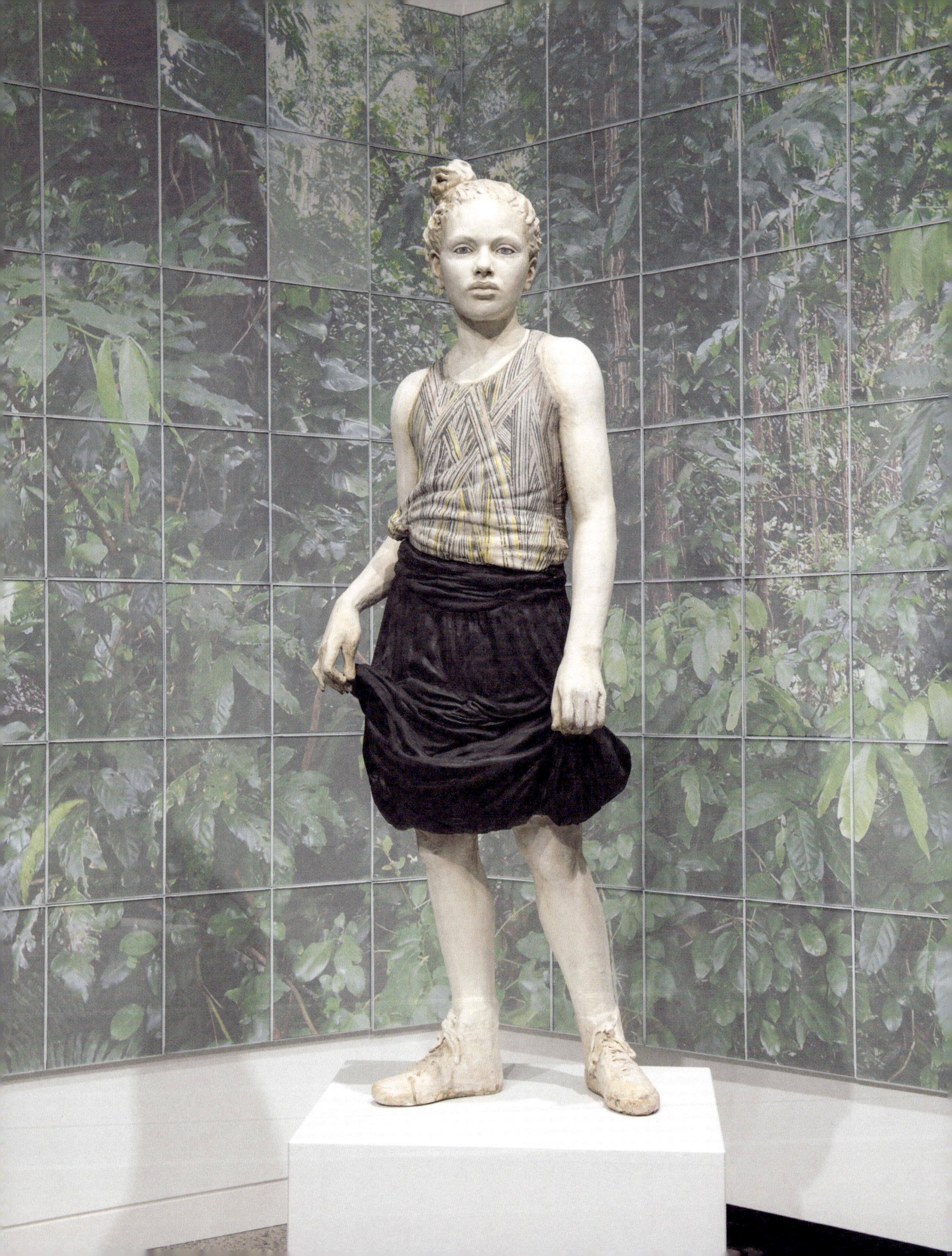

INTRODUCTION

WHAT I SHARE with you in this book is the accumulated technical insight gathered from my journey to the crossroads of two great artistic traditions. The first is ceramics, that incredible technology that includes everything from the humblest pottery to the most exquisite statuette. The second tradition is figurative modeling, historically practiced by sculpting solid forms, which would then be molded and cast.

Both ceramics and figurative sculpting are among the most ancient and universal of all human cultural expressions. The discovery of the space between these two worlds offered me an exciting, fertile landscape from which to create fireable, representational compositions. My sculpture methods draw on the observational methodologies of traditional modeling and combine them with the immediacy and expressive potential of clay.

This space between the figurative and ceramic traditions is not bound by either the rigor of naturalism or the demands of functionality, and offers innumerable points of entry for you to create without inhibitions. In this book, you will learn observational strategies and anatomical insights that will help you create figurative forms of any style, be it representational or abstract. You will also learn how to build hollow sculptures in wet clay, expanding the boundaries of traditional ceramics.

HOW TO USE THIS BOOK

There is no wrong way to engage with this book, but if you would like to follow the step-by-step instructions to build a full, 25 inch (64 cm) figure, first start by printing out the photographic references found in Appendix A. These are pictures of our model from the four cardinal views: front, back, left, and right. Follow the enlargement instructions on the photos to print them to the right size, then pin them up on your studio wall at approximately the same height as your work surface.

It is important to understand that these pictures are an exact, one-to-one representation of the figure you will be sculpting in clay. You will take direct measurements with calipers from the photographs and transfer them to your sculpture, and you will be looking back and forth from sculpture to photographs at every stage of the process. The cardinal views are your anchors, while the intermediate views, found in Appendix B, simply give you more information as you begin refining your emerging figure from all angles.

Next, print the templates found in Appendix C, also following the enlargement instructions to make them the proper size. You will use these templates by laying the paper onto your clay slabs, cutting around the perimeter, and transferring any reference marks from the template

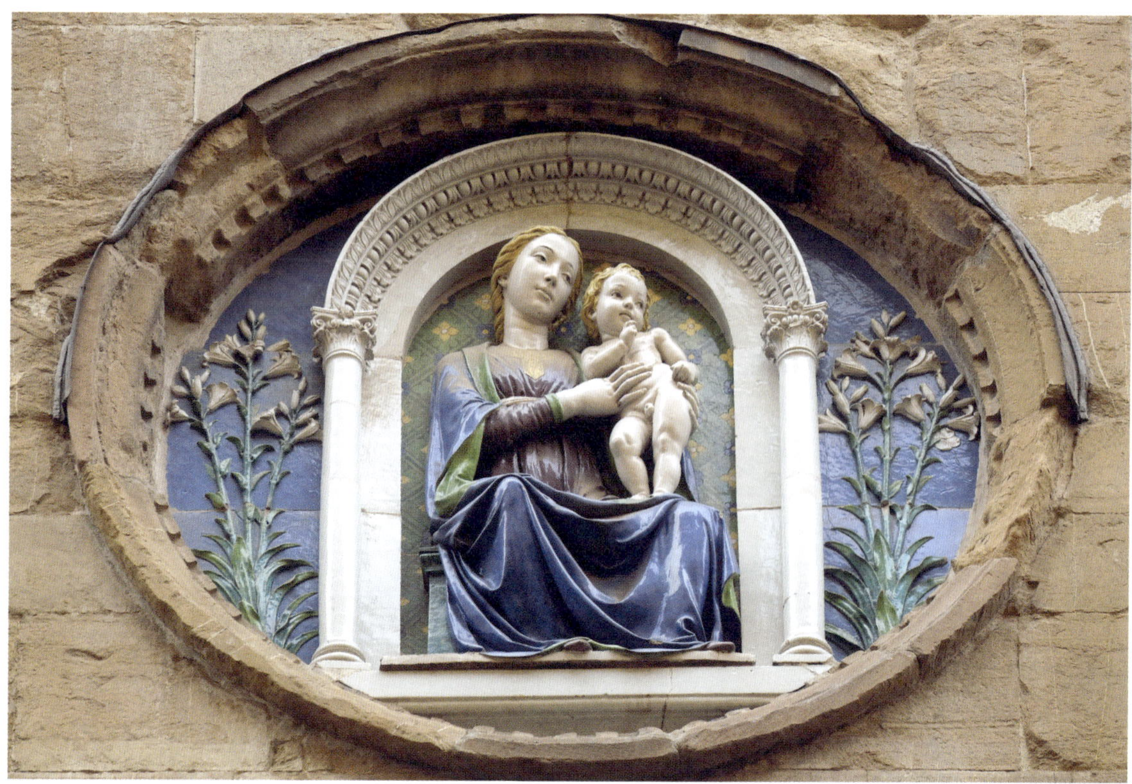

Medallion with Virgin Mary and child by Luca della Robbia, Florence, Italy, glazed terra-cotta.

to the clay. Following the instructions, you will turn these slabs into hollow forms, the starting points for the major volumes of the body, then assemble them and refine them through successive rounds of sculpting.

The rest of the book, the historical and personal perspectives on figurative sculpture, as well as the artist galleries and interviews, offer new vistas to expand your sense of creative possibilities within this practice and to deepen your understanding of the boundless technical and conceptual possibilities in this field. I hope you find it as rich, challenging, and satisfying as I have!

MY STORY

I have memories of my childhood in Puerto Rico, attending church and looking up at the sculptures of angels and saints surrounding the congregation. They looked down with faces full of ecstasy, torment, and serenity—a biblical range of emotion that simmered below the surface of life. In those sacred spaces, I began to understand how every gesture and every set of upward-cast eyes could tell a story.

In the context of Catholicism, introduced to Puerto Rico while under Spanish rule, figures play a key role in the act of worship. They offer cues to elicit heightened emotional states, orienting our attention to the transcendence and pathos at the core of the Catholic doctrine. For me, they were magnificent and otherworldly, and it would have never occurred to my younger self that they were not divinely created. Building layers of detail into my own pieces, I am often amazed at the sentient qualities that begin to ensue from the gradual reorganization of this telluric material. This feeling echoes my childhood sense of disbelief around the possibility of inciting the illusion of life through a creative practice.

I also practiced dance and movement from an early age, which is another big childhood connection to figurative language. The insight into the mechanics of movement and the expressive potential of choreographed bodies grounds me to this day in the figurative vernacular. This language works through the sociocultural coding we recognize, as well as through the endless somatic expressions that fall just outside what is readily acknowledged, opening a vast field of possibilities that appeal to our different mechanisms of understanding the corporeal, from the conventional and conscious, to the latent and subliminal. All our stories are encoded there, in the language of the body.

My devotion to the figure found a powerful mechanism for expression when I was formally introduced to clay by the Puerto Rican ceramic artist and architect, Jaime Suárez, during my third year of studies at the University of Puerto Rico. Suárez's influence on the contemporary ceramics' movement cannot be overstated. As an architect, his groundbreaking vision and implementation of clay to express ideas of time and space at impressive scales proved profoundly inspiring. Through the work executed during that semester, I began to understand clay as a material that could capture my vital energy through touch.

Through my trajectory down the path of figurative ceramics, I began to make connections between the figurative sculpture I had experienced in the context of spirituality and my own sculpture oriented towards a secular viewer. I gradually understood how the deep conceptual ties I had cultivated with devotional figures, both in church and in my childhood home brimming with my mother's collection of saints and virgins, were present in my artistic practice. My connection with devotional objects allowed me to recognize that my sculptural work plays on a similar process by seeking to orchestrate an emotional experience through the careful selection of the gesture, scale, and

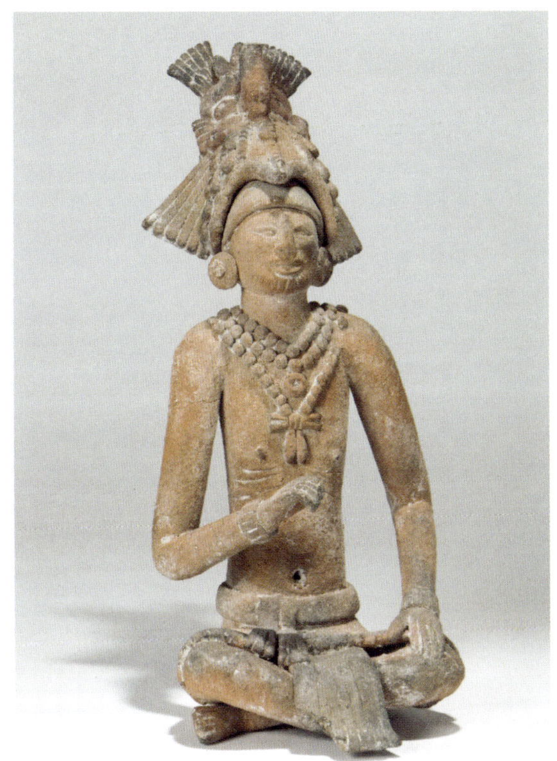

Mayan Jaina king classical period clay figure (c. 1100 CE).

surface comprising a figure, appealing to our innate human disposition to connect with the self-referential.

I believe clay has a voice and a disposition. In my practice, the greatest synergy between material and concept is the result of a careful negotiation between traditional hand building approaches, guided by observational systems drawn from the world of naturalistic rendering.

THE FIGURE THROUGHOUT HISTORY

As human beings, we are primed to react to our reflection. You connect with a figure, identify with it, and through that phenomenon tap into a sense of a shared story.

Within the vast world of artistic figuration, clay has been used to form representational sculptures throughout history. From the Neolithic periods in Eurasia and Africa to Pre-Columbian indigenous communities in the

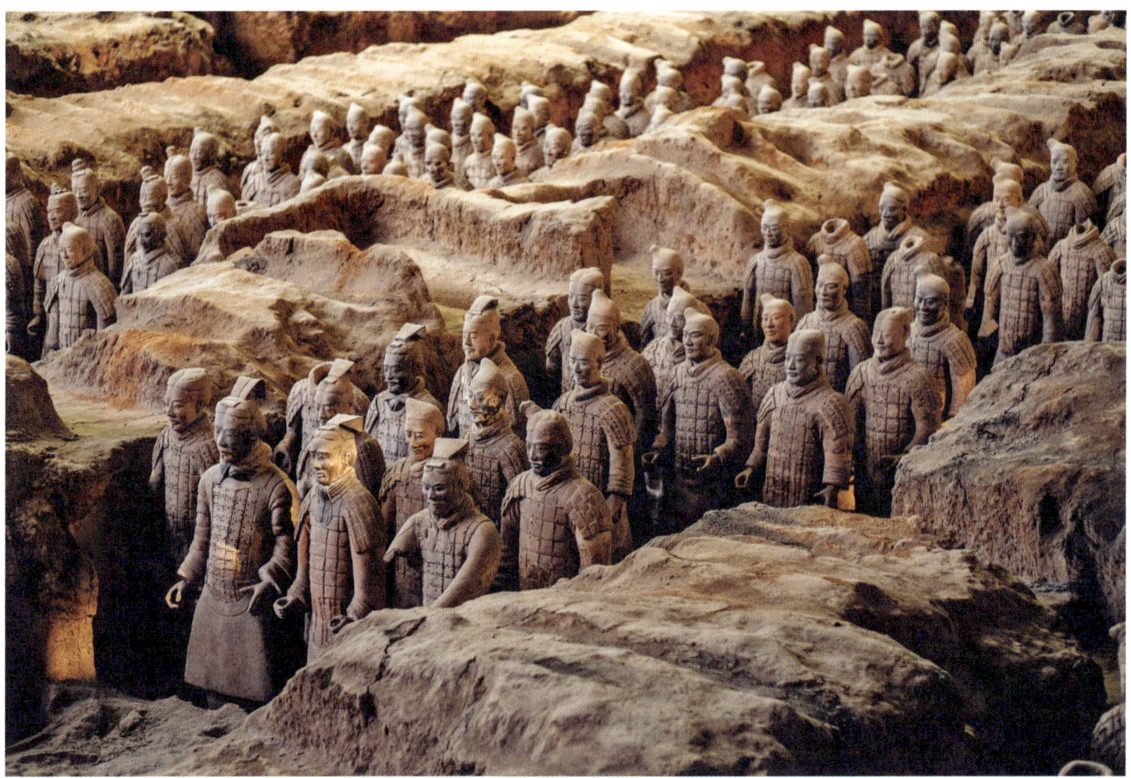

Terra-cotta army of Qin Shi Huang, who reigned in China from 221 BCE to 210 BCE.

Caribbean and the Americas, clay has served as a means to create anthropomorphic objects that speak to the longings, fears, and beliefs of a community. Examples such as the Nok terra-cotta figures from Nigeria (1500 BCE–500 CE) or the elaborate Jaina terra-cotta sculpture (300–1200 CE) from present-day Mexico exquisitely embody a full range of impressions from daily life. In the case of the Jaina sculpture, used primarily as funerary accompaniments and created in a naturalistic style, the figures are an anthropological treasure, offering a view into the physicality, dress, and customs of the late Classic Maya civilization.

Amidst the myriad of extraordinary representational clay objects held within the annals of history across different cultures, let's take a brief stop along the way at a few objects and periods that have deeply captivated me. First, there's the terra-cotta army of Qin Shi Huang, the first Emperor of China, created to accompany him in the afterlife (210–209 BCE). Comprising more than 6,000 life-sized warriors, the scope of this effort, driven by the unique beliefs of the period, still amazes me.

Across the world, the magnificent Ife terra-cotta busts from Nigeria (1000–1400 CE) offer a highly evolved and realistic record of the time, complete with detailed body ornamentation that transports us into this remote African kingdom. They add so much to our knowledge of the rich landscape of tribal renderings throughout the continent.

Shifting our focus to Europe, let's take a look at the use of clay throughout the Italian Renaissance. During this time, the use of terra-cotta by artists gained increasingly more importance, which lead to its full revival during the 15th century. In one form or another, clay played a role in the studio practice of most sculptors. One of

THEMES IN FIGURATIVE SCULPTURE

When surveying the vast realm of figurative sculpture, one notices two main categories of expression that emerge and repeat across times and cultures. Most figurative sculpture is either symbolic, offering a means to metaphorically connect with experiences and concepts through a distillation of the human form, or it is documentary, presenting figurative renderings that serve as chronicles, embodying more literal depictions of reality. And sometimes, compositions can combine elements of both. Some examples include:

- Shamanistic or talismanic figures

- Decorative figures

- Mythological or religious figures

- Humanistic figures driven by anthropocentric ideals

- Political/commemorative figures

- Portrait/representational figures

- Funerary figures

The two themes from this list that resonate in my own work are mythological/religious depictions and portrait renderings. Having grown up immersed in a devotional culture with a strong allegiance to Catholic saints, I see votive statues as distillations of ideas— miniature vehicles through which devotees can summon a sense of presence. This type of composition draws from reality but is neither specific nor absolute; it exists in an archetypal, symbolic realm. My second drive is to use the figure as a record of transcribed reality. In these compositions, I am more closely adhering to naturalism and looking to capture likeness, often combining the modeled and glazed object with photographic backgrounds to create an imaginary dialogue sourced from reality.

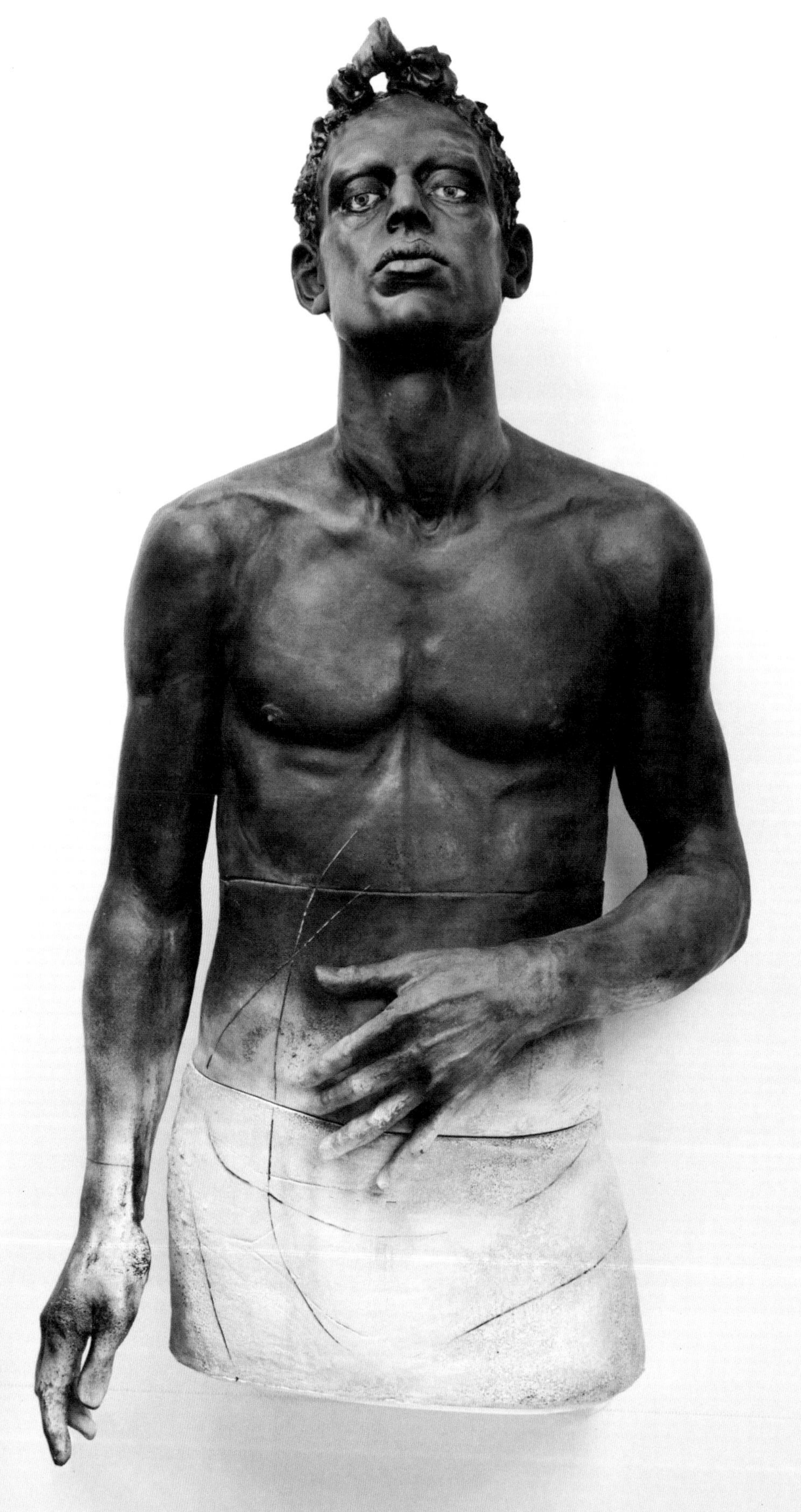

its key roles was to help articulate ideas and create models or prototypes that would inform works in bronze, marble, or stone. Amidst all the highly evolved art of the period, it is these rough, ephemeral objects that ignite my imagination. Though fragile and modest in size, many of these artifacts summon the urgent energy underlying the invocation of ideas. They offer dynamic versions of monumental compositions that were ultimately rendered in much more controlled and conventional manners with sterner materials. Michelangelo's contorting terra-cotta models of Hercules and a slave, and Giambologna's sketch of a river god, offer examples of this practice of creating bozzetti to explore possibilities and inform their creative practice. Later, during the neoclassical period, Antonio Canova would continue the wide use of gestural and lively clay sketches to speak to the ideas of the sublime and heroic.

In addition to these maquettes and standing apart from the bevy of sculptural artists of the Italian Renaissance, Luca della Robbia's figurative terra-cotta sculpture broke new ground in the implementation of ceramics. Through technological discoveries involving the firing of tin- and lead-glazed terra-cotta to higher temperatures, the objects became stable and long-lasting. They were also covered with glossy, vivid surfaces. At times emulating marble, his pieces, and later those of other family members, revolutionized the potential of this medium to convey the sculptural ideals of the time, specifically in the context of religious iconography.

THE FIGURE IN CLAY TODAY

The last twenty years have seen great advances in the field of contemporary figurative ceramics as methods and techniques have continued to evolve. There are now both a myriad of entry points into the practice and a dizzying number of sculptors worth investigating. Nonetheless, I would like to point out a few giants who broke ground both technically and conceptually, adding diversity and dynamism to our field.

Starting in the 1970s and 1980s, artists like Robert Arneson, Viola Frey, Stephen de Staebler, Akio Takamori, Jean Pierre Laroque, George Jeanclos, and Patti Warashina began utilizing the language of the body as a way to articulate powerful commentaries through satire and pathos. In the realm of naturalism, Judy Fox, Doug Jeck, Dirk Staschke, and Tip Toland pioneered the creation of compelling, hyper-detailed, and emotionally charged compositions. These days there are too many extraordinary artists to point to, but Beth Cavener, Simone Leigh, Matt Wedel, En Iwamura, and Vanessa Beecroft are creating seminal, extraordinary work that uses the language of representation in clay to attest to their unique places within our shared human experience. I encourage you to research all the above and more whenever you are in need of inspiration.

In this book, I hope that by guiding you through my process you will discover for yourself how rich and dynamic working with the human figure can be.

Cristina Córdova, *Adentro*. Courtesy of the artist.

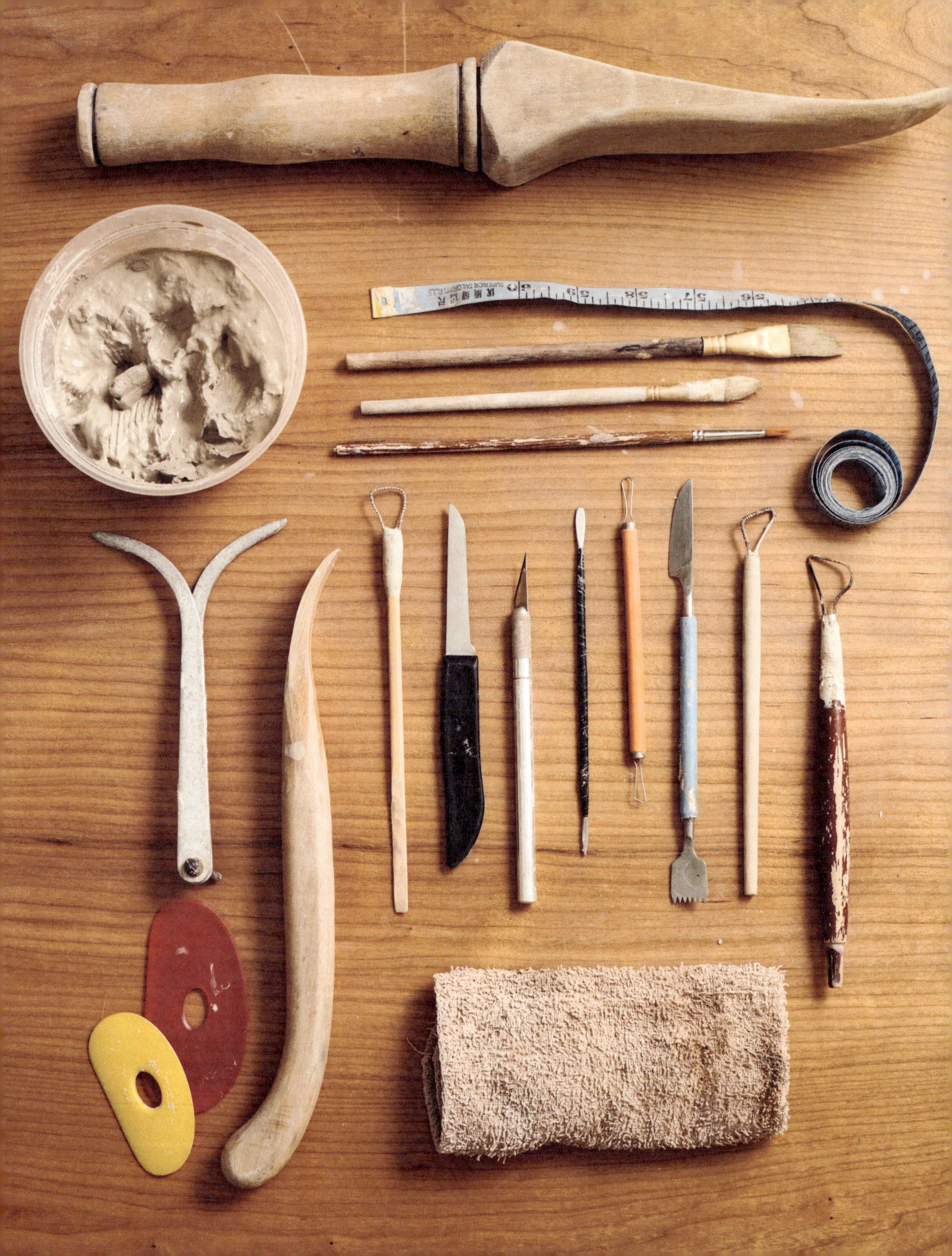

● **1**

PREPARATION

SCULPTING IN CLAY is delightfully simple. It can be done without a specialized space or elaborate tools. All you truly need are clay, water, and some inspiration. That said, understanding how to prepare your workspace to both safeguard your health and optimize your creative output will help you nourish an effective studio practice. By familiarizing yourself with tools and equipment related to ceramic sculpture and then practicing your technique, you will learn to unlock the potential of this wonderful material.

To me, a studio is successful when it is safe, environmentally aware, and streamlined to fit your needs. In this chapter, I will explore what it means to cultivate a studio environment that frees you to create meaningful work.

STUDIO SETUP

After years of working on sculptural ceramics, I feel there are several key considerations that ensure the safest, most productive time in the studio. In this section, we will not only address the tools and equipment I use, but also important considerations like lighting, work surfaces, and safety.

SAFETY IN THE STUDIO

It is important to work in a space that has good air quality and proper ventilation, particularly with respect to kilns and glaze mixing. My kilns are on the covered porch that wraps around my studio, so fumes and gases are dispersed and do not enter the work area. If the kiln you will be using is located indoors, there are several downdraft and updraft kiln vent systems that you can purchase and hook up to your kiln to keep off-gassing chemical compounds out of your workspace—and lungs.

Although I do not mix my own clay, I routinely mix slip and glazes. When measuring and combining the dry materials that go into my glazes and slips, I work outdoors in my spray booth while wearing a respirator. I keep my respirator on until the glaze is hydrated and thoroughly integrated. The spray booth offers a contained space with good light and an exhaust system to move the particles away as I work.

Inside the studio, I do not have any special ventilation other than a gentle cross draft from open windows and doors during the warmer months. To keep dust down, I try to tidy the floor after each sculpting session with a wet rag and a dustpan. Cleaning scraps while they are still wet helps to contain the dust that ensues when clay dries and becomes pulverized.

Periodically I will do a deep cleaning. First, I move through the studio, picking up large scraps of clay with my wet rag. Next, I use a hose to pour water onto my concrete floor and then use a squeegee to push that water into a trap with a drain at the center of the workspace. If your workspace has no clay trap, you can achieve the same results with a wet/dry vacuum. Mopping takes more time but is also a good option.

Sweeping is best avoided as it is an easy way to make minute silica particles airborne and compromise your workspace. Unless I am using some sort of sweeping compound, which helps to capture the clay and dust particles, I do not sweep under any circumstances. Long-term exposure to clay dust can have cumulative, irreversible effects. I urge you to bring mindfulness into your studio routine by implementing simple cleaning strategies to keep yourself and everyone who enters your space healthy.

WORK SURFACES

In my studio, I work on either a sculpture stand or one of several rolling tables with sealed plywood tops. All of my work surfaces are easy to clean and move around. I am 5 feet 4 inches [1.6 m], and my 36 inch (91 cm) tables come up to the level of my hips, which works well for me. When sculpting from photographic references that I have taped to my wall at the same height as my sculpture, I use a wooden sculpture stand with a rotating top. Built onto casters so that it can be easily moved into alignment with a particular reference image, my sculpture stand can also be adjusted to come up or down as needed. For larger pieces I use a steel turntable with a circular wooden base.

When looking to purchase a sculpture stand, you will find a wide variety available. These range from basic wooden stands that hold around

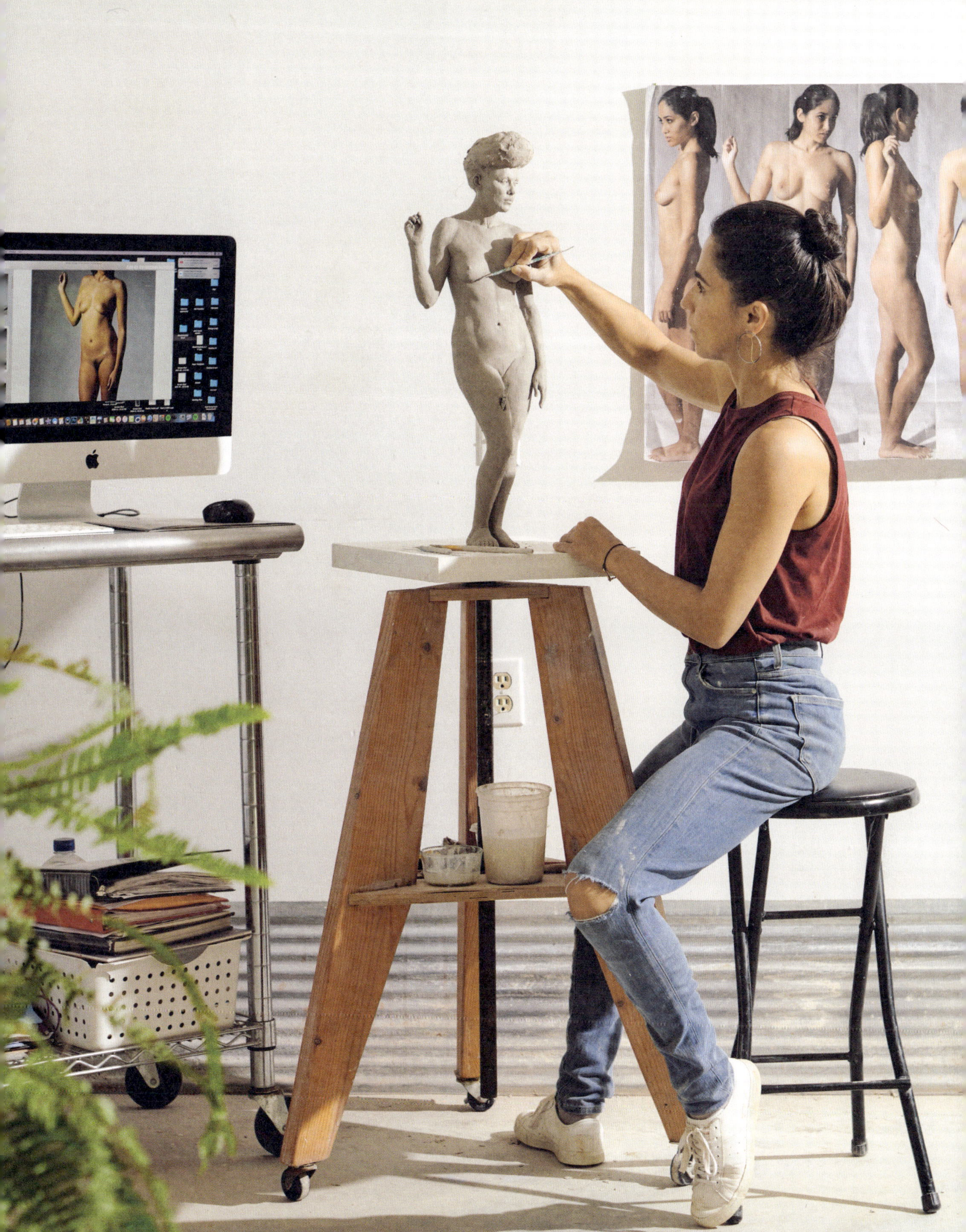

80 pounds (36 kg) to heavy-duty crank stands that can hold upwards of 700 pounds (317 kg). When making your selection, ensure that the stand you choose is rated to hold the weight range you will be sculpting in.

For the purposes of this book, I recommend you work on a rotating surface at the height of your photographic references. You want the top of your sculpting surface to line up with the bottom edge of the images. The idea is to be able to look through the sculpture and onto the references. I find that using an adjustable sculpture stand on casters near a wall offers the most effective way to easily move across your line of photo references, making adjustments and building accuracy as you go. I also like being able to move the piece to different parts of the studio to refresh my perception by viewing the work at a distance or in different light. As an alternative to a sculpture stand, you can place a turntable or banding wheel on top of a table that is located in front of the vertical surface where your photographic references are hung.

LIGHTING

A critical part of the sculptural process, lighting is what allows your eye to discern and articulate forms effectively. Make sure you work in a well-lit space to optimize your ability to understand and develop volumes. I am always blown away by the impact good lighting can make in both helping me understand the ins and outs of a composition and keeping my eyes and brain fresh throughout a long workday.

Diffused natural light is the best option, but adding in some artificial boosts can help create a bright environment that will enable you to sculpt with clarity and ease. I like to use clamp lights with 10 watt daylight LED bulbs to compensate for low or shifting natural lighting in my studio. Sometimes I put these lights on stands, and sometimes I clamp them to ceiling beams.

Note: I try to avoid harsh lights, particularly ones coming from side angles, as these can confuse the eye's ability to decipher forms.

TOOLS

Wood and rods for armature: For the sake of stability, I often make my sculpture base thick, using two 14 x 14 inch (35.6 x 35.6 cm) pieces of plywood glued together. I am using ¼ inch (6 mm)–diameter metal rods to construct a simple armature and lend support to my sculpture during the construction process. By embedding threaded inserts within my wooden base, I make it easy to unscrew and remove the rods without damaging my piece before drying and firing.

Rolling pin: In generating slabs onto which I will trace my templates, I use rolling pins of varying sizes to compress my proto-slabs and roll them out to an even thickness, often with the help of thickness strips.

Thickness strips: Thickness strips are two long pieces of wood of even height. I use them as rails to guide either my wire tool or my rolling pin during the multi-step process of converting a block of fresh clay into slabs of uniform thickness. I have a 1 inch (2.5 cm) set of thickness strips that I place on either side of my block of fresh clay to guide me as I cut slices of clay off my block to send through my slab roller. When I don't have a slab roller at my disposal, I use sets of ⅜ inch or ¼ inch (1 cm or 6 mm) thickness strips to create tracks over which my rolling pin will run as it compresses my proto-slab into a ⅜ inch or ¼ inch (1 cm or 6 mm) slab (my

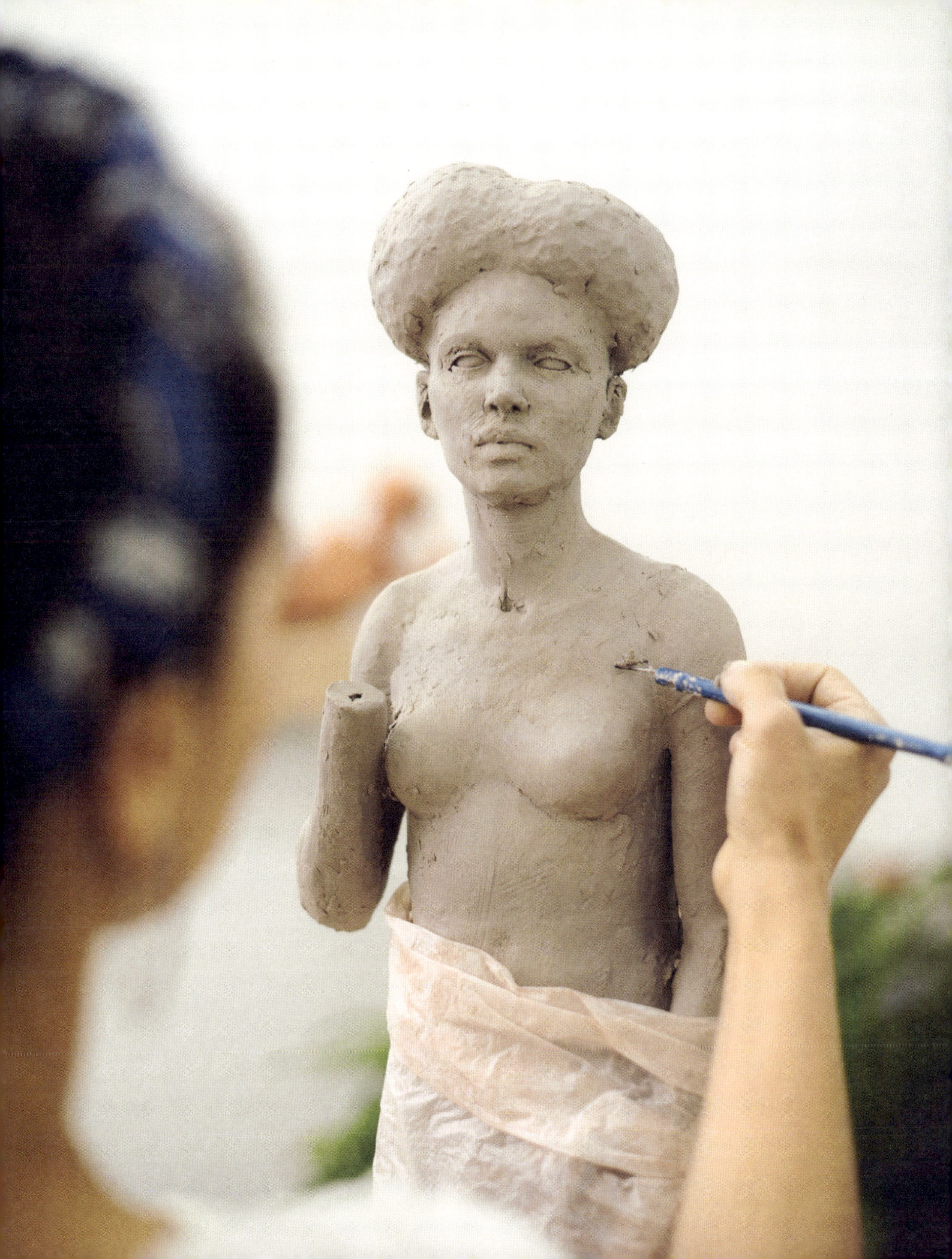

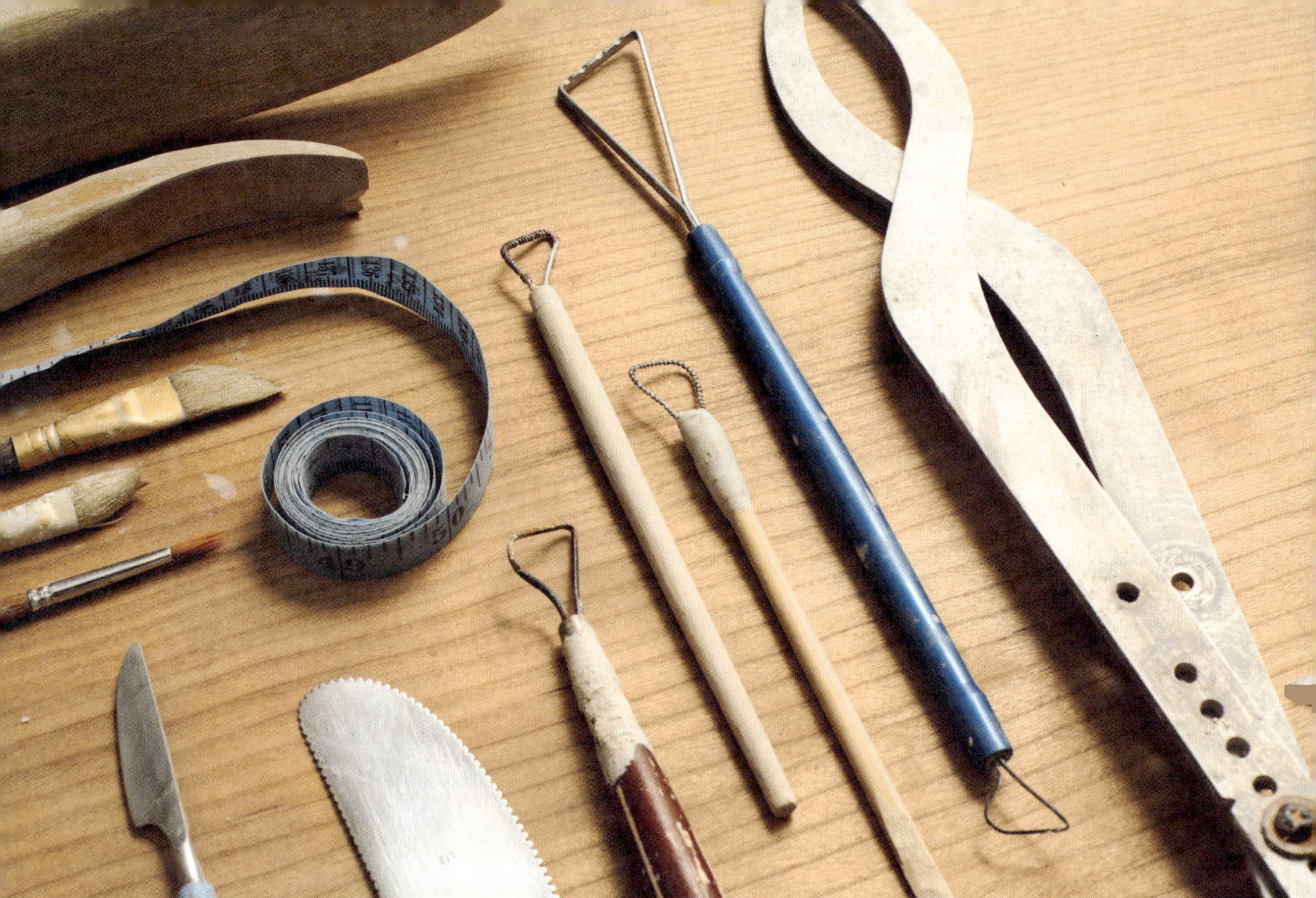

target slab thicknesses for the shapes used in this book and most of my work).

Mirror tile: Having a 12 x 12 inch (30 x 30 cm) mirror available in my studio not only lets me use my own face and body as an occasional figurative reference, but also enables me to observe my sculpture in its mirror image. Looking at my evolving figure through a mirror helps me perceive mistakes and inconsistencies that I do not catch as easily from the perspectives my brain has become accustomed to. The inverted image helps spark new insights around symmetry, rhythm, and balance in the composition as the brain is forced to reset and perceive outside its regular framework.

Clay: When choosing a clay body for figurative ceramics, select one with good sculptural capacities: plastic with a good amount of fine/medium grog. Although I use a number of clay bodies in my practice, my favorite for large-scale works and full figures of any size is Max's White WC-953 Paper Clay from Laguna/Axner. This versatile clay fires gray-stony white in reduction at cone 10, buff-white at cone 5 oxidation, and off-white at cone 04 to cone 2, my preferred firing temperatures. It contains a moderate amount of fine and medium mesh grog as well as paper pulp, which lets you build vertically quickly. It has lots of dry strength and has very little shrinkage (4% to cone 06 and 8% to cone 5). Not all clays will work with this hand building technique, so I recommend testing.

Tip: If you have a good sculpture body you know well you can wedge shredded nylon fibers or toilet paper sheets into part of the clay that will be used for the weight-bearing part of the sculpture to add dry strength and stability as you work up. You can also experiment with adding a small percentage of fine or medium grog to the clay that will be used to build the foundation of your piece.

Wire tool: Your wire cutter tool will enable you to break your block of fresh clay into sections that can be combined into slabs using a rolling pin or pressed on a slab roller to reach our target thickness. I also use it to trim parts of my sculpture that need to be reworked or reset.

Biodegradable plastic: Because I work in a water-based medium, plastic is essential for keeping my pieces workable and controlling moisture throughout a composition. To reduce the environmental impact of plastic waste generated through my practice, I use biodegradable plastic and reuse each piece for as long as possible, washing them and hanging them out to dry on my back porch when they become coated in clay dust.

Shop towels: Thicker than regular paper towels, reusable shop towels are great for preserving the moisture of delicate areas on a sculpture. I run them under a faucet and squeeze them out until they are damp, then I lay them over areas of my sculptures that are prone to rapid drying, such as ears, hands, thin wrists, and other small extremities. I then cover these areas in plastic. I also use damp shop rags under plastic to protect seams of my sculpture that will need to receive new forms when I resume my work after a break. For example, once I have finished building the lower body, I will place moistened shop rags around the top perimeter of the pelvis form where I will later attach the torso.

Calipers (small and large): Calipers enable me to cross-reference the measurements of my sculpture against my reference images and vice versa. I use them to plot bony landmarks, features, and overall measurements onto a sculpture. They also come in handy when checking the width and height of various features, as well as the distance between designated points on my reference photos. When I use my calipers, I remember that I am moving from 2D photographs to a 3D sculpture, and I keep in mind that my reference photos do not account for z-axis displacement, or the measurement that describes depths and projections. It is also important to make sure that the wingnut at the bottom of the calipers is tight enough that the calipers will not slide out of position after having captured a measurement. For the purposes of this book, a simple pair of steel calipers will do, but for scaling up or down from life-size castings, you might consider investing in a pair of proportional calipers.

Seamstress tape: I routinely use seamstress tape to capture the circumference of various points on a human form. When working from a live model, I measure circumference at the top and bottom of each form. For example, for an upper arm, I measure the circumference at the armpit and just above the elbow. Then, when I go to lay out a trapezoid that will roll up into my upper arm cylinder, I know how wide to make the top and bottom of that trapezoid. I tend to make my measurements a little bit less than those that I capture on my model so that I have room to develop the forms with fresh clay once my core form has set. If I am not working at full scale, I can use a conversion ratio to adjust all the measurements that I capture with my seamstress tape and bring them into my target scale. For example, if my model is 5 feet 4 inches (64 inches or 1.6 m) and my target scale is 18 inches (46 cm), I will divide all the original measurements by 3.56, acquired by dividing 64 inches by 18 inches. Once I have rolled up each cylindrical component that will comprise my figurative sculpture, I check its circumference with seamstress tape before compressing my seam.

Sculpture rakes: A sculpture rake is a steel loop tool with a serrated edge that allows you to move clay around in a different way than a straight edge loop tool. This is one of the tools that I use the most to articulate the volumes throughout the figure. My rake helps me tie my forms together visually and create a sense of dynamic flow. Rakes tend to break after a lot of use, but if the wire head pops off your rake you can always use epoxy putty to re-adhere it to its shaft.

Clay modeling eye tool: I use a 7 inch (17.8 cm) plastic eye modeling tool by Philippe Faraut to help me define the eye without flattening the arching surface of the cornea. The concave surface of this tool lets me easily articulate a convex form.

Knife with small scoring tool attached: I love this tool. On one end, the large flat surface of its steel knife allows me to smooth areas on my sculpture or make drawn marks and cuts. The other end functions much like a wire brush— its small, serrated edge helps me score and stitch the ends of slabs as well as small areas of my sculpture that are hard to reach with a serrated rib.

Serrated rib: After cutting out my patterns from slabs of clay, I use scoring tools to score and slip the edges of my clay patterns where they will come together as seams when I assemble the slabs into three-dimensional forms. After I have thoroughly compressed all areas of a seam, I use my serrated rib in a cross-hatching motion over the new seam to integrate the clay from both sides of the new connection and to smooth down the small ridges and valleys created by my fingers during compression. I like using a fine edge serrated rib that has 18 teeth per inch. These toothy ribs are fantastic for unifying, scraping, and shaping clay. Made from high quality stainless steel, these scrapers are flexible.

Mudtools ribs (yellow and red for varying levels of hardness): I use ribs to groom my surface. I can hold my red rib in an arch and run it over a particular muscle to compress, unify, and smooth the surface in one fell swoop. The denser yellow rib is used for more aggressive passes where the clay form might need a bolder adjustment. I also use these when applying underglaze transfers to my surfaces.

Favorite stainless steel tools: These tools have both a straight edge and a curved edge. They help me articulate detail without flattening volumes. I use them to model and finesse facial features, nuances on hands and feet, creases where components meet, etc.

X-ACTO knife: I use a fresh X-ACTO knife over a cutting mat to prepare reference images that I will work from during my sculpting process. With the help of either a website called PosteRazor or Adobe Illustrator, I print my reference images over multiple pieces of printer paper and then use my X-ACTO blade to cut off the white margins of those 8.5 x 11 inch sheets, adhering them together with clear tape. X-ACTO knives with fresh blades also help me cut up underglaze transfers that I sometimes use to decorate my surfaces. Once my sculpture is in the hard stage where I am making refinements, I also use a dull X-ACTO knife to clarify the edges of the eyelids or define the lip partition.

Clay knife: When I overlay a paper template on top of my slab of clay, I use a paring knife to both mark my interior guidelines and cut around the perimeter of the pattern. When marking the inner marks, I use the back of my knife so as not to accidentally make a deep incision.

Small wire loop tools: These small wire loop tools are great for articulating and refining features. I use them in the corners of my sculptures' eyes, around nostrils, or wherever there are tight areas that need to be finessed.

Goat hair brushes: Because their soft, absorbent quality allows me to load them up with material, goat hair mop brushes are my favorites for glazing and applying slip. In sculpting, I use them in the last steps when applying my finishing slip.

Small nylon brushes: I use these medium stiffness nylon brushes both to smooth and clean my surface and to move clay around in a sculptural way. I like having an assortment of these brushes of various shapes and sizes on hand. When used in a cross-hatching motion, these brushes can be great for smoothing out transitions between small-scale forms.

Wooden paddle: I use several paddles of different sizes and shapes to pound my sculptures from the outside into the forms I observe in my reference photos. Paddles are great for compressing seams and establishing planes that I will later flesh out with fresh clay.

Wood point head tool/finger tool: Rounded on one end, this tool is great for reaching into small forms and pushing out from the inside. Just as my paddles enable me to modify my forms from the outside, my wooden finger tool acts as an extension of my hand and lets me adjust my forms from the inside while I am gauging those changes from the outside.

Slip in lidded plastic container: I look for a sticky peanut butter consistency in my slip. If I initially add too much water, I leave my slip container with the lid off to let some of that moisture evaporate. I use slip as an adhesion aid any time I am joining a seam together. I like to score and then grab it with my scoring tool, like a small spoon, to lay it over the seam. I use slip liberally on my seams and clay surfaces that will be further developed, especially when my clay is already pretty firm. To finish my sculpture, I also use slip that is more hydrated and run it through an 80-mesh sieve. This creates a much smoother slip that will be used to finish the sculpture and impart a sense of skin onto the surface.

Rag/terry cloth: I use terry cloths in the later stages of my sculpting process to push back surface noise and slowly articulate my final layer of skin. Terry cloths work very nicely with Max's White Paper Clay, which is strong enough to take a lot of scrubbing. When working at a large scale in Max's mix, I move my damp rag over the surface of my sculpture in long, wide strokes from multiple directions to clean and unify my surface. Damp rags can also be used as alternatives to shop towels: I place them over areas of my sculptures that are vulnerable to drying when I am wrapping up my pieces.

Spray bottle: My favorite spray bottles are the fine-mist sprayers used by hair stylists. When my working sculpture is unwrapped from its plastic covering, I am spraying it regularly throughout my sculpting process—a light misting at least every ten minutes.

EQUIPMENT

Banding wheel: It is hard to overstate the importance of seeing your sculptural pieces in the round. Using a banding wheel is a simple way to make sure that you are considering your piece from all perspectives on a regular basis. A banding wheel on a table is a good alternative to a sculpture stand that has casters. I prefer heavy, sturdy banding wheels.

Wooden boards: I keep a series of large plywood boards in my studio for cutting and carrying slabs, keeping work contained, and keeping tables clean. I also have smaller boards to hold work in progress that I want to more easily move about the studio. My boards are cut from thick ¾ inch (2 cm) plywood so they will not warp when I wash them in my sink.

Sculpture stand: My sculpture stand can move up and down, and it rests on casters so it can be wheeled around the studio or in front of a particular reference image that is taped to the wall. Make sure that your sculpture stand is rated to support the weight of your sculpture.

80-mesh sieve: I use my 80-mesh sieve during my process of mixing glazes to ensure that no clumps of dry materials make it into my final glaze. After measuring out and thoroughly stirring my dry materials, while wearing a respirator and gloves, I hydrate the glaze, stir it again, and then use a spatula to push the glaze through my 80-mesh sieve at least one time. I also use an immersion blender to further integrate my glaze.

I also use my sieve to strain watered down joining slip to convert it into finishing slip at the end of my process

Slab roller: If you plan to do a lot of slab-based work in your studio, it may be worth investing in a slab roller to expedite this process and quickly generate slabs of uniform thickness. Much like a printing press, a slab roller consists of a metal roller positioned over a tabletop. You can use a crank to adjust the thickness of your slabs. It is important to sandwich your clay between two long pieces of canvas before sending it through the slab roller. The canvas protects your metal roller from becoming covered in clay.

Computer: I keep a desktop computer in one corner of my studio. On this computer I store all my reference images for each pose I am working on. While I print out my four cardinal views to the scale I am sculpting in, I generally do not print the transitional or "in between" views of my pose. When I get to the stage where I am looking at my transitional views, I move my sculpture stand close to my computer and observe the screen directly, cross-referencing what I see on my sculpture with what I see in the digital images. I also use my computer to scale and tile my photographic references before printing them. Finally, my computer comes in handy when I want to gain artistic inspiration from the work of other artists using either my Pinterest boards or the web.

Clamp lights or other lights to support sculpting: I use clamp lights with 10W daylight LED bulbs to compensate for low or shifting natural lighting in my studio. The flexibility of such lights lets you move them around with ease, clamping them to stands or other static features. Daylight bulbs have color temperatures that begin at 4600K (Kelvins) and range up to 6500K or higher. Emitting a bluish white light, they illuminate the workspace in a crisp, invigorating way that resembles midday light and provides optimal contrast among colors.

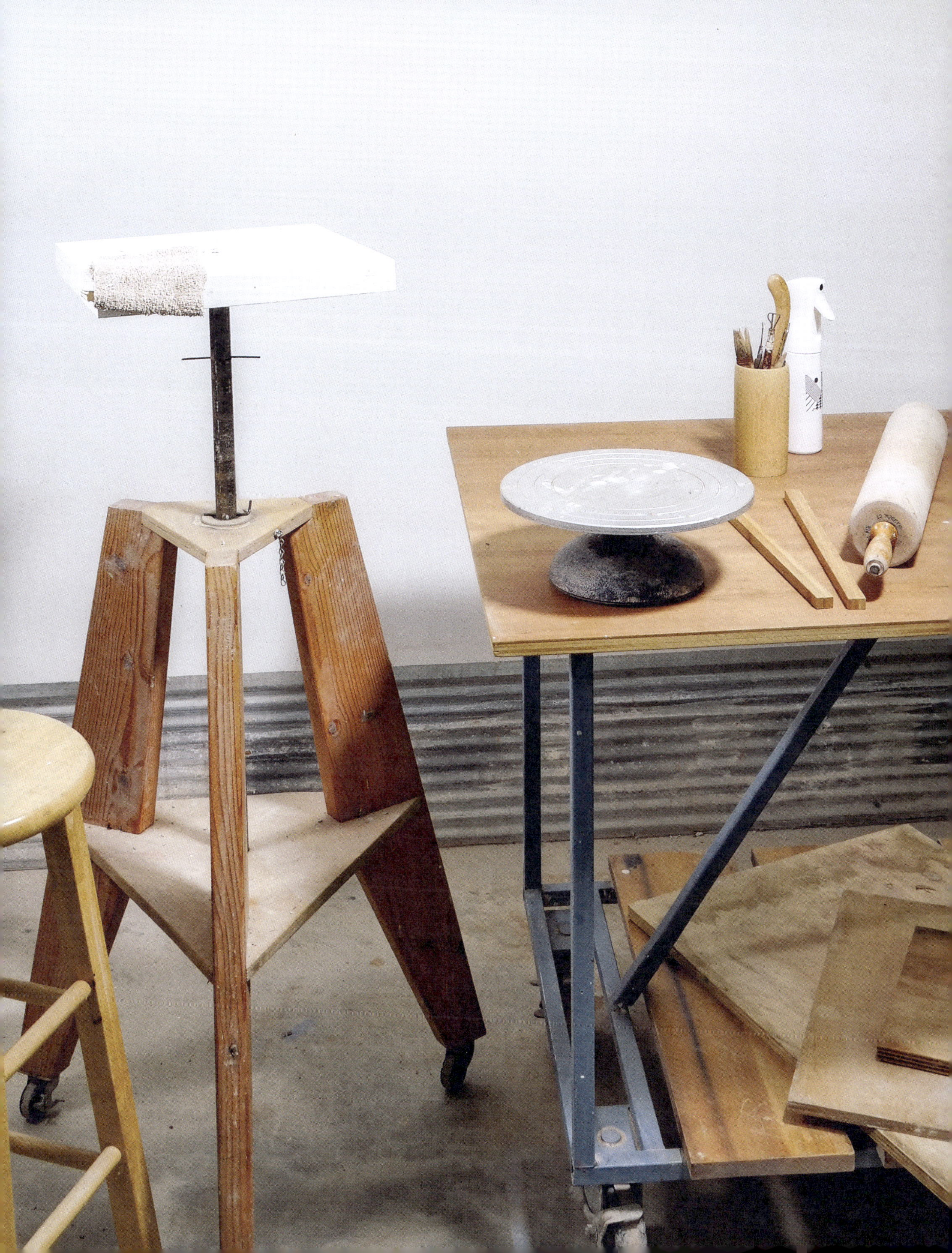

Kiln: I work with kilns of different sizes and shapes to support my practice. I fire most of my work at low- or mid-range temperatures, using ramping schedules that I have designed to suit the needs of my pieces. To prevent my pieces from cracking during the firing process, I use shrink slabs made from the same clay body as my sculptures. I also use a thin layer of sand—which acts like tiny ball bearings—beneath both my shrink slab and sculpture. Sand also protects my kiln shelves from potential glaze drippage during my glaze firings. When assembling and disassembling my kilns or loading and unloading pieces, I move slowly and treat my kilns gently to protect the fragile firebrick that they are made from.

Spray booth: Located on the porch of my studio, my spray booth is where I work with dry materials that may be harmful to my lungs (glaze components, dry slip, etc.). Once I turn it on, the spray booth continually sucks air from its chamber into a vent, moving particles away from me and into a filter. My spray booth is also where I spray my glazes. Its plastic walls catch the excess glaze that does not make it onto my sculpture, and these walls are easy to clean. I use caution and wear a respirator when mixing dry materials and spraying glazes.

Compressor: I turn on my air compressor when I am spraying glazes in my spray booth. If I have a piece of bisqueware that has been sitting around for a long time gathering dust, I may also shoot compressed air over its surface prior to glazing to move away any particulates that may cause crazing.

Heat gun: My heat gun comes in handy when I am pressed for time and am looking to speed up the drying process on a particular part of a sculpture. I prefer to let my pieces air dry, and I use my heat gun more frequently on less precious pieces of work, such as test tiles.

FINDING INSPIRATION

The process of exploring ideas and researching possibilities is a key part of any studio practice. Years into making, I realized that my most successful projects were preceded by a period of investigation where I clarified my ideas and translated them into formal possibilities through sketches, maquettes, and surface tests.

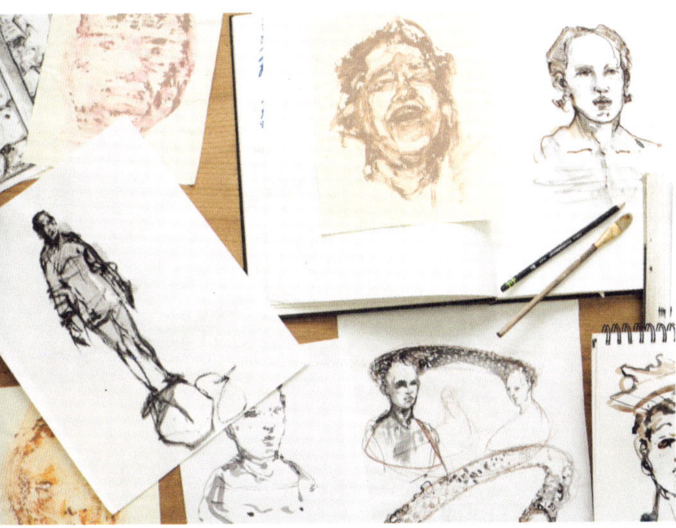

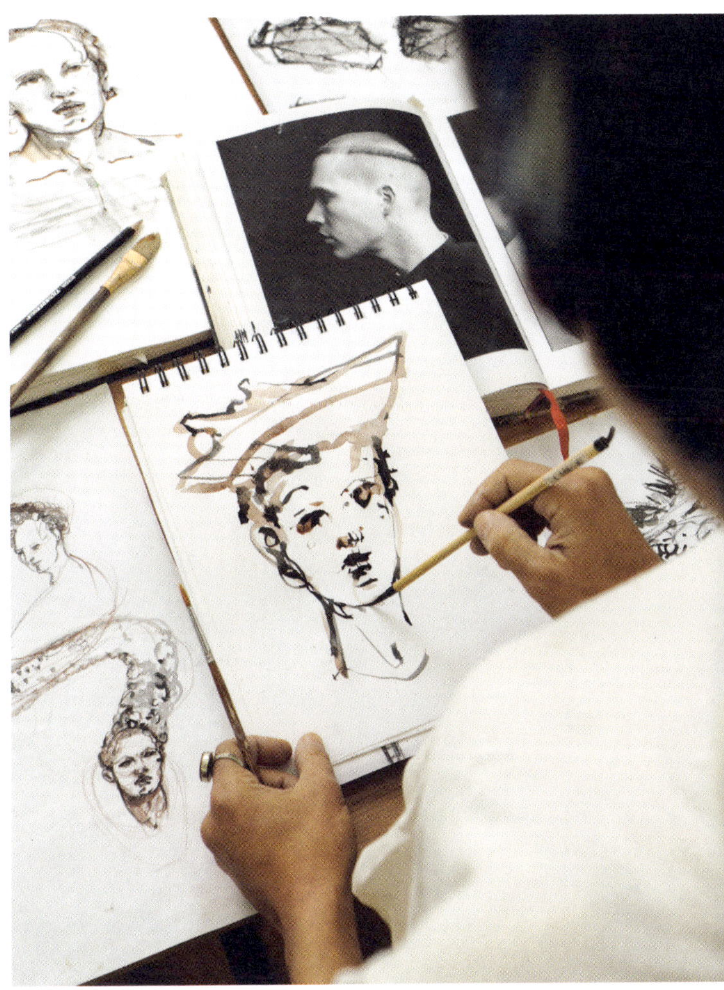

Depending on the scope of the work I am setting out to do, my approach to this preparatory stage varies in depth. At a minimum, I draw simple watercolor or charcoal renderings to understand where my creative energy wants to flow and experience my reaction to different scales and formats. I also take some time to look at books, old sketchbooks, and online images to facilitate this exploratory process. In the most comprehensive permutations of this preparatory stage, I move from sketches to clay models that I then photograph and print out to different scales to understand the potential of the idea as closely as possible before investing time and resources into executing it (see page 40). Working at this small scale unlocks a free-flowing exploration process, allowing me to be more playful as I develop an assortment of shapes and figurative ideas to pull from. As an artist, it is easy to fall into the safe, established grooves of the tried and true. Understanding how to activate your practice is an essential part of sustaining a meaningful and inspired connection to what you make.

Time consuming yet deeply grounding, this process allows you to discern what is most in alignment with your formal and conceptual inquiries at a given moment.

If you aim to be naturalistic in your figurative rendering, the next step involves finding or generating photographic references to support your sculpting.

For life-size pieces, I work with models who are close to me, like my daughter, Eva. The physical accessibility of my models opens a number of beneficial possibilities:

- I can do an exploratory photo session to investigate an assortment of poses and garments before selecting the final composition from which to generate my reference photos.

- I can take direct measurements of all the parts of the model to facilitate the construction process and help counteract lens distortion in my photo sets.

- The model can come into the studios to pose for me directly, infusing the work with a real interpersonal connection.

GATHERING AND PROCESSING REFERENCES FOR SCULPTING

SOURCING PHOTOGRAPHIC REFERENCES

When I am sculpting full-size figures, I prefer to take the images of the model in the studio on the same rotating base that I will use to sculpt. First, I cover the stand with a layer of sturdy plastic and place it in front of a clean white wall. I explore a variety of poses before settling on my final choice.

With a bright yet diffused light from above, I illuminate the model, minimizing shadows and hot spots as much as possible. I position my camera about 10 feet (3 m) away from the figure and set it on a tripod so that the camera's height is lined up with the middle of the figure. This will minimize lens distortion. My current studio camera is a Canon Rebel with an 18-55 mm lens. When I feel ready to capture a position, I will have someone rotate the base in 15-degree increments as I take the images until I come back to my starting point, generating about 24 views.

Before releasing the pose, I trace my model's feet onto the plastic covering the base. I take measurements from the model, such as the distances between bony landmarks and widths of arms, legs, neck, and torso, with my seamstress tape to create a blueprint that I will reconcile with the photographic references printed to scale, which helps me compensate for any distortion in the pictures.

Although I prefer photographing my model when rendering a life-size sculpture, the majority of my work is smaller-scale, so the ability to acquire pre-established photo sets has been invaluable. In the resources section of the book, I have included several of my favorite websites where you can browse through pose options and acquire references to inform your work.

PROCESSING AND PRINTING FILES TO SUPPORT SCULPTING

After selecting a pose and downloading a photo set (my own or purchased), which is generally comprised of 24 to 28 images in the round, I pick out the four cardinal views (direct front, back, and left- and right-side views) and then adjust them in Photoshop. As I seek to optimize my images for sculpting, I both color correct them and enhance the value range to better understand volumes and clarify external contours.

Next, I place my four cardinal views into one wide Photoshop document (see image on page 32) and work to align them. Note that simply aligning the tops and bottoms of each photograph will likely not align the figures contained within each frame, as these photographs tend not to be taken at consistent distances from the model. It can be useful to drag guidelines down into your document, as these consistent horizontals will span across all four cardinal views. You can then select the visual landmarks on the figure that seem least affected by camera distortion and align them with your horizontal guides. If my gesture has a good measure

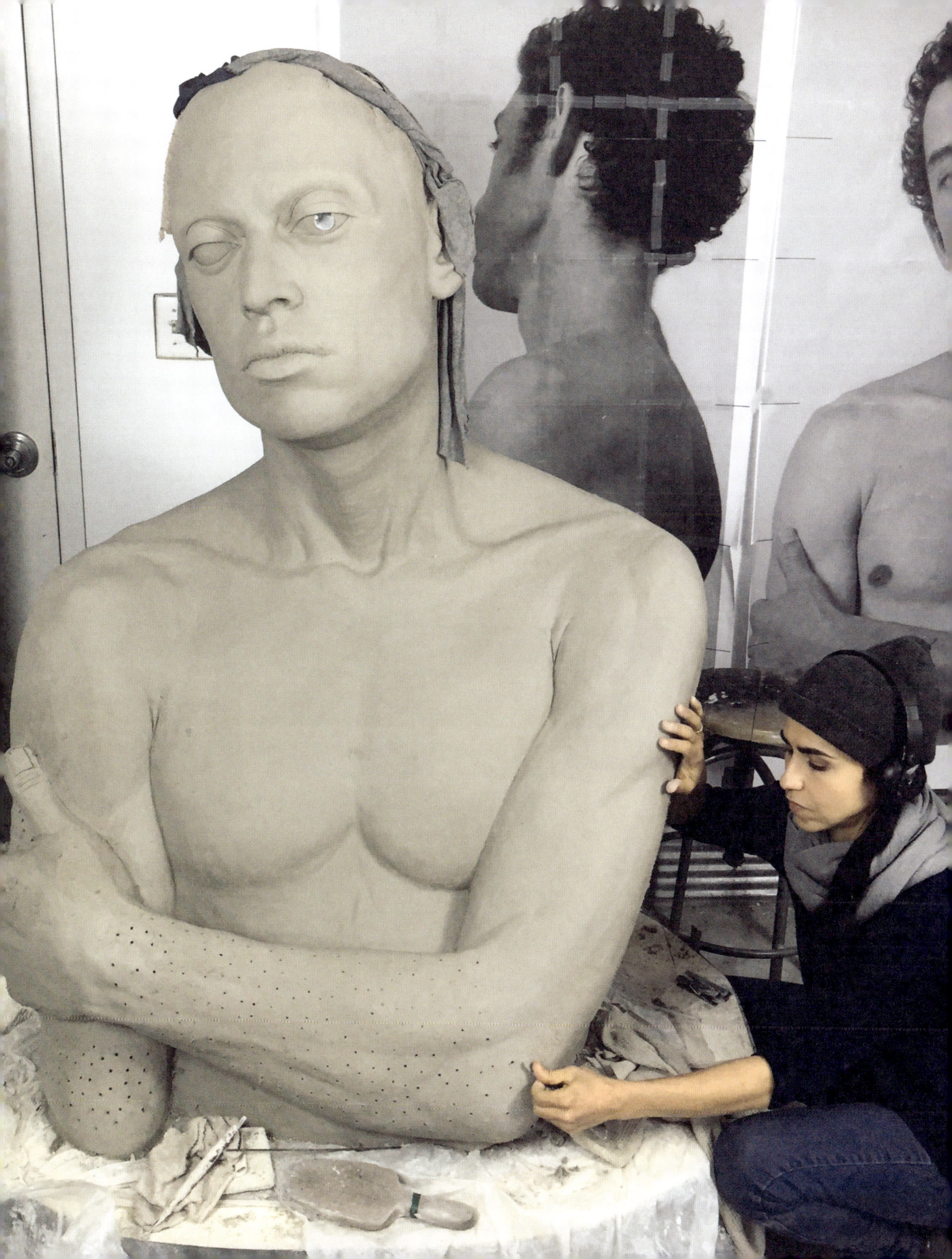

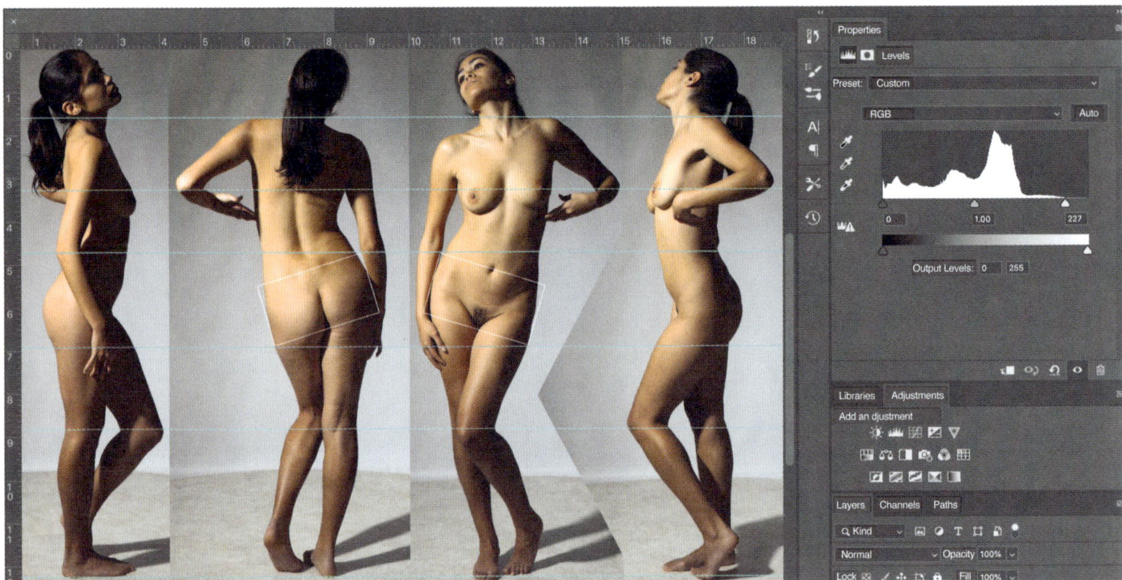

of torque, making it harder to establish front and side alignments, I will determine the views based on the position of the pelvic box.

Next, I crop the images as close to the top of the head and the bottom of the feet as possible before putting them through a tiling software that will allow me to print out posters of any size using a standard home printer. (You can also send the original, untiled file to a print shop with large scale printing capabilities.) Printed to my target scale, these tiled images will serve as my blueprints as I construct my sculpture.

I use this same approach to process images of my small clay maquettes when I want to experience the impact they have at different scales (see page 46).

In addition to these four cardinal images, you can print out your additional "in-between" poses and hang them up on your vertical surface. Often, I reference these transitional photos directly off of my computer screen. I use them to inform the development of the gesture by providing additional insights into how the forms evolve in space.

As with any blueprint, interpretation is required to translate the two-dimensional information contained in these images into a three-dimensional rendering. Some aspects will be easier to resolve than others. Equipped not only with these scaled, printed images but also with additional photographic views, a generic proportions guide, knowledge of bony and fleshy landmarks, and additional tools for anatomical insight that can be sourced online or in books, you can confidently navigate any roadblocks you meet on this journey. Finally, your own intuition will be a constant companion, guiding you as you transform an image set into a form that speaks to your own experience and aesthetic values.

SIMPLE ARMATURE CONSTRUCTION

In the context of figurative sculpture, an armature is a structure that stabilizes the malleable material being formed into a figure. Depending on the technique being used, they can vary in complexity, ranging from carefully considered versions that provide measurements and gestural placement, comparable to a skeleton, to simple uprights in alignment with a pose that help stabilize the foundation of a figurative composition.

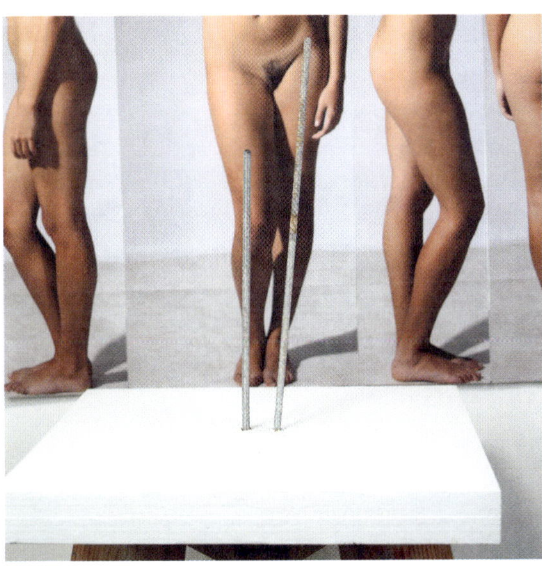

Because most of my work is built hollow, I use the latter, simplified approach to guide and stabilize the legs and pelvic area of a piece before stacking the upper body, which is sculpted without any internal support. In combination with the right clay body, this approach offers enough stability to achieve the results I am after without being overly complicated and makes it easy to dismantle when preparing the piece to dry fully before firing.

The first step is creating the right base, and the first thing I consider when deciding on the shape and size of my base is how big my piece will be. Larger pieces will need to be built over armatures that are secured to a heavier base to counteract the torque created by the height of the form. I build larger pieces on a rotating steel table with a wooden base cut round to make it more contained as the piece is rotated throughout the process.

For this piece, I am using a square 14 x 14 inch (35.6 x 35.6 cm) piece of wood, 1½ inch (3.8 cm) thick, and two ¼ inch (6 mm) threaded rods (with 20 threads per inch), one cut 13¾ inches (35 cm) long and the other cut 10¾ inches (27 cm).

MATERIALS

- ¾ inch (2 cm) plywood

- Two threaded inserts (¼ inch, size 20, sold by internal diameter) or 4 hex nuts (¼ inch-20)

- Two 18 inch (45.7 cm) lengths of steel threaded rod (¼ inch-20 size, and stainless or coated to inhibit rust)

- Printed full-size figure reference photos

- Hack saw (if steel rod is not pre-cut)

- Allen wrench ¼-inch

- Drill

- Two drill bits approx. ³⁄₁₆ inch and ⁵⁄₁₆ inch (5 and 8 mm)

- Ruler (14 inches [35.6 cm] or longer)

- Bevel gauge or protractor

- 3½ inch (8.9 cm) mil plastic to cover the top with clear tape to stabilize

INSTRUCTIONS

Cut two 14 inch (35.6 cm) squares of ¾ inch (2 cm) plywood. Spread wood glue on two faces of the plywood boards and either clamp them together or secure them with screws. Allow the glue to dry overnight.

Once the glue is dry, find the center of your square. An easy way is to draw two diagonals connecting opposing corners and the center will be the point where they intersect.

With the ruler, measure the distance between the center of the heels from the back view of your photographic references and mark that distance on your base, centered on the midpoint and parallel to an edge of the base. In this case, that distance is 1⅛ inches (3 cm). These will be the marks for the rod placement. Ⓐ

Now place your rods over your photographic references to understand the angle at which they will come out of the base. Make sure to check the alignment of the rods in relation to the photographic references from all views: front, back, and sides. In this pose, the model's left leg is fairly straight, with a slight incline forward and to the right as the leg moves up. Ⓑ

With the right leg, which rests at an angle, place the shorter rod over the left-side view of the photographic reference and use a bevel gauge to capture the angle. For more complicated leg placement, it can be helpful to use two bevel gauges to check front and side angles simultaneously. Bring the gauges to your base and align your drill with the angles from the side. Ⓒ

With a ³⁄₁₆ inch (5 mm) drill bit in place, drill a straight hole slightly deeper than ¾ inches (2 cm, the length of the inserts) followed by drilling with a ⁵⁄₁₆ inch (8 mm) drill bit. It is recommended that you make your way up to the final hole by starting with a smaller drill bit to ensure accuracy. Ⓓ

Tip: It can be helpful to have a second pair of eyes to ensure your drill remains straight from the front (not tipping left or right) as you go through the process of pre-drilling and drilling the second hole.

Once your holes are drilled, screw in your two ⁵⁄₁₆ inch (external diameter) threaded inserts into the drilled holes with a ¼ inch (6 mm) Allen wrench until they are flush with the top of the base. Once you are done, screw the rods into the inserts, making sure they are all the way in, and check that the angles are consistent with your reference photos. If necessary, you can make minor adjustments by slightly bending the rods. Try to get the rods in as close to the reference as possible but keep in mind that this simple armature offers a margin of play. Ⓔ Ⓕ

VARIATION

An alternate route for more complicated positions, where the angles of the legs move more dramatically along both axes, involves following the same steps as above, but drilling 1 inch (2.5 cm)–diameter holes (as deep as the inserts) to receive the inserts. That extra space will be packed with epoxy paste (I use PC-7 or PC-11) to allow for more play in finding the right alignment of the rods from all angles. Once your holes are drilled, start by adding epoxy both within the 1 inch (2.5 cm) holes in your base and around the sides of your inserts, near their bottoms. You should have the rods already screwed into their inserts, and be mindful not to get epoxy into the threads on the rods.

You can then place the epoxied inserts, rods screwed in, into the epoxied holes in the boards. Using your angle bevel, match the angles of the rods to the angles of the legs in your front view reference photo, and then turn the board and adjust the angles of the rods to also match the side views. Once you have your rods positioned to match the angles of the legs from all views, prop them up with sturdy objects from your studio so they won't move while the epoxy cures. Allow the epoxy to cure for 24 hours, or according to the package directions. Unscrew the rods to ensure that the epoxy has not stuck in the threads, then screw them back into the board as far as they will go. If the rods are stuck, you can grip the end with pliers or a vice grip to help you twist them free. Then screw them back into the board as far as they will go.

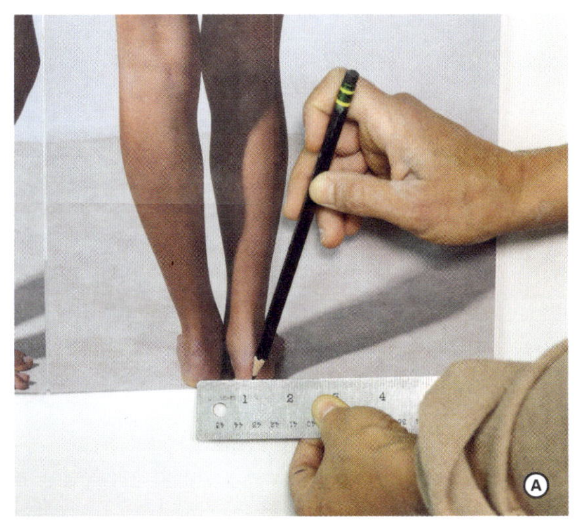
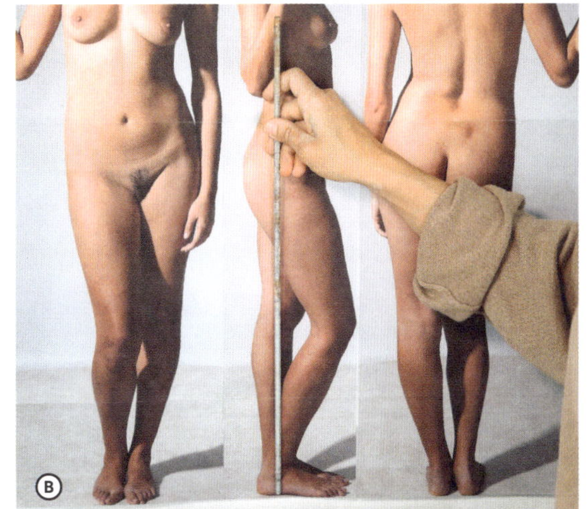
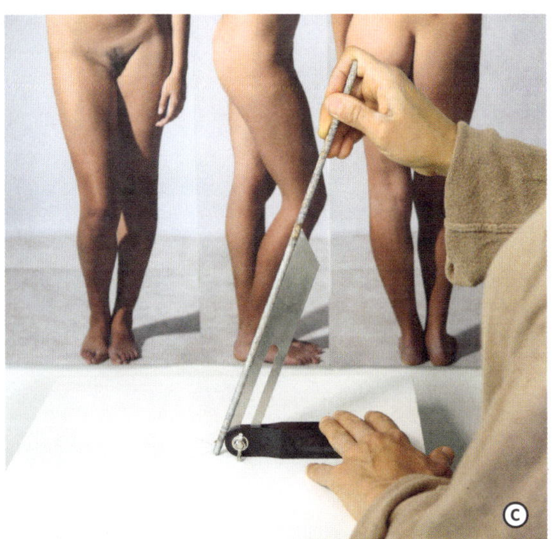
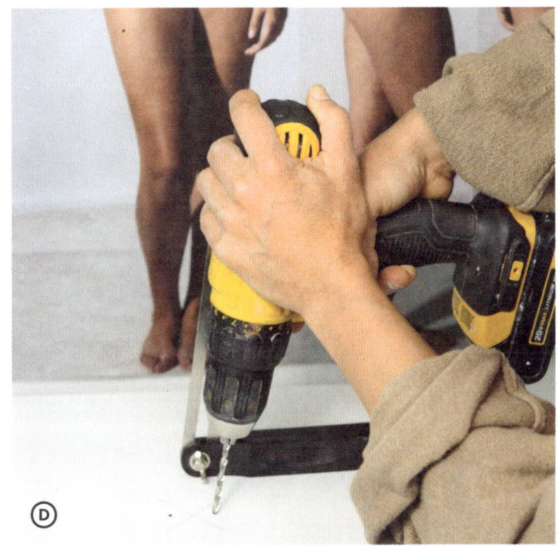
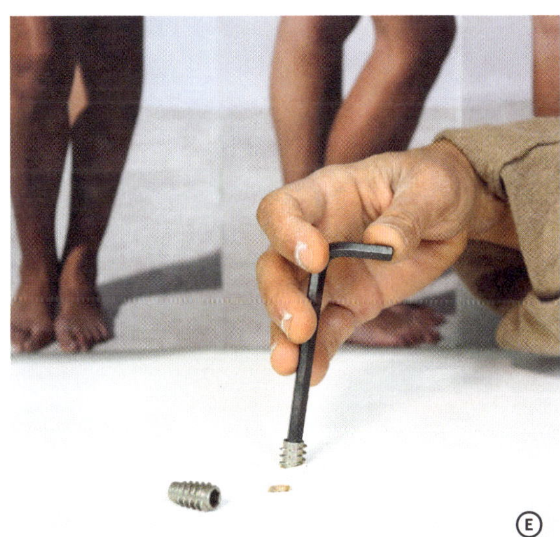
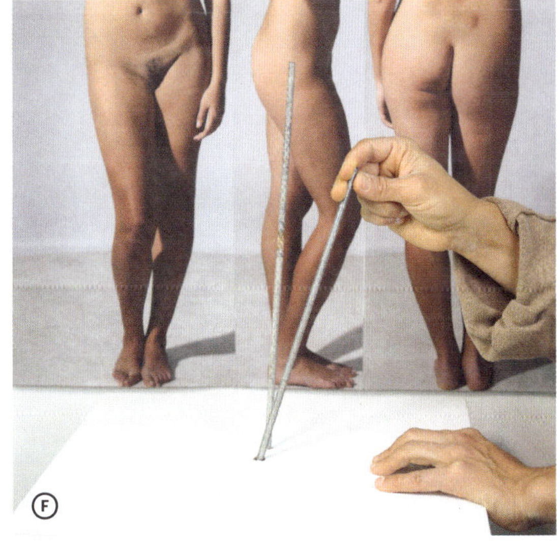

EXTERNAL SUPPORTS

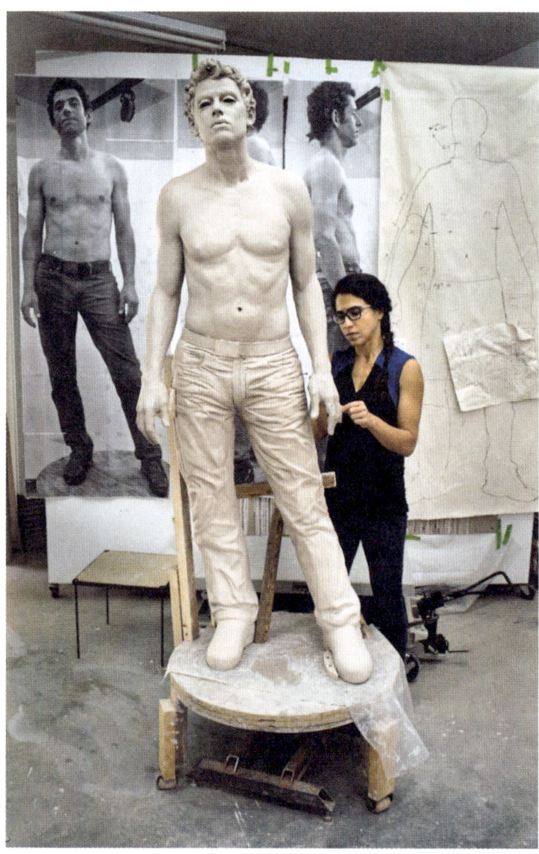

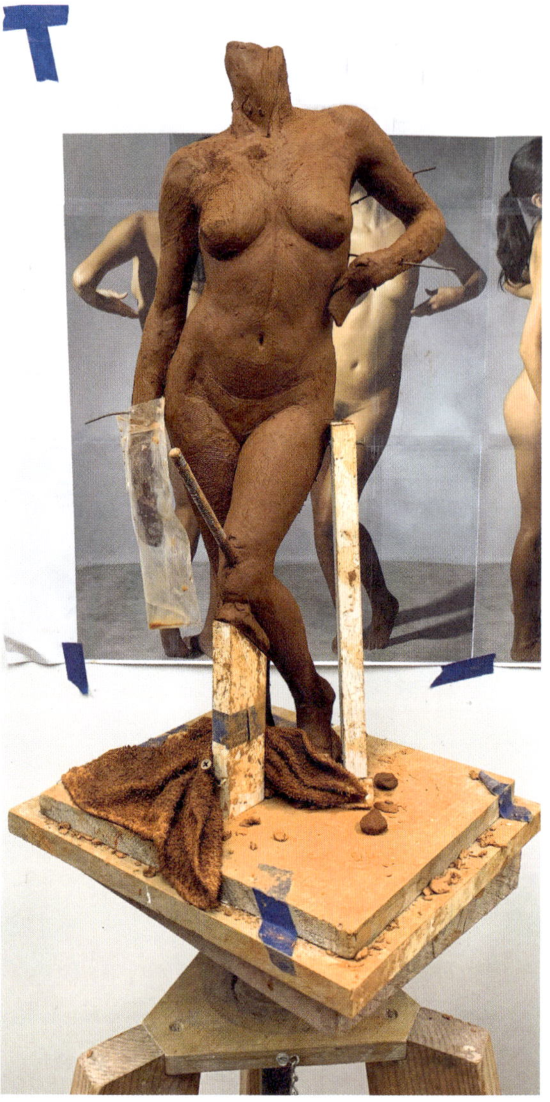

Depending on the pose you will be developing, as well as the scale of the work, you might need to add some external support to your composition to secure the gesture. This is needed as more vertical weight is added and the figure runs a risk of distorting, or when adding appendages that may succumb to gravity before weight-bearing joints dry. To do this, I take a pre-drilled piece of wood or custom fabricated steel support and run it from the base to the hip area of the figure at a diagonal, securing it with screws directly into the clay. It is important to note that paper clay has a wood-like quality that accepts this type of intervention without cracking. This might not be the case with other clay bodies, so I recommend doing tests to make sure this strategy is viable if you are not using the recommended clay.

Other options for external supports, depending on the scale, include metal rods or stiff wire, which I will use to support cantilevered arms or acutely angled heads by running them from the body part to the torso to take weight away from a soft joint and safeguard its position while it dries.

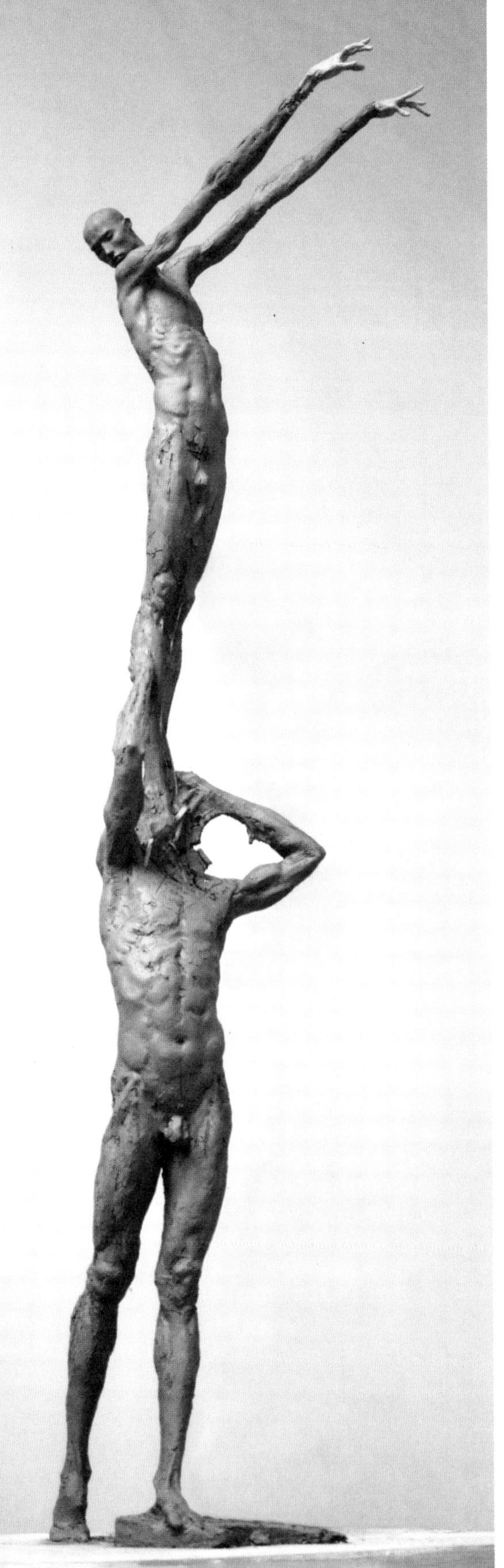

Eudald de Juana

Why do you work with clay?

I work with clay because it is a material that allows the whole process to be recorded. I like it because when you see a piece in clay, you can see the marks of tools, the fingerprints of the artist. I think this helps the viewer connect more with the piece because it feels more alive. If we use computers or molds, all these leave no trace of the process. They are mechanical processes that feel colder and, I think, keep the viewer at a distance, unable to engage as much. Clay is a material that captivates me and when it comes to working with it, I truly enjoy it. It does not make noise; it is a natural material you mostly work with your hands, then you just wash your hands with water. The truth is that it is a very generous material that allows you everything, from cutting and adding, and offers a lot of flexibility.

Your work appears and disappears simultaneously through a game between an exquisite figuration and a sensation of disintegration or erasure. How do you conceptually interpret these formal/ stylistic decisions?

For me, it is a game. Representing reality as it is does not excite me. I want to contribute something more to the world I see around me, reinterpreting it in my own way. For me, this game of allowing forms to appear and disappear helps me connect more with the viewer because you leave things to be resolved. I don't like it when things are obvious. When something is subtle, it is there but it gets the viewer more involved, inciting their imagination. When everything is very explicit and burdened with too much detail, it feels very chewed up, like you are saying things too many times, being

Eudald de Juana, *The Piano*. Courtesy of the artist.

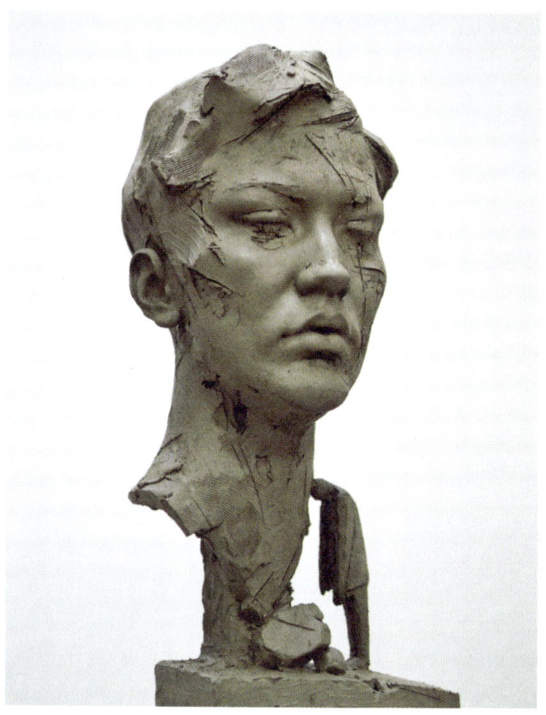

Eudald de Juana, *The Stone.* Courtesy of the artist.

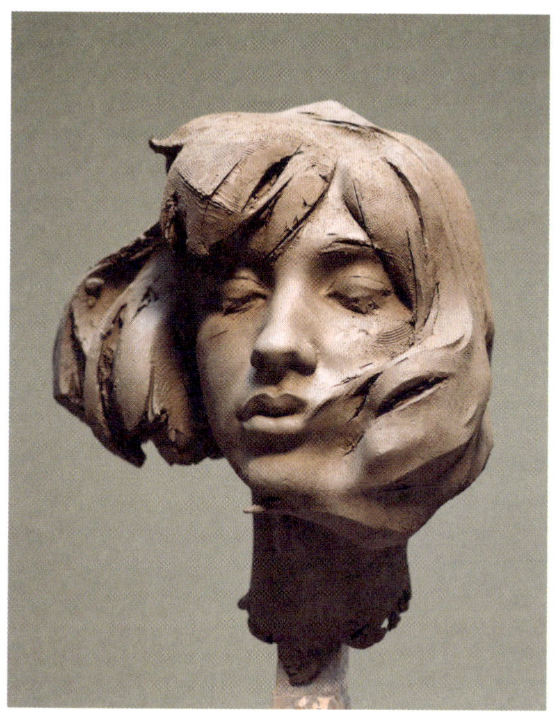

Eudald de Juana, *Wind.* Courtesy of the artist.

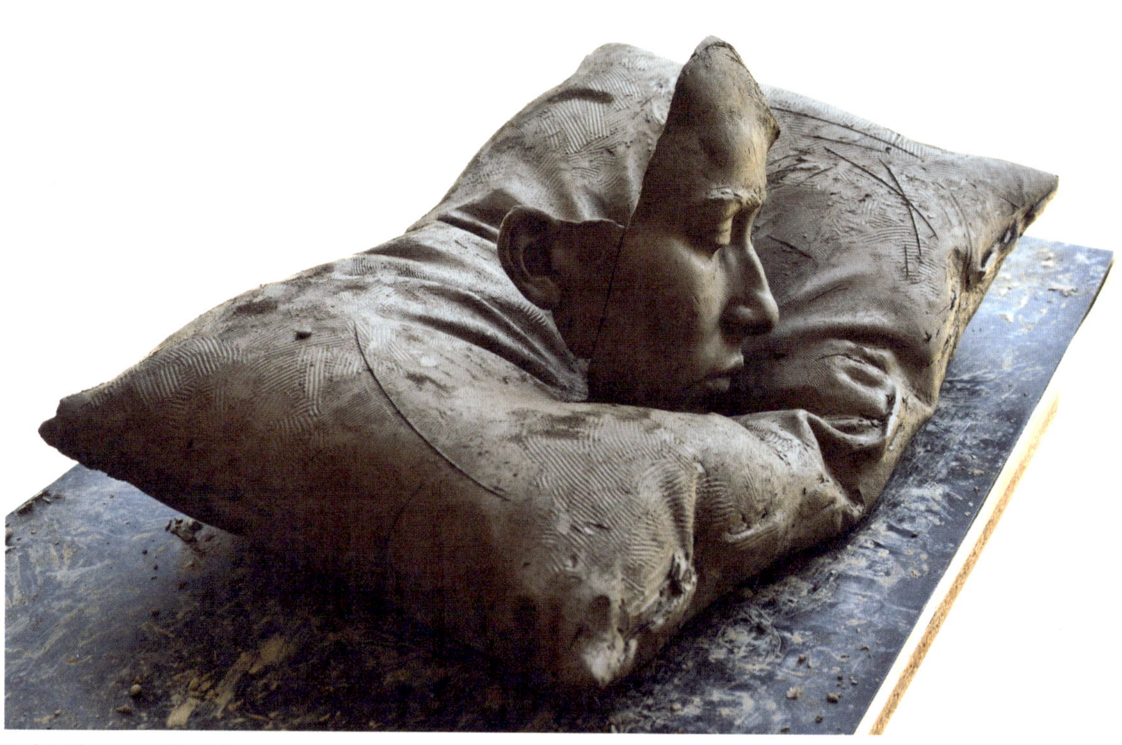

Eudald de Juana, *The Offering.* Courtesy of the artist.

too obvious. I think something is lost in these instances and the work becomes boring. I try to give just enough so that the viewer can make his own story, his film, and then erase anything that doesn't add to that end.

I also like to take a sculpture, which is something so physical and seemingly explicit, and play with the illusion of light, which is something painting does, to transform the planes and the surfaces. Through these modifications, when the light interacts with a piece, it can give you the sensation that there is an atmosphere, that there is a fog enveloping the form. It conceals and lets you see at the same time in a transformative way. It is a very interesting game between the form, which must be supported at a constructive and anatomical level, allowing everything to be in its place, and the simultaneous act of erasing the specificity of what is there, leaving parts unexpressed, latent. This subtle dance gives the sensation that the clay, which is such a solid conglomerate of particles, especially as it hardens, is something that can be perennially soft to the touch, or that it is ethereal as if it were fog. I feel this is very interesting for the viewer but also for me when creating. When I start a piece, I have a general idea, but during the process, as I start to evolve the form, deciding what to strengthen and what to subdue, one part takes you to another. And that is the beauty of this practice: When you let yourself be surprised and let yourself go.

Despite your youth, you have had a prolific career. How do you keep renewing your artistic vision and your purpose within this sculptural medium? And related, how do you prepare to start a new piece?

I have been doing quite a few commissions, several of them that have not yet come to light. Of course, I had always wanted commissions. For me, it was an explosion of joy every time I received a request, because I felt that I could live from doing what I love and this gave me a feeling of progress. But for the past years, because of the commissions, I haven't had much time to do my personal work. Nonetheless, these commissions luckily have given me a lot of creative freedom, so I still feel the work is my own, not subdued by someone else's vision. There is a second look, a second opinion from the client and an opportunity to modify. Each time you adjust a sculpture, there can be a thousand options, but it is interesting to use that other point of view from the client to help me leave my comfort zone.

I feel that if I had to do my personal work, everything would go in a predictable direction. When you get a commission, it is a new challenge. You are given some parameters. For example, make a sculpture of an angel for the Milan cemetery. Since this premise is an angel for the cemetery, from here on, how do I develop my own version that connects with this idea and feels harmonious with my body of work? Now I'm doing a head of a Spartan soldier for another company, a topic that, surely, I would never have done. But now I think, *wow, super interesting,* because it allows me to do things I wouldn't have considered, opening my horizons.

Sometimes, the innumerable quantity of ideas can paralyze you, leaving you blank. A commission, or any thematic directive, can close the range a bit and facilitate that narrowing of focus, and from here, even more ideas can come out. So, I would say I have two primary ways of engaging with ideas. When working on commissions, I sit down with paper and more specifically think about the idea: what do I want to express, the aesthetics of characters, the composition, etc. Other times, I start in an organic way. I am attracted to a face or the shape of a body and from there the piece unfolds.

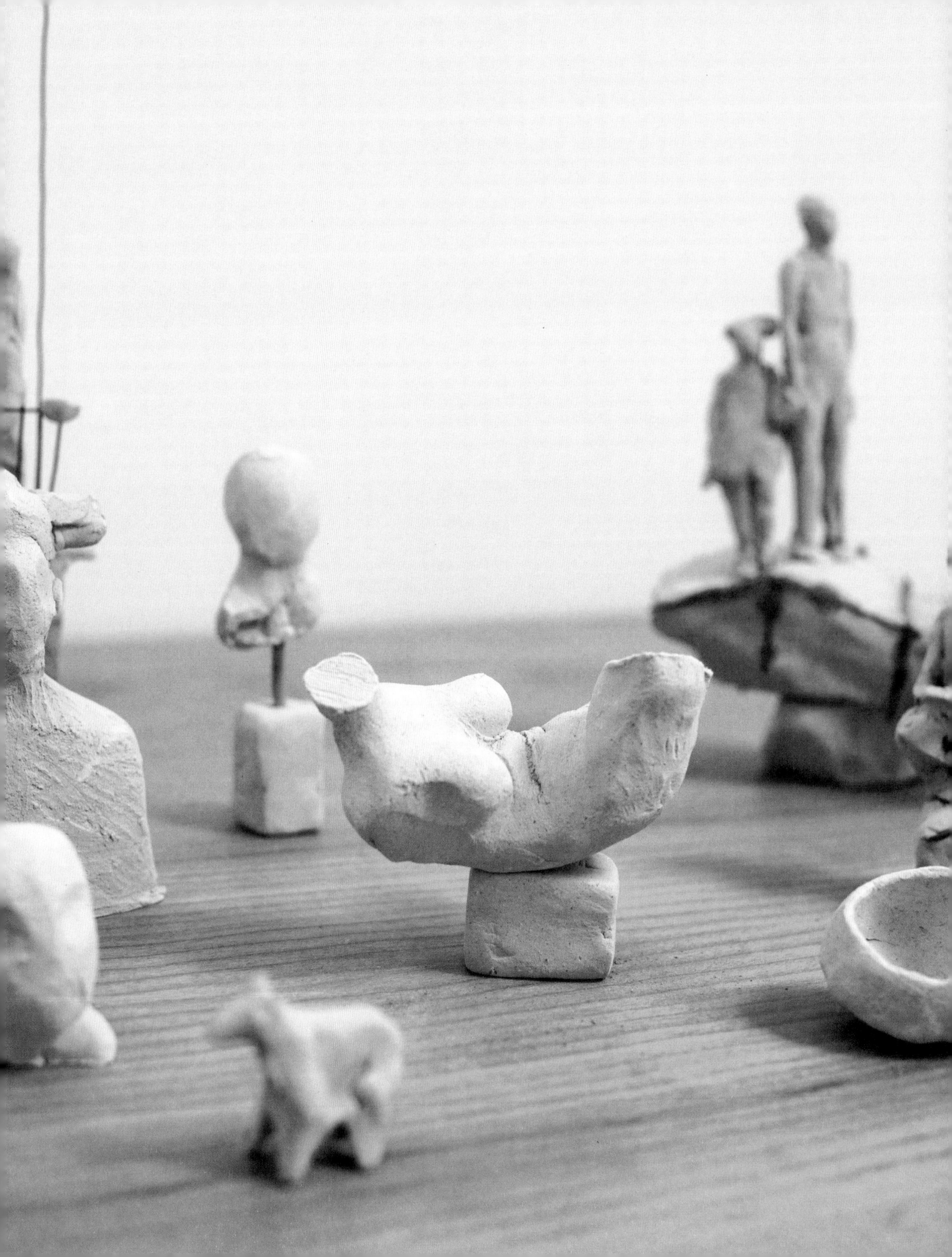

GETTING STARTED

I FIRST BEGAN sculpting with clay slabs as a means of building forms quickly and creating objects that could go straight into the kiln, with only minor adjustments at the end of the sculpting process. This system has enabled me to build sculptures with limitless forms at almost any scale.

This technique will allow you to turn flat planes—clay slabs—into complex, curvilinear forms that come together in dynamic ways. Working this way, everything starts with a block of clay that is turned into a slab through the use of a rolling pin or a slab roller. By using either formal paper patterns or intuitively cutting and darting slab-formed cylinders, you can quickly construct core shapes. Next, we'll adjust these hollow core forms by pushing the walls in or out, which offers a dimension of engagement that is unavailable in solid building. After developing the forms on a musculoskeletal level, you'll move toward the realm of fat pads and skin by adding pieces of fresh clay onto the stiffened core. As you hone your forms through incremental modifications based on a deep level of observation, the very breath of life can seem to enter this inert material. In this chapter, I'll explore the initial steps in more depth, offering different ways to begin sculpting the figure.

HOW TO MAKE A SLAB

There are multiple ways to prepare a slab, depending on the tools you have at your disposal. The most expedient way to make slabs is with the use of a slab roller. I use a Bailey DRD/II 24 Direct Drive S/R with a 69 inch (175 cm) table. I highly recommend this tool as an addition to your studio if most of your work will use slabs, especially if you are interested in delving into large-scale compositions. However, you can also make perfectly good slabs with a sturdy rolling pin and some strips of wood. I will cover both methods in this section.

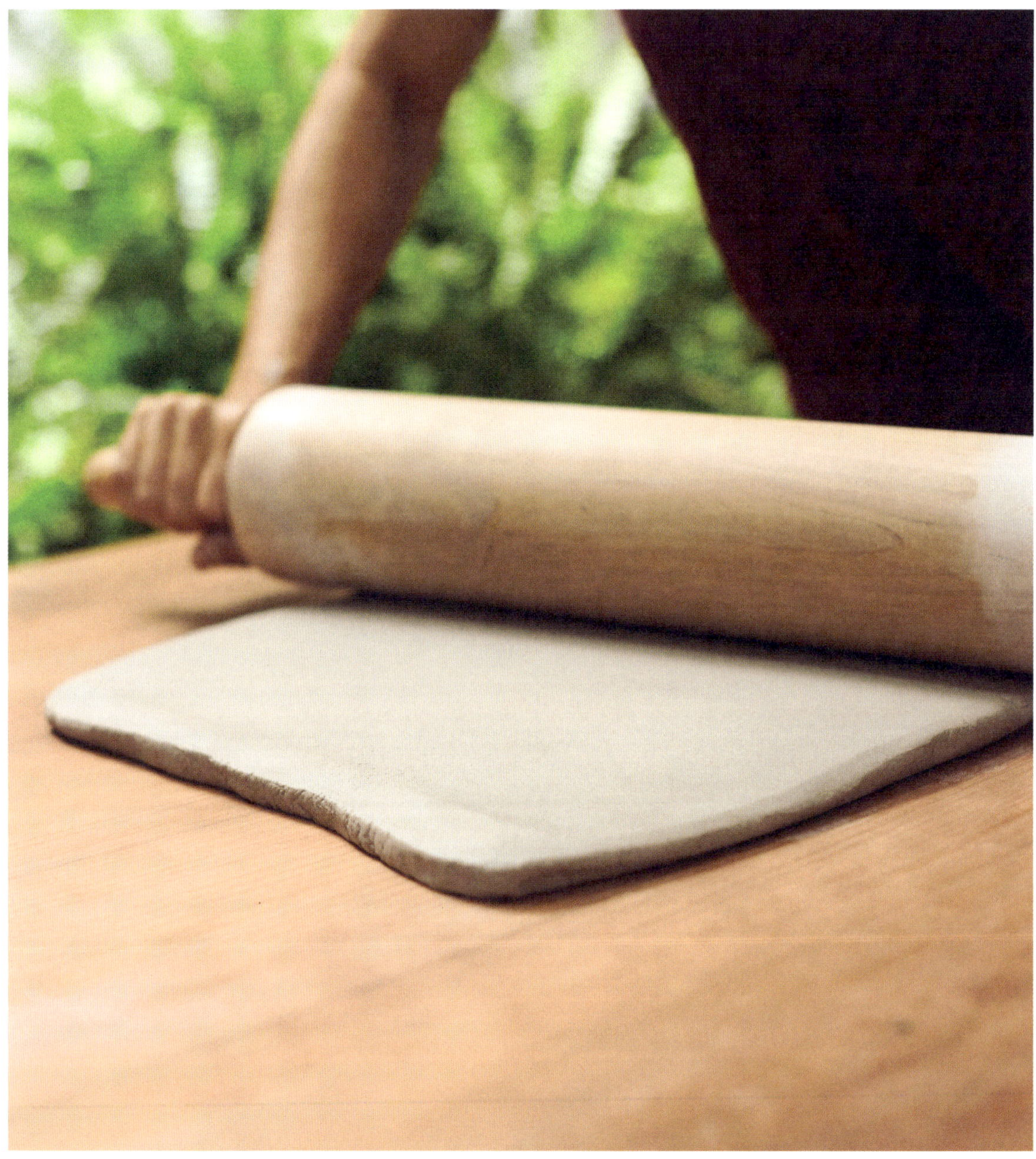

No matter which method you choose, the goal is to make a slab that is a consistent thickness. For the tutorials in this book, you will also need to make sure your slabs are large enough in length and width to fit your templates. Throughout the construction process, I recommend working with ⅜ inch (1 cm)–thick slabs.

MAKING A SLAB WITH A SLAB ROLLER

Much like a printing press, a slab roller consists of a large metal roller, or sometimes two rollers, depending on the style, centered over a flat surface. The roller can be raised and lowered with a crank to adjust the thickness of your slab. You will lay your clay between two pieces of canvas when it is going through the slab roller so that the clay does not stick to the roller and present a cleanup challenge. Your canvas should be slightly narrower than the roller, so it does not get bunched up when going through the press.

Set the gauge to ⅜ inch (1 cm) plus a little more to account for the thickness of your canvas. Next, lay the piece of canvas down on the slab roller table (feeder side, if applicable) and smooth out all the wrinkles.

If you are using pre-wedged clay straight from a fresh bag, use your wire cutter to take an even slice off of the long length of your clay cube and place that slice directly onto your canvas. If you would like, you may use rails— two pieces of wood of identical height, located on either side of your block of clay—to guide your wire cutter through your block of clay.

If you are using reclaimed clay, wedge your clay thoroughly and then whack it with a rubber mallet both horizontally and vertically to achieve a proto-slab of consistent thickness. Alternatively, you can throw your clay down in an angled motion onto a smooth concrete floor or canvas-covered table to generate this proto-slab. Your proto-slab needs to be thicker than ⅜ inch (1 cm) in all areas. I tend to aim for a slab roughly 1 to 1.5 inches (2.5 to 3.8 cm) thick.

To help the roller catch the clay, tamp down slightly on the edge of your proto-slab that will first make contact with the roller, creating a subtly tapered edge. Feed the front edges of both pieces of canvas beneath the roller and then pull gently on those canvas ends while turning the large wheel that rotates the roller. If any wrinkles emerge on the canvas as you are turning the roller, smooth them out before they go under the press, taking care not to let your fingers get too close to the roller. You never want to reduce the thickness of your slab by more than half of its initial thickness, so you may require more than one pass to get to ⅜ inch (1 cm).

Note: It takes more clay and more passes through the slab roller to generate larger slabs, but you can always use scoring, slipping, and compression to knit small slabs together at their edges into one large slab.

MAKING A SLAB WITH A ROLLING PIN AND THICKNESS STRIPS

To make a slab using a rolling pin, begin by cutting a slice of clay off your bag. You want your slice to exceed your target thickness, but if it starts out too thick, you risk overly displacing the vertical alignment of the clay molecules. Clay has "memory," and such displacement could invite undesired warping or cracking later in the sculpting or firing process. For a ⅜ inch (1 cm) finished slab thickness, I try to start with a slice that is 1 to 1½ inches (2.5 to 3.8 cm) thick.

Cut another similarly sized slice off your clay block and use a fork to thoroughly score and slip an area of at least 1 inch (2.5 cm) along the long edge of each slice. Next, overlap the edges of the two slabs so that the scored areas meet.

Compress along this seam using first your palm, then a serrated rib and finally a rolling pin. Move the serrated rib in a cross-hatching motion to integrate the clay particles.

Flip your slab over carefully and use your serrated rib on the other side of the seam. Using a rubber mallet, start beating your clay with even, rhythmic hits. Go from one side to the other in vertical strokes, then turn your slab or reposition yourself to repeat the same process using perpendicular strokes. Your clay should start flattening and expanding.

As your clay approaches your target thickness, roll the rolling pin from various directions, applying more pressure to high points. If you have access to ⅜ inch (1 cm) wooden "thickness strips," you can place these strips on either side of your slab to create a track for your rolling pin to roll on and make your thickness uniform. Once you meet your target thickness, you can trim the organic edges into straight lines and add additional sections to create a larger slab.

Working with patterns expedites the construction of basic forms and creates a consistent starting point for different figurative compositions. Inherently pliable, clay allows us to plot dimensions onto a flat slab and then configure that slab into a three-dimensional form that can be repeated and adjusted for endless applications. The beauty of a pattern within the context of figurative ceramics is that it holds anatomical information yet is not overly prescriptive; one can generate myriad compositions from the same set of templates. Patterns also help mediate shifts in scale. By enlarging a template extracted from a small sculpture, one can resolve artistic decisions at a manageable scale before embarking on projects that involve a significant investment of time and resources.

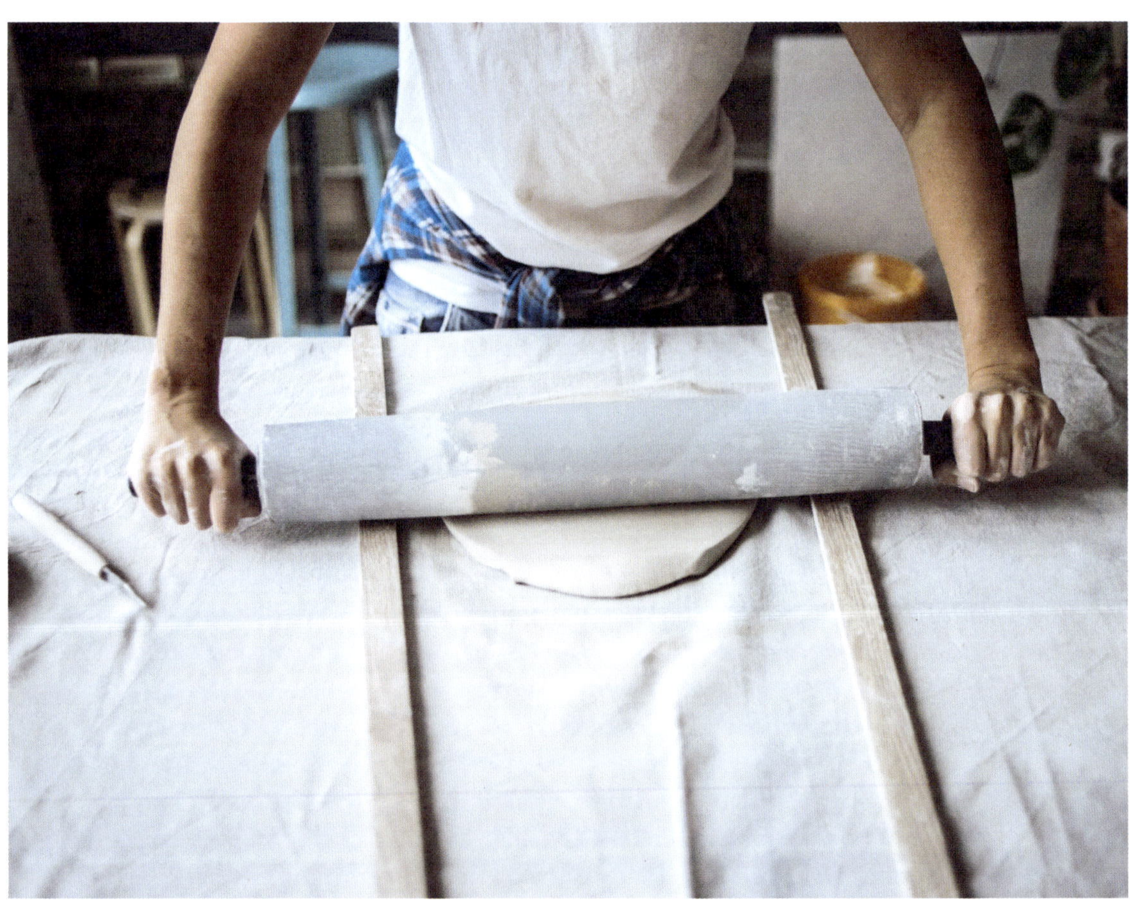

USING PATTERNS

This book contains a set of general patterns for all the parts of the body to construct a figure and explore this hollow building technique. When working in conjunction with photographic references, templates allow us to create well-proportioned, generic forms onto which you can then model more specific features and gestures using photographic references. We will use them to build a 25 inch (63.5 cm) standing figure on a basic rod armature. You will need to enlarge each template page by the indicated percentage before using. Note that throughout this book, I will use the terms pattern or template interchangeably to indicate a flat paper guide with markings used to support the cutting of a slab to generate hollow clay forms.

Although these templates offer a great starting point, you can also develop your own shapes through simple observations, opening a world of compositional possibilities.

HOW TO CREATE YOUR OWN PATTERNS

There are innumerable ways to generate a shape that could serve as a template. In my practice, I either extract measurements directly from a model or photoset or base my patterns on sketches drawn at my target scale. The precision of the former method can be grounding, yet the freedom with which I am able to express anatomical information in my drawings lets me capture gestures that are less focused on naturalism. Let's explore pattern making in the context of a head and show you how to easily generate your own set of forms to integrate into your practice.

MAKING A HEAD SHAPE PATTERN WITHOUT UTILIZING PHOTOGRAPHIC REFERENCES

Entering the realm of figurative sculpting without any references is a bit like entering into a jungle. Guided by your own intuition and aesthetic compass, you may discover a rich landscape of possibilities, but there is also the chance to get lost and untethered amidst so many creative prospects. For this reason, even if you are not using photographic references or a model, I recommend beginning every project with a session of two-dimensional or three-dimensional sketching (see Chapter 1) that you can photo-graph and print out to scale. In this case, we will be building a head using a quick clay sketch printed to scale with two views, leaving plenty of space for discovery.

To start, you will need to determine the dimensions of the slab from which you will build your head. Begin with either scaled sketches or printed images of a small clay study digitally adjusted to your target size. Make versions of these references in both front and profile views. Your references should be the size of the head you are hoping to sculpt. First, turn to your profile sketch and measure the distance from the front to the back of the head along two horizontal lines: Once across the midline, below the nose, and once from the top of the chin to the back of the neck. Then, measure the vertical distance between these two points and record these three measurements on a piece of paper. Next, use your front view sketch to measure the width of the head at the same vertical levels you used when taking your profile measurements: right below the nose and above the chin. Multiply these values by 2 and add these to the first horizontal measurements to establish the widths of your slab (front width x 2 + side width = total width). Because we are not measuring a cube, these measurements will be "soft" (as opposed to absolute), meaning they will need to be adjusted to describe the dynamics of a curvilinear plane and to allow extra material for overlapping vertical seams. As a rule of thumb, I select the narrowest and the widest points throughout the shape I am trying to recreate to extract measurements, multiplying the front measurements by 2 before adding the side measurement just once.

To determine height, I measure from the base of my printed sketch to the top of the head and add about 30 percent (15 percent in each direction) to that dimension. This tolerance will both provide extra material to support the head under the chin and enable you to articulate the dome of the head. With these five values, sketch a diagram of your starting shape to know how big your slab will need to be. The width of the top line will be the same as that of the below nose line and the width of the bottom line will be the same as the above chin line. Once all measurements have been established on paper, you can connect the outer edges and create your cutting guide. Roll a slab that is ⅜ inch (1 cm) thick, plot your starting shape onto the surface, and cut accordingly. Ⓐ

Once the slab is at the proper state of dryness, able to hold its weight on edge but still pliable, stand it on its side to make a tapered cylinder. Adjust, cutting away and resetting the proportions, until you feel satisfied with the feel of this preliminary form. Next, make additional adjustments by pushing in and out, articulating soft shapes to begin to describe primary features before capping the form to complete the shape. Finally, make additional notes around

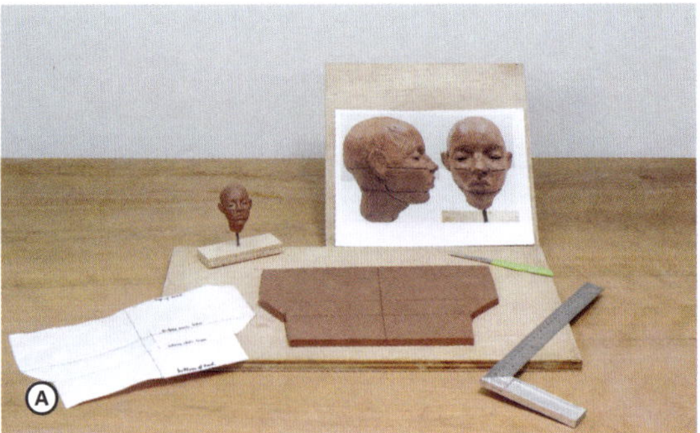

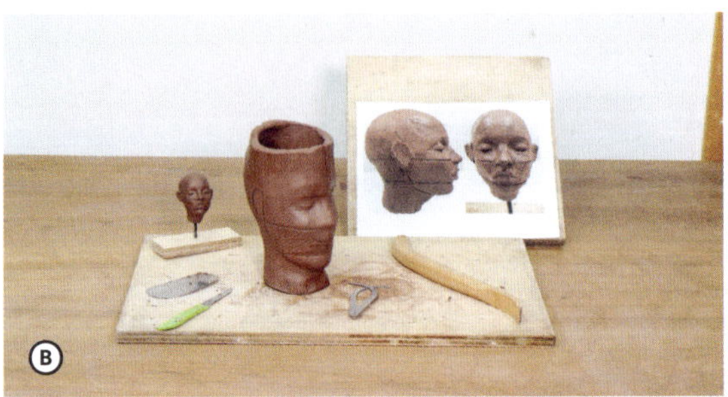

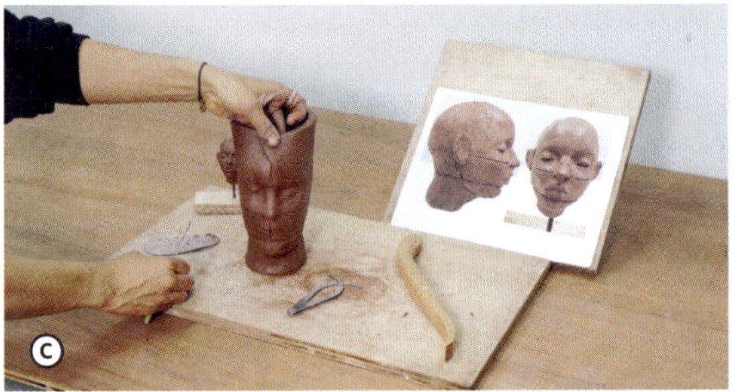

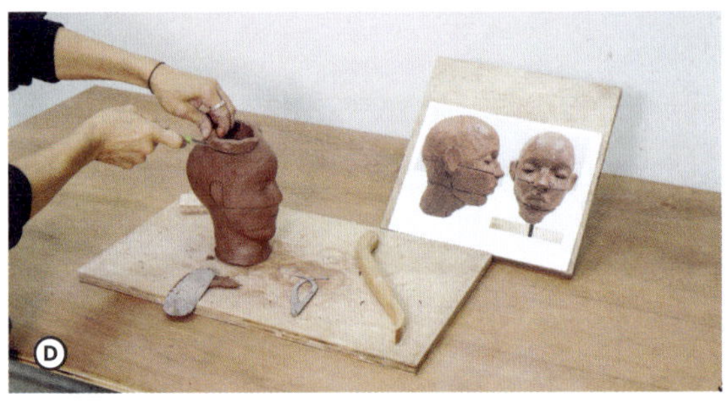

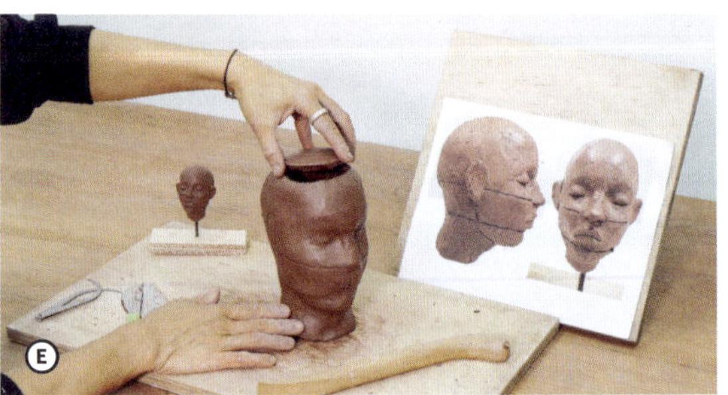

the key landmarks on your piece by drawing onto the surface noting the placement of the eyes, brow, nose, mouth, jawline, chin, and ears. ⒷⒸⒹⒺ Wait for your piece to set—it should be beyond a "sticky" stage, but still pliable—then begin to cut the form apart and flatten the shape in order extract your pattern. ⒻⒼ

CUTTING A HEAD SHAPE TO CREATE A PATTERN USING ANY HOLLOW FORM THAT IS STILL PLIABLE

If you have a sculpted head that you'd like to make a template from, start by cutting a small circle out of the very top of the head. (In our model, this step is done.) Set this clay disc on a piece of paper and trace around it with a pencil. Next, find the vertical centerline of the back of the head and cut down this line from top to bottom. The head is now open on top with a slit running down the back. Gently open the head at this back seam and uncurl the clay, laying it down on a piece of paper with the face up. The areas with the most curvature, the upper part of the head and the chin, will not want to lay flat easily. If the head is small, I will simply press these areas flat. If it is a larger head, cut short slits at the places with the most curvature to help these areas lay flat. These slits will open and create triangular darts in the eventual paper template. When the clay head is lying flat, I trace all the way around the edge. Next, take a needle tool or thin knife and cut through the flattened clay face to transfer key features to the paper underneath.

Cut slits to mark the eyeline, the bottom of the nose, the mouth, the mandible, the brow line, and the chin. When the clay is lifted off the paper, you'll have the rough draft of your head template. This paper will be stained, damp, and wrinkled from contact with the clay. The lines drawn with pencil and cut with the knife may be faint. To create a more durable, clear tem-

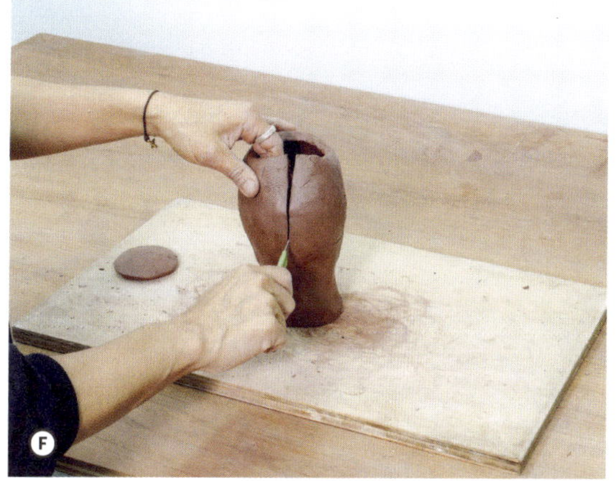

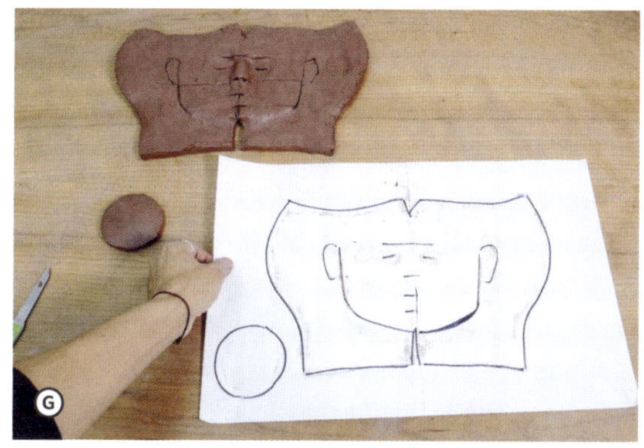

plate, let the paper dry and then cut out the traced head shape. Using an X-ACTO knife, cut through the lines that mark the facial features. Next, lay the rough paper template on a clean piece of paper or plastic sheeting and trace around the perimeter with a fine-point marker before drawing through the slits in the paper to transfer the facial feature marks. Add about ¼ to ½ inch (0.64 to 1.3 cm) to one side of the seam at the back of the head so the slab can overlap there for a strong connection. You now have completed your pattern! You can use this template to reproduce multiple small heads at the scale of the maquette shown here, or you can enlarge it to use the captured information at different sizes.

This approach can be used to make shape patterns for any form where you have a scaled front and side view. Ⓖ

Judy Fox

How do you research and ground yourself around a subject before committing to the long process of making a new piece?

The process of making a figure begins in my mind. As I would look at cross-cultural art or read the newspaper, I would always be on the lookout for images. I want an iconic gesture that might be read, or even misinterpreted, in an interesting way by a contemporary gaze. From a striking historical character or image, I'd start to imagine a figure and tinker with it. I would then find a model of the same ethnicity as the prototype and take many photos from all angles. Working from the photos and with my knowledge of anatomy, I put together a portrait of the model in the predetermined pose. My rendering was specific and concentrated so that the spirit of the individual would be channeled, creating a sometimes awkward drama as they balanced in a contrived position. Superimposition of individual and type was reinforced by styling a historically sourced hairdo atop an otherwise naked body. The impact of the piece that emerged from its conflicted elements can be a surprise. Are we seeing an actor or a victim of projected meaning?

Could you talk briefly about your process as it relates to clay?

Clay is the most versatile material I know as far as creating form straight from the mind. Each piece is hand built gradually to its general shape from the bottom up and then maintained at leather-hard. There are removable metal rods in the legs. The rigid clay is carved with plaster rasps so that the form is controlled and the surface has a firm look. I add details in soft clay as I work and carve them when they firm up. Larger works are carved and fired in pieces and glued together after firing. I then fill the seams with plaster so they are not visible after the surface is painted with casein.

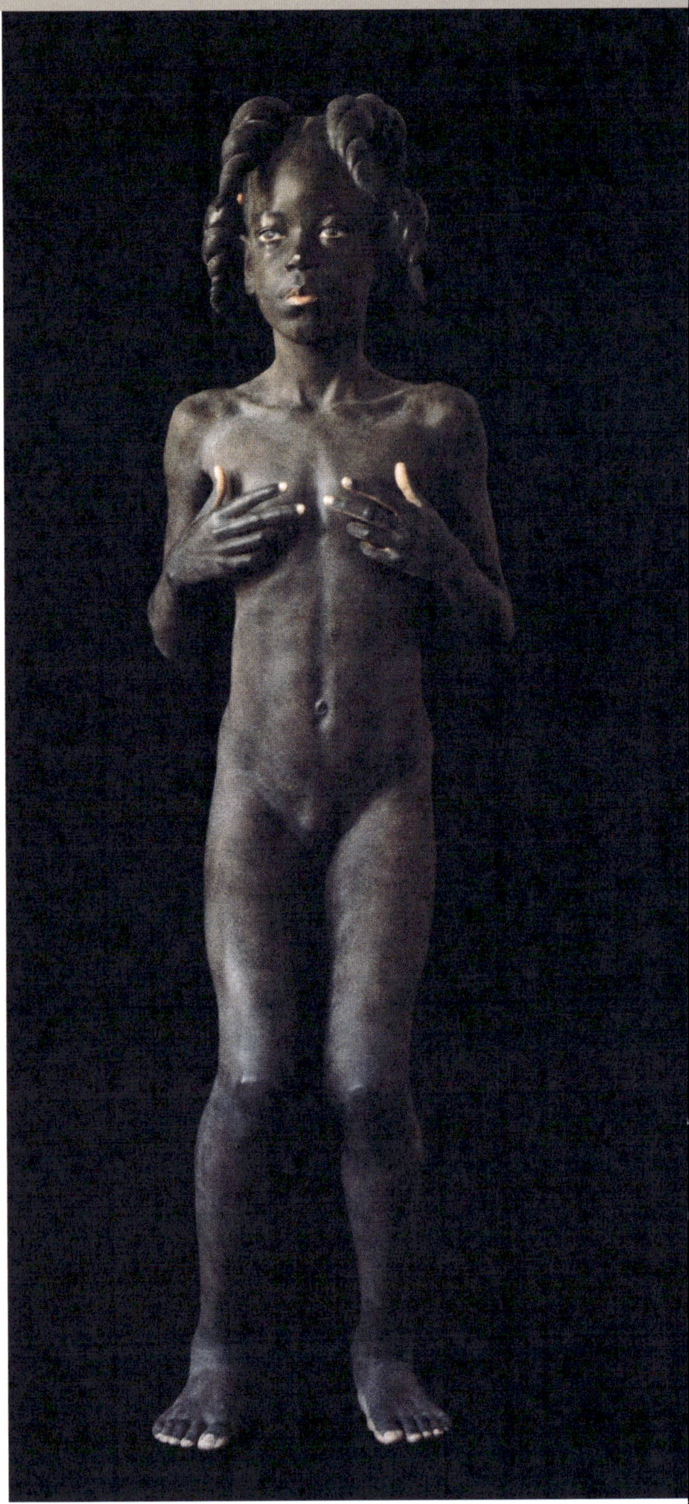

Above: *Onile.* Clockwise from top left: *Sphinx, Snow White,* and *Guardian.* All courtesy of the artist.

THE FIGURE IN CLAY

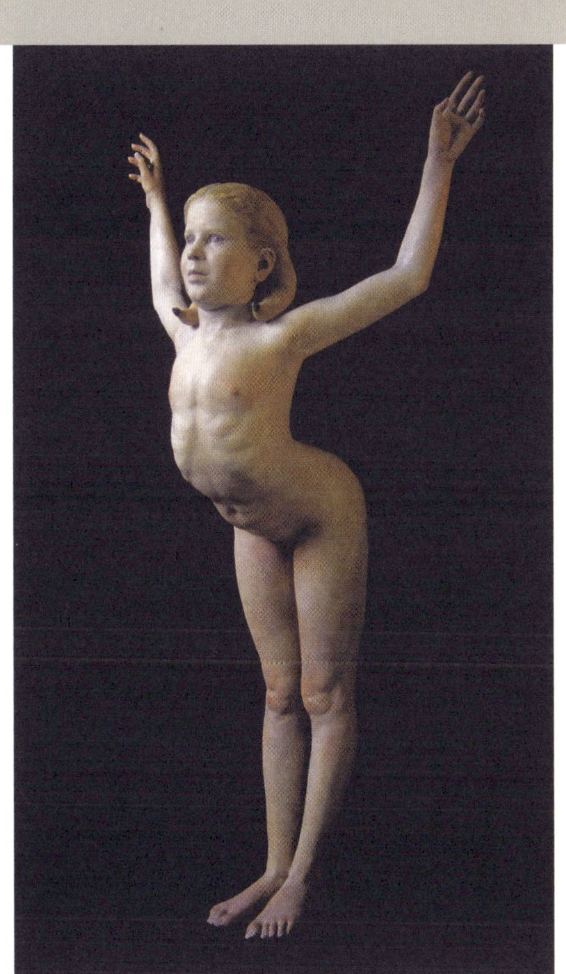

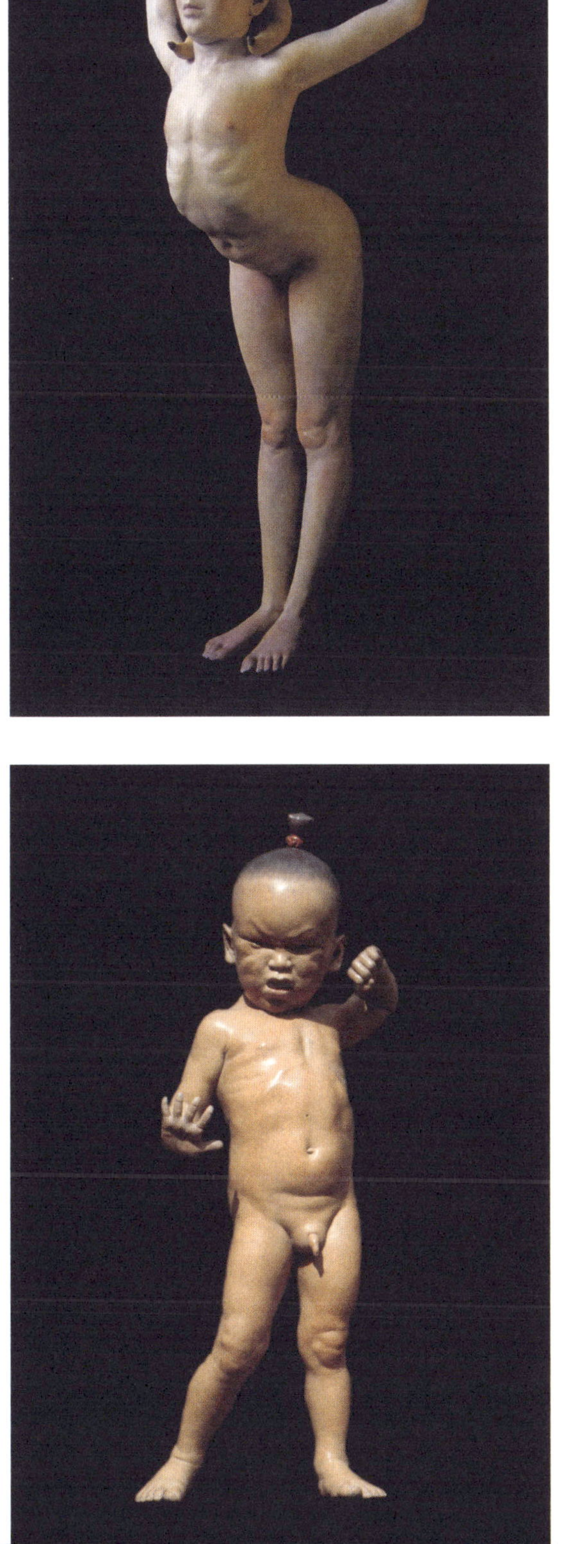

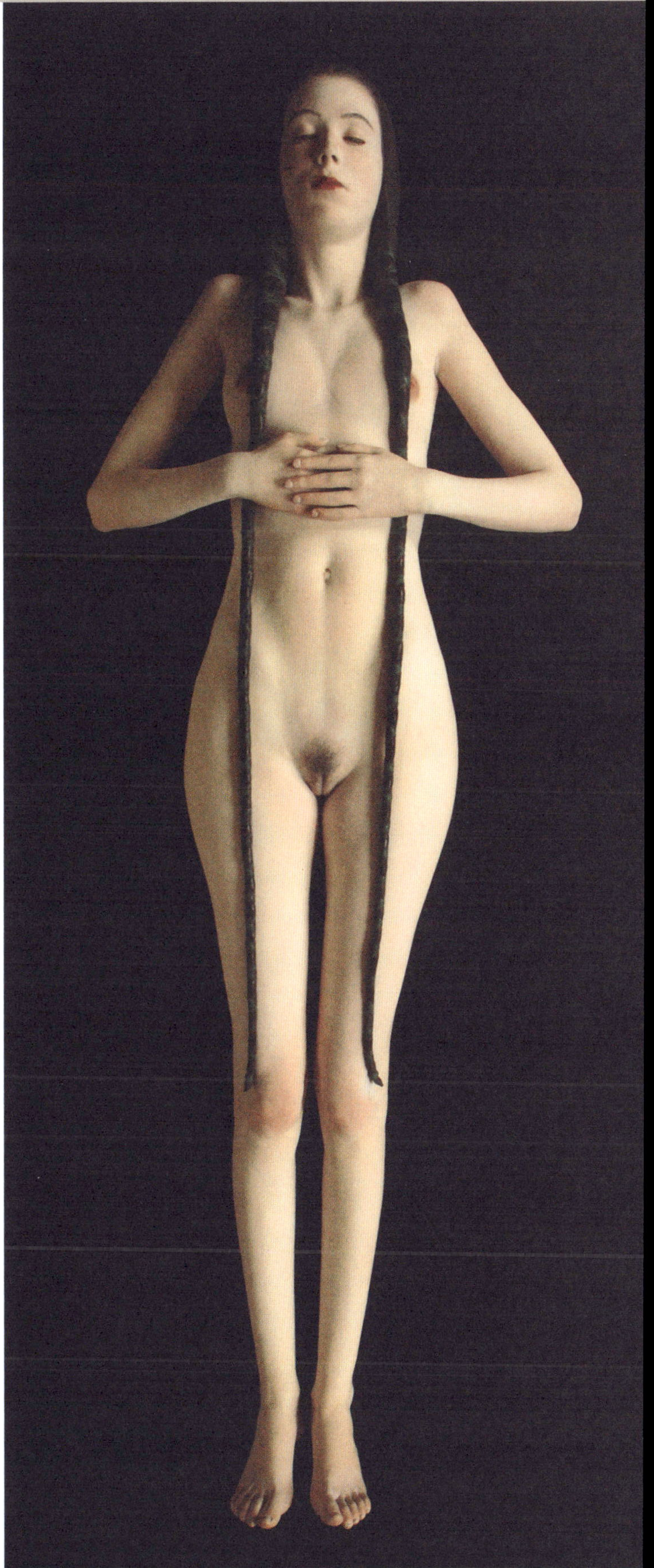

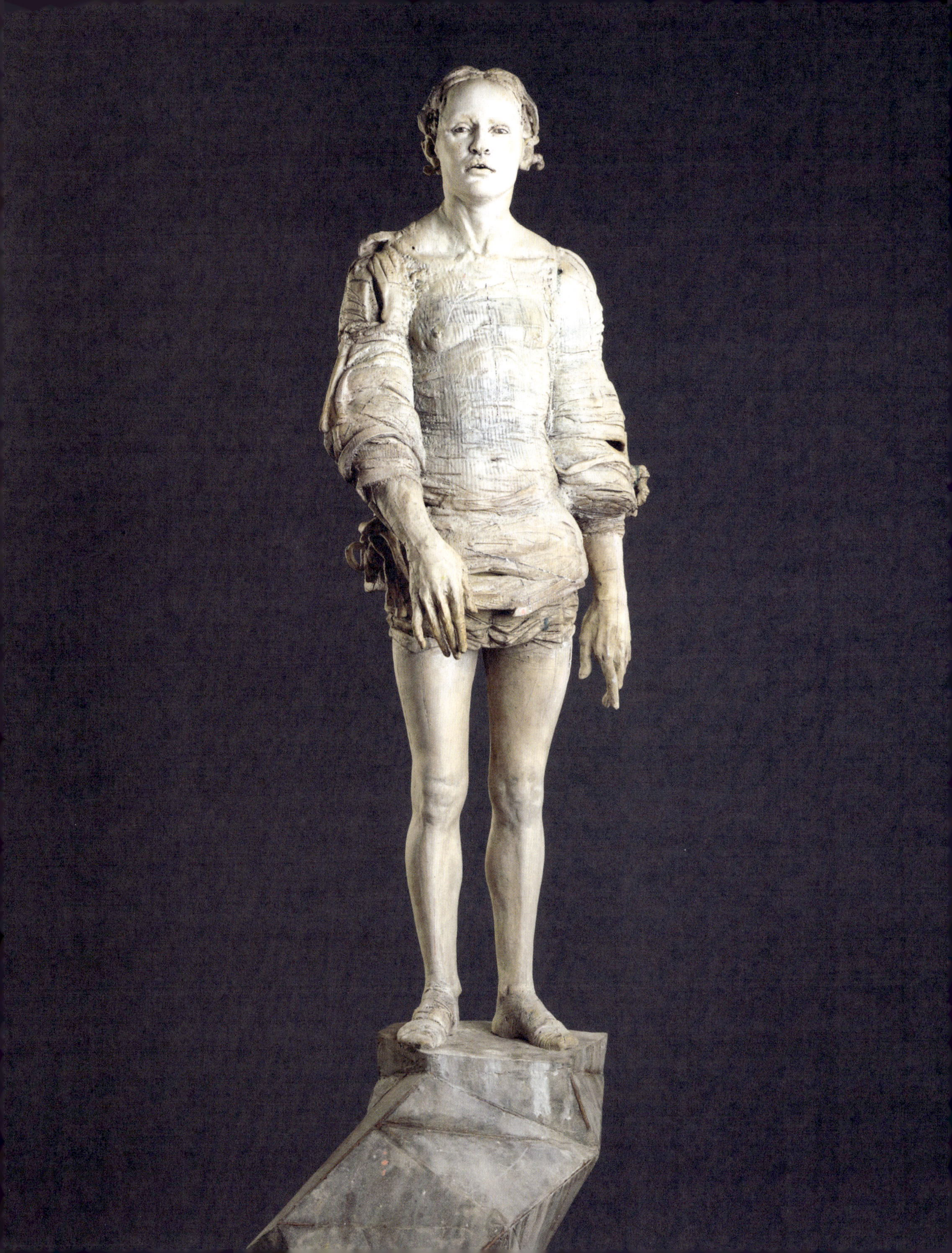

3

ASSEMBLING LOWER BODY PARTS ON ARMATURE

NOW THAT YOU have prepared your space and assembled your tools, materials, and references, you have reached the most exciting part of the figure sculpting process—creating your forms and assembling your sculpture over its armature from the ground up. You will start by preparing the base. Next, you will slide your clay footprints onto the armature and establish the placement of the lower legs. With lower legs in place, you will elaborate the structures of the feet and then continue to the upper legs, reconciling the pattern-generated shapes with specifics observed from your reference images as you continue stacking form onto form. Finally, you will assemble the pelvis and fine-tune its alignment in relation to the legs, capturing the contra postural gesture created by the interplay of the engaged leg and the angled pelvis.

While the pattern-generated shapes you will be using hold useful information, it is important to understand that they will need to be modified in accordance with your photographic references to hone in on the dynamics of the gesture and articulate your volumes to their full extension. However, you could also consider using the pattern-generated forms more loosely to create open, stylized figurative compositions that do not adhere as closely to a naturalistic agenda. This process offers many possibilities and space for discovery at every stage!

WHAT YOU'LL NEED TO GET STARTED

- Armature

- Footprint, lower leg, and upper leg patterns

- ⅜ inch (1 cm) slab that fits your lower body templates

- Joining slip

- Fresh clay to work over seams

- Knife

- Scoring tool

- Metal or wooden dowel (⅜ inch [1 cm] thick)

- Serrated rib

- Rake tools

- Brushes

Cristina Córdova, *Isla,* part of the collection of the Asheville Art Museum.

PREPARING YOUR ARMATURE

As you begin to build your sculpture onto the armature, the four photographic views printed to scale should align with the four views of your sculpture from each of the four edges of your armature base. In other words, for a square base, one edge of the square will be facing you when looking at the sculpture from the front, and another when looking at the left side, and so on. This setup creates an easy way to ensure your perspectives remain consistent and that the information you are referencing matches the angle from which you are sculpting. Later in the sculpting process we will introduce additional photographic references of our model. These transitional views impart visual information that cannot be gleaned from our four cardinal images alone. To orient these new views, you will approximate the vantage point by aligning the outer edges of the reference model and negative spaces created by her position with that of your sculpture.

JOINERY

HOW TO MAKE JOINING SLIP

To make joining slip, roll or pinch out flakes of clay, as thin as possible, and let them sit out until they are completely bone-dry. (You can also do what I do and save the cutoffs and scraps that I generate throughout my sculpting process so that I have a supply of bone-dry clay to turn into more joining slip when I run out.) Place the small pieces of clay in the base of a lidded plastic container. Run water over your flakes until they are just covered, and then listen for the pleasant fizzing sound of slaking clay. I like to let my clay sit for several hours or overnight before stirring, adjusting water content if needed before putting it into a covered container for use.

Note: For this process, you want your joining slip to be thick like toothpaste. If in slaking (or breaking down) your bits of clay you end up with a slip that is too soft, just leave it out, stirring it often until it reaches the right consistency, or add more dry clay to balance the mix.

KEYING

In the context of figurative sculpture, keys are drawn registration marks that record the placement of various sculptural components while those pieces are temporarily separated. Like a bookmark, a registration key helps you find your place. There are numerous instances in which registration keys can be helpful. For example, keys are crucial in the hollowing out of solid-built sculptures. In this book, we primarily use them after we have made choices about the final positioning of a new body component, for instance, how the torso will join the lower part of the body. At this point, we are ready to slip and score the edges of our cylindrical forms to permanently attach them. This task involves removing the top form to access the seam with our scoring tool, but we don't want to lose the alignment we have so carefully chosen. This is where keys come in, making sure we can easily find our way back.

Because our figurative compositions are complex—aligned along the x, y, and z axes—I recommend drawing at least three keys across every line of separation. Keys should be clearly visible and roughly perpendicular to the line of separation across which they are drawn. It may be helpful to smooth or clean up a heavily textured surface before drawing in keys. While single perpendicular lines are certainly sufficient, it can also be helpful to create some variation among your keys: a single line for one, two parallel lines right next to each other for the second, three lines for the third. Use whatever method works for you. Be sure to draw your keys long enough so that you don't accidentally erase them when you score and slip the inner edges of the forms you are attaching.

SLIPPING, SCORING, ATTACHING, AND CLEANING SEAMS

Throughout this process, you will be joining clay together, when first forming your slabs into your preliminary shapes, and later as you begin to combine different body segments. When joining clay, you will score, or rough up, both sides of the joint and stick them together using a tacky clay slip, paying attention to the water content of your slabs or forms and making sure to compress thoroughly to ensure proper adhesion. Slipping and scoring is the common term used to describe this process.

As a rule of thumb, when creating the initial forms from slabs, you want to assemble them while the clay is still very pliable, as soon as the clay can hold the shape without collapsing, to ensure the joined areas are completely integrated and the seam isn't visible in the final product.

When attaching the different body parts, such as the torso to a pelvis, it is helpful to have the pieces be of comparable dryness. As clay dries, clay particles shrink together, and it is important to have this shrinking rate be consistent in adjoining segments to avoid any cracking.

Pieces that are being attached should be firm enough to hold their shape and withstand the firm pressure of compressing one form against the other. Each clay body has its own window for joining two pieces together, and it's import-

ant to get to know these properties in the clay you use. If the clay becomes too stiff, it will not adhere properly. In cases where the joining edges seem too dry, you can rehydrate the area by placing moist rags or shop towels over the edges and covering the joint with plastic to gradually bring the clay to a proper water content for joining.

Things to keep in mind:

- When unifying two body components, slip and score along the outside of the seam to pack fresh clay, reinforcing and disappearing it.

- Have an assortment of scoring tools for different scales. In my practice, I use a fork for the larger pieces and a toothed stainless-steel tool to score in tighter locations. I also use a wire brush scoring tool or an X-ACTO knife for the most delicate work.

- Score deeply enough to create plenty of texture for edges to adhere properly. The drier the clay is the sharper your scoring tool will need to be.

- Make sure your joining slip is tacky and not watery.

- Once the seam or joint has been compressed and recovered, allow some time for it to set before putting it under any strain. If you are joining body parts that stand against gravity, like outstretched arms, be prepared to use external supports such as clay, metal rods, or stiff wire, to take the weight off the joint until the clay begins to dry and is firm enough to hold weight.

CLAY DRYNESS FOR SLAB BUILDING

After I have rolled out my slabs, I generally must wait to let them firm up enough to support their own weight when standing on edge. If I pick up the corner of my slab and it feels floppy like fabric, the slab is too soft and is at risk of stretching when lifted. When I can lift a corner of my slab and it holds that shape and doesn't fall all the way back to the table when released, I know it is ready. Conversely, a slab is too dry to work into a form when you try to bend it into a cylinder and deep cracks (and not surface cracks that can be easily compressed) form on the outside.

It is very important to monitor the water content of your slabs, forms, and sculpture throughout this process. Add moisture regularly with a mister or spray bottle to keep your piece workable. Wait for the clay to absorb that moisture before spraying again. Cover your work strategically by using moist rags, shop towels, and plastic to ensure some parts start to set to hold weight and offer stability while others remain in a softer, workable state.

THINGS TO KEEP IN MIND:

- If a slab has dried too much to turn into a form but hasn't yet entered the bone-dry stage, it is still possible to rehydrate and regain its pliancy, especially when using paper clay. To accomplish this, mist both sides of the slab and wait for the moisture to be fully absorbed. Take a moist towel, squeezed of any excess water, and cover the slab top and bottom before putting it under tight plastic for 6 to 12 hours so that the slab gradually reabsorbs moisture. If this is done gently, the slab should be ready for sculpting again.

- There are three primary stages that describe the dryness of a slab: soft, leather-hard, and bone-dry. Within each of those there are many in-between stages that correlate to the different steps of this process. In general, the slabs are cut and assembled into shapes when the clay is at a soft leather-hard stage. The parts are assembled and joined together when the clay is at the leather-hard or mature leather-hard stage—when you can still join parts and add material to refine the surface, but the core form is no longer flexible and would break apart if cut open. This stage is often described as having a chocolate-like consistency. As the piece continues to dry, it will enter the bone-dry stage, where no more wet clay can be added, and the surface acquires a soft, powdery quality.

FOOTPRINT AND LOWER LEG

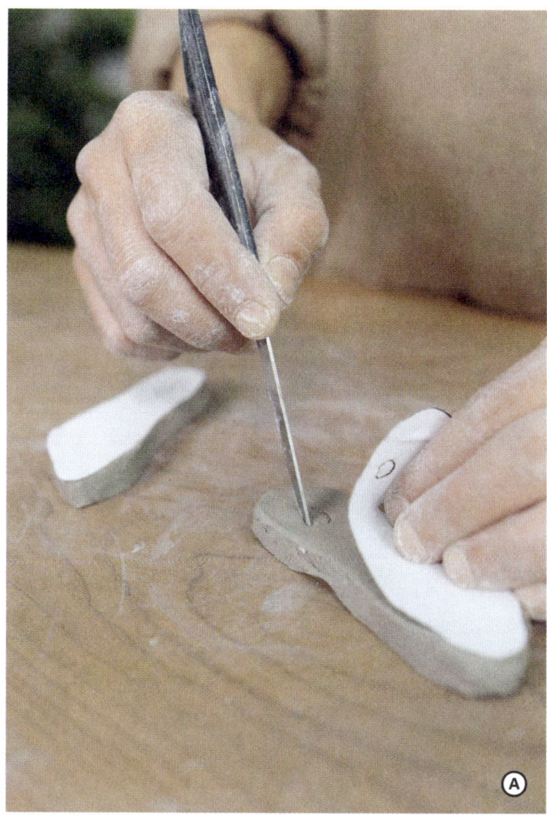

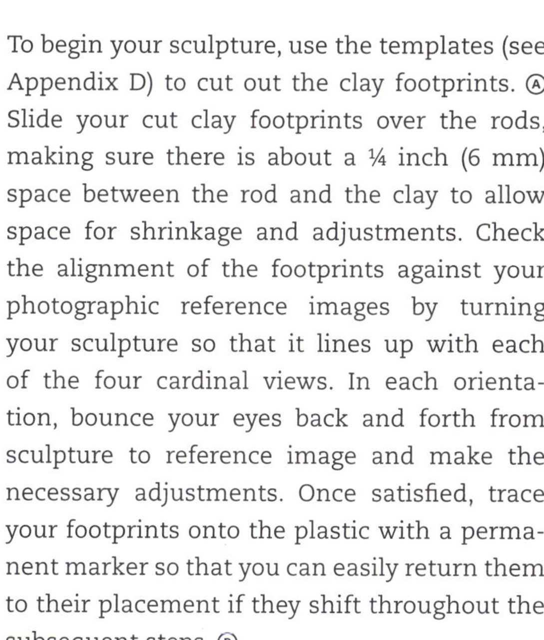

To begin your sculpture, use the templates (see Appendix D) to cut out the clay footprints. Ⓐ Slide your cut clay footprints over the rods, making sure there is about a ¼ inch (6 mm) space between the rod and the clay to allow space for shrinkage and adjustments. Check the alignment of the footprints against your photographic reference images by turning your sculpture so that it lines up with each of the four cardinal views. In each orientation, bounce your eyes back and forth from sculpture to reference image and make the necessary adjustments. Once satisfied, trace your footprints onto the plastic with a permanent marker so that you can easily return them to their placement if they shift throughout the subsequent steps. Ⓑ

Place your printed lower leg templates on top of a ⅜ inch (1 cm)–thick slab and use a knife

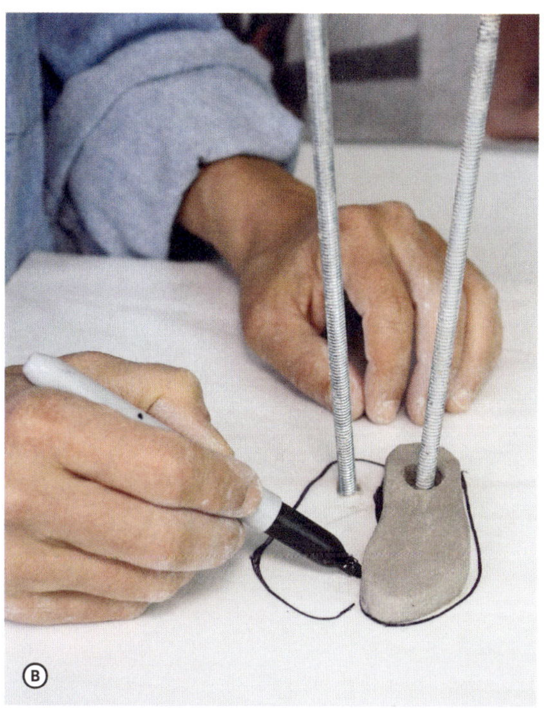

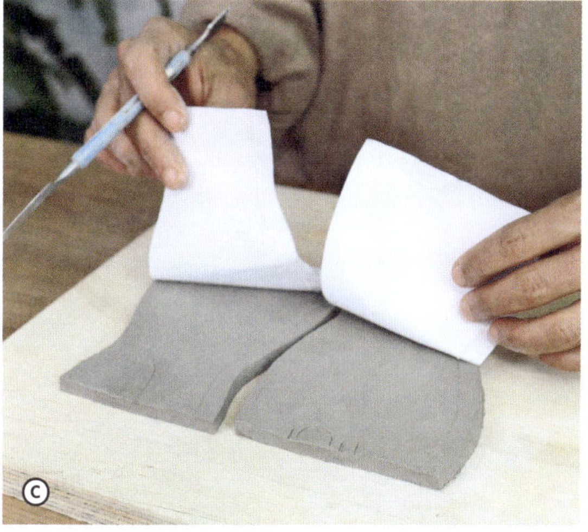

to cut the edges and trace guidelines of these templates. Remove the templates and lightly redraw the guidelines so that they are more legible. Ⓒ Next, curl each slab until the two long edges come together and overlap along the guideline.

Slip and score these edges where they will touch and compress the seam together. Move

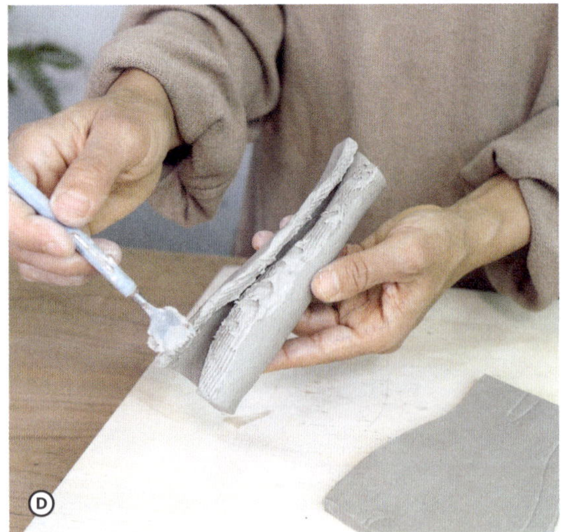

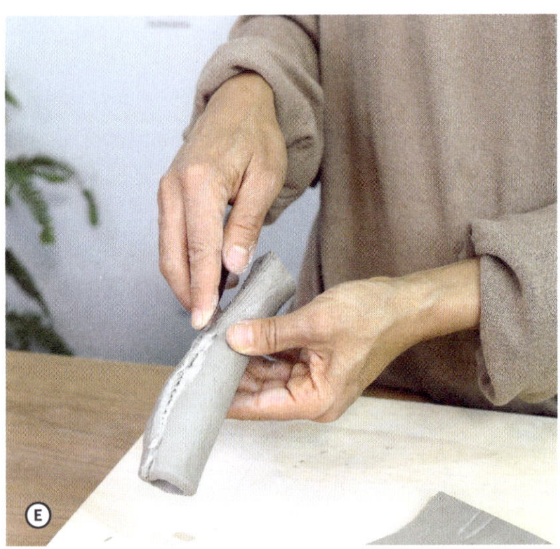

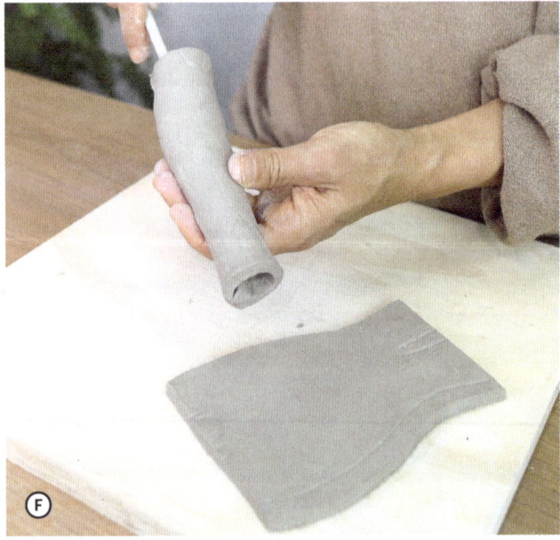

your serrated rib across the outside of your seam in a cross-hatching motion to interlace the clay particles and strengthen this connection point. On the inside areas of the seam that you cannot access with your fingers, use a dowel or your threaded rod to help with compression. Slide the rod through the lower leg form and turn it gently as you support and guide pressure with your hand from the outside. Apply enough pressure to secure the seam but not to distort the shape. Make sure the opening through the cylindrical form is at least ½ inch (1.3 cm) to allow for shrinkage and small adjustments. Ⓓ Ⓔ Ⓕ

Once the lower leg cylinders have set enough to hold their shape against the pressure of your fingers without distorting, compare them with your photographic references by holding them up to your printouts at each cardinal view while making adjustments. Look at the relationship between the shin bone and the calf muscles, and make note of how the form narrows as it transitions to the knee. (This narrowing is even more pronounced at the ankle.) Add or remove bits of clay as needed to begin articulating the subtleties of these forms.

Slide the lower legs over the rods and bring them down to meet the footprints. Find the alignment of the lower legs by turning your sculpture to match each photograph's orientation and make adjustments accordingly. Stabilize the legs with bits of clay to hold them in place as you turn your sculpture. Once you feel satisfied with the placement of the legs, trace around the outside of each leg onto the footprints and draw several vertical keys, or alignment marks, through both ankles and footprints to have a record of their alignment. Ⓖ

Next, remove the legs to slip and score them before attaching them permanently. Once the lower legs are affixed to the footprints, slip, score, and pack fresh clay around the outside of this seam to enhance stability.

Note: *In larger pieces, the lower legs can compress under the weight of the subsequent layers before the clay fully sets. For this reason, I often make these slightly longer than the photographic references to account for that shortening due to compression.*

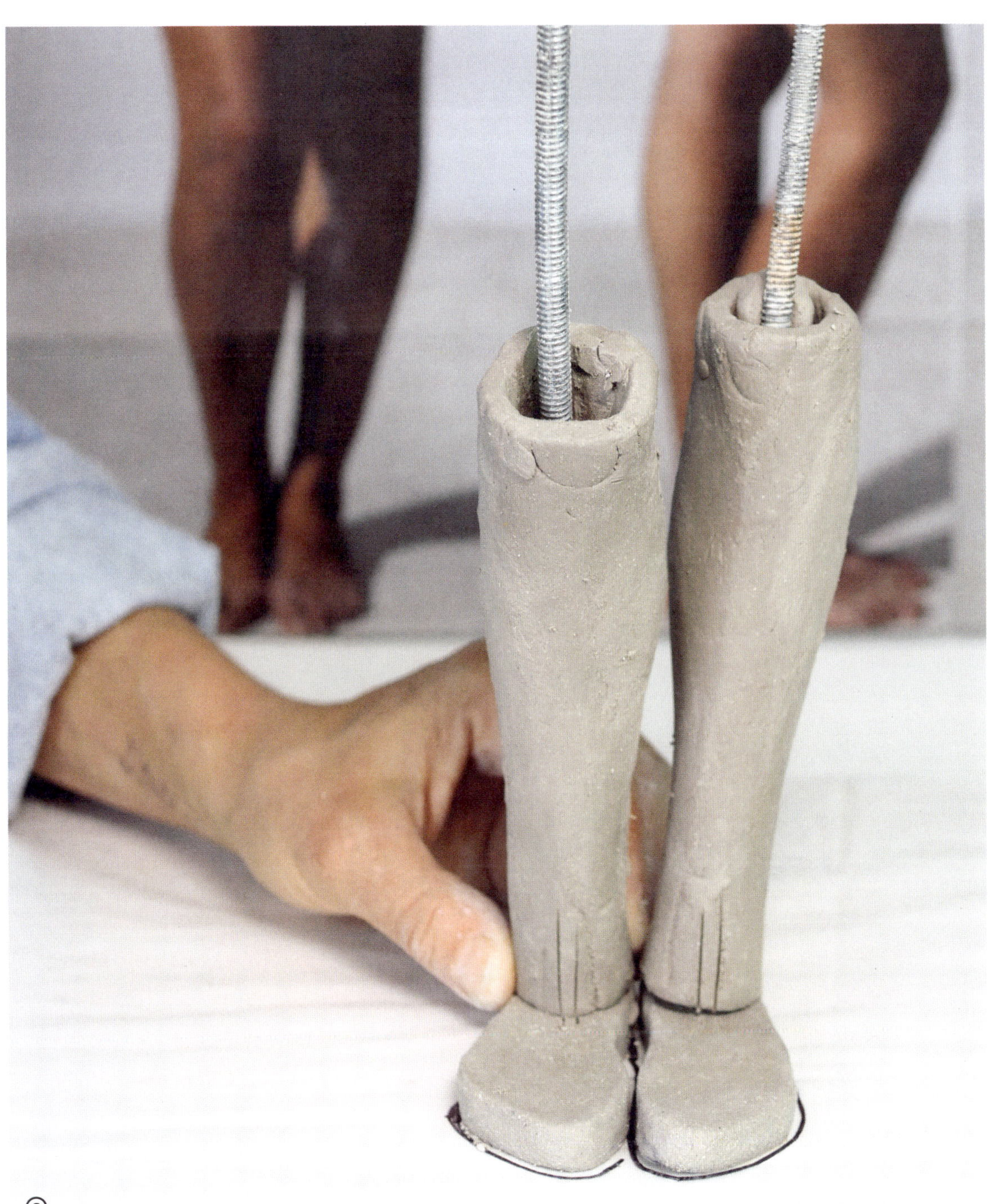

THE FOOT

The widest part of the foot is just below the toes. It spans from the big toe's first metatarsal phalangeal joint to the base of the pinky toe's fifth metatarsal on the outer part of the foot. ④ The outward facing diagonal drawn between these points mirrors the tilt in the ankle bones between the fibula and the tibia. The fibula is located on the outside of the ankle and is lower than the tibia, which rests on the inside of the ankle. ② ⑤

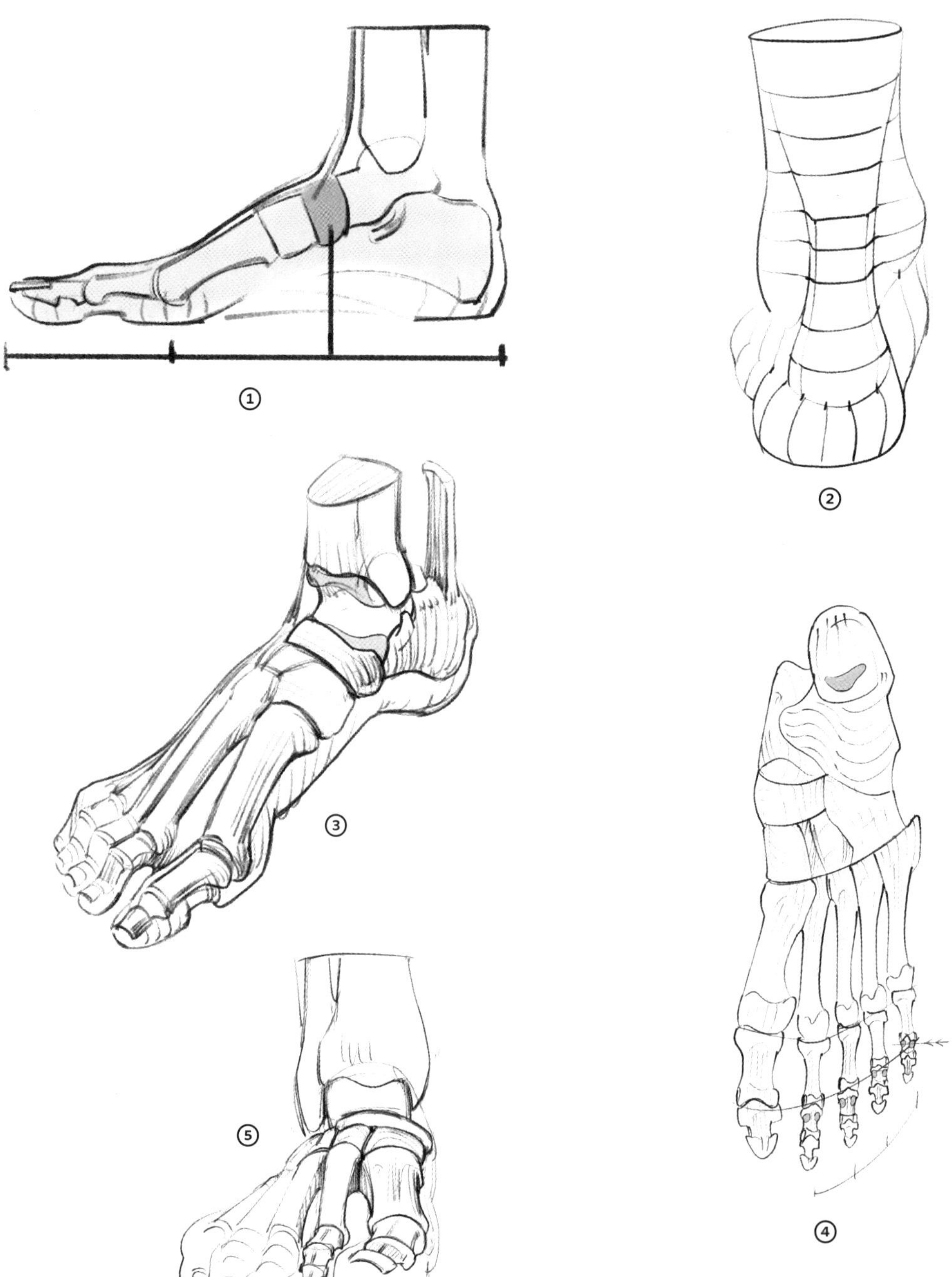

THE FIGURE IN CLAY

Illustrations: *Morpho Mains et Pieds* de Michel Lauricella © 2019 Editions Eyrolles

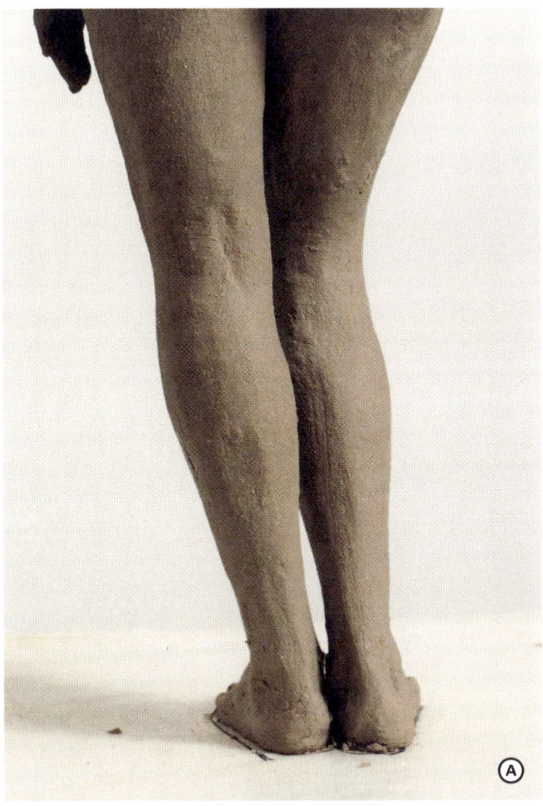

(A)

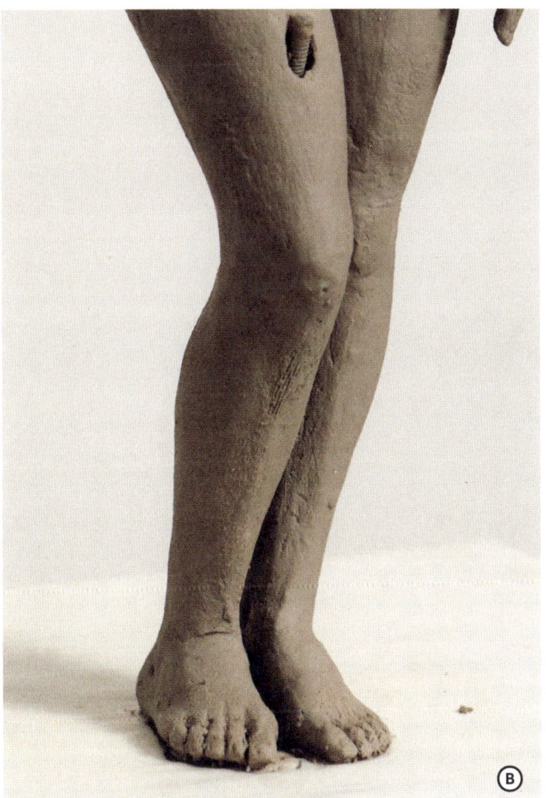

(B)

When seen from above, the foot appears like an elongated triangle. From its widest point at the knuckle line, the outer edges of the foot angle inwards to meet the ankle. Moving from the knuckle line forward, into the toes, there is an inverse angling inward along the side of the big toe and the pinky. Note that the arc of the toes follows the diagonal established by the widest part of the foot. ④

Tip: The size of the foot is roughly equivalent to the distance between the wrist and the elbow crease on the inside of the arm. When working without patterns, you can use calipers to capture that forearm distance and use it to plot the length of the foot, scaling it to match the overall size of the sculpture.

At their most basic level, the foot and leg can be understood as an assortment of acute and obtuse cones. Viewed from the side, the foot's profile forms a squat triangle between the toes, the ankle bone, and the heel. Viewed from the front, you can see another triangle created by the widest part of the foot, right below the toes moving back on either side to meet the ankle. Viewed from the back, you'll notice yet another triangle form created by the heel, where it connects to the Achilles tendon at the level of the ankle bones. Ⓐ ⑤ Ⓑ

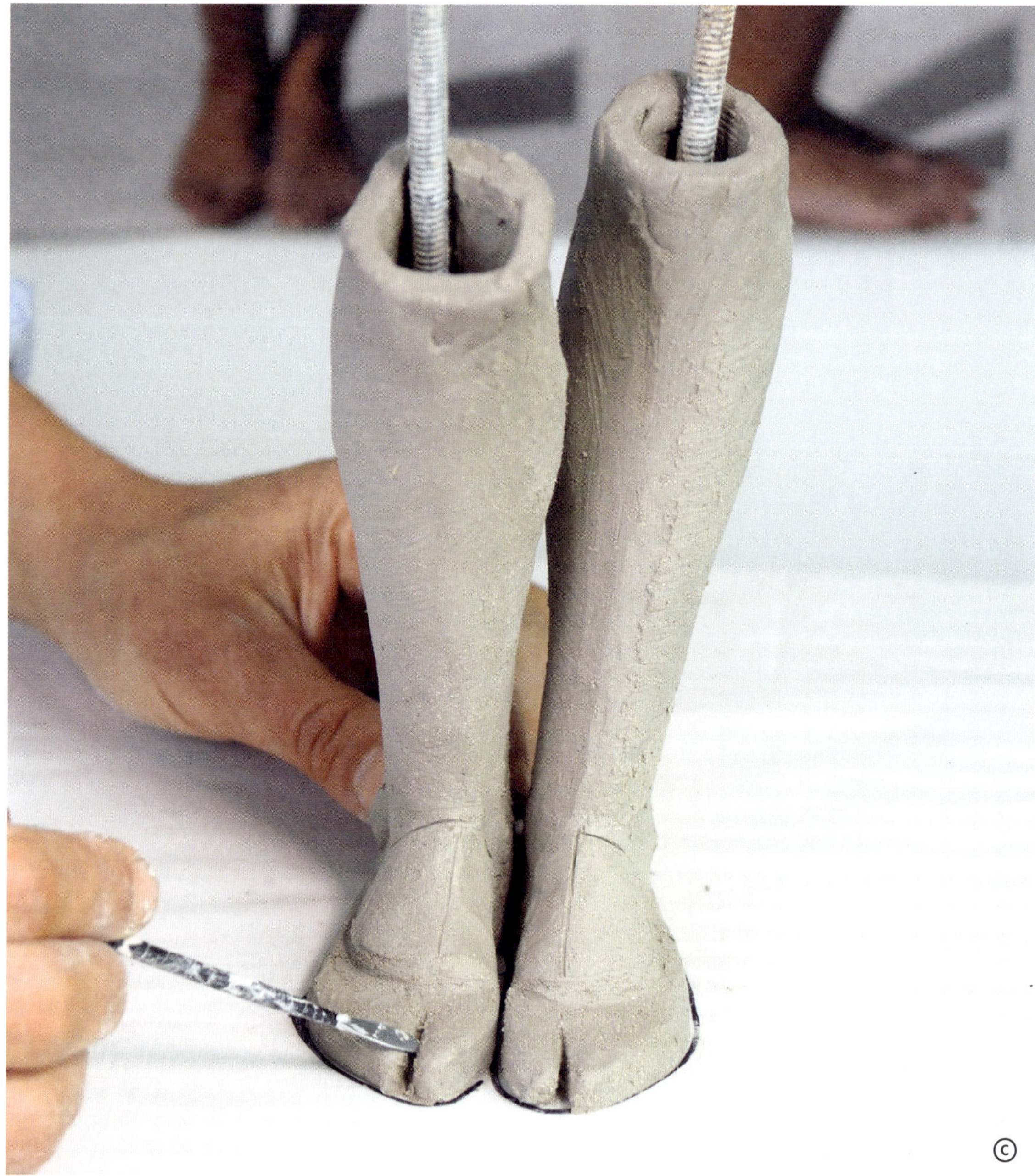

THE FIGURE IN CLAY

Once you have the basic size and shape of the footprint, continue to add bits of clay to articulate the preliminary volumes of the foot: the mound, adjacent to the ankle, and the platform from where the toes will be developed. The apex of the mound aligns with the break between the big toe and the rest of the toes, so go ahead and create a demarcation to separate your big toe from your other toes. © To the inside of that dividing line, the mound slopes down sharply towards the inner part of the foot, leading into the arch. To the outside of that line, the mound slopes more gently towards the outer part of the foot where it meets the tail of the platform. The platform occupies about a third of the overall length of the foot toward the front, where the toes are, and moves in a sliver along the outer part of the foot and toward the heel.

It will move below the fibula, or the diamond-shaped outer ankle bone. The fibula is lower and slightly further back than the tibia, or inner ankle bone, which has a rounded shape.

Once you have established your mound and platform along with the demarcation of the big toe, you can mark the rest of the toes radially, following an outward curve that runs across the widest part of the foot. When the foot is in a standing position, the three middle toes shift planes at each joint to reveal a stair-step design. While the big toe has just two bones, the rest of the toes contain three each. Ⓓ Ⓔ Depending on how much pressure is being exerted on the phalanges, the three center toes will either point forward or downward. The big toe tends to point upwards while the pinky toe points down and inwards, burrowing under the fourth toe.

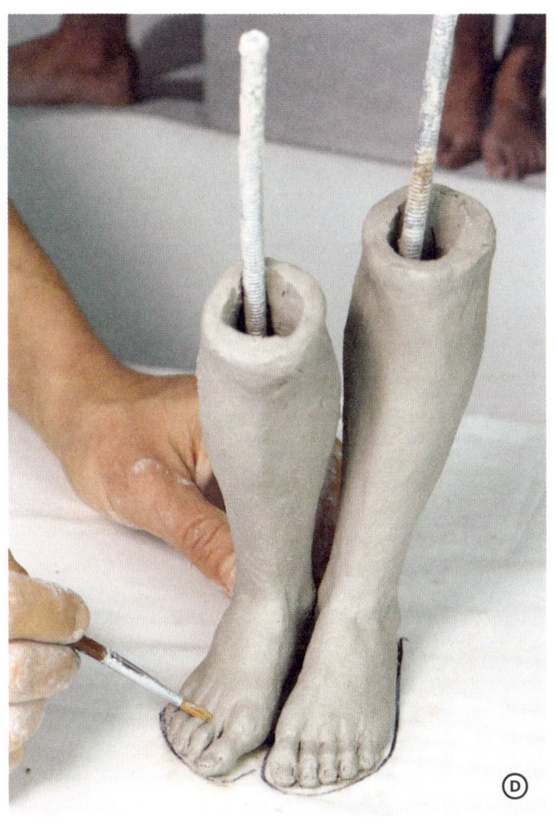

Ⓓ

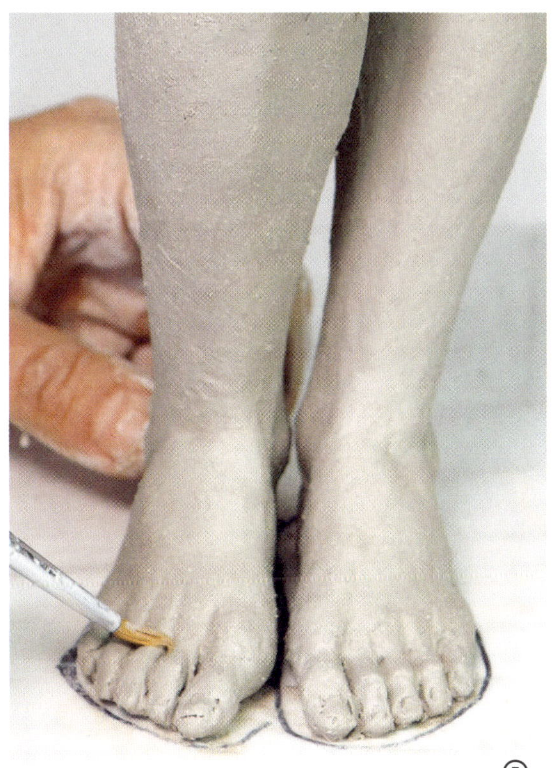

Ⓔ

NAILS

The nail bed rests on the last phalange of each toe and has a rounded quality that presses onto the soft form at either side, causing the flesh to bulge up around it. Toenails also have a slight upward incline as they move outwards from the base of the nail to the end of the toe.

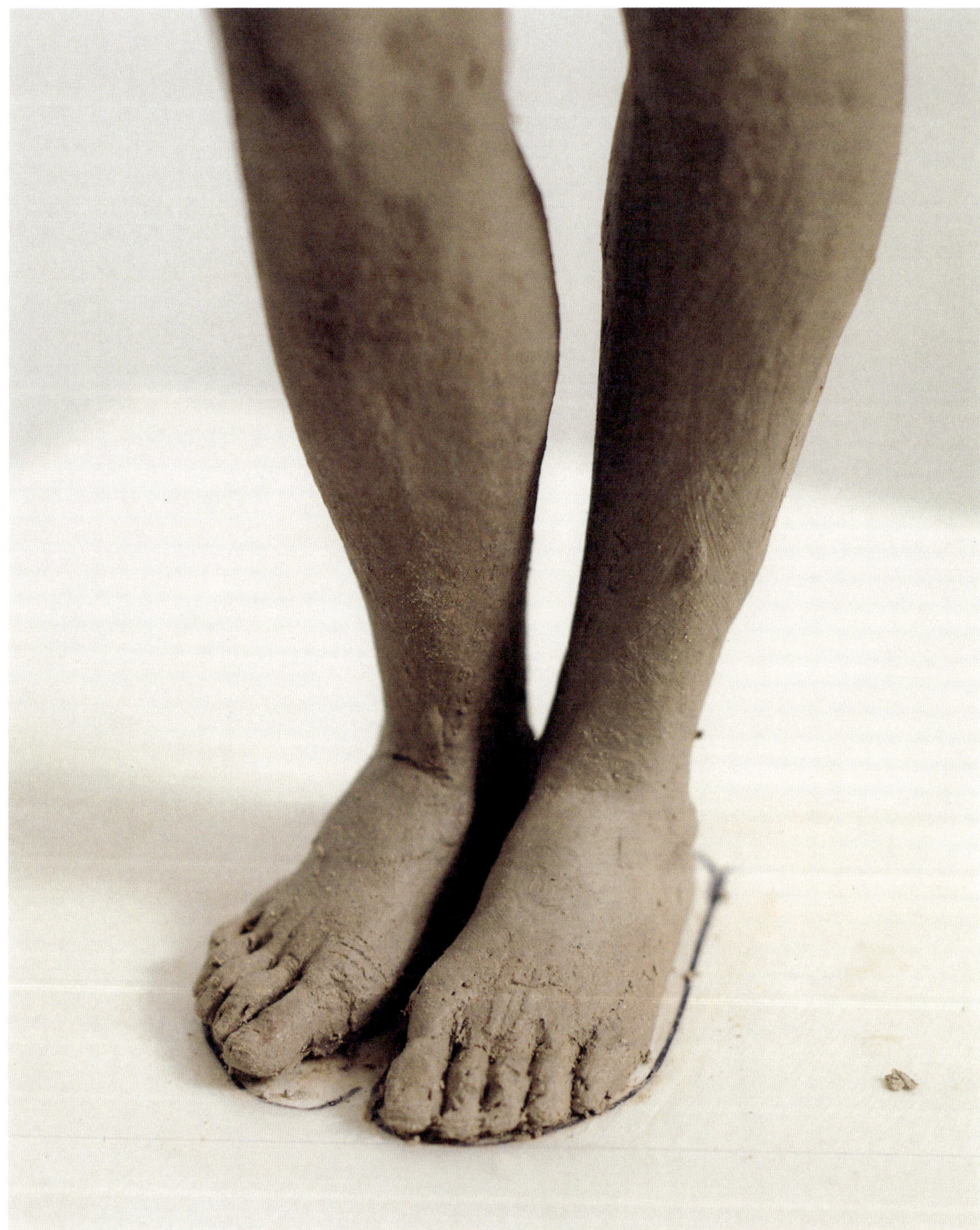

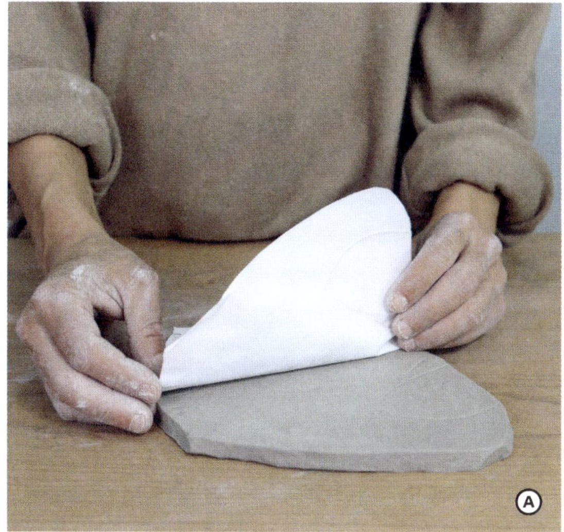

UPPER LEG

Place your printed upper leg templates on top of a ⅜ inch (1 cm)–thick slab. Using a knife, score the guidelines and cut the perimeter of each template. Ⓐ Next, curl each slab until the two long edges come together and overlap along your guideline. Slip and score these edges where they will touch and compress the seam together thoroughly, moving your serrated rib across the outside of your seam in a cross-hatching motion just as you did with your lower leg cylinders. Ⓑ If you have trouble accessing the inside of this seam with your fingers, use a dowel or threaded rod to apply pressure from within. Ⓒ Turn your rod gently, supporting from the outside with your hand. Apply enough pressure to secure the seam but not enough to distort the shape. Your goal is for the seams to become strong and integrated—compressed to a similar wall thickness as the rest of the upper leg cylinders, with superficial lines eliminated by the cross-hatching of your serrated rib.

Once the upper leg cylinders have set enough to retain their shape under the pressure of your fingers, hold them up to your printouts at each cardinal view and make adjustments. Ⓓ Add or remove bits of clay as needed to begin articu-

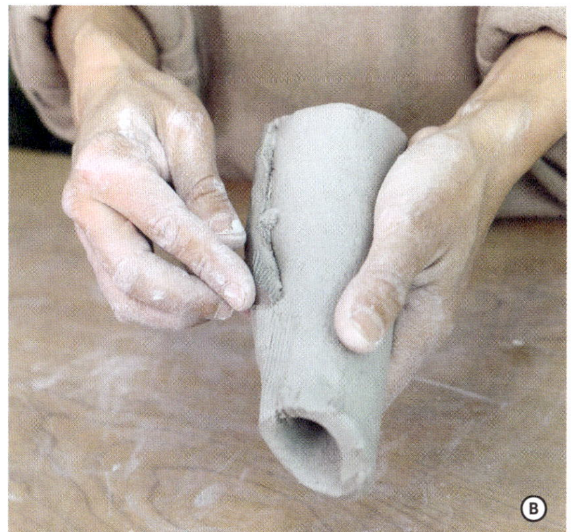

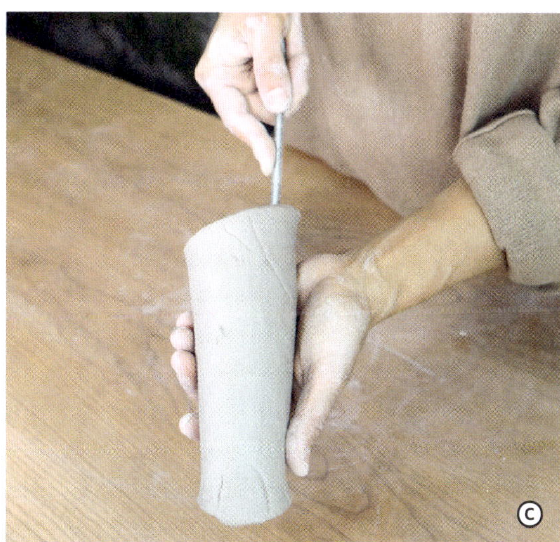

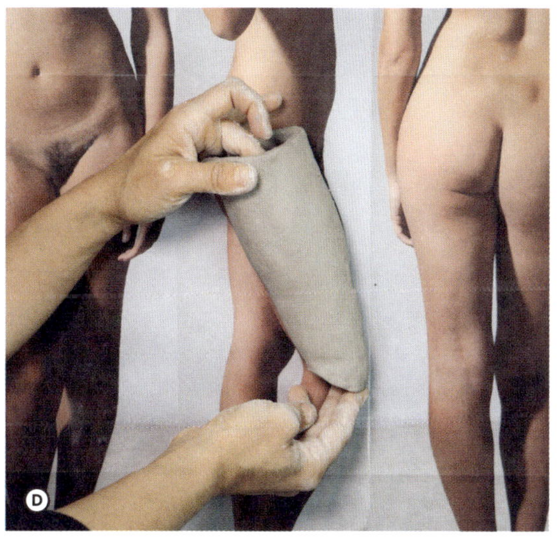

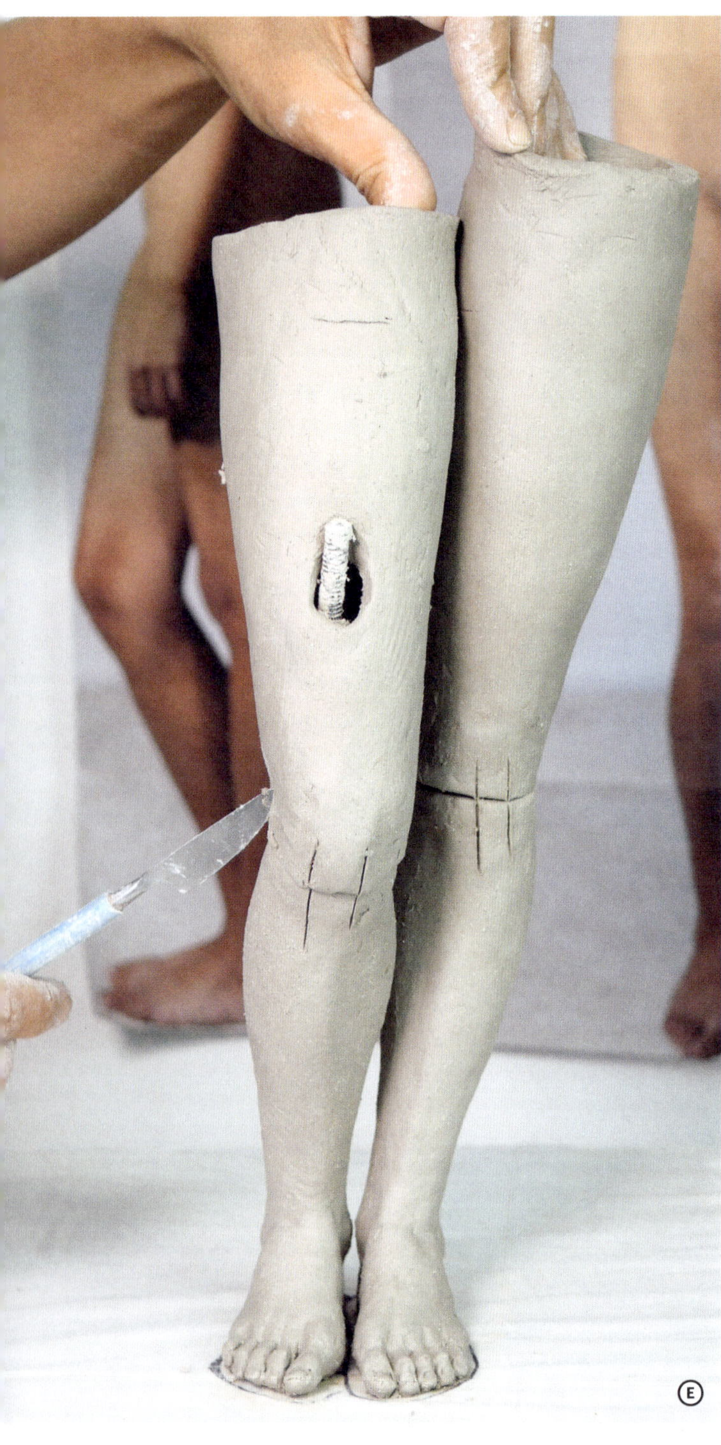

lating the subtleties of these forms. Push out gently from the inside to develop the projection of the quadriceps muscles and hamstrings. Using your photographic views as blueprints, seek to echo the outer shape of the leg form from all perspectives. With your calipers, confirm the thickness and height in relation to your photographic references.

Once you are satisfied with this preliminary modeling, place your upper leg shapes onto the armature and begin finding their proper alignment.

Because we are working with a contrapposto pose in which the left leg is mostly straight while the right knee is bent, only the left leg will thread over the armature through its central cavity. By contrast, the threaded rod on the right leg will shoot out through the lower thigh, so the upper right leg will be devoid of armature. This difference is structurally acceptable because the left leg bears much of the weight of the pose. Ⓔ

On the right side, hold the upper leg form up to the lower leg form and draw lines to find the angle at which these two forms connect. Trim the ends of each cylindrical form so that their angles match up in accordance with your reference images, and then temporarily affix the two forms. You will need to locate where the armature piece will emerge from the right thigh and cut a hole large enough to leave some space around the rod to ensure that your sculpture does not crack as it shrinks around the metal.

Repeat the same process with the left leg by fully sliding the upper leg over the lower leg and slightly trimming the edges to allow for the two shapes to come together, capturing the gentle forward incline of that upper leg.

Take your time, observing and adjusting the forms as you turn the piece to engage with each photographic perspective. Refrain from permanently scoring and slipping the upper and lower legs together at this point; you may still want access to the inside of these forms.

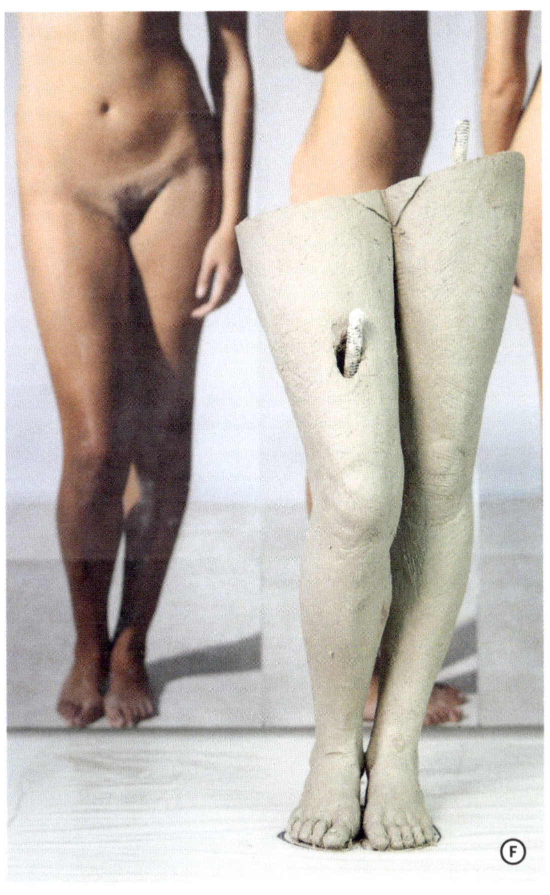

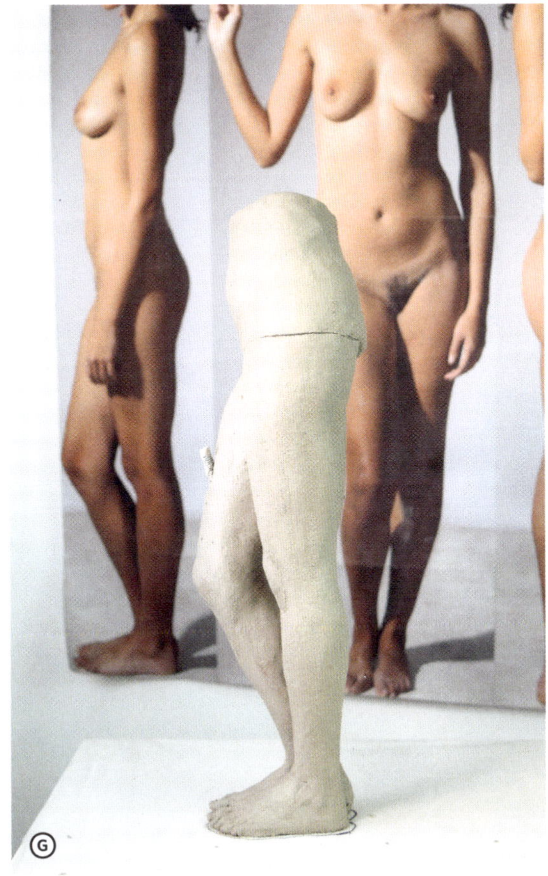

Instead, add bits of clay to hold the forms in place as you visually integrate this new layer. You can also pinch the tops of the legs together to hold them in place as you continue to make adjustments.

Compare the overall gesture of the legs to what you see in your reference images. Use your calipers to capture information from your blueprints and verify heights and thicknesses in your sculpture. How do the large diagonals of the legs change angles from each of the four views? Consider the shape of the negative space between the legs. Next, note the s-shaped forms that run throughout the whole of the leg, creating subtle undulations that move from the inside towards the outside of the leg as well as front to back and vice versa. Find these undulating rhythms in each perspective. ⓕ ⓖ

Step back periodically to gauge your progress at a distance, making sure that your sculpture is turned to the same perspective as one of your reference images. Use the edge of the armature's base in relation to the wall to ensure proper alignment. Moving away from your piece shifts your perception from the micro to the macro and helps you grasp the dynamics of the composition in a different way. Bounce your eyes back and forth from reference to sculpture to find inconsistencies.

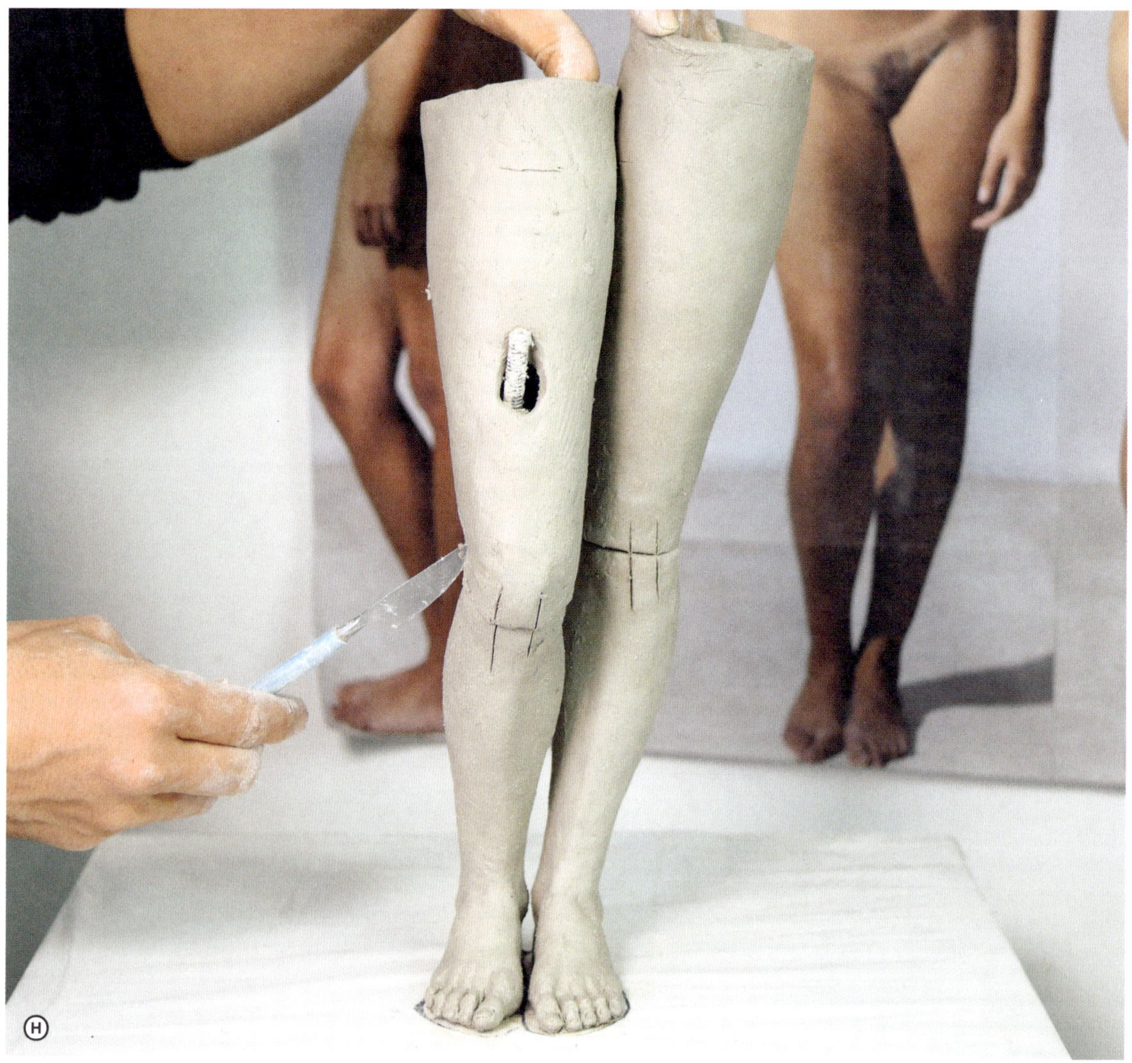

Next you will affix the upper legs. Draw two or three vertical keys across the horizontal seams between your upper and lower legs, marking their placement. Remove the upper legs and then slip and score both sides of each seam before reattaching. As you are applying downward pressure to the upper right leg, support the front of the knee area with your free hand to stabilize the lower leg. This support will both provide resistance to aid in compression and preserve the alignment of the leg parts. Because the left leg is straight, your downward pressure should not affect the position of the lower leg. Join the legs by slipping and scoring the inner thigh areas and pressing them together from within the upper leg cavities, helping to stabilize the posture. To further secure the form, you can add some clay on the inside of the upper left leg between the inner clay wall and the rod. Once your upper legs are fixed into place, slip and score the outside of your two horizontal seams and pack fresh clay into these joints to strengthen them, making small adjustments as needed. Check your alignments to ensure that everything remains consistent with your references before letting your seams set. Ⓗ

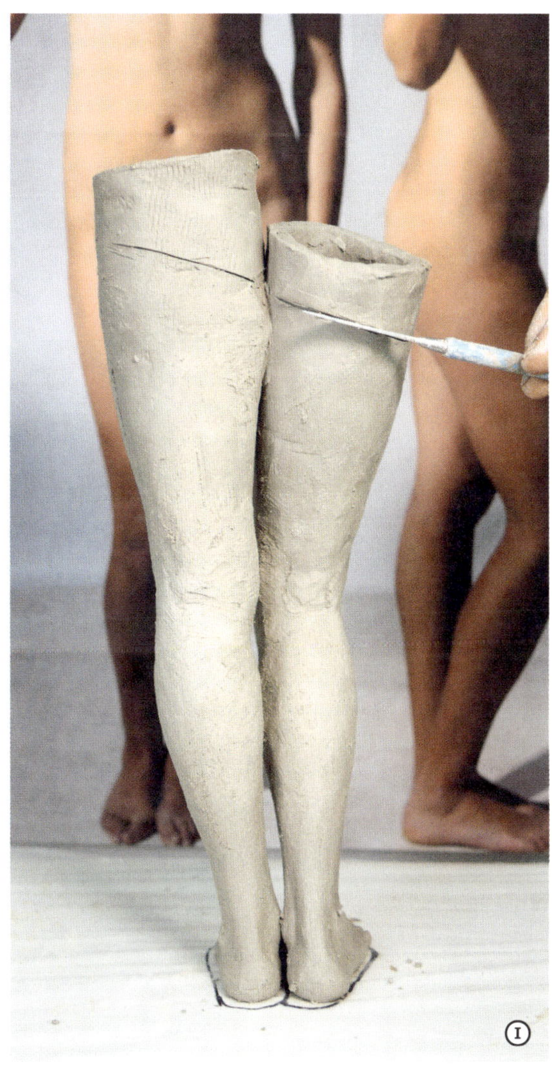

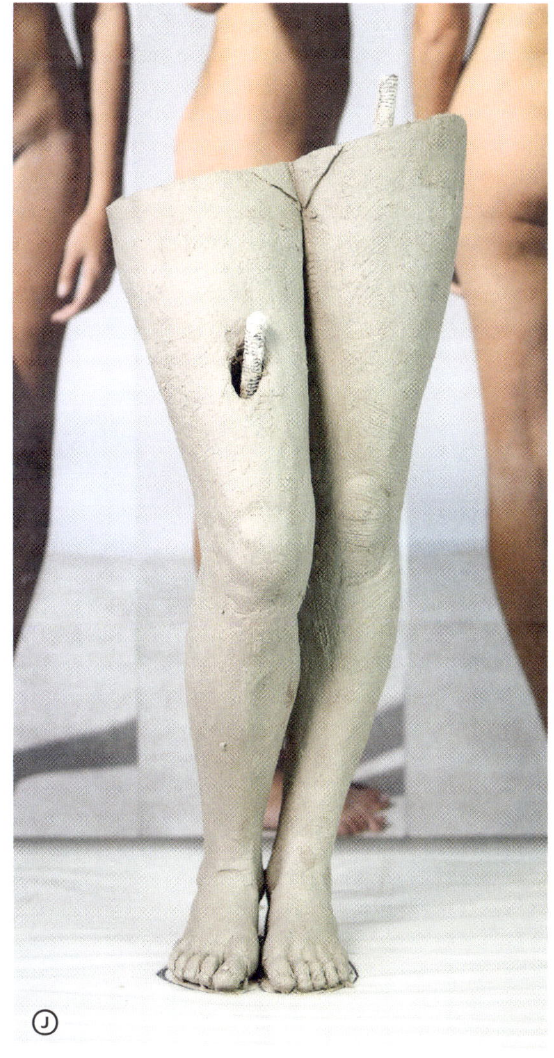

To prepare the legs to receive the pelvis, you will trim the tops of the leg forms to create a single angled plane. Because the pelvic tilt in this pose is most apparent from the front and back views, turn to your back photographic reference image. On either side, take a measurement from the bottom of the heel to just above the gluteal crease, towards the center

of each leg. Mark those two points onto your sculpture front and back. Connect those two marks to form a diagonal line on both the front and the back. Continue these lines around the sides to establish your cut line, and then follow that line with your knife to trim away excess material from the tops of the legs. ⓘ ⓙ

PELVIS

Place your printed pelvis templates on top of a ⅜ inch (1 cm)–thick slab and use a knife to mark the guidelines and cut around the perimeter. Ⓐ Next, bend each slab into a cylindrical form until the two short edges come together and overlap along the guideline. Ⓑ Slip and score these edges and compress the seam together. Move your serrated rib across the inside and the outside of your seam in a cross-hatching motion to interlace the clay particles and strengthen this connection point. Use enough pressure to gradually compress this seam without distorting the shape. Ⓒ Ⓓ

Bring the pelvis to your photographic references and compare it to your four cardinal perspectives, making adjustments by pushing in or out as needed. Using calipers, capture height and width measurements from your photographs and compare them to your form, paddling in or pushing out if necessary. Once you are satisfied, hold the pelvis over the legs to align the edges, reconciling any discrepancy by pushing out or tucking in to allow for good surface contact.

When the pelvis has dried enough to hold its shape without distorting when squeezed lightly, set it over the legs and the composition with each of your photographic references, using your calipers to compare heights and thicknesses. Because the pelvis will sit lower towards the front of the legs, you will have to trim some material to bring that front edge of the pelvis slightly down. Once the position matches the references, you can add bits of clay to even out the edges of the legs and pelvis, ensuring that they echo each other and are making good contact.

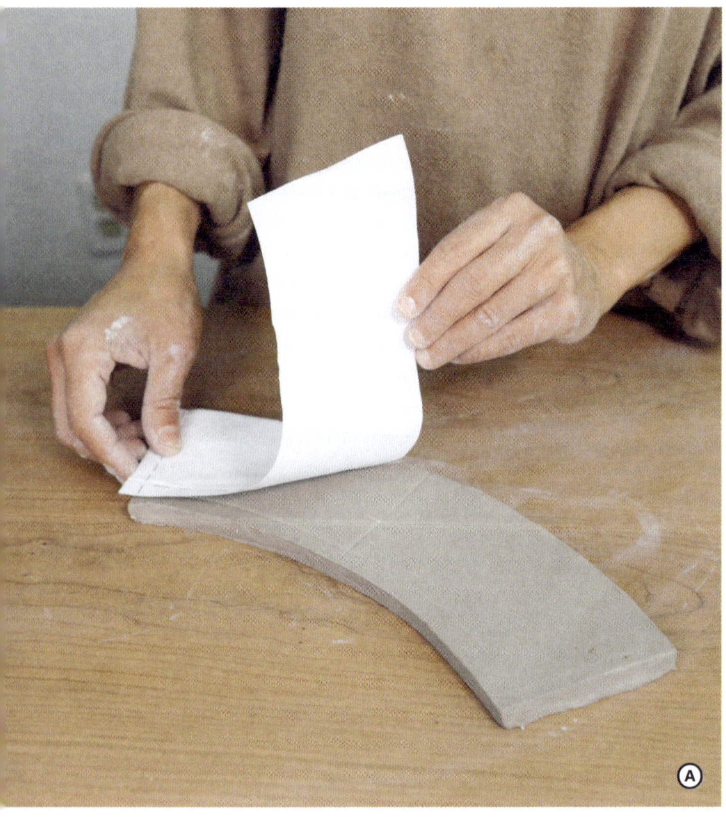

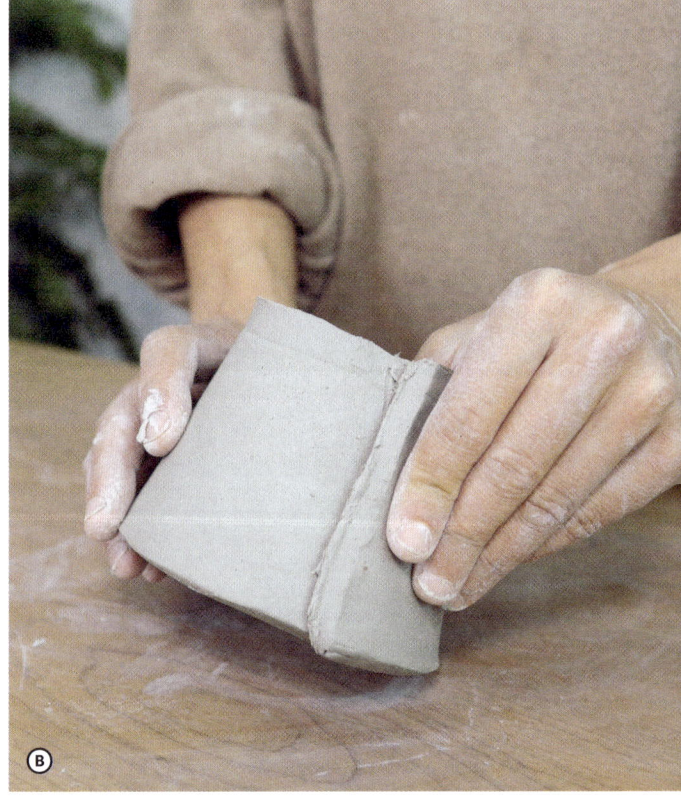

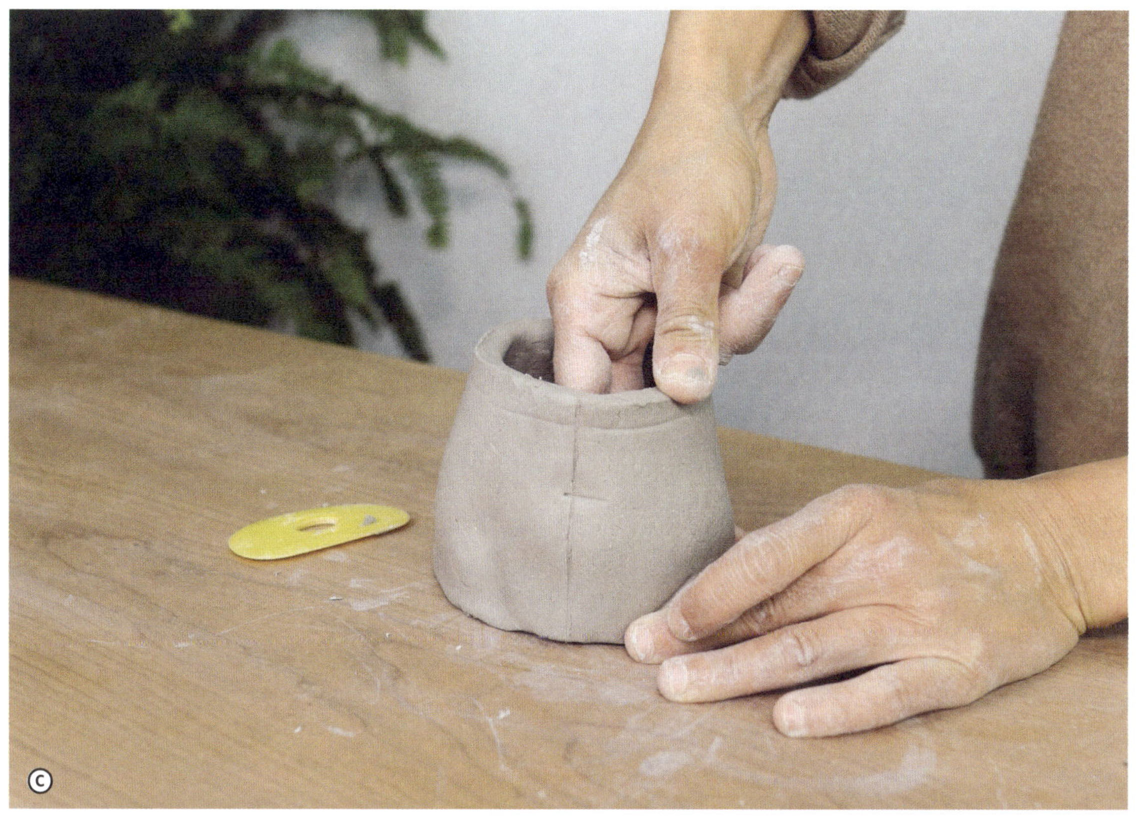

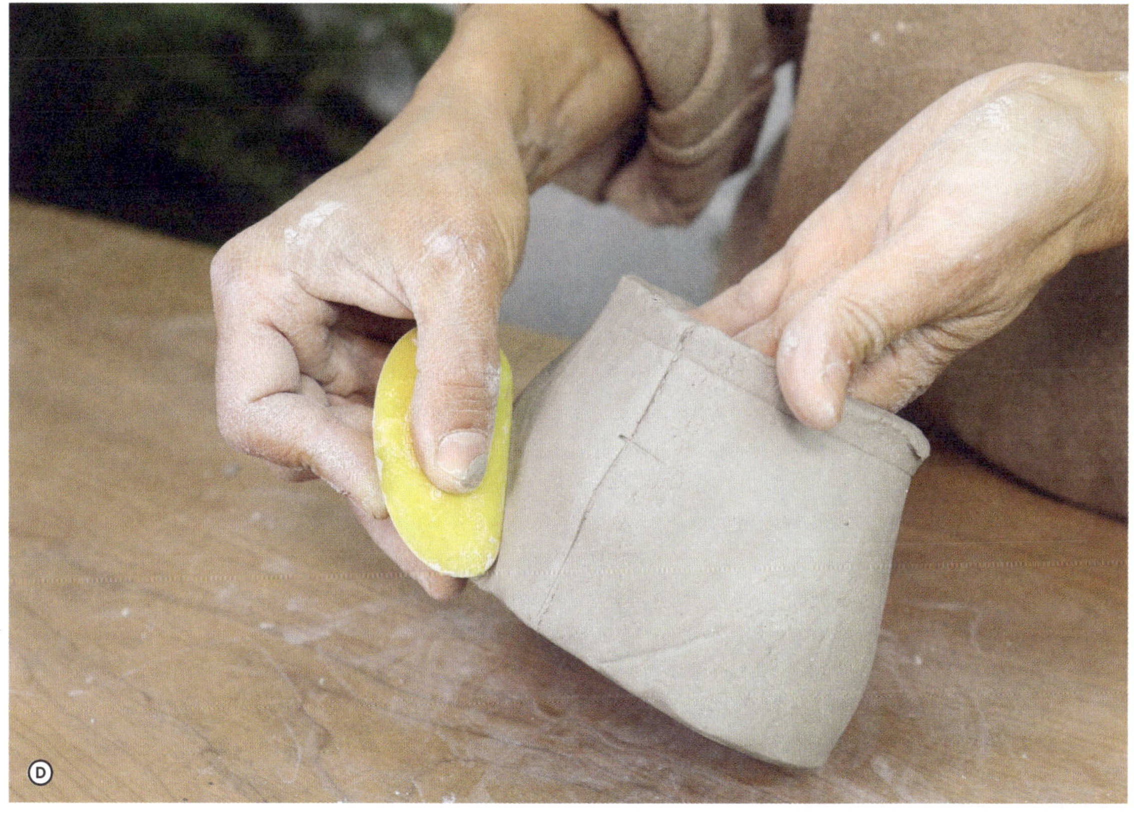

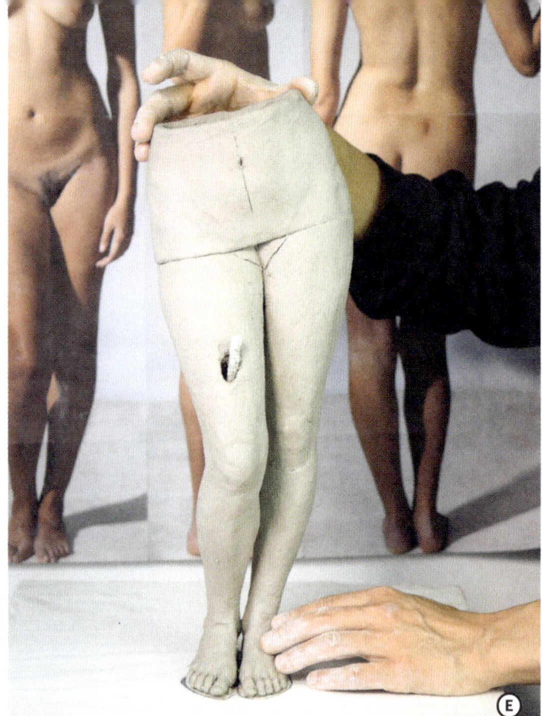 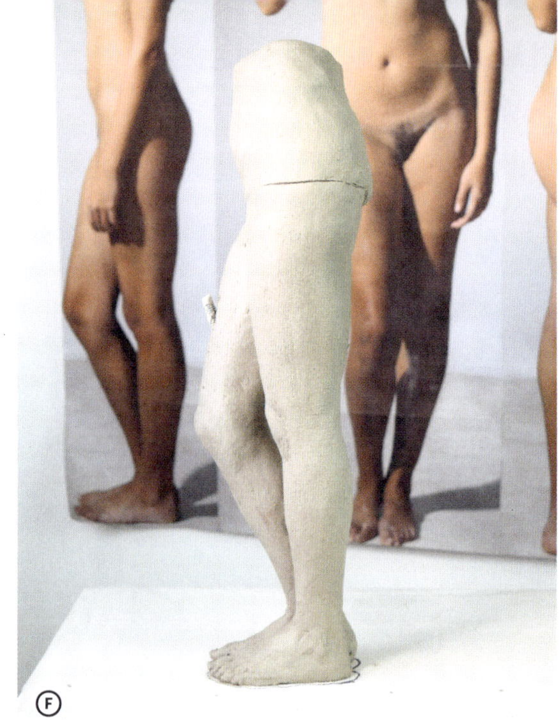

When you are satisfied with the tilt of your pelvis, draw your vertical keys, marking through the pelvis and the upper legs so that you can find the proper alignment after slipping and scoring all edges. Often, when working on larger forms where the insides of the forms are accessible to my hands, I will add coils of fresh clay to the insides of my seams, to facilitate a stronger connection. Ⓔ Ⓕ Compress the pelvis onto the legs with firm and careful pressure and then score the inside and outside of the seam, adding fresh clay to secure the connection and fill any gaps. There will be a small gap towards the front, in the pubic area, and another in the back, at underside of the intergluteal cleft. Slip and score these areas and pack fresh clay to fill the gaps, fully integrating your forms. In preparation to receive the torso, add a coil of fresh clay to the figure's right side at the opening at the waist to bring the top of your sculpture to level. Be sure to slip and score before integrating this coil. Finally, return to your references. Turn your figure and compare it to your four photographic blueprints. Using both your eyes and your calipers, verify that all the forms and measurements remain consistent with the photographic material.

At this stage, you will need to let your sculpture dry in a strategic manner before moving on to the next layer. To encourage some parts to stiffen up more than others, you must carefully monitor the moisture throughout your composition, leaving some parts temporarily exposed to stiffen while applying plastic or moistened towels to safeguard or rehydrate other components. At this stage, you want to keep your feet, legs, and pelvis stiff without becoming bone-dry. Protect the edge of the pelvis that will be receiving the torso by covering it with an extra layer of plastic or a moistened shop towel if it needs extra hydration.

It is important to understand the specifics of your particular clay body. The more you work with a clay body, the more you will appreciate how dry it needs to be to hold weight, and how moist it needs to be to remain workable and receptive to further attunements. Small appendages such as feet, hands, and ears are important places to keep hydrated with moist shop rags under plastic, as they are more vulnerable to quick drying than larger areas of form.

Gallery

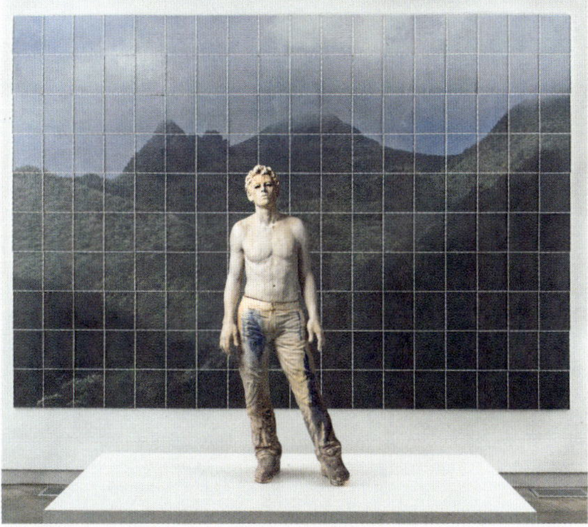

Cristina Córdova, *La persistencia del verdor*. Robin Dryer.

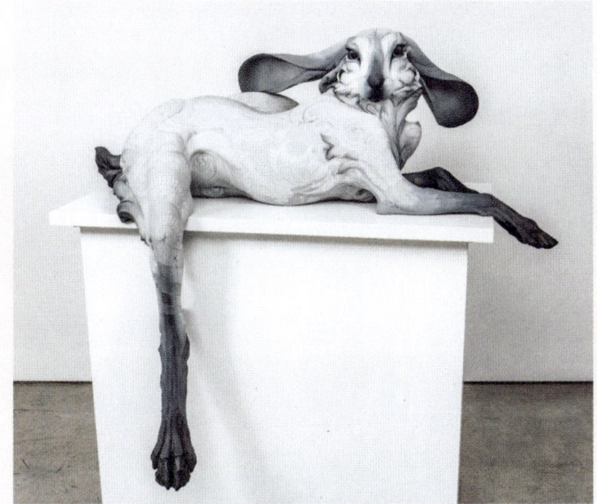

Beth Cavener, *L'Amante*. Noel Alum.

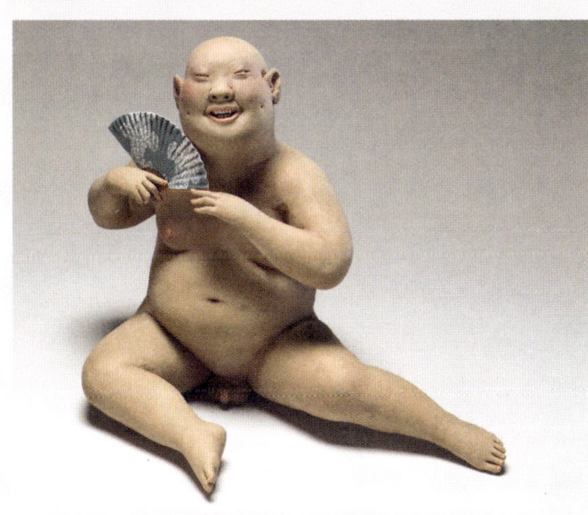

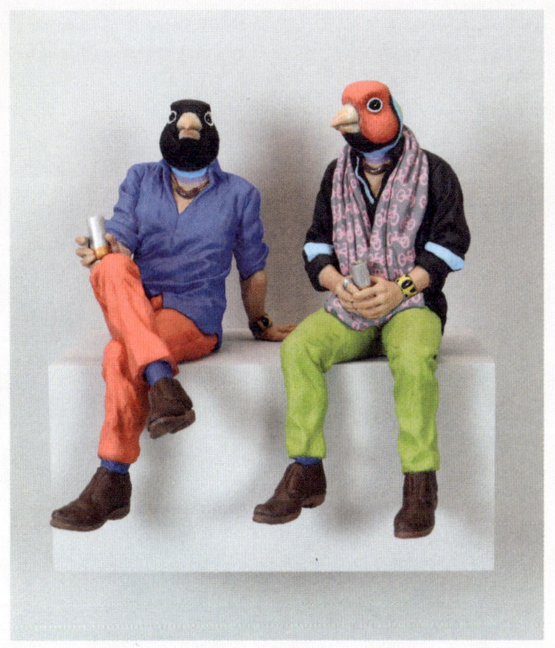

Cristina Córdova, *Colonia*. Steve Mann.

Alessandro Gallo, *Brooks and Oliver*. Courtesy of the artist.

Esther Shimazu, *Warm Green.*
Paul Kodama, courtesy of the John Natsoulas Gallery.

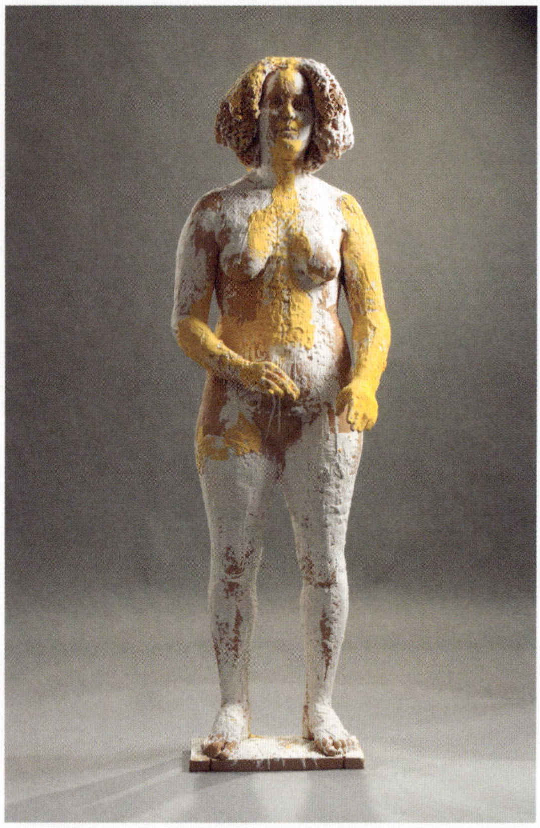

Kathy Venter, *Coup D'oeil.* David Borrowman.

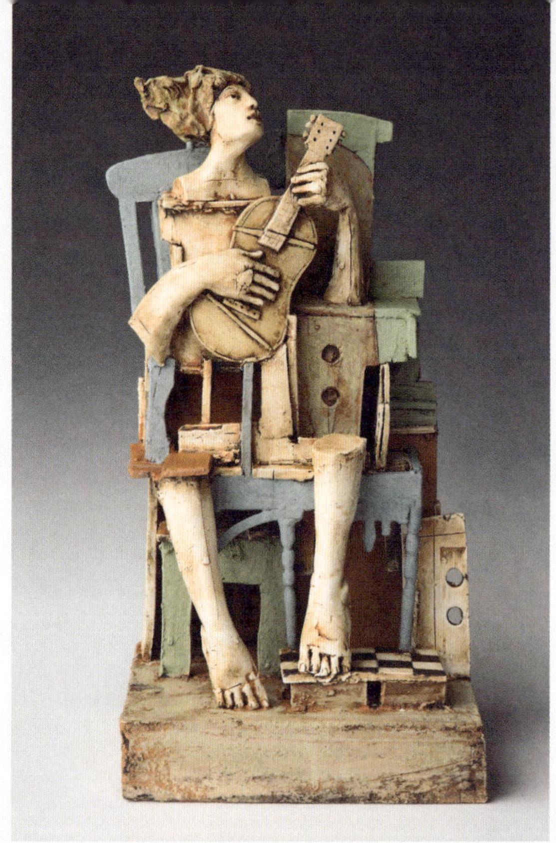

Christy Keeney, *Guitar Player.* Fergal Megannety.

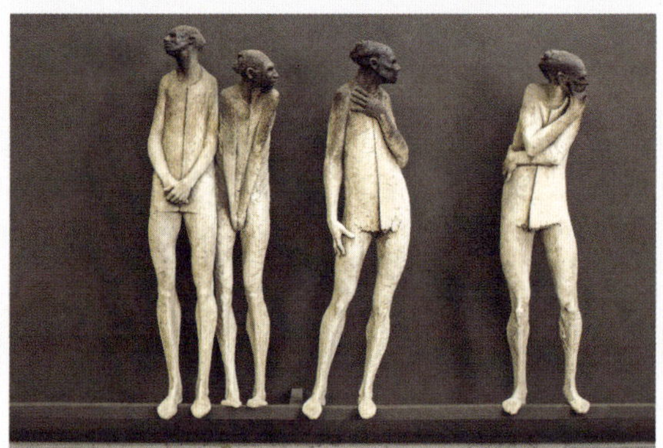

Max Levia, *Horizonte.* Jose Carlos Flores.

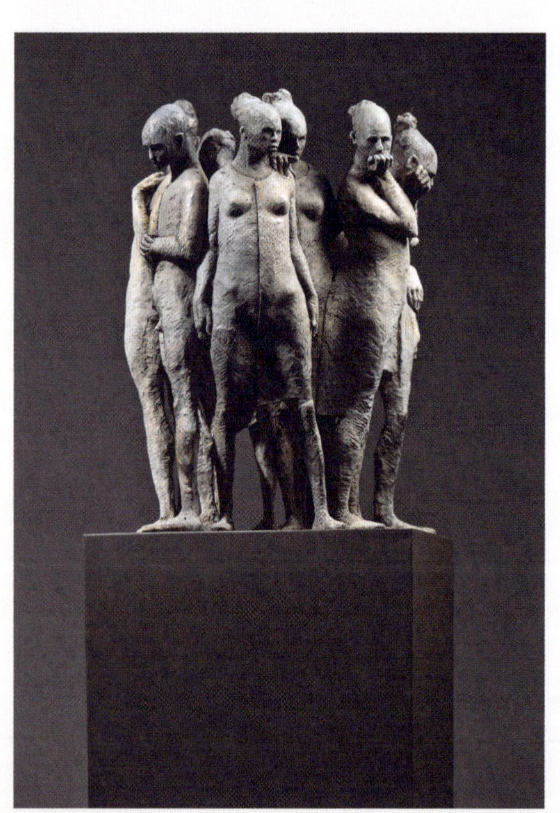

Max Levia, *Múrmuros.* Jose Carlos Flores.

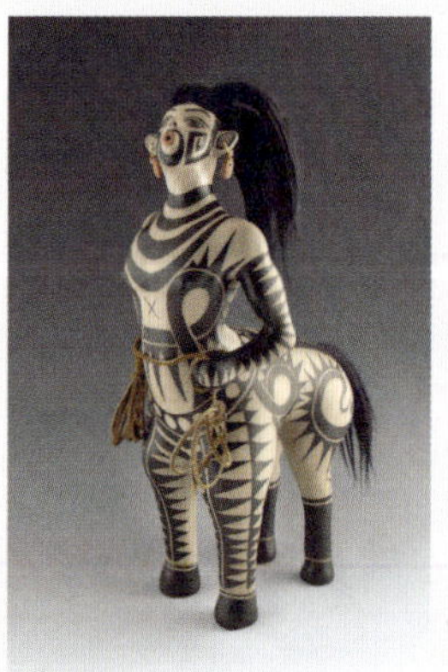

Virgil Ortiz, *Centaur.*
Courtesy of the artist.

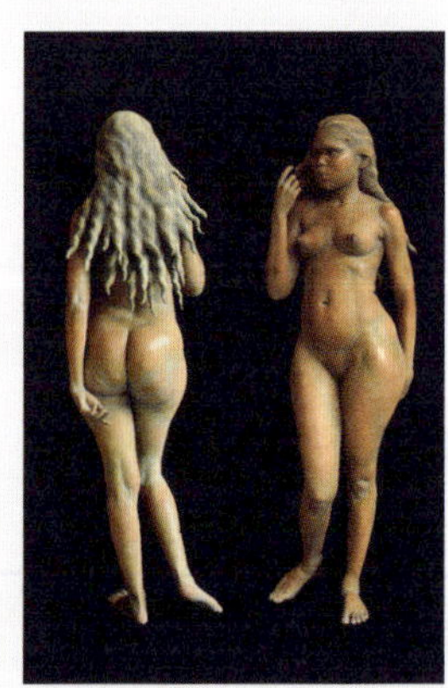

Judy Fox, *Eve.*
Courtesy of the artist.

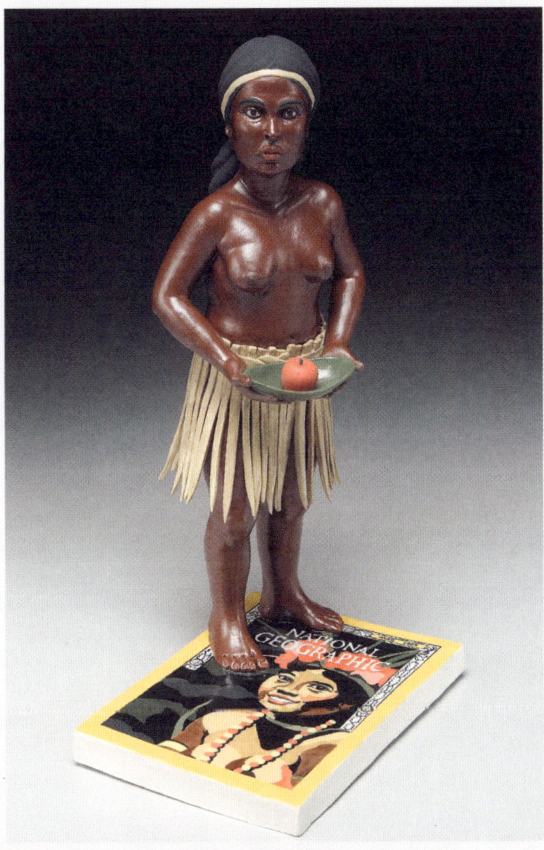

Russell Biles, *Kiddy's Porn (Thanks NG)*. Tim Barnwell.

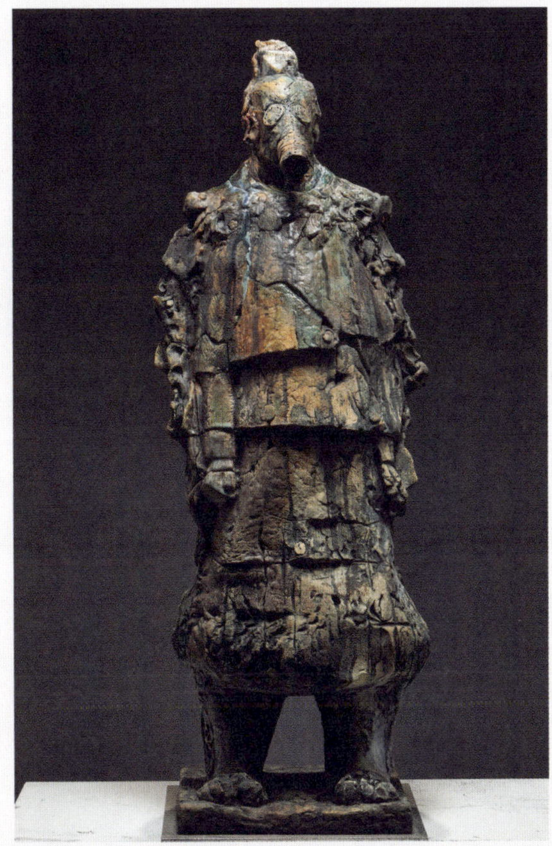

Wanxin Zhang, *Wanderer*.
Courtesy of the artist and Catharine Clark Gallery.

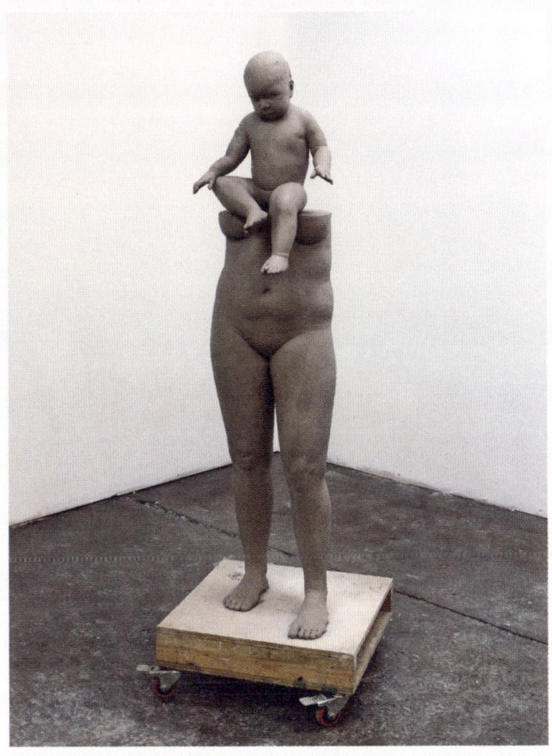

Ashley Lyon, *MOTHER*. Courtesy of the artist.

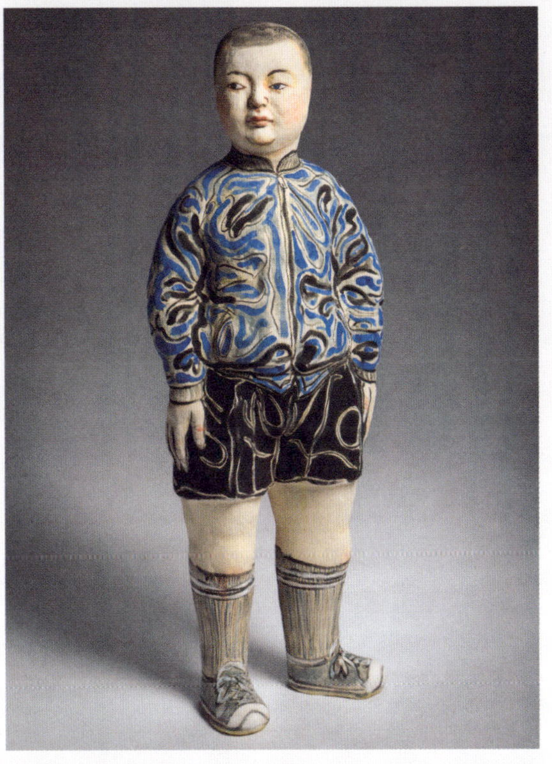

Akio Takamori, *Boy in Blue Jacket*.
RJ Sánchez | Solstream Studios.

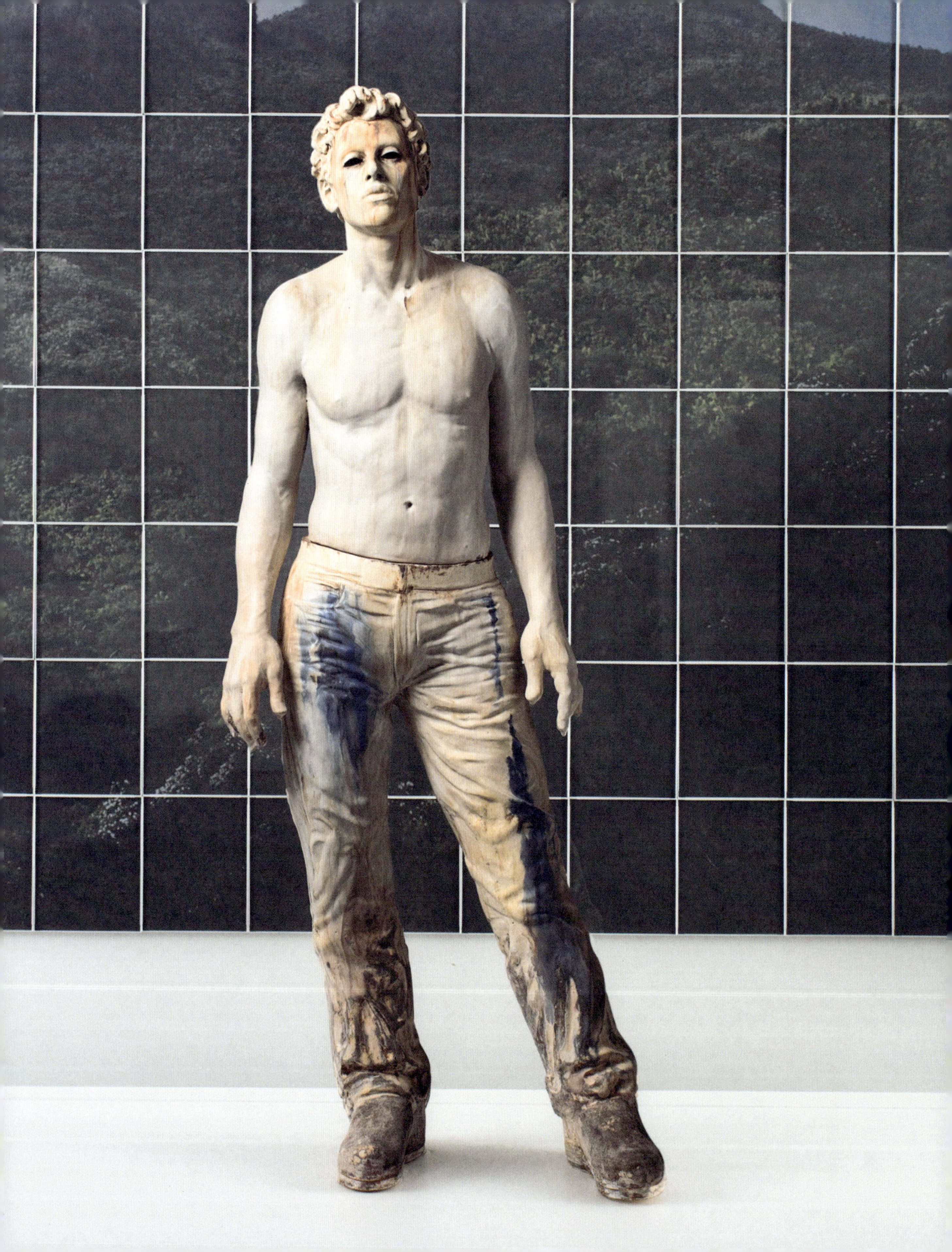

4

ASSEMBLING THE UPPER BODY

AS WE MAKE our way into the upper body, comprising the torso, arms, and neck, we engage with regions of immense expressive potential. The upper body houses key bony structures such as the rib cage, clavicles, and scapulae, which are overlaid by the abdominal muscles and the flesh around the mid torso, the pectoral tissue, and the breasts. In the shoulders and arms, we have the deltoid, biceps, and triceps muscles. Finally, we add in tissues around the neck that will create visual cohesion between the head and body, connecting the cervical spine to the cranium on the back of the body and linking the mastoid process to both sternum and clavicles in the front. Collectively, these components add to the gestural information begun in the lower body and articulate a crescendo that completes the story of the figure.

WHAT YOU'LL NEED TO GET STARTED

- Templates (torso, neck, breasts)

- Slabs (¼ inch, ⅜ inch [6 mm, 1 cm]) that fit your upper body templates

- Fresh clay to work over seams

- Joining slip

- Ruler

- Wire brush scoring tool

- Calipers

- Wooden finger tool

- Metal or wooden dowel

- Seamstress tape

- Paddle

- Stainless modeling tools

Cristina Córdova, *La persistencia del verdor,* part of the collection of the Everson Museum of Art.

GETTING STARTED

Now that we have the legs and the pelvis articulated and stable, we will continue with the torso, head, arms, and hands. At this stage, the lower body should have dried enough to be firm, with little to no movement. You will need to carefully monitor the dryness to ensure that the lower legs and feet do not enter the bone-dry stage before the composition is finished.

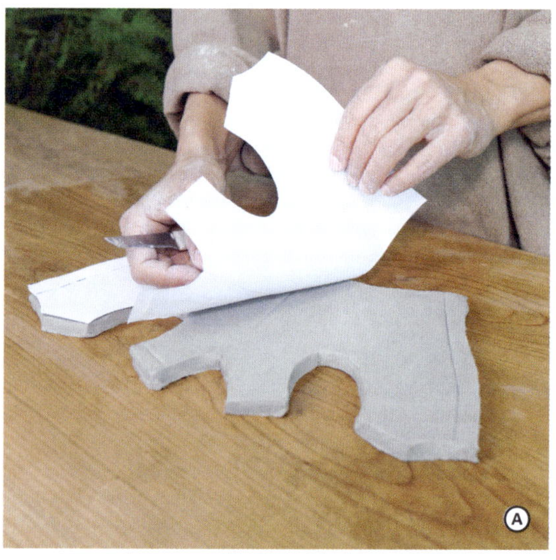

Mist the piece regularly while keeping the legs and pelvis covered in plastic as you work on the upper parts of the body. Protect the edges of the composition receiving the next addition of clay by adding extra layers of plastic over moistened cloth or paper towels.

As you add each new layer, it is helpful to step back and look at the figure in its entirety to assess the full gesture. Seeing all parts of the composition enables you to make alignment correlations and ensure that all elements are in proportion.

Place the torso template on top of a ⅜ inch (1 cm)–thick slab and use a knife to cut the edges and trace the guidelines. If needed, remove the templates and lightly redraw the guidelines so that they are more legible. Make sure your center guideline is shallow enough that it will not cause your slab to split. Ⓐ

Next, curl the slab until the two short edges come together and overlap along the guideline. Ⓑ Slip and score these edges where they will touch and compress the seam together. Move your serrated rib across the outside of your seam in a cross-hatching motion to interlace the clay particles and strengthen this connection. On the inside, use your fingers or threaded rod to help with compression. Ⓒ

Note: *Remember to counter that inner compression with outside pressure from your supporting hand, applying enough force to secure the seam without distorting the shape.*

After the back seam is fully integrated, curl the two flaps that will comprise the top of the torso forward to meet the overlap lines before slipping, scoring, and compressing. Ⓓ Ⓔ

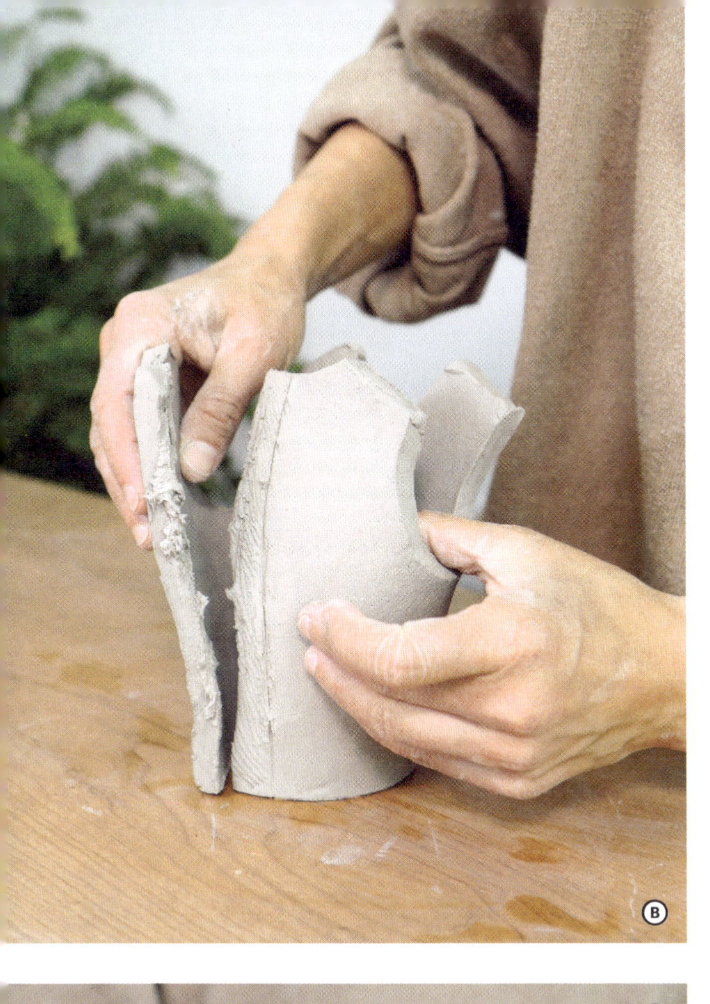

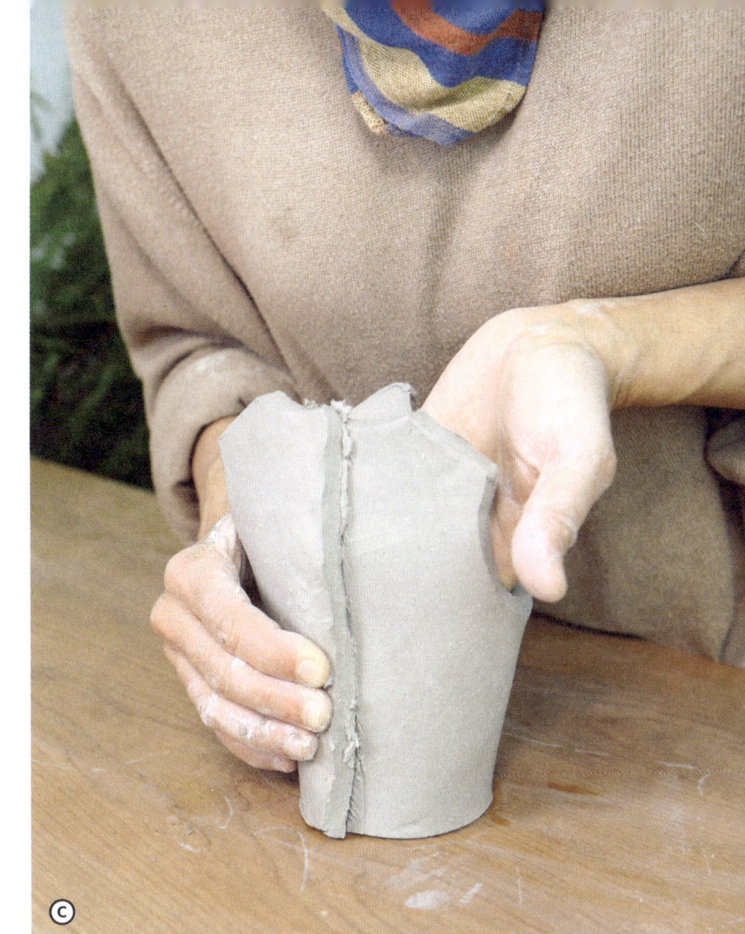
C

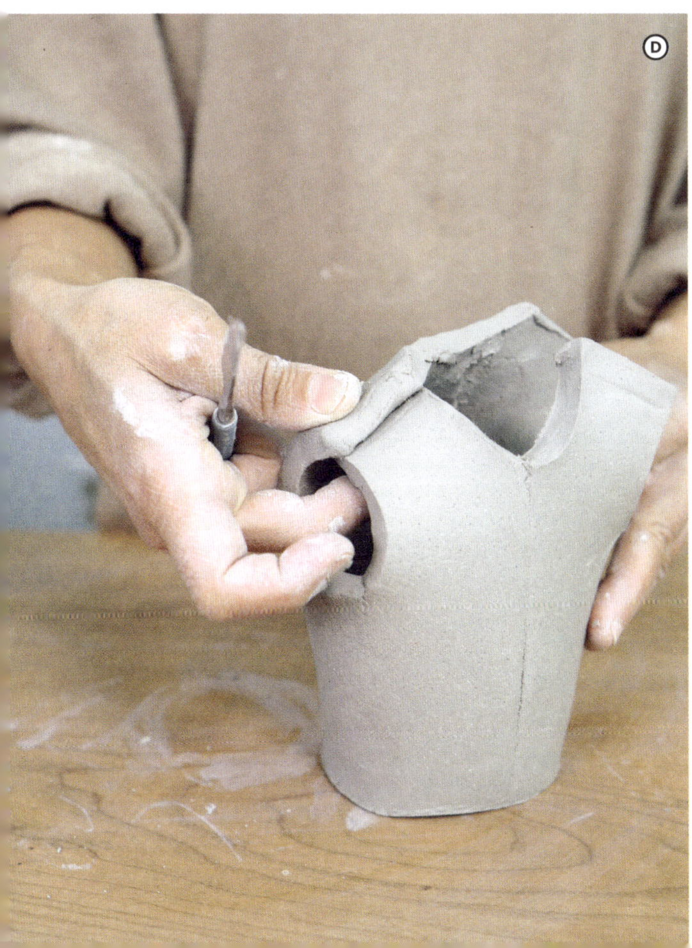
D

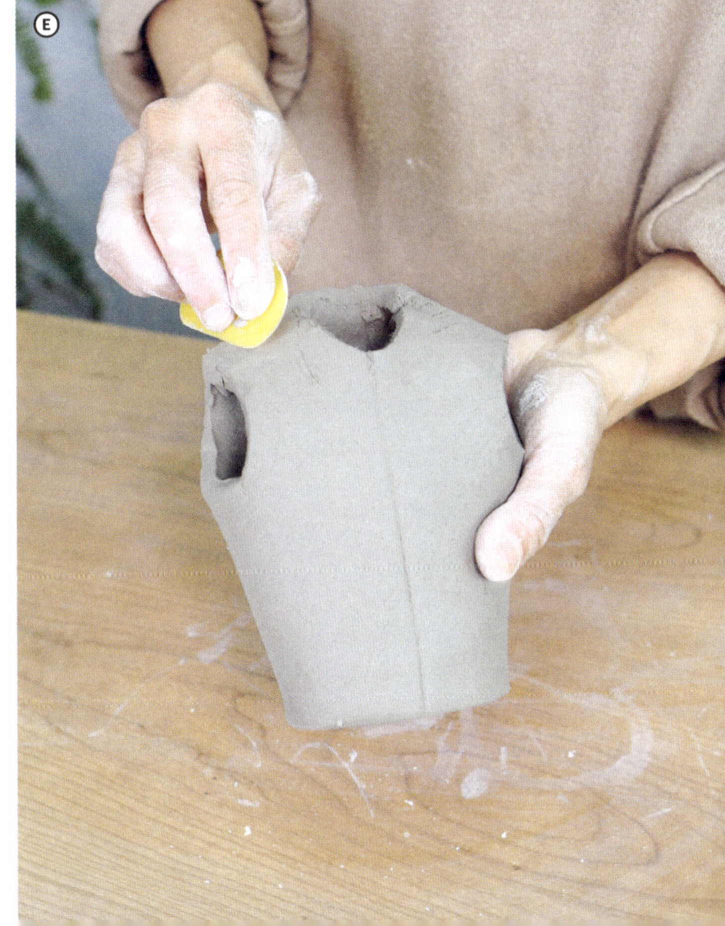
E

ATTACHING TORSO TO PELVIS

To prepare the torso to meet the pelvis, we will first make several adjustments.

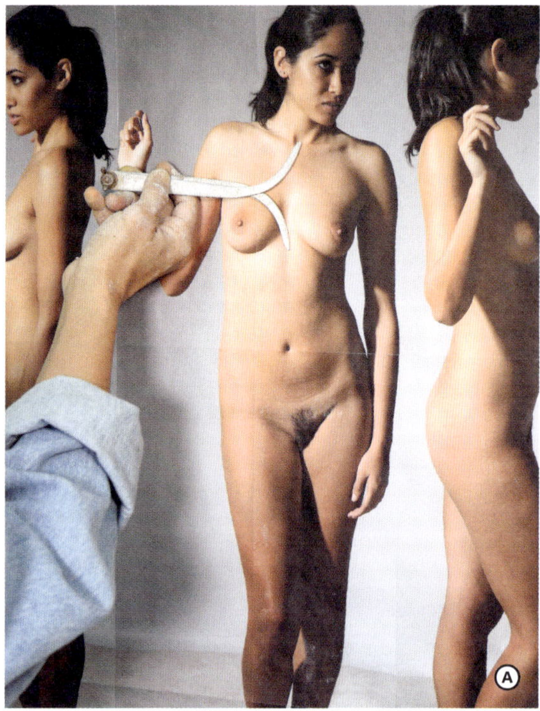

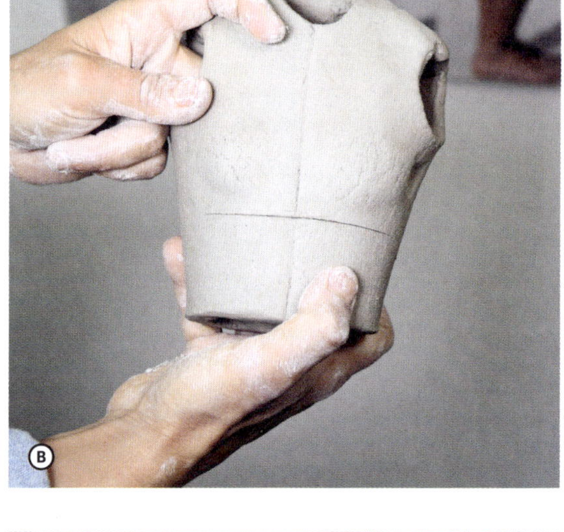

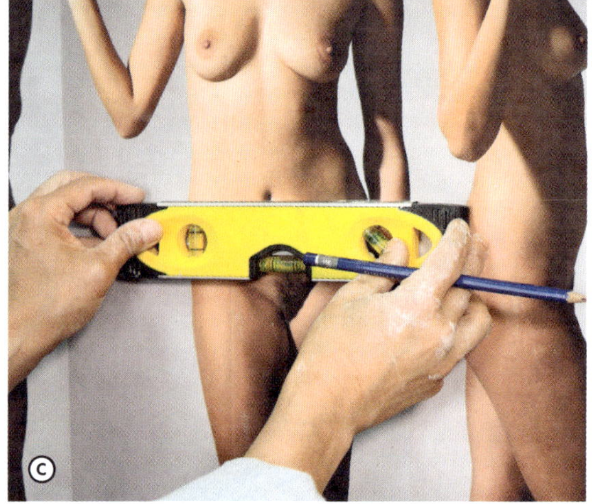

Turn to your forward-facing reference photograph and measure with your calipers the distance between the base of the neck, or jugular notch, and the bottom of the breasts. Place the bottom prong of your calipers along the centerline when taking this measurement to split the slight difference in height between left and right breasts. Ⓐ This is just a starting point; we will address this discrepancy more carefully later in the process.

Carry this distance to the torso and, placing the top prong of your calipers at the base of the neck opening, draw a horizontal line with the bottom prong to mark your breast line. Make sure that the calipers remain perpendicular and do not incline back to follow the slope of the chest. Use this new mark as a guide in relation to the centerline imprinted on the form from the pattern. Push out gently on either side of the centerline and above the breast line

to develop the breast area to use as a visual reference. Ⓑ

Stack the torso onto the pelvis. Holding your calipers up to your front view reference photograph, draw a level line across the navel of the model with a pencil. Take a measurement of the distance between the bottom of both breasts and the navel. Ⓒ Compare this measurement with its corresponding distance on your sculpture, utilizing the breast line you drew in the

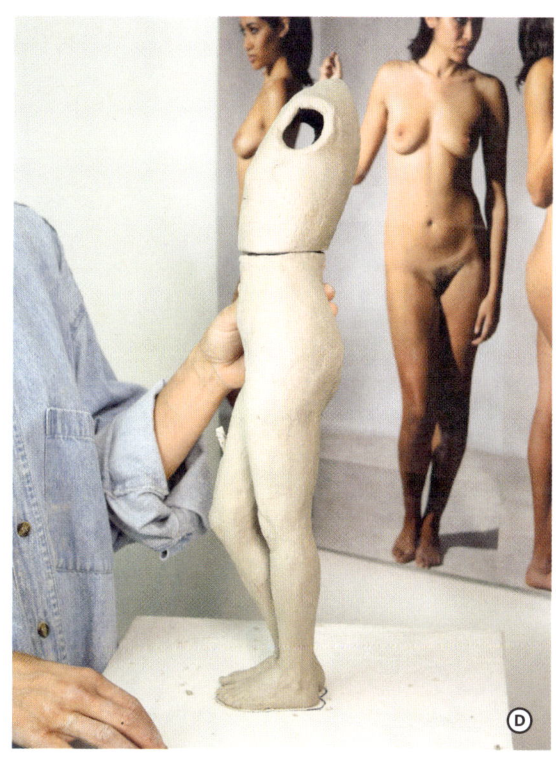

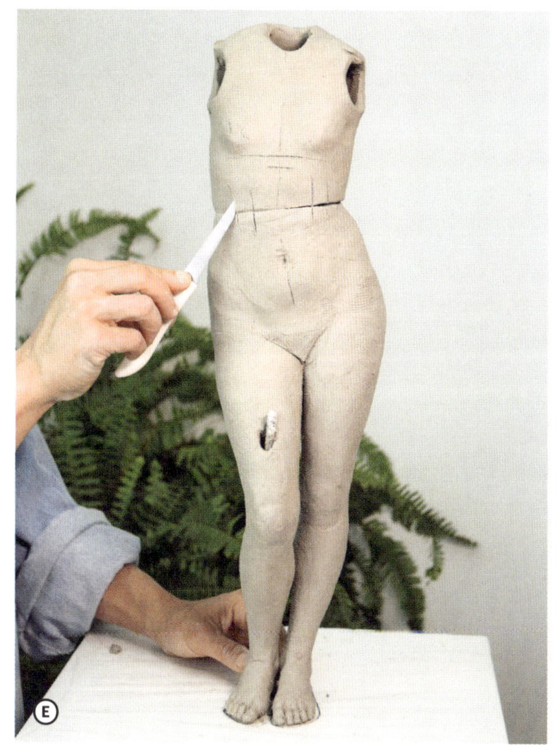

prior step. The length between the belly button and the bottom of the breasts should be slightly greater on your sculpture. This is intentional. Rather than cutting the torso straight across to correct the height discrepancy, use the excess material to help establish gesture by strategically trimming away material.

Note that in the side-view reference photos, our model's torso sways slightly back. From the front and back views, notice the torso's slight shift towards the left leg, in opposition to the pelvic alignment. To account for these shifts, we will trim the lower edge of the torso gradually to echo the positioning of the model. I normally start by resolving the front-to-back tilt before addressing the lateral movement. First trim roughly ½ inch (1.2 cm) from the back edge of the torso and paddle gently to even with the rest of the edge. Replace the form on top of the pelvis and visually compare your alignment against the two side view images.

Next, using the front-view reference image and your calipers, measure the distance between the base of the sculpture and the breast line again, checking the measurement on either side of the centerline. Once you are satisfied, establish the side tilt by trimming about ⁵⁄₁₆ inch (8 mm) from the right edge of the torso to bring that side down and gently paddle to even out. Place the torso form onto the pelvis once more and check your alignments against the photographs, using your calipers to recapture measurements. Take the time you need to gradually move toward the best alignment, adding bits of clay to shim and adjust your torso's position if necessary. If you feel you have trimmed too much material, you can add a coil to reset the correct distance. When you are satisfied, draw your vertical keys into either side of the piece. Slip, score, and connect the torso to the pelvis by firmly pressing down. Work over that seam with your serrated rib and add fresh clay to further bond these components together at the waist, filling in any gaps and securing the connection. Ⓓ Ⓔ

With your torso in place, take some visual notes and incise them onto the surface of the sculpture. Drawing marks onto your sculpture is a great way to guide the sculpting process and enhance your eye's ability to ground and prioritize the abundance of information offered by the photographic references. Ⓕ

After aligning your composition with the front photographic blueprint, reset your drawn centerline so that it curves slightly to follow the pelvic and upper body shifts. Use your calipers to check the distances between the pubic area and the navel, the navel and the bottom of the breasts at either side of the centerline, and the bottom of the breast to the top of the shoulders, comparing each measurement with your sculpture and making marks and adjustments where needed.

Observing the play between light and shadow in your front view photograph, draw the clavicles, the deltoid, and the triangle of the sternum onto your sculpture. Once you have drawn in these landmarks, make your way to the outer edge of your sculpture and compare its silhouette with those of your photographic references from each cardinal view. After placing your sculpture stand parallel with the wall so that your sculpture aligns with its respective reference photo, add, push out, and carve away clay when necessary to echo the gestures

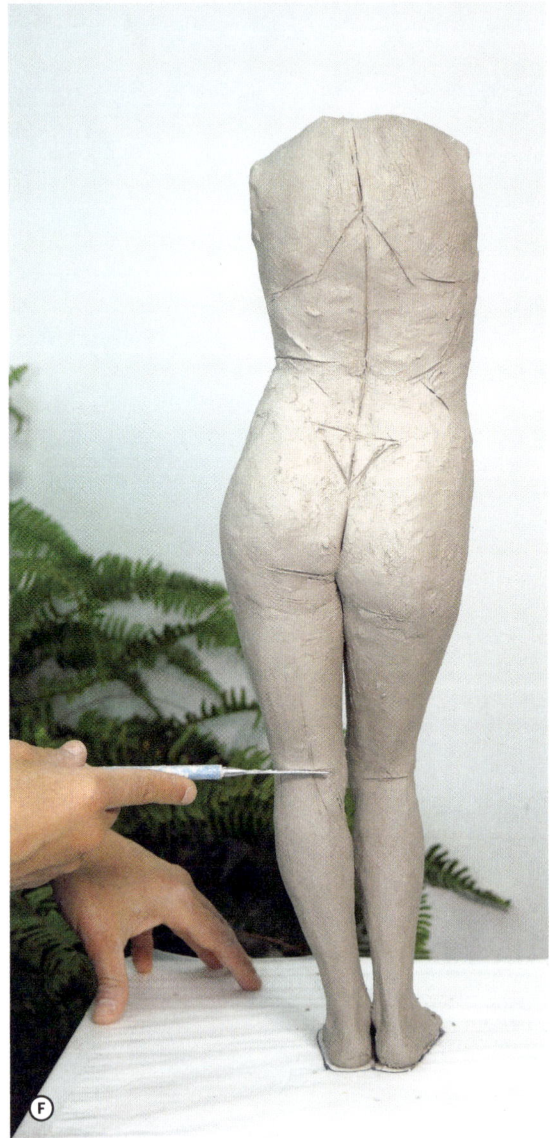

you observe in the photographs. At this point it is helpful to have your wooden finger tool handy to make adjustments by sliding the tool through the top opening of the torso and gently pushing out to articulate volumes as you compare your piece to the photographic references. The ability to push from the inside is one of the great benefits of this technique and the wooden finger tool allows access to the deeper parts of the form. Do this from each perspective.

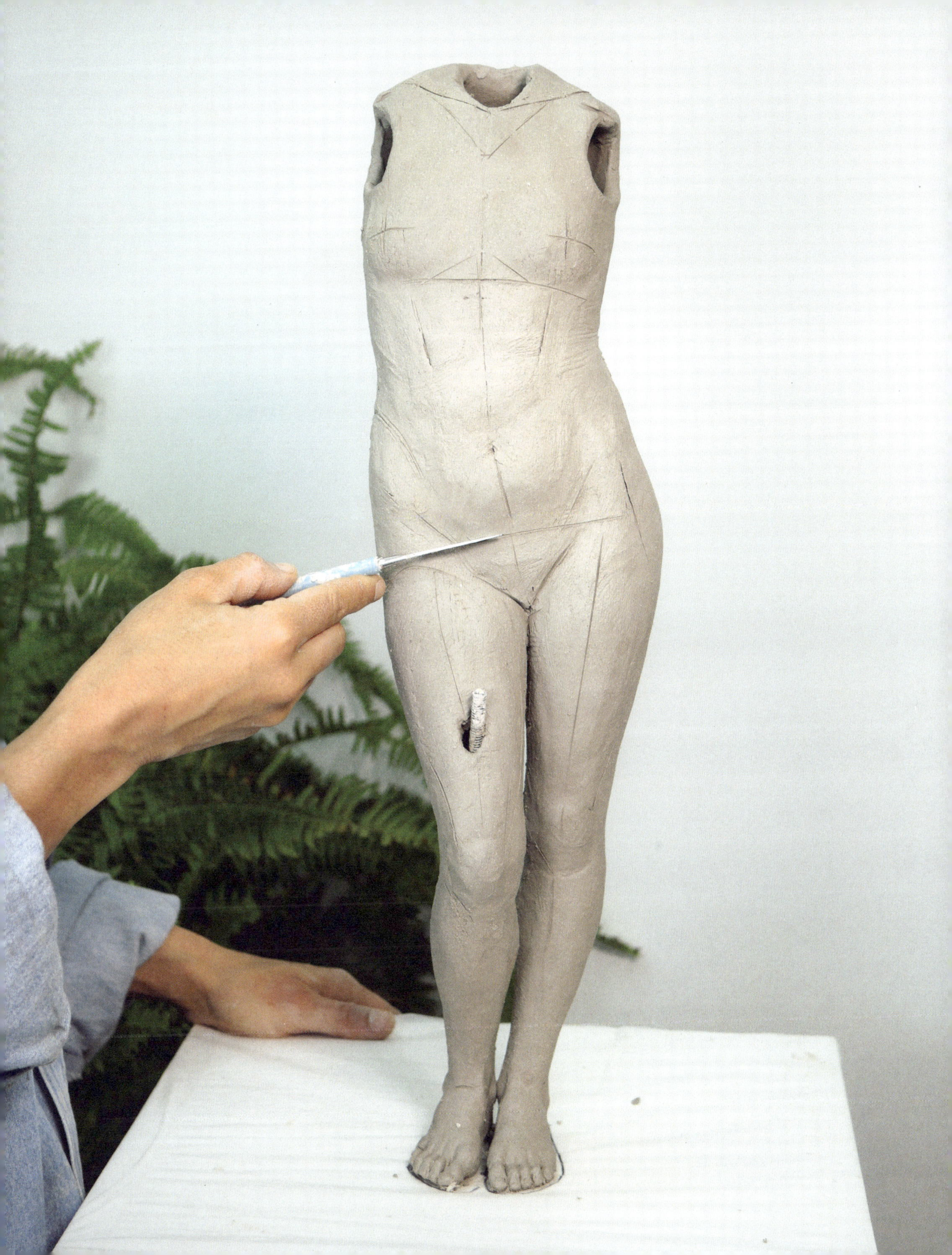

THE NECK

Once you feel satisfied with your torso, cut a rectangle 3½" (8.9 cm) wide by 3" (7.6 cm) high from a ¼" (6 mm) thick slab and curl it into a cylinder, slightly overlapping the edges at the seam. Compare it with your references, trimming any excess if needed to match the width of the model's neck before slipping, scoring, and compressing your seam from the outside with a serrated rib and the inside with a threaded rod. The neck will be longer than we need it to be, but this is intentional to protect the edge and allow for options in the positioning of the head.

Next, use a paddle to gently bevel the bottom edge of the neck cylinder so it can more easily fit within the opening on top of the torso. On the back side of the neck opening, use gentle strokes of pressure from within to lift the clay and begin to articulate the upper trapezius muscle in accordance with your reference images. Bring the new cylinder to your torso and adjust the opening to fit the neck shape and facilitate a good connection. Looking at your references from all vantage points, adjust the placement of the neck front to back and side to side. When ready, score your keys onto the surface, slip and score, and attach the neck. To revise the seam, you can slide your dowel through the neck opening to offer counterpressure from the inside of the narrow shape. At this stage, it is okay if the neck seems longer than necessary. We will adjust the height in later steps as we attach the head.

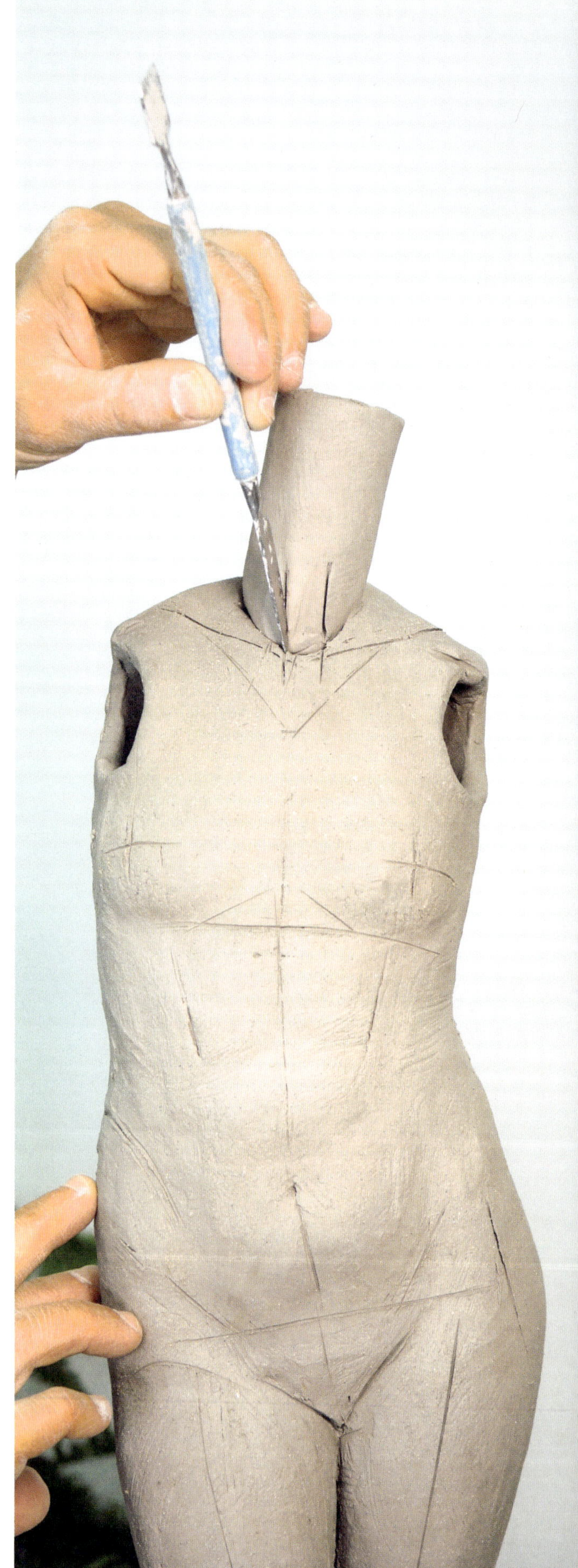

THE FIGURE IN CLAY

BREASTS

To assemble the breast shapes, place your templates onto a ¼ inch (6 mm) slab. Because these shapes are smaller and more delicate, they will be easier to form and articulate from a thinner slab. Trace and cut the circular forms with pie-shaped darts. Bringing the two straight edges together, gently slip, score with a wire brush, and compress with your fingers. Ⓐ Ⓑ To develop the breast forms, dip your thumb and index fingers in water and move them from the center of the cone outwards, along the seam towards the pointed edge, softly pinching either side of the cone along the seam, gently elongating the form to create a teardrop shape.

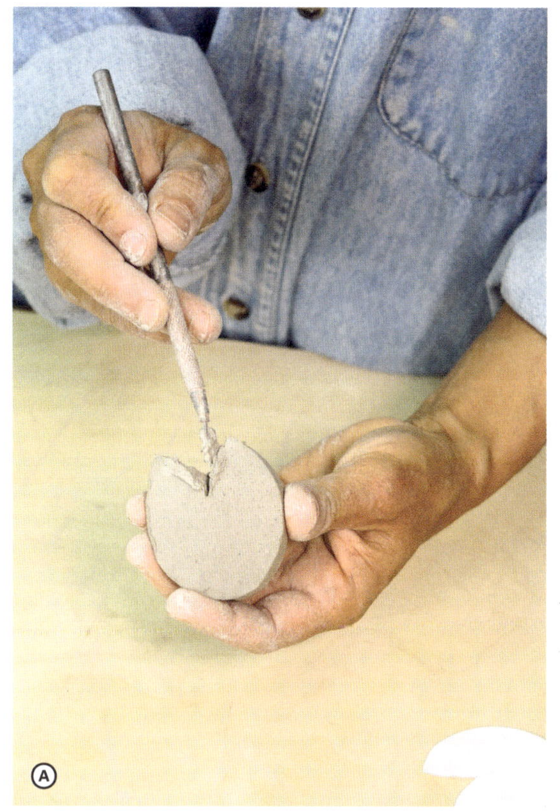

Ⓐ

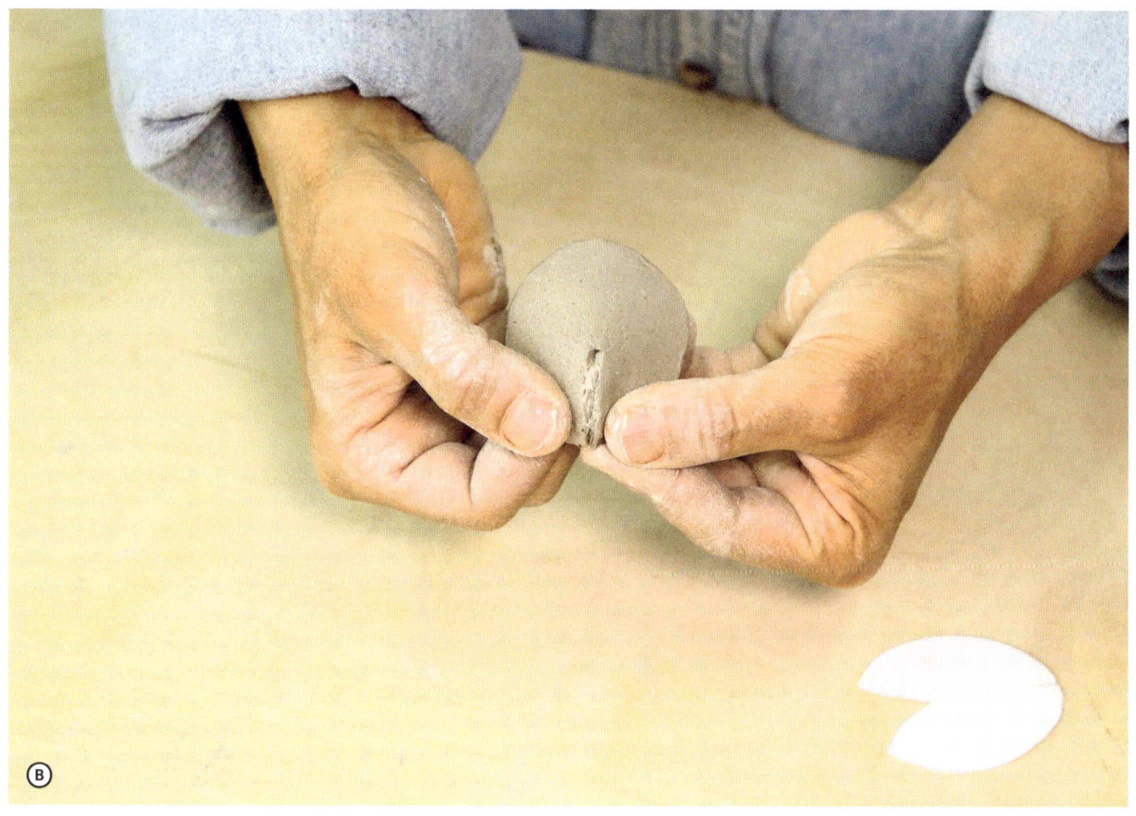

Ⓑ

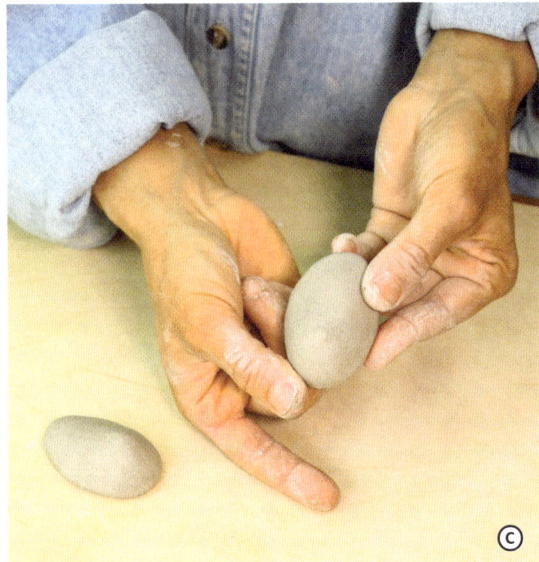

To develop the bulge of the breast, start at the widest part of the form and gently push out from the inside to create a convex mound along the underside of the teardrop shape. Note that this pushing out does not happen along the whole of the shape but only towards the bottom half and that it creates a bowl-like shape with the edges tucking back in instead of flaring out. Gravity dictates that the bulk of the breast tissue will gather at the bottom of the form, while the top of the breast will move in a gentle sloping. ©

Make sure to keep these shapes well hydrated until you apply them to the sculpture. I often keep several tightly lidded containers or "wet boxes" to hold the assembled bits and pieces of a composition and keep them properly hydrated until I am ready to use them.

To attach the breasts to the figure, find the bottom of breast line from the previous step and, with your calipers, measure the distance between each nipple. Transfer this measurement onto your sculpture with two horizontal marks on or near the bottom of breast line. Make a vertical line through each of these marks. Next, take a measurement of the distance between the bottom of the breast and the nipple. Use this distance to measure up from where your vertical lines intersect the bottom of the breast line and make two marks, establishing the location of the nipples.

With these guides in place, align your breast shape with the bottom of the breast line and nipple mark and press gently toward the upper part of the form. Make your keys, slip and score, and attach permanently by pressing firmly but gently. Add fresh material to mediate the transition into the surrounding tissue. You can perforate the underlying surface for venting before attaching breasts permanently or pierce a venting hole at the finishing stages, making sure it goes all the way into the thoracic cavity before sealing from the outside. Ⓓ

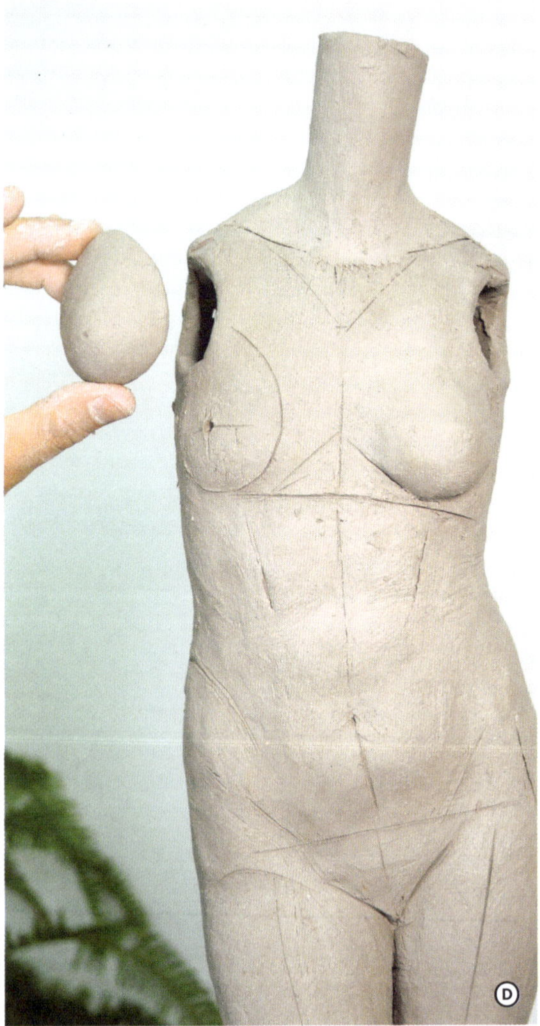

Claire Partington

Your pieces are viewed around the world but they are born in the U.K. How do you feel your studio setting informs your creative voice?

It's fantastic that we are so connected (virtually) with images shared instantly to a global community. The downside being my work is primarily viewed as a tiny digital reproduction, which doesn't convey the scale or surface details. I also wonder if some of my colloquial references are lost in translation.

My location totally informs my work. I live and work in London, in a normal residential part of the city and my studio is in an old warehouse next to a park. There aren't really defined cultural or ethnic enclaves in London anymore (only the division between rich and poor) and everyone just rubs along together. I think Londoners have a pride in the city and a unique identity that sits alongside whatever heritage they may have—and that really is what city life is about: change and adaptation.

My exposure to art was also very informed by my location. Britain is full of art. I was at art school just around the corner from the National Gallery and British Museum and I worked at the V&A Museum. Contemporary British art in the late 1990s was very abstract and conceptual and not interesting for me, so I really immersed myself in the Old Masters and Colonial spoils which make up British National Collections. At the time, I didn't question the historical and social exclusions or ethics of that art, but the iconic imagery and compositions definitely feed into my work.

What techniques come into play when constructing your figures and developing their surface?

The figures are all coil built from the base up. Sometimes I construct the bases from slabs with an internal support structure.

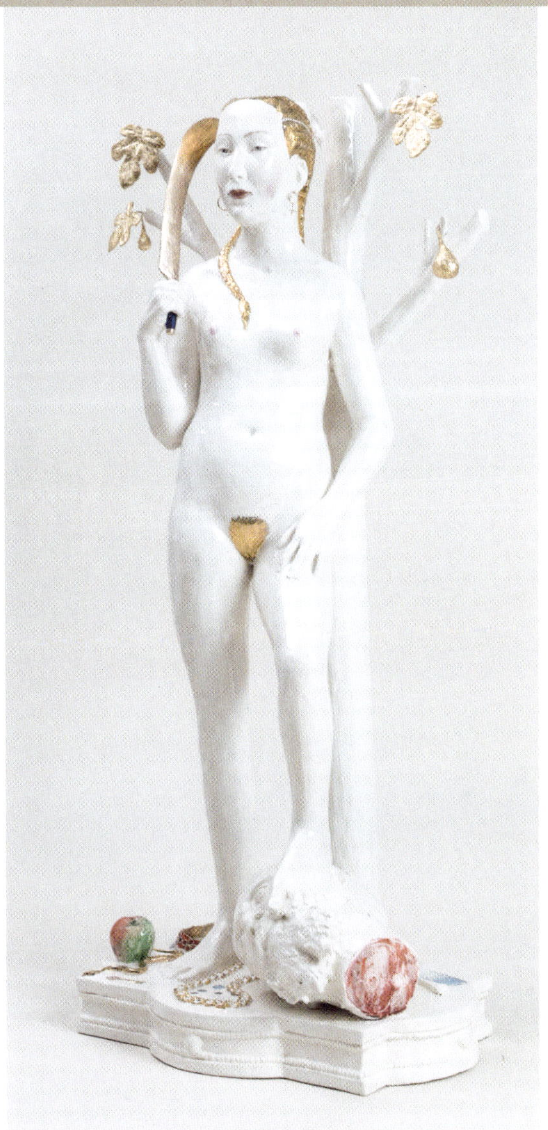

Claire Partington, *Judith with the Head of the Artist (Cranach)*. Dan Weill.

I'm building from an image I have in my head. Sometimes I'll adopt a pose myself to help me visualize the position of limbs, or I'll search online and print out some reference images (for specific clothes or dog breeds), but I don't draw first. I think making in clay is similar to making a preparatory sketch which gets refined as you work the surface, similar to the process of oil painting.

The figures are usually glazed and then I'll make my own surface decals for each piece to reflect a specific narrative.

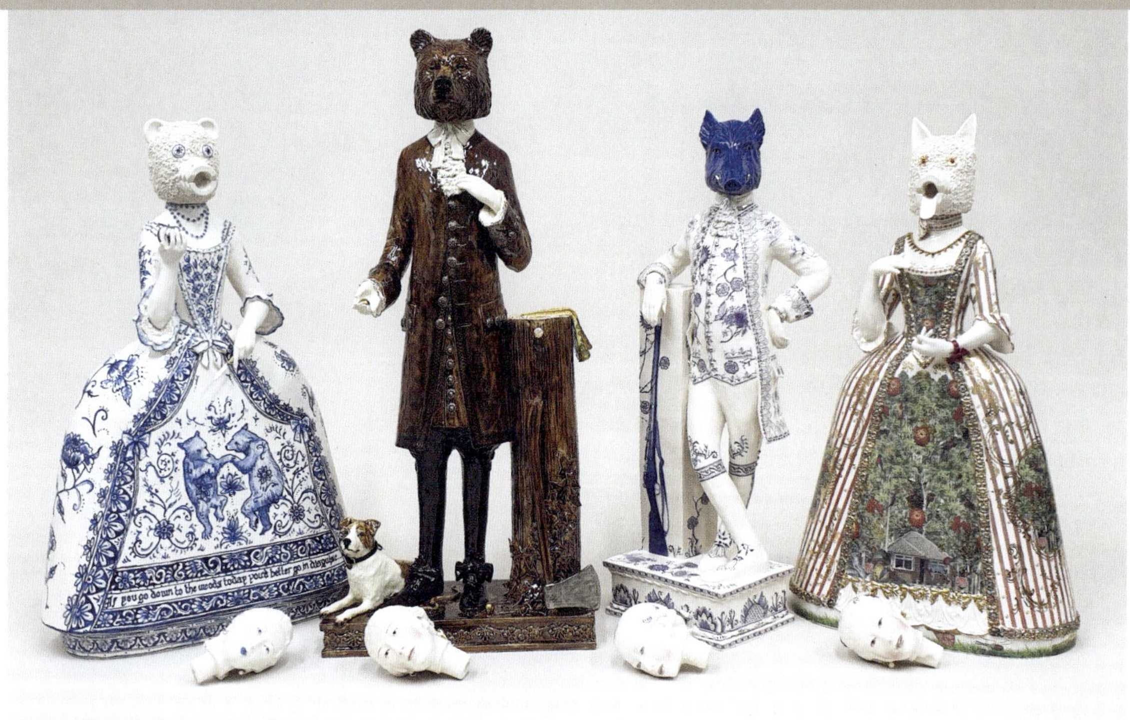

Claire Partington, *The Hunting Party*. Dan Weill.

I have a mixed media approach to my work and I usually buy or make metal accessories for the figures too.

What strategies do you use to develop content?

My main issue is finding time to get my ideas out of my head. I don't have any shortage of content; however, I'm better at editing myself now—before I get to the building stage. My work takes a long time to produce and, during the building, the ideas can evolve.

My figurative ceramic work started out as illustrations to European folk stories, but over time it has evolved into more of a comment on human nature. A lot of my figures are based on people I know or encounter in daily life: people in the schoolyard or park on my way to work. I do a lot of people watching and will spot a person's style or pose that may remind me of a character or artwork and I'll make a mental note to use an aspect of that in my work.

You've been on this path for years, keeping up an impressive creative rhythm both in terms of an abundant production and the degree of quality and complexity of the work. What practices support you?

I started making ceramic figures at night school when I had young children and it was a release to focus my mind on something away from work and home life. My kids are older now and my work is making my art, but being in my studio is still a luxurious novelty for me—a space to think and listen to music.

With regards to making practices, I studied sculpture at art school and I have always been very practical and intuitive in terms of making in all types of materials.

ARMS

To create the arms, you will plot dimensions onto a ¼ inch (6 mm) slab and create two tapered cylinders, which will be the simplified foundations for our upper and lower arms. Once attached, you will continue to articulate this core by pushing out, cutting, and pressing in. After these core forms have set, you will add another thin layer of clay and engage in nuanced modeling to bring the forms to their full fruition. Let's begin.

On your slab, draw a 10¾ inches (27.3 cm) vertical line and two horizontal lines, perpendicular to and centered with the first at either end. Make one 6⅔ inches (17 cm) and one 4 inches (10.2 cm). After connecting the outer edges of these lines, cut along the outer shape and down the centerline to extract your two arm shapes. Ⓐ

Curl the shapes onto themselves, using a gentle pinching action to guide the tight bend of these small forms. Ⓑ Bring each form to your photographic references and compare its width at various locations with the arm on the image. When you feel that you have the correct thickness, trim any excess material beyond the overlapping edges. Carefully slip, score, and enclose your cone, using your dowel or rod to compress from the inside by rotating each cone as the rod gently moves up and down within the form. For this part of the process, I particularly like a threaded ⅜ inch (1 cm) metal rod: the serration helps stitch the clay together and the weight aids in compression. Once the seams are integrated, cover them well and set them aside to stiffen. Ⓒ

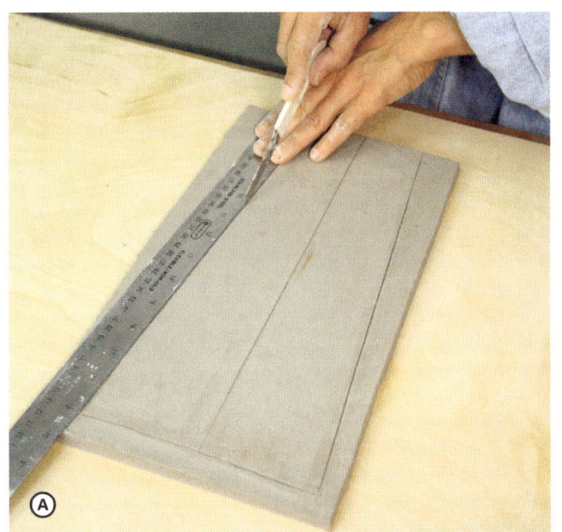

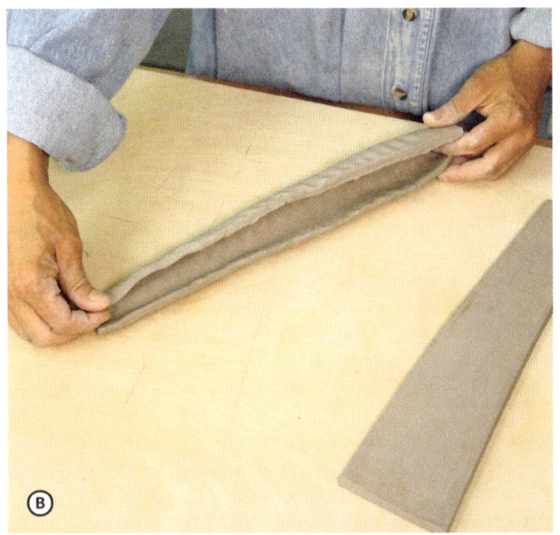

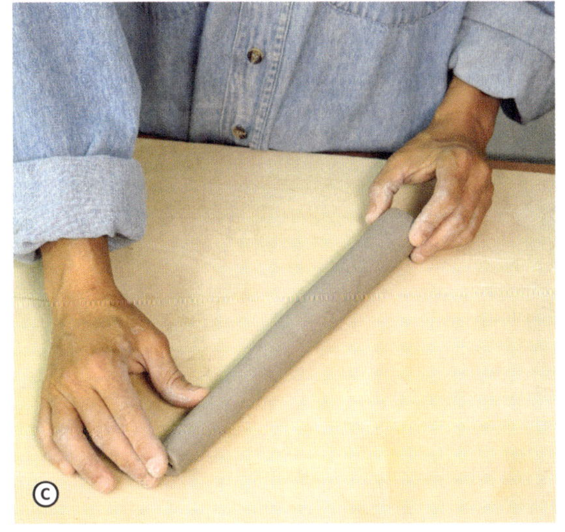

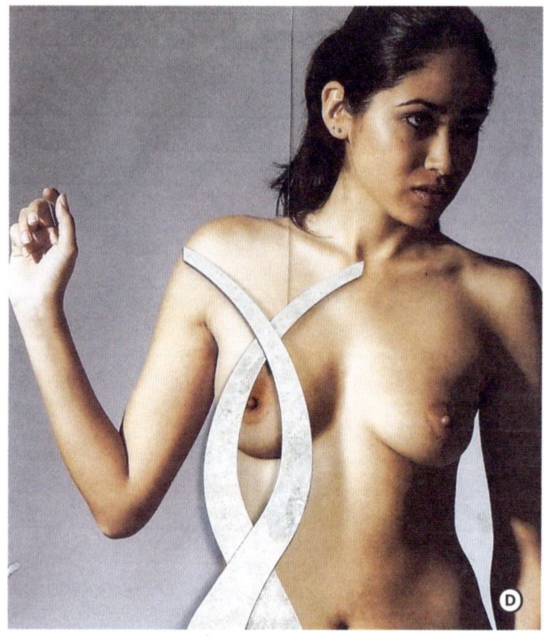

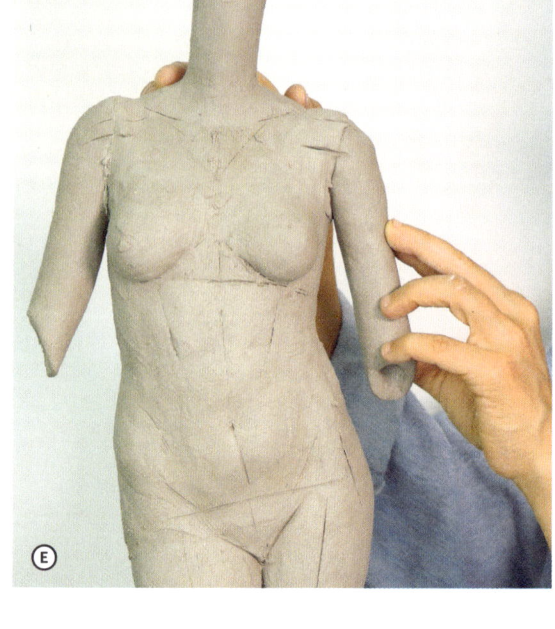

To attach the upper arms, you will uncover your arm cylinders and compare them against the photographic references. With calipers held to your front-view reference image, measure the distance between the top of the arm, just inside the shoulder, and the elbow joint. Next, hold one arm cylinder up to the front reference photo and slide the tapering cylinder up or down until its width matches that of the reference image. This is how you will decide which part of the cone to cut from. Mark the measurement from your calipers onto your cone, adding about a ¼ inch (6 mm) of extra length onto the thinner side, and then cut a segment from your arm cylinder that approximately matches the height and width of the upper arm.

Next, trim the top part of your cone segment at a diagonal where the arm will meet the torso and round the top of the form by pushing gently with your finger from the inside. Once you have prepared your upper arm segment to meet your torso, hold your calipers to your front-facing photographic reference and take a measurement of the distance between the centerline (sternum) of the torso and the outer part of the shoulder. Ⓓ

If necessary, trim the width of your torso around the armholes to prepare to receive your upper arms. Place your cylinders against the torso to both check for alignment and ensure sufficient surface contact for a strong connection. Use your calipers to once again grab the distance from the centerline to the outside of the upper arm, around the outer apex of the deltoid.

Make sure this distance on your sculpture is consistent with the measurement from the photographic reference by trimming, adjusting, and adding bits of clay where necessary. Observe the negative space between the arm and the torso from both front and back views, cross-referencing these shapes with those in your reference images to guide lateral placement. Add a bit of clay to the armpit to protect the distance between the torso and the arm, ensuring that the form will stay in place. Once you have evaluated the placement of the upper arm from all vantage points, draw your keys before slipping, scoring, and finalizing your seam. Ⓔ

Once the shoulder joint has set enough to hold the weight of the upper arm, measure with your calipers against your reference the dis-

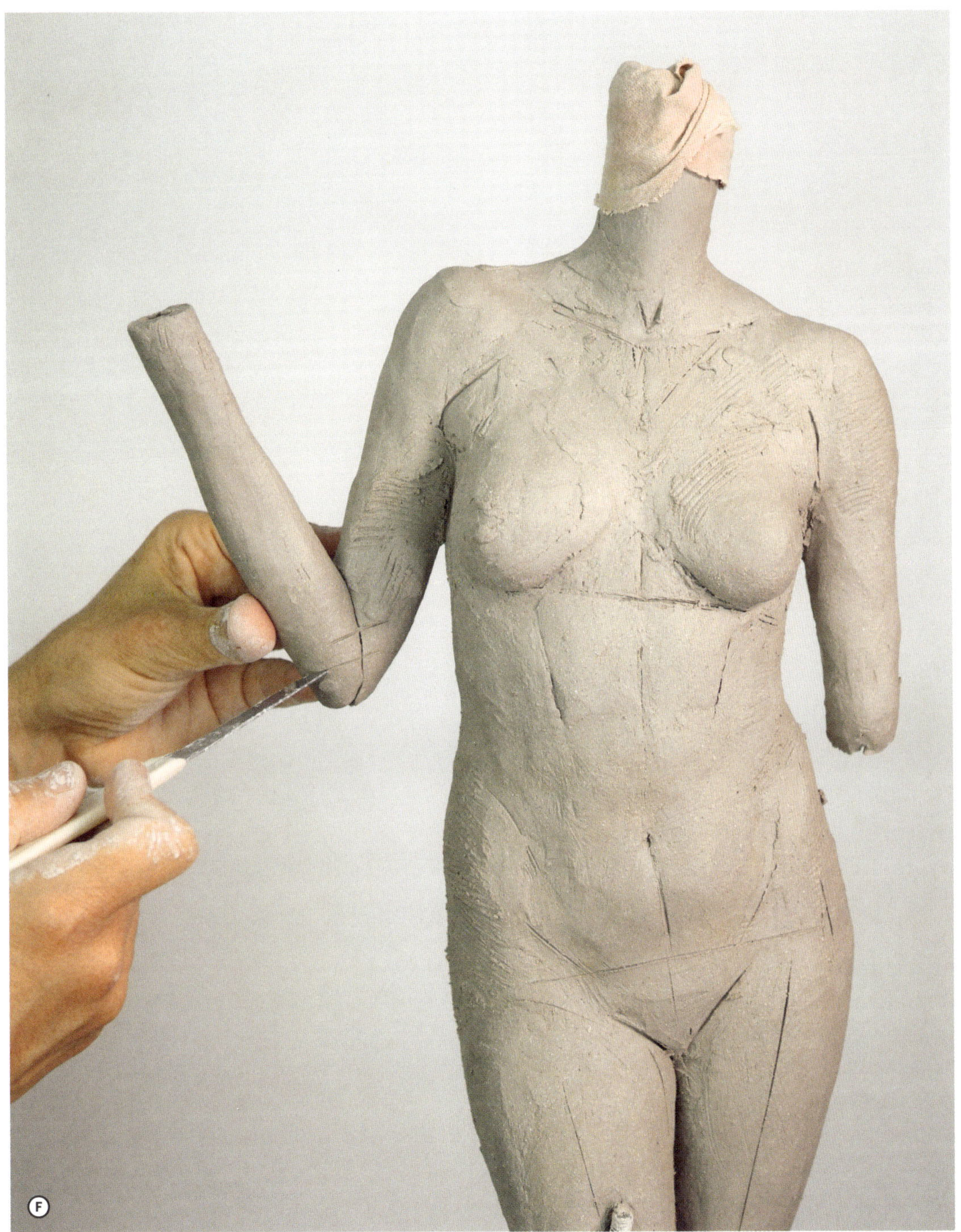

tance between the elbow and the wrist, right before the hand. Add about ¼ inch (6 mm) in length. Compare this segment to your photographic references to ensure it is the proper width and length. Starting with the bent right arm, take a measurement with your calipers of

the distance between the top of the shoulder to the tip of the elbow from the side photographic view. Compare this measurement to the length of the arm on the sculpture and trim the lower edge at an angle to match the diagonal creased elbow established by the bending arm. Ⓕ

Repeat this process for the lower arm segment by trimming a matching diagonal on the wider side of the cone. 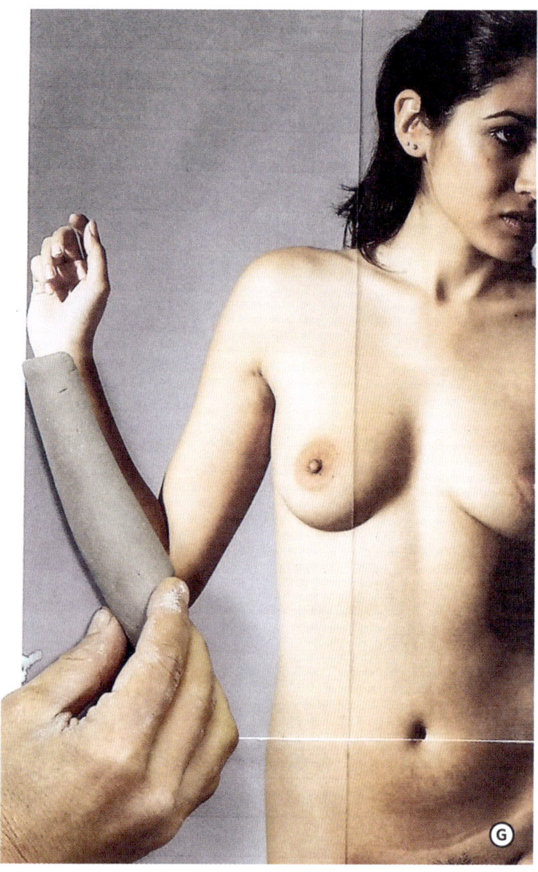 Position the lower arm against the upper arm to check for alignments. Make adjustments where they are necessary, perhaps adding bits of clay to articulate the proper angle. As with the upper arm, look at the shapes of the negative space from the front, back, and right views of your photographic references and use these to establish alignment. When you are ready, set your keys and slip and score before attaching firmly and revising your seam. If necessary, pin a thin metal rod or wire from the lower arm into the torso to support the elbow joint before it sets. 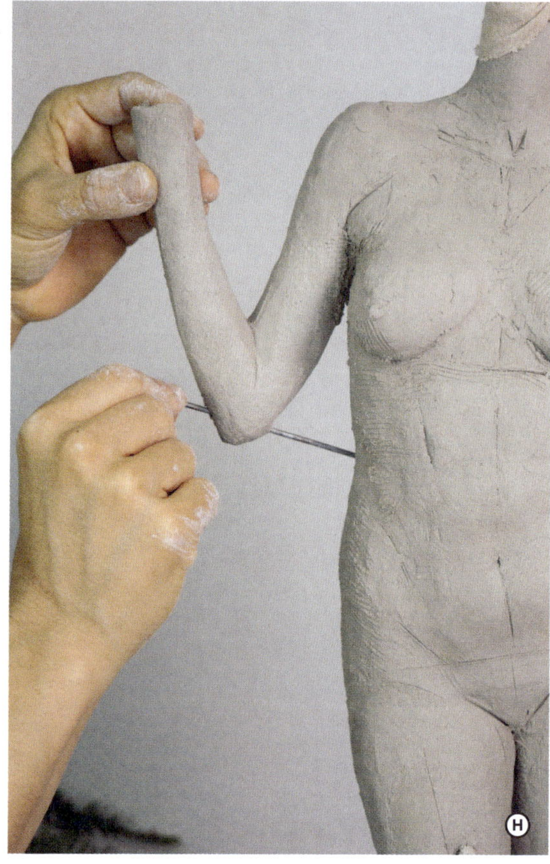

Follow the same process to cut and attach the extended arm. Note that on this side, there is a subtle internal rotation on the lower arm as it rests on the upper right thigh. You can use this point of contact to help support the weight of the lower arm. ⓘ

As your figure compounds outward, the appendages become more vulnerable to drying. Make sure you protect the receiving edges of the neck and arms with extra plastic and moistened shop towels or cloth as needed. Spray your composition often, and whenever possible, keep the legs covered as you continue to develop the upper body.

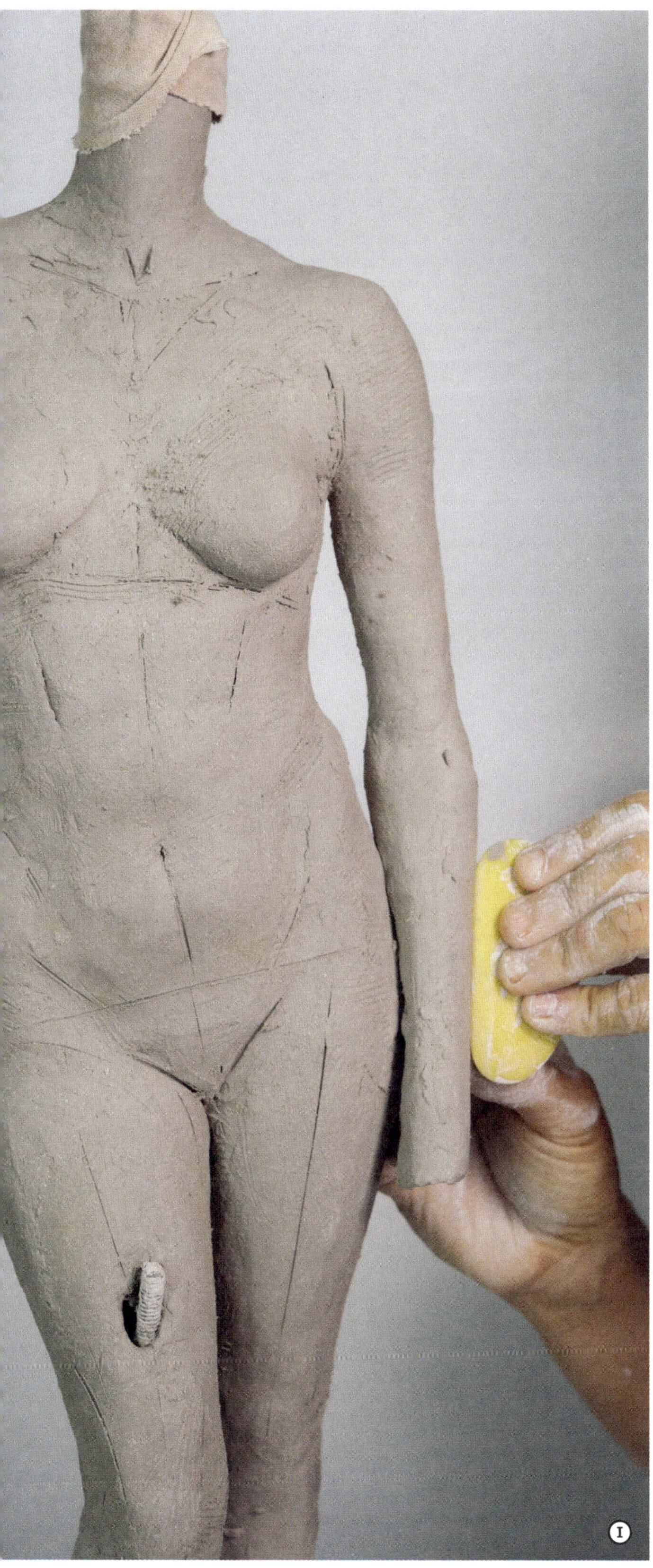

- Before attaching the arms, make sure the arm cylinders are dry enough to be able to hold their form against the pressure of your fingers.

- Cut more material than necessary to allow for adjustments to the form as it is integrated into the composition. This extra material also protects the edges from drying as you move on to subsequent steps.

- In the context of life-size compositions where the shoulder joint will need to bear more weight, you can take extra steps to reinforce the shoulder seam. As one option, you can pinch a phalange out of the upper arm that will fit snugly into the arm-hole on the torso, creating more surface contact. You can further fortify this joint by cutting a flap on the back of the torso and inserting your hand into the sculpture to compress the clay at the joint from the inside, adding fresh clay to the inside as needed. Once finished, you can slip and score the flap before recapping the opening and cleaning the seam.

- As with every part of the sculpting process, these cylindrical cones will establish the general proportion and positioning of the arms, offering a "core" onto which we will sculpt the subtleties of our forms by carving and adding bits of clay once that substrate has set.

- To offer support while the arm joint dries enough to hold its position, you may use stiff wire or metal rods to pierce through the arm onto the torso, relieving some of that vertical weight.

Gallery

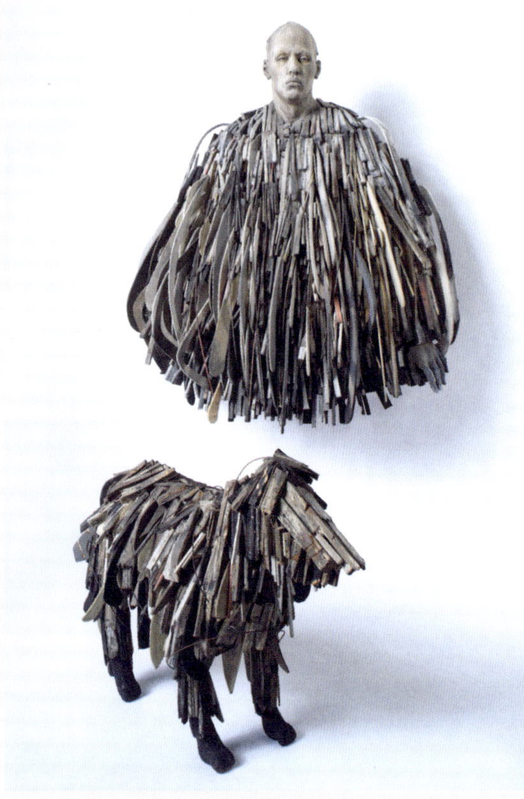

Cristina Córdova, *El rey*. Steve Mann.

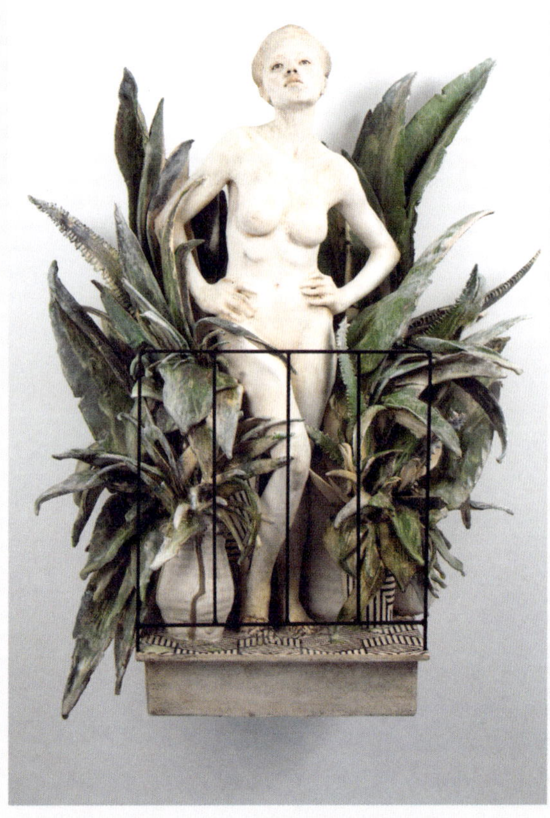

Cristina Córdova, *Del balcón.* Courtesy of the artist.

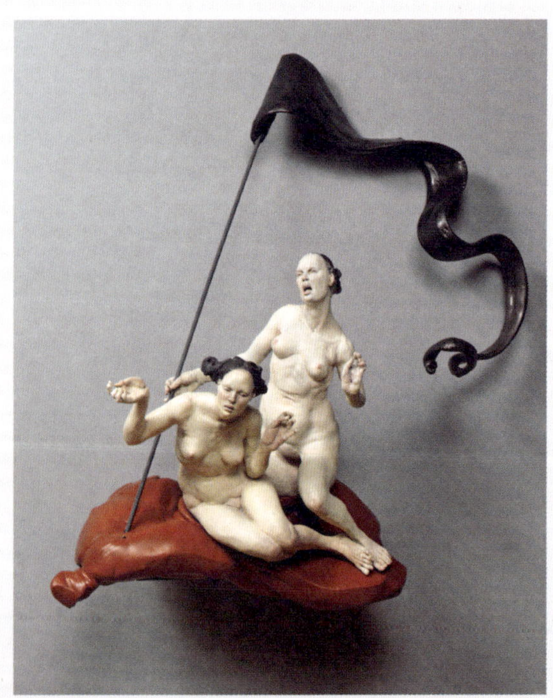

Cristina Córdova, *Hermoso naufragio.* Courtesy of the artist.

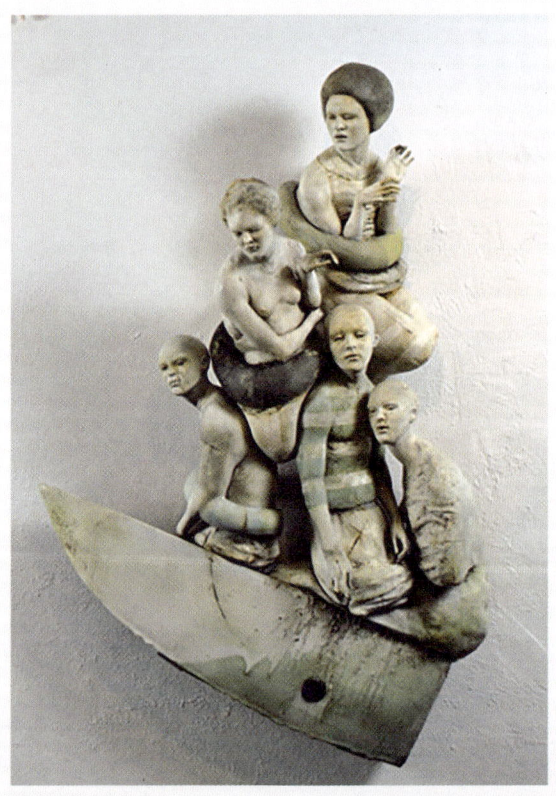

Cristina Córdova, *La huida.* Johnny Betancourt.

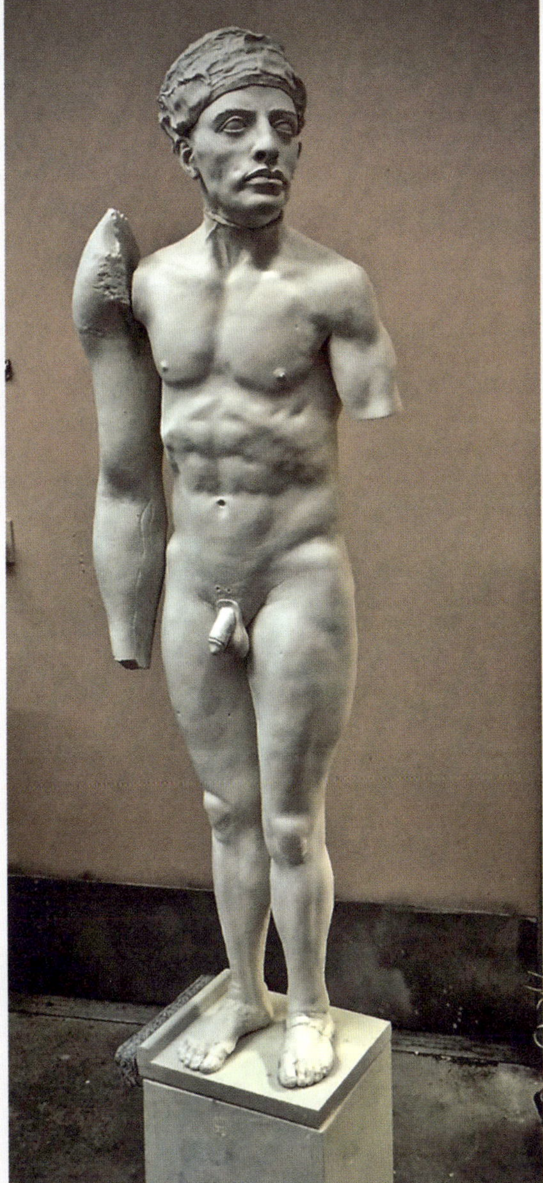

Doug Jeck, *David*. Courtesy of the artist.

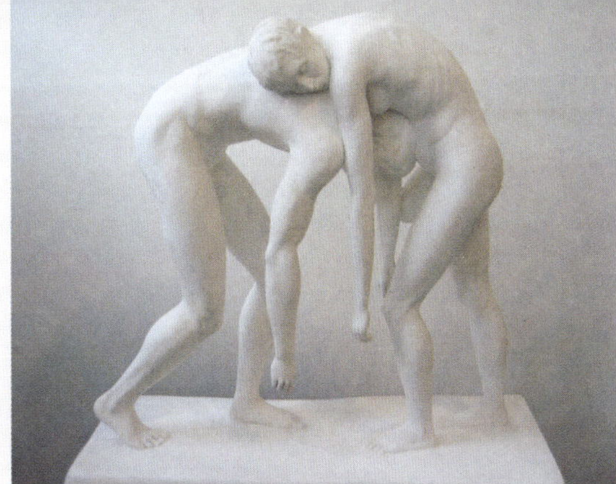

Kathy Stecko, *Elegy*. Courtesy of the artist.

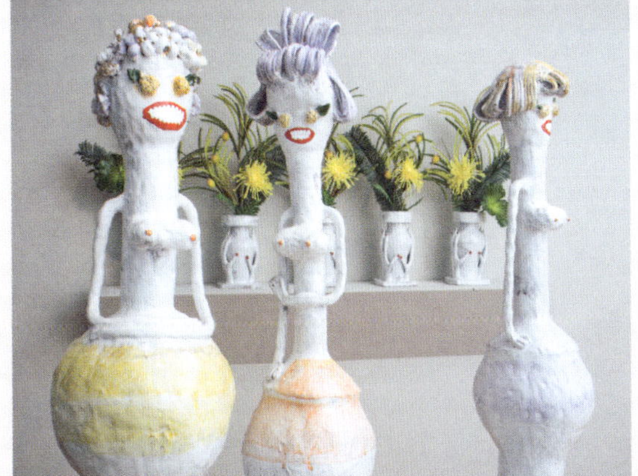

Joanna Powell, *Women from "She Ain't Pretty That Way."* John Carlano.

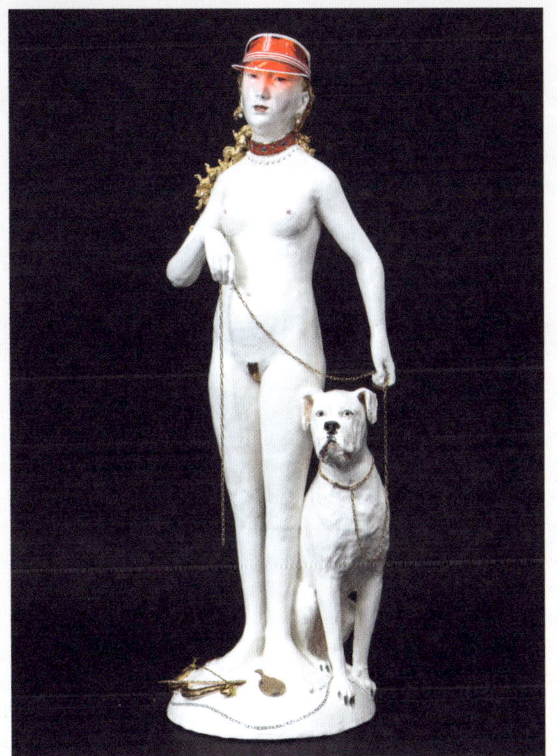

Claire Partington, *Venus and Cupid*. Dan Weill.

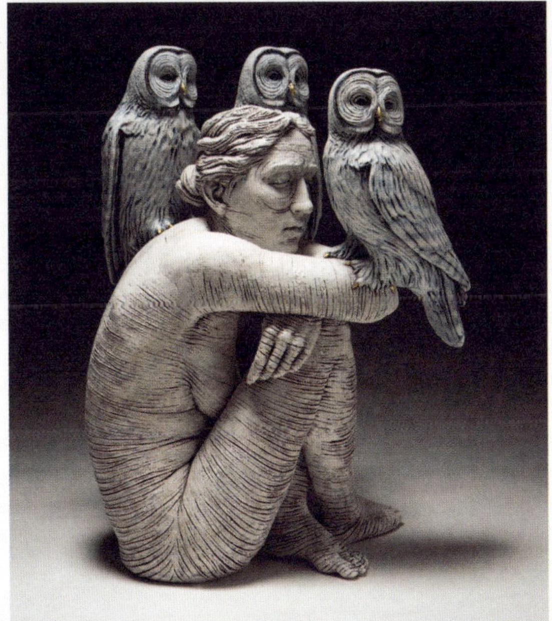

(left) **Adrian Arleo, *Great Greys*.** Chris Autio.

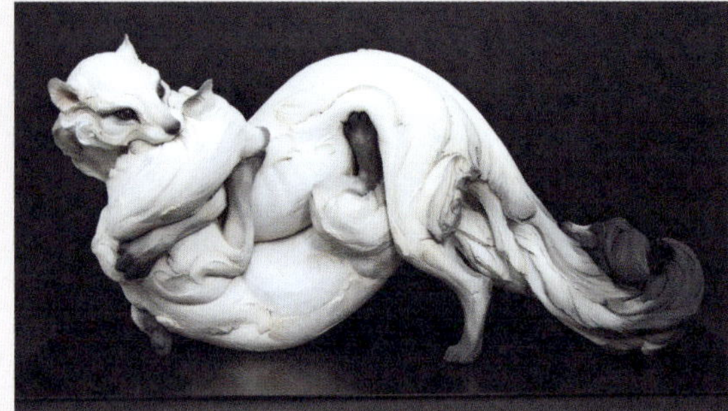

Beth Cavener, *Limerence.* Courtesy of the artist.

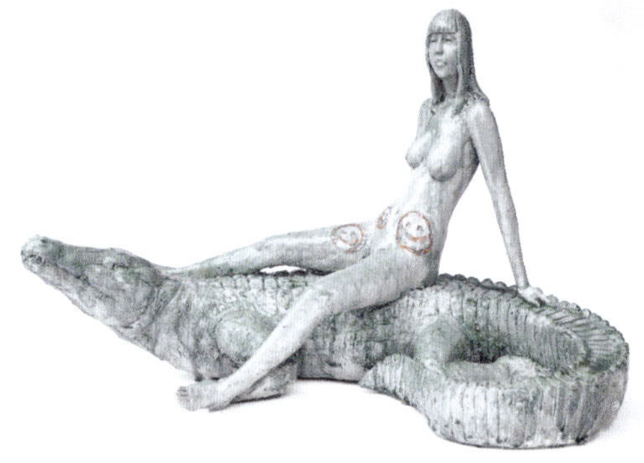

Lars Calmar, *Happy.* Grethe Aasted Therkelsen.

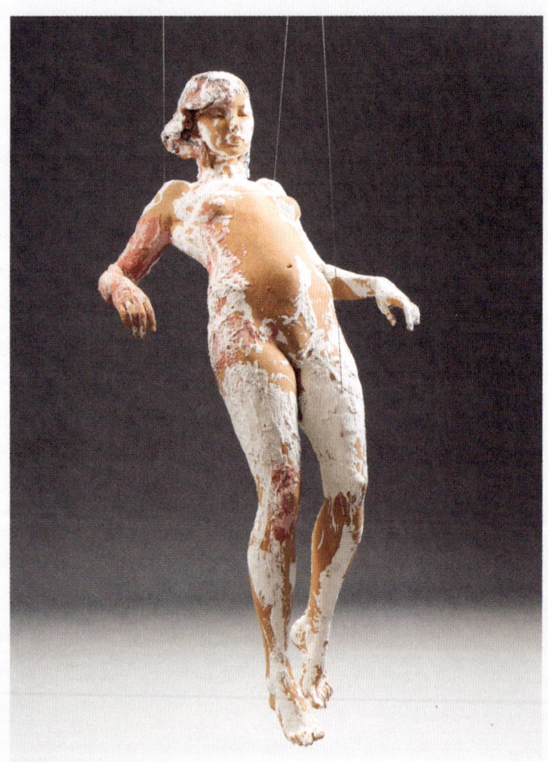

Kathy Venter, *Immersion #19.* David Borrowman.

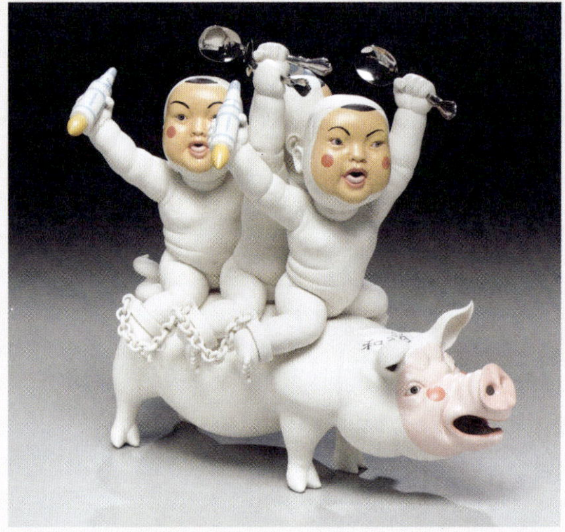

Russell Biles, *Crazy Train.* Tim Barnwell.

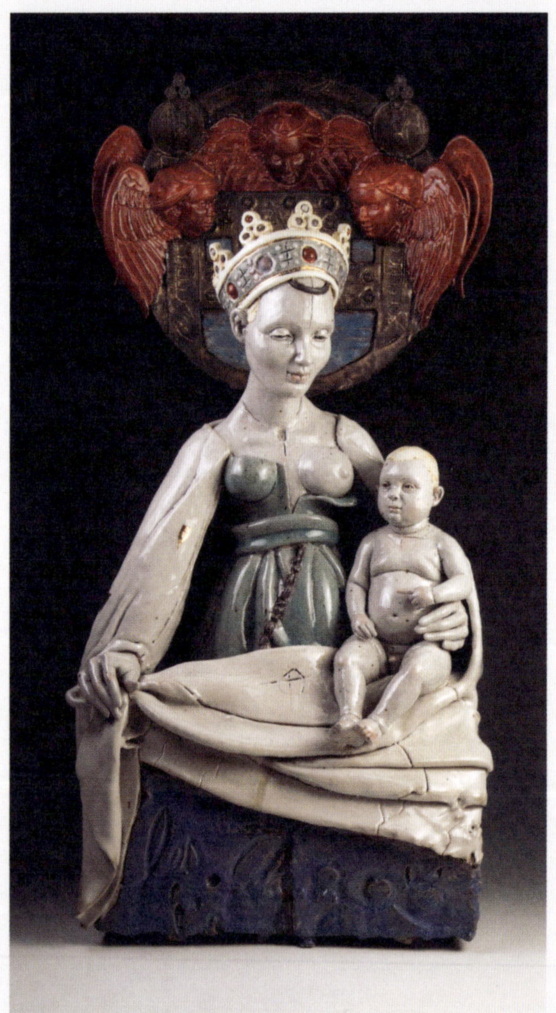

Kelly Rathbone, *Jean Fouquet.* Ryan LaBar.

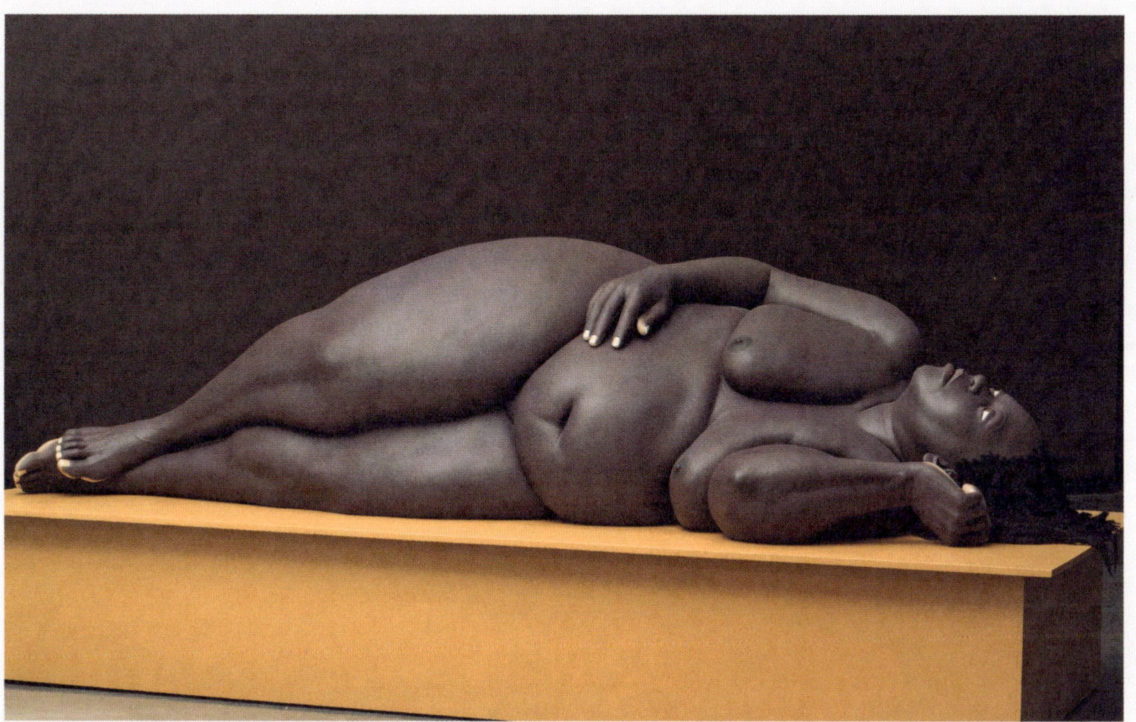

Tip Toland, *Africa*. Dan Kavita.

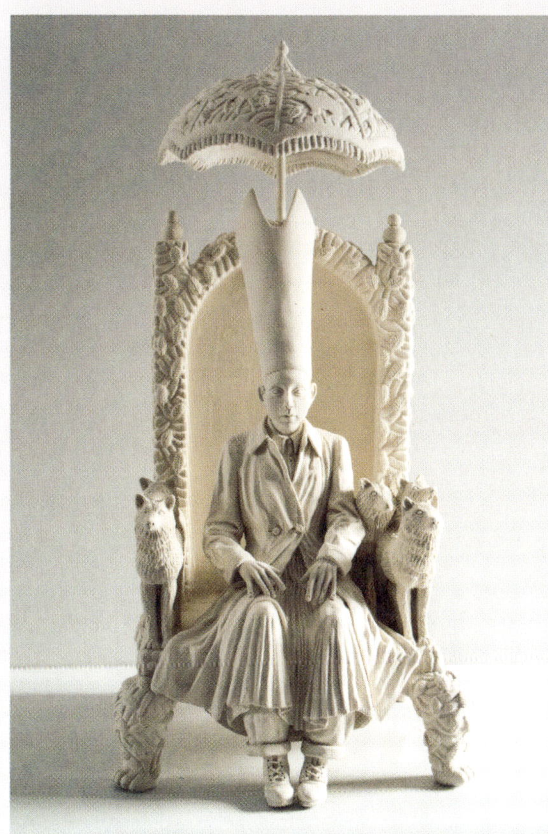

Tricia Cline, *Pope Joey*. Courtesy of the artist.

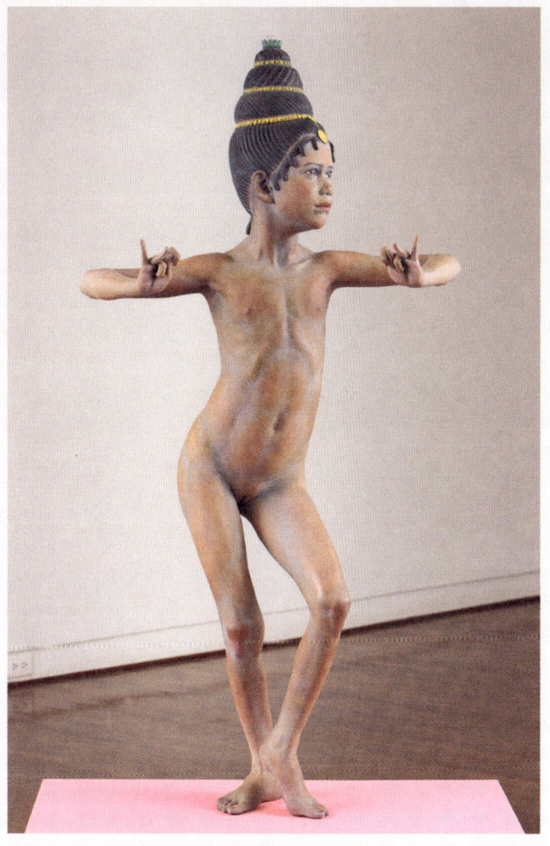

Judy Fox, *Lakshmi*. Courtesy of the artist.

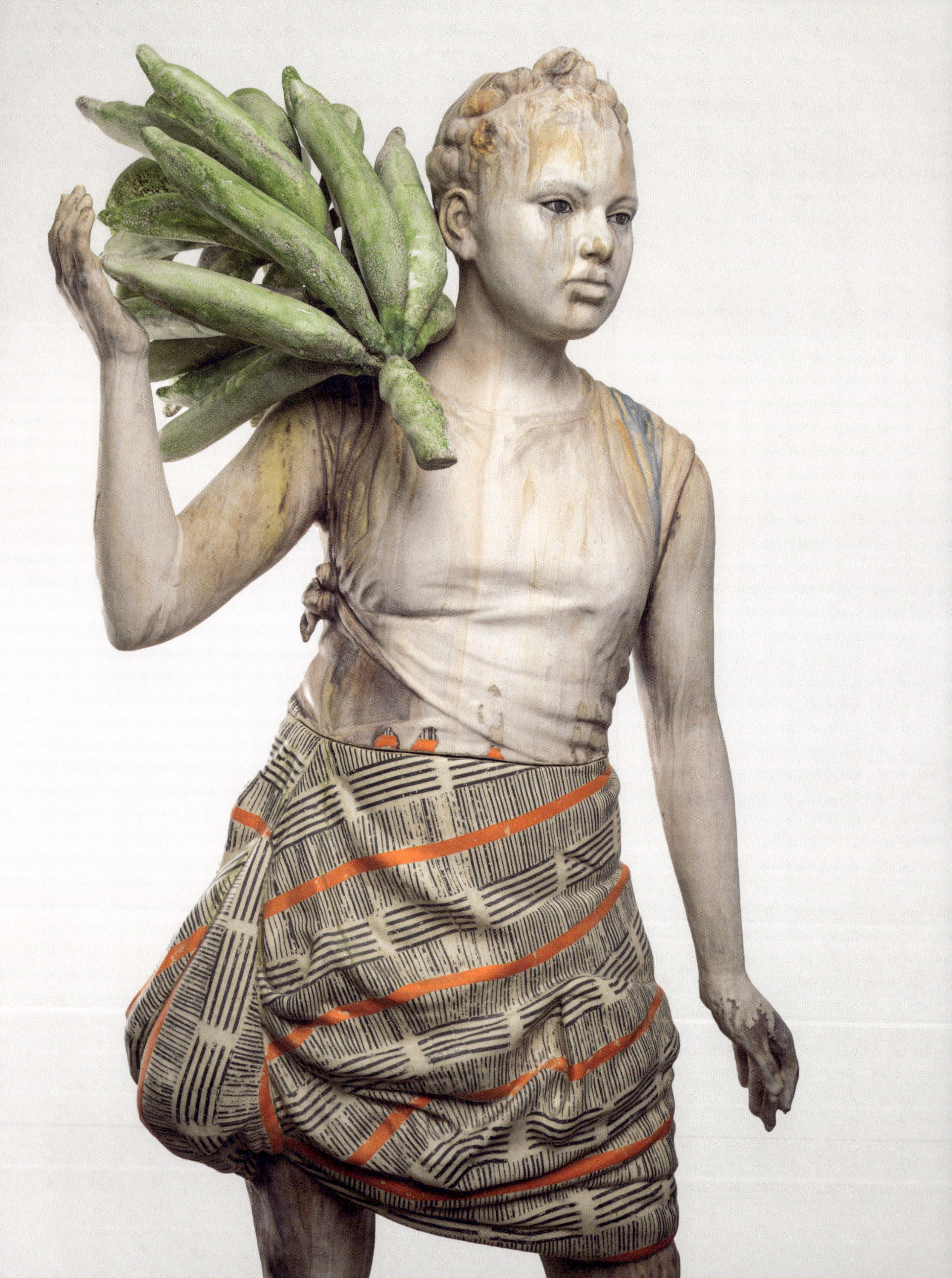

THE HEAD

THE HEAD STANDS as the universal archetype of consciousness and reason, of power and inspiration. It is a symphony of movement—a richly eloquent dance between the bony structure of the skull and the muscles, cartilage, and skin. As the most expressive part of the body, it offers a boundless array of communication possibilities, expressed through the myriad of muscles that contract and release in accordance with our thoughts and emotions.

I am drawn to many different artistic presentations of the head, ranging from the poetic archetypes of Benjamin Lira to the hyperrealistic human echoes of Tip Toland and Ron Mueck. Across the board, there is something primal about imbuing a head with a sense of aliveness, gradually building up layers of information, then suddenly tipping into the realm of the sentient. In my own practice, I usually sculpt a head using anatomical and photographic guides. However, at times I may choose to sculpt more freely, seeking symbolic or archetypal attributes that are not always apparent in direct, realistic renderings.

What follows is a basic sequence of steps to create a generic head in clay, drawn from both universal proportions and my own discoveries. You may combine these steps with specific reference information to render a portrait or expand on them through a process of free interpretation. In this book, we will be working on a small head to fit our 25 inch (63.5 cm) sculpture, but I invite you to print the pattern at different sizes to continue your exploration.

WHAT YOU'LL NEED TO GET STARTED

- Template (head)
- Slab (⅜ inch [1 cm]) that fits your head template
- Fresh clay to work over seams
- Joining slip
- Ruler
- Wire brush scoring tool
- Calipers
- Wooden finger tool
- Metal or wooden dowel
- Seamstress tape
- Paddle
- Stainless modeling tools

Cristina Córdova, *Cosmología isleña,* part of the collection of the Smithsonian American Art Museum.

USING A PATTERN TO CREATE A HEAD SHAPE

Before you begin this section, print and cut out the head template from page 187. Prepare a ⅜ inch (1 cm)–thick slab of clay and place the template over it, cutting around the outside profile and marking all the reference lines with the back of your knife. Ⓐ Ⓑ Ⓒ

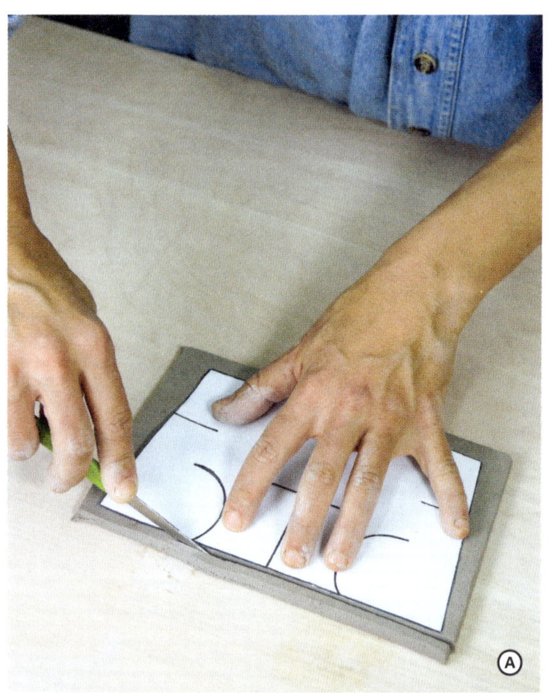

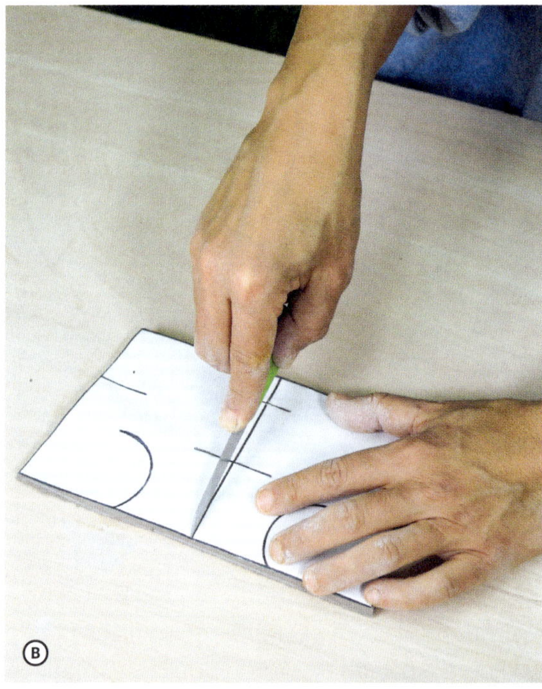

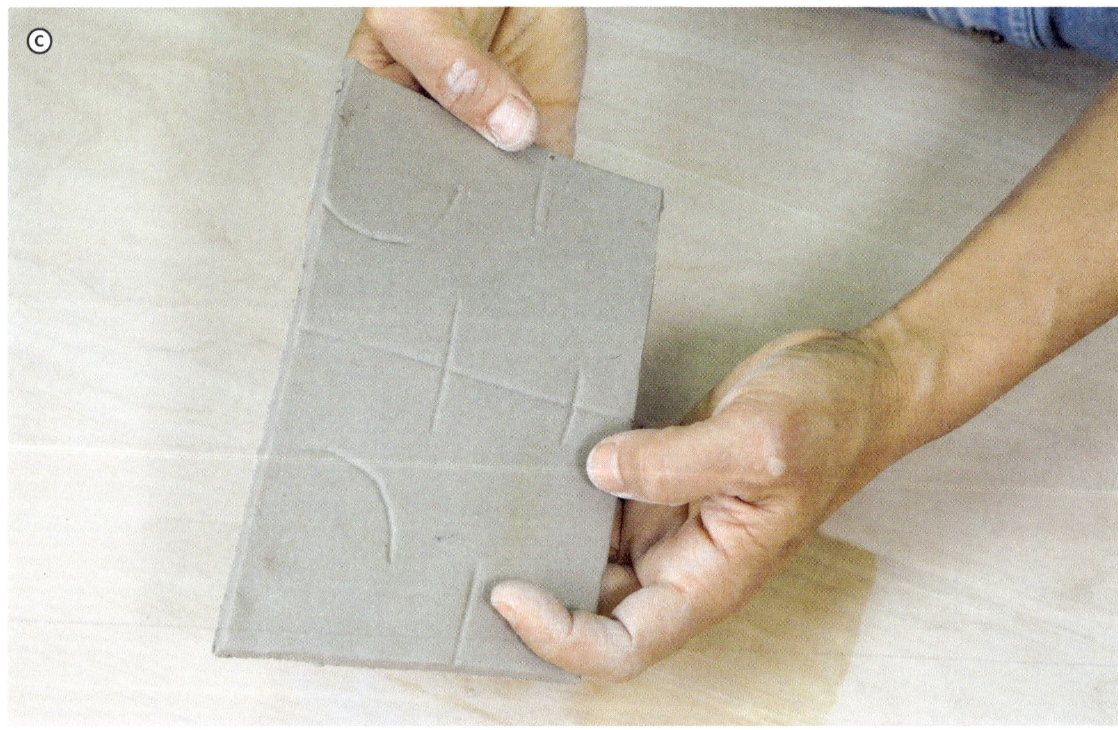

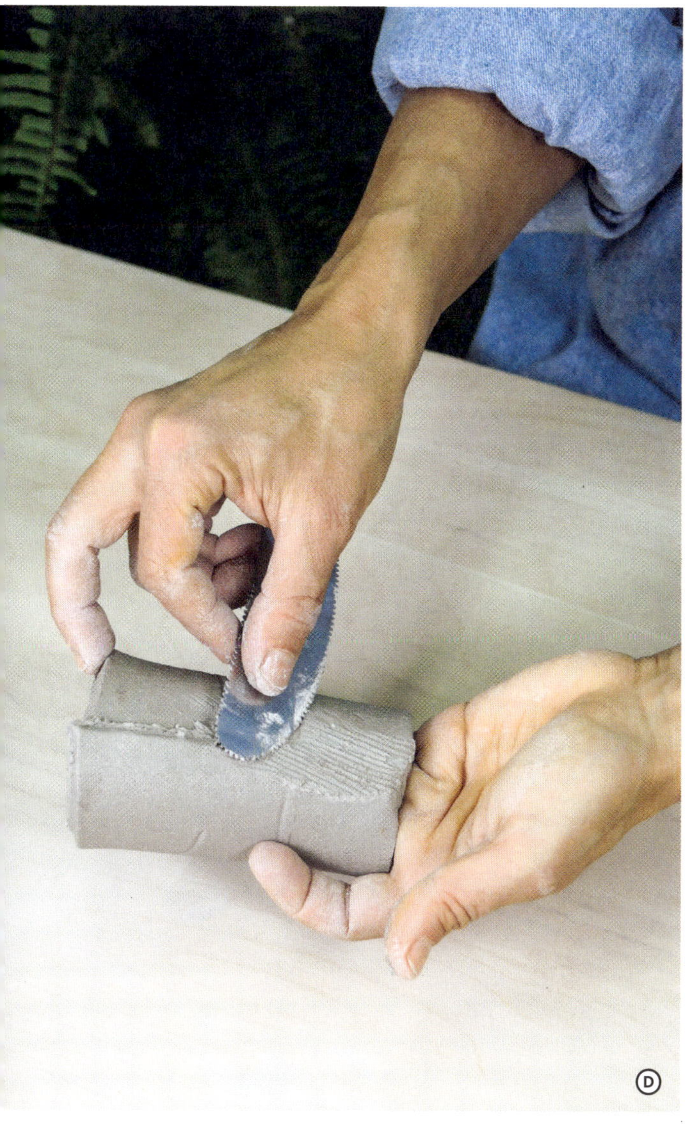

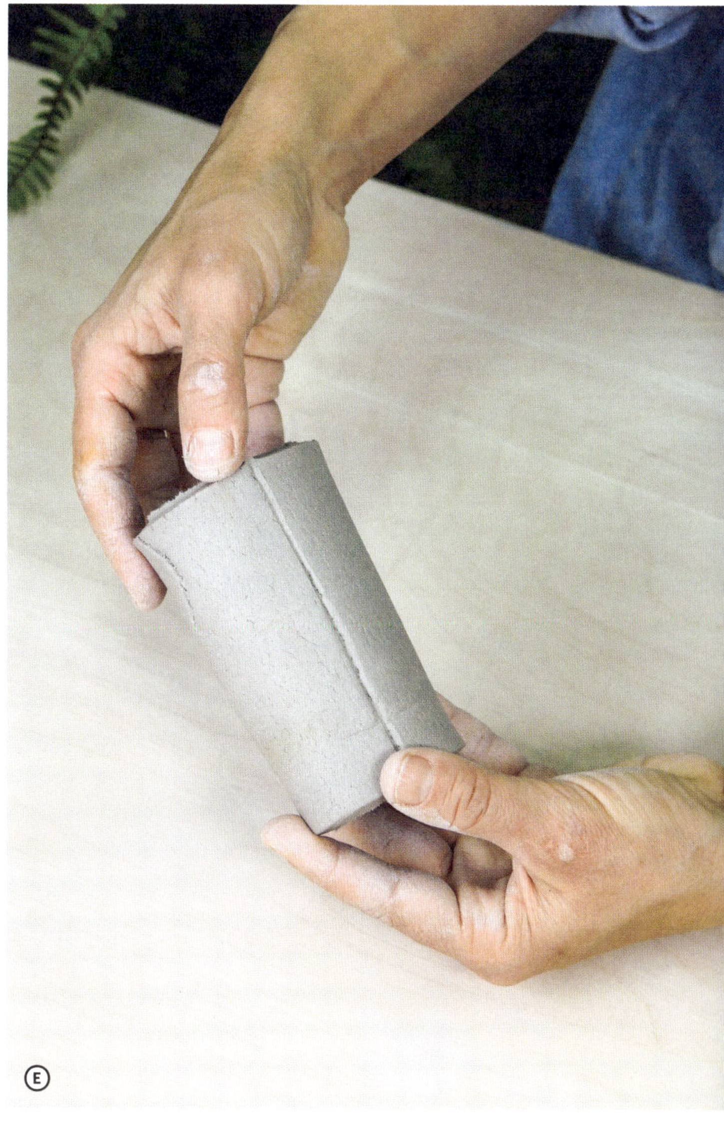

Ⓓ   Ⓔ

Assemble your primary shape by overlapping the edges of the slab by ¼ inch (6 mm) before slipping and scoring, and then compressing that vertical seam to create a cylinder. Remember, your reference lines should end up on the outside of the form. Ⓓ Ⓔ

For the step sequence that follows, we will begin adjusting the form by establishing the jawline, cutting darts, pushing inward and outward to articulate the bony landmarks of the skull, and drawing onto the surface to guide the placement of the features. Let's jump in.

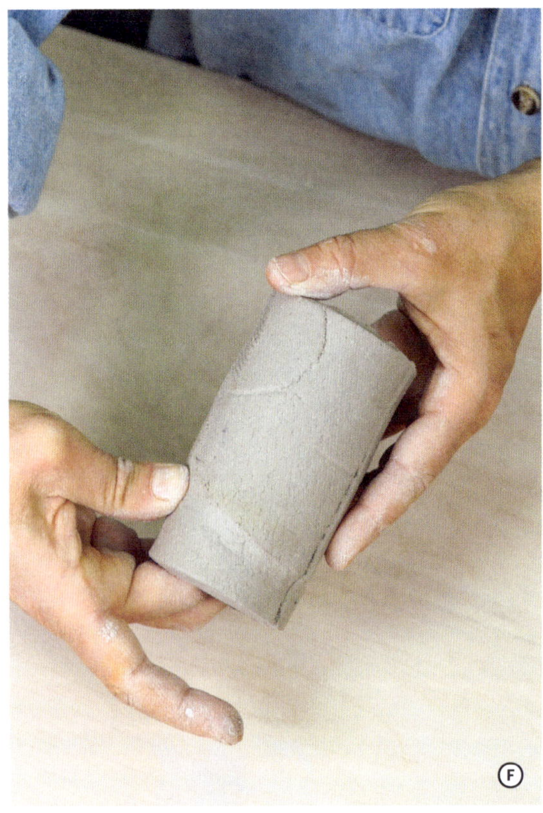

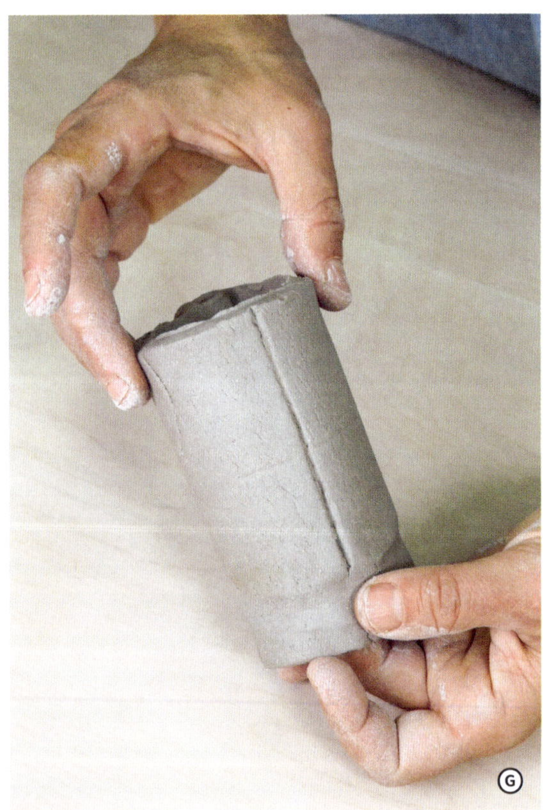

DEVELOPING THE CRANIAL FORM

1. Find the lowest reference mark (last down from the top on the front of the face) and move your finger from there to the mark toward the back of the cylinder, pressing firmly in a diagonal motion to establish the jawline and the back of the skull. Ⓕ Ⓖ Ⓗ

2. Focus on articulating the curve at the top of the skull. With smaller heads, you can just pinch and tap the curve into shape. With larger heads, you will need to cut four darts, at the front, back, and on each side, to develop the cranial curves.

3. Once the curves are established, create a small cap to sit on the cranial opening to close the form. This piece will stay unattached throughout most of the process so you can access the inside of the cavity while sculpting, but putting it in place periodically will help you visualize the whole form and allow you to take measurements from the very top of the head. Ⓘ Ⓙ

4. Now that the boundaries of the skull are defined, remove the cap and move your finger vertically along the inside of the shape, starting with the middle vertical line that you transferred from the template. Begin rounding the form gently, taking care not to exert excessive pressure that could distort the form too aggressively. As you gradually push from the inside, you are supporting and guiding the pressure from the outside with your other hand. Your goal is to begin articulating a spherical shape as seen from the front and back of the head and an egg-like shape as seen from the side. Ⓚ

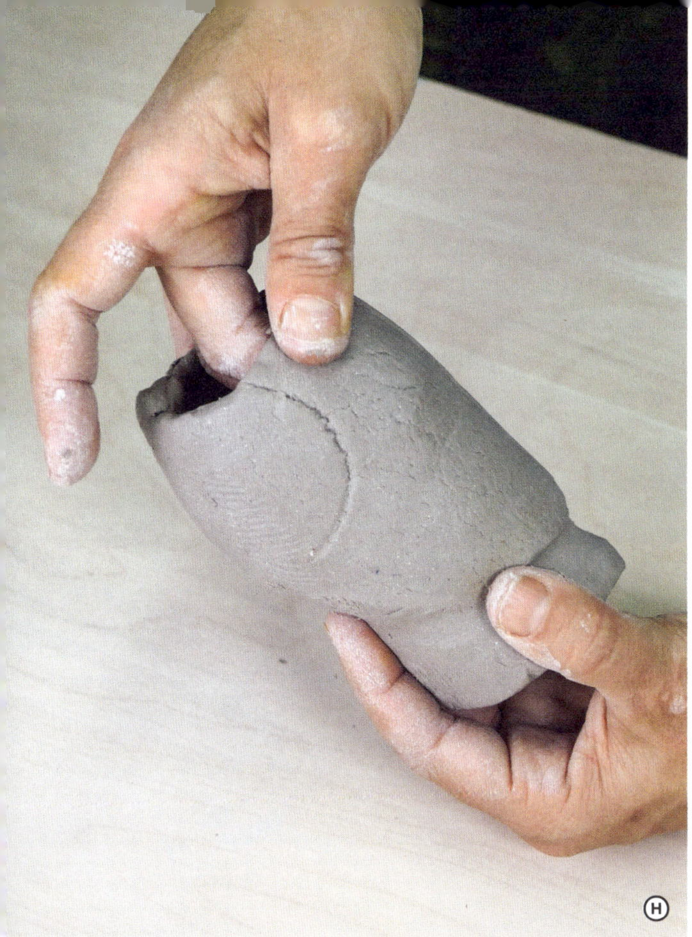

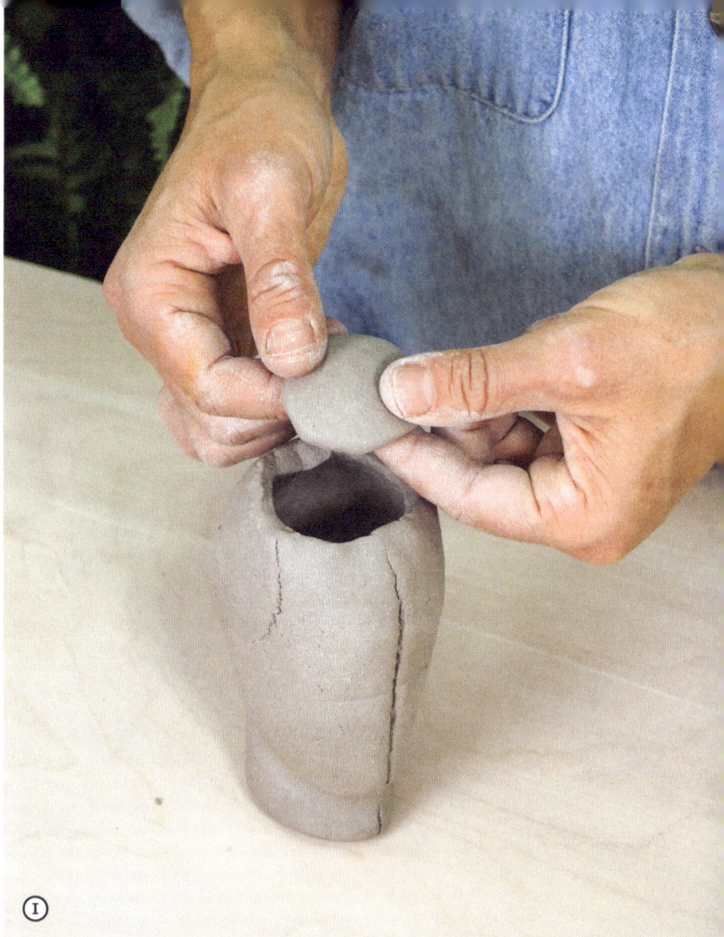

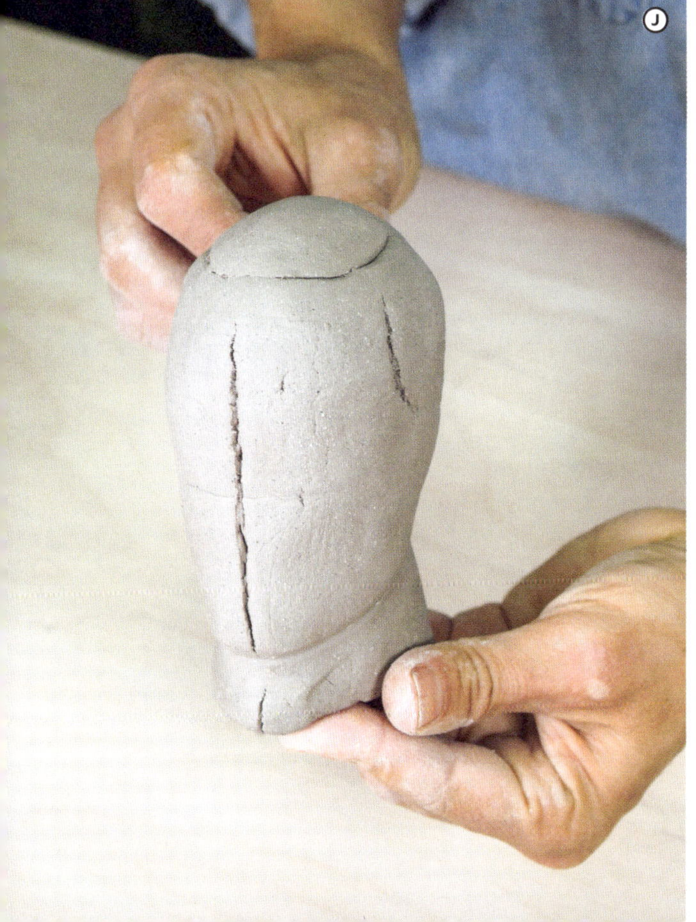

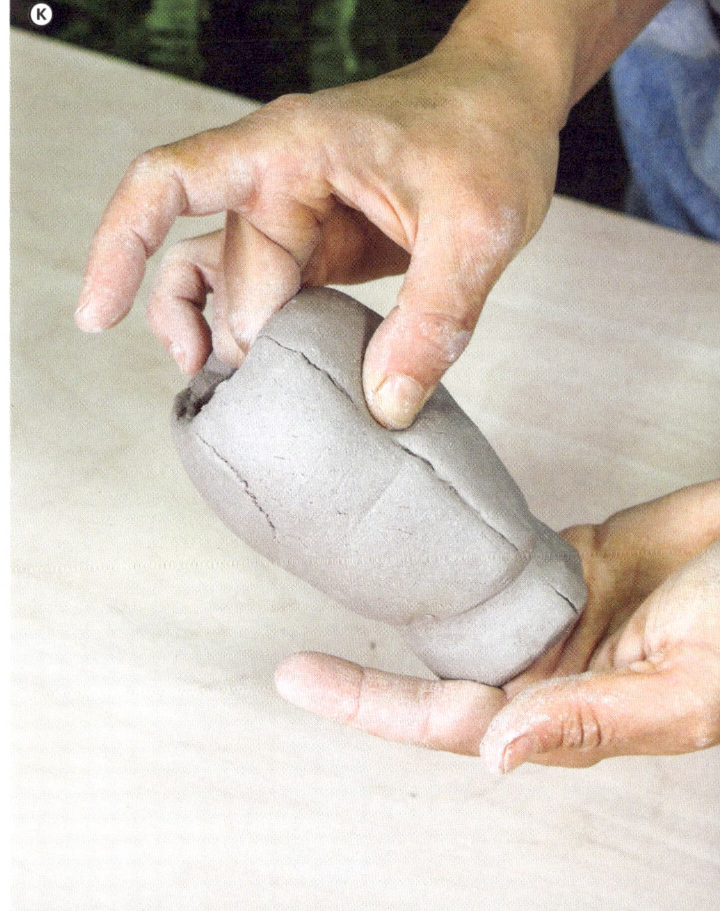

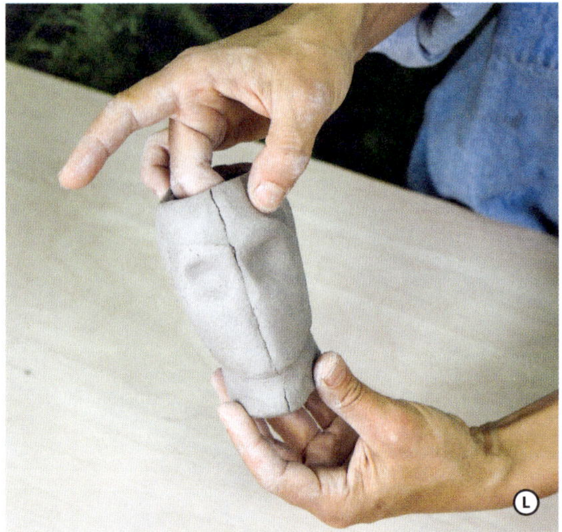

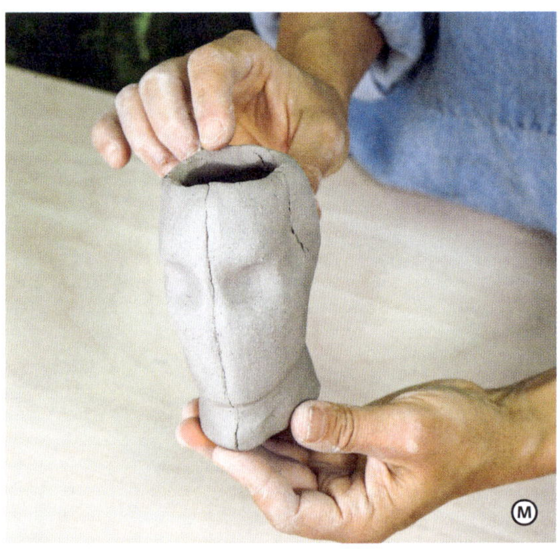

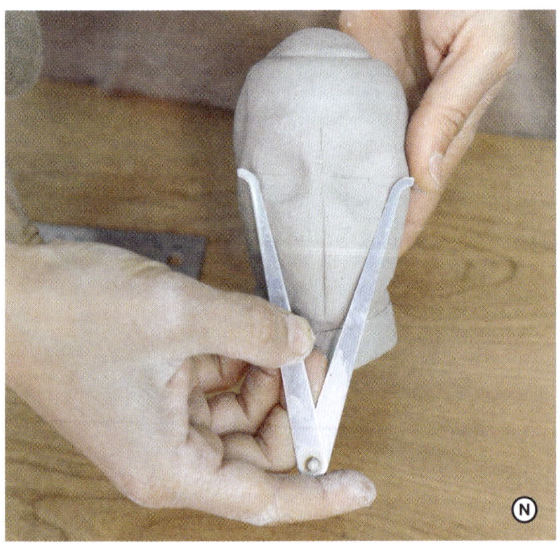

5. Once the basic head shape is articulated, push inward, just above your horizontal center reference line, while supporting with your finger from the inside. These indentations will be your ocular cavities. By offering support from the inside both above and below the cavities as you push in from the outside, you will start to develop the brow line and the cheekbone area.

6. Gently press inward in the shape of a squat "M" over the brow area to articulate the glabella and the contiguous brow bones. You are still working on the cranial, or bony interior, structure of the head, so remember that the final articulation of the form will happen through the addition of a layer of soft clay onto that core. Ⓛ

7. To further develop that bone structure, you will now create a shift in plane between the forehead and the temples by moving your thumb along the curved reference line from the template while offering internal support around the outside edge of the ocular cavity to establish the zygomatic arch and the temporal line. Ⓜ

8. With the help of calipers, a ruler, and photographic blueprints, you can establish new reference marks that will guide the placement of the facial features. The first measurement will capture the distance between the top of the head, or vertex, and the bottom of the chin. Using your calipers and your ruler, find that measurement, divide it in half, set your calipers to this new value, and mark that distance onto your skull. Make a horizontal line through this point across both ocular cavities. This will be your eye-line. Ⓝ Next, use your calipers and ruler to measure the width of your head at its widest point, around the cheekbone area. Divide this value by 5. Adjust your calipers

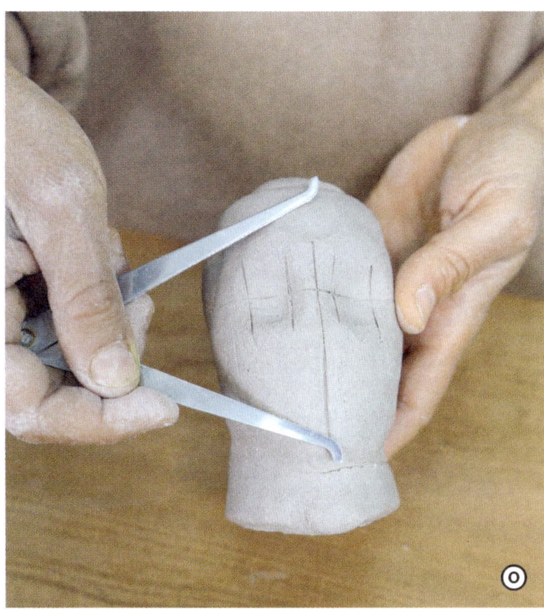

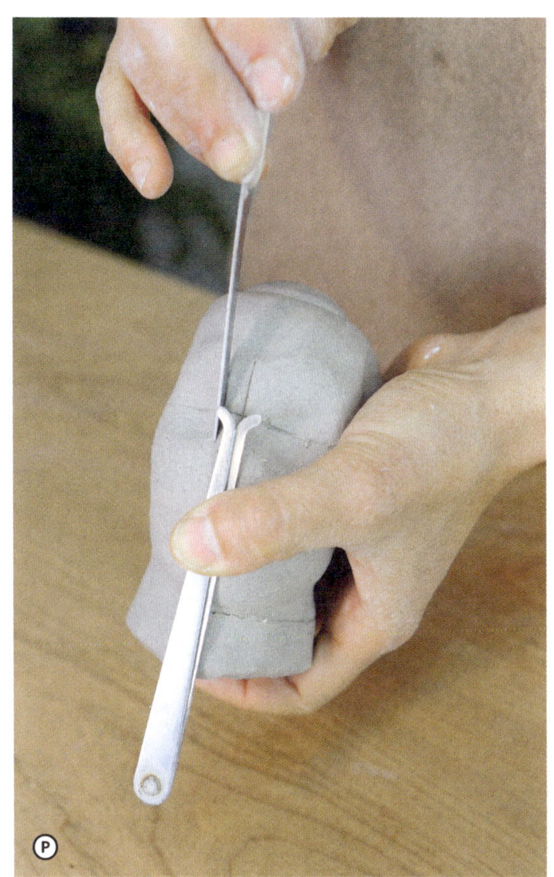

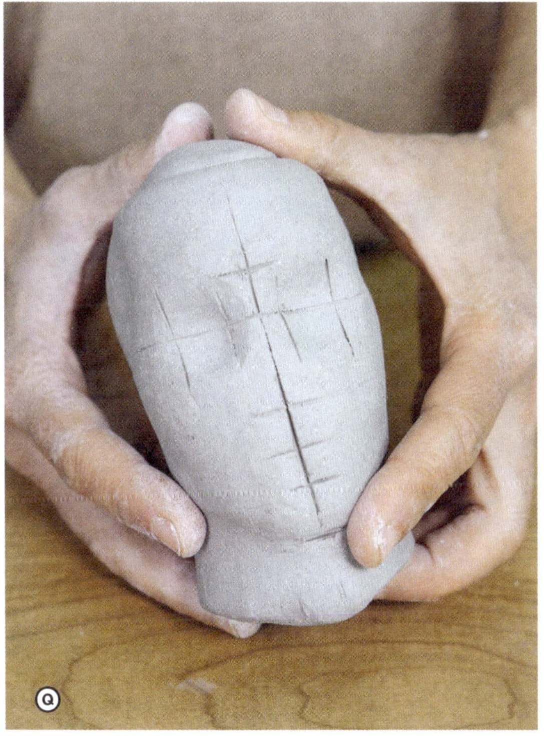

to this new measurement and divide your eyeline into five equal segments. 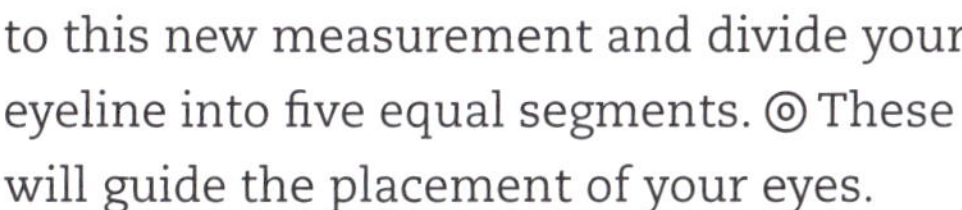 These will guide the placement of your eyes.

9. To find the placement of the nose, use your calipers and ruler to find the measurement between the hairline mark and the bottom of the chin. Divide this measurement by 3, adjust your calipers, and use them to plot two marks that divide the distance between the hairline and the chin into three equal segments: the hairline to the brow; the brow to the bottom of the nose; and the bottom of the nose to the bottom of the chin.

10. Using the same process, divide the distance between the bottom of the nose and the bottom of the chin into three equal segments. Draw horizontal lines dividing these segments. The upper line marks the site of the mouth, and the lower line is where the top of the chin will be. (Also see Appendix C.)

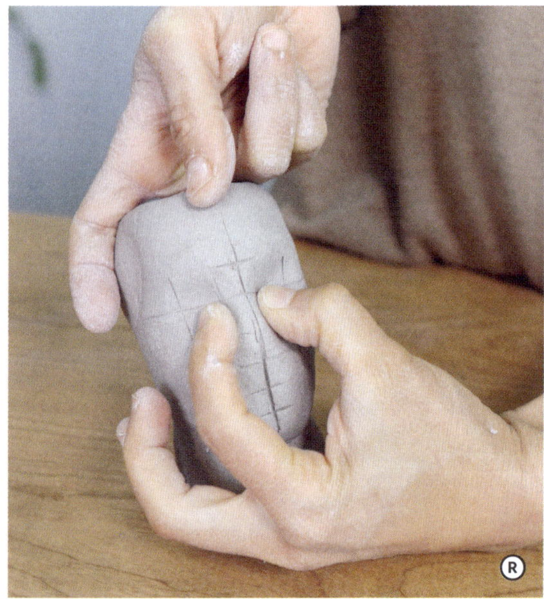

11. Using these reference lines, push outwards from the inside, starting to articulate the projection of the nasal bone, while supporting and helping guide the gesture from the outside with your other hand. ⓡ Again, the goal is developing volumes that represent the bone structure. The final, fleshy features will be achieved by adding material in subsequent steps.

12. Moving down, push out at the upper horizontal mark between the bottom of the nose and the chin. You are looking to articulate the arch of the maxilla, the bone that holds teeth in a semicircular formation. To control this projection, place your thumb and index finger at the edges of the curve from the outside as you gently push out from the inside. ⓢ

13. To finish up this section, push out to accentuate the chin or mental protuberance. ⓣ

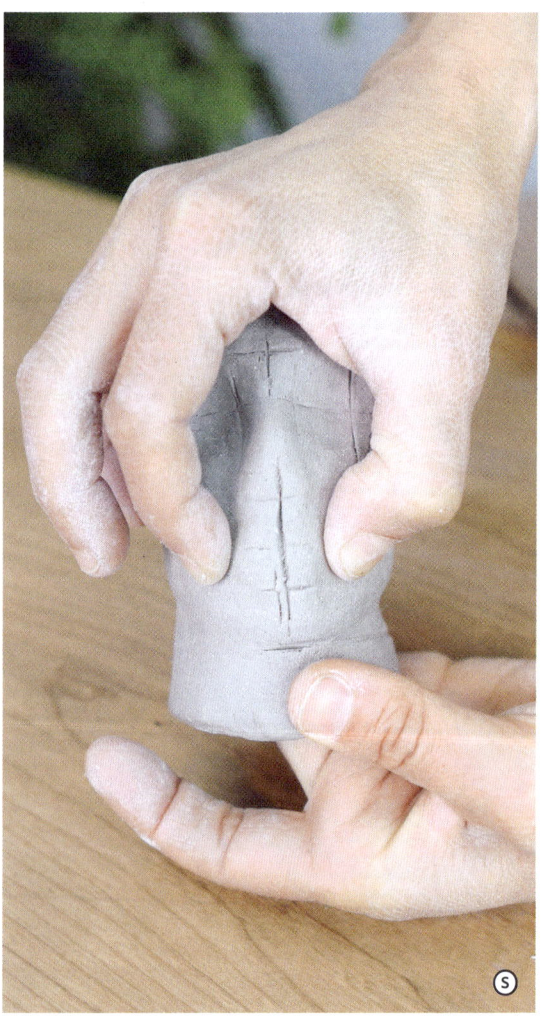

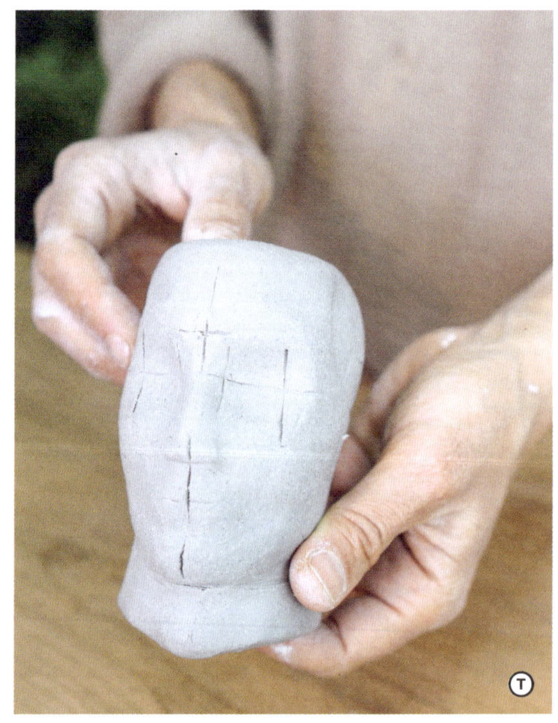

ADDING FACIAL FEATURES

At this stage, it is a good idea to take measurements from your photographic references with your calipers to ensure the head feels proportionally aligned with the rest of the body. Once the cranial core has dried enough to hold its form under the pressure of your fingers, you will begin adding more features over the bony landmarks you have established. Note that your clay must still be wet enough to receive a new layer of clay, so tracking moisture level is an important part of this process. You are now shifting into the realm of cartilage and tissue. For smaller heads like the one we will be developing, it works well to hydrate a specific area with a brush and then model over that area with soft clay. For larger heads, it helps to slip and score before adding any new material to ensure proper adhesion.

The following steps describe my process to develop generic features that will serve as the foundation for a more specific facial rendering in subsequent waves of refinement.

ADDING PRIMARY FACIAL MASSES

1. Let's start with the eyes. Locate the vertical marks perpendicular to the lines inside the ocular depressions. To guide your eye placement, use a stainless modeling tool and draw in the shape of the eyes in relationship to these marks. Next, roll two small balls of clay of equal size. Keep these small bits of clay hydrated and place one in each ocular cavity, moistening the surface with a brush or slipping and scoring if necessary or to ensure a good connection. Ⓐ Shape these mounds into half spheres with your tool by moving it across the top and bottom edges. As you move your tool across the front of the eye volume, let up on your pressure to avoid flattening the mass. Our goal is to preserve the convex nature of these half spheres. Ⓑ

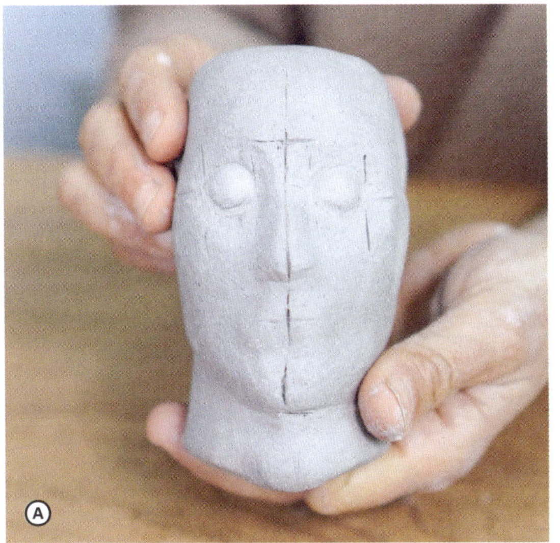

Ⓐ

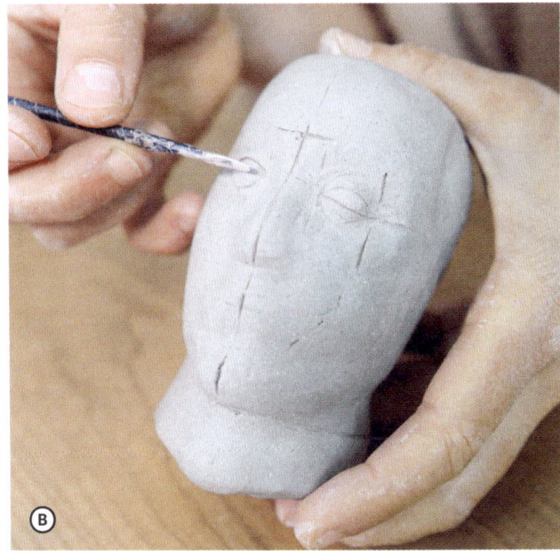

Ⓑ

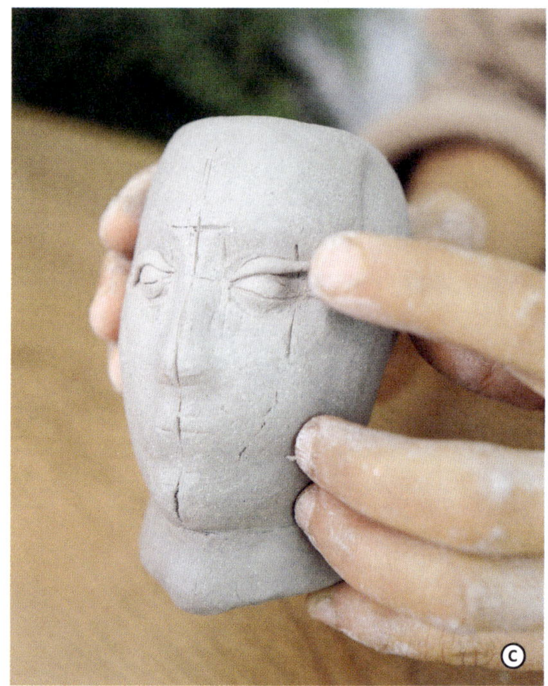

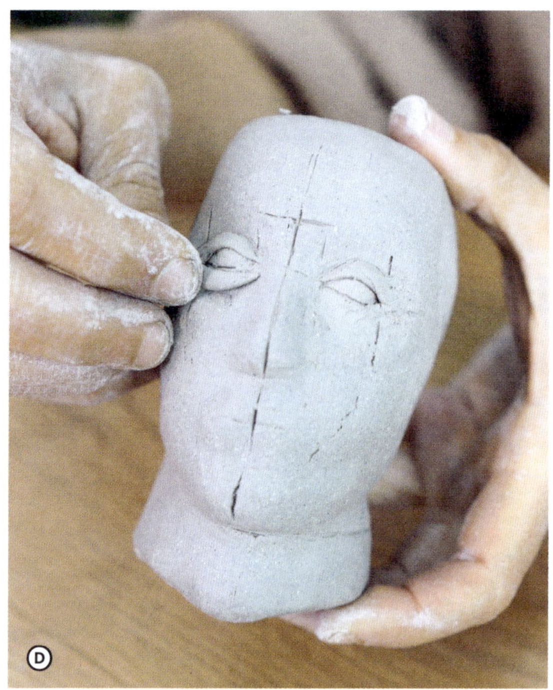

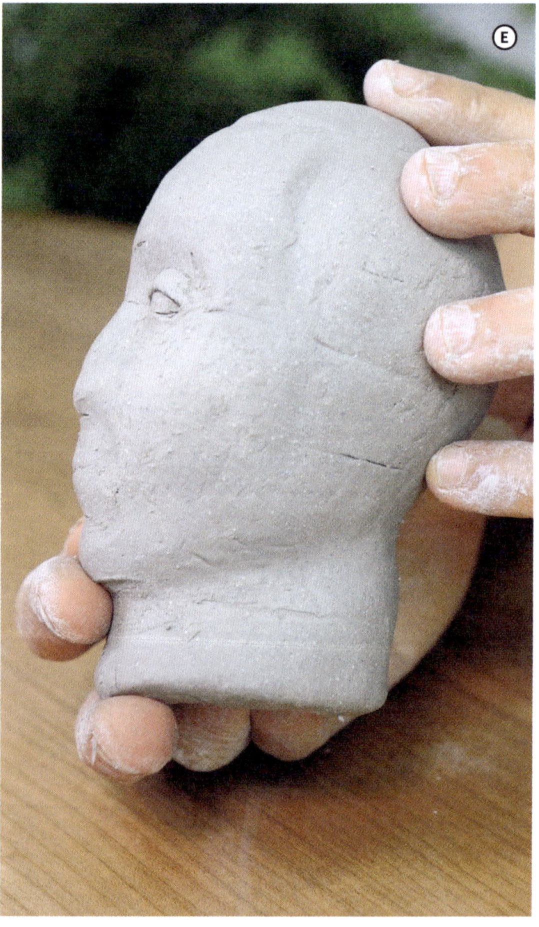

2. Next add lids, top and bottom, using small tapering coils that will be compressed and adjusted against the eyeballs with your small stainless tool or knife. Ⓒ Ⓓ It is important here to check your head from the side to ensure the eye is not projecting beyond the brow bone. Ⓔ

3. Add some clay in a teardrop shape to the outer eye area. This area is also known as the superior orbital compartment. Orient your teardrop with the thin end pointing inwards toward the nose and place it above the upper lid and below the brow bone. Ⓕ (Also see Appendix C.) You are looking to create a convex shape at the outer part of the eye that turns gently into a concave hollow as you approach the inner eye, right below the eyebrow. Use a small brush to integrate this new material, while preserving the projection of the convex curve. Ⓖ

4. Next, add a bit of clay, also in a teardrop shape, to accentuate the brow. Ⓗ

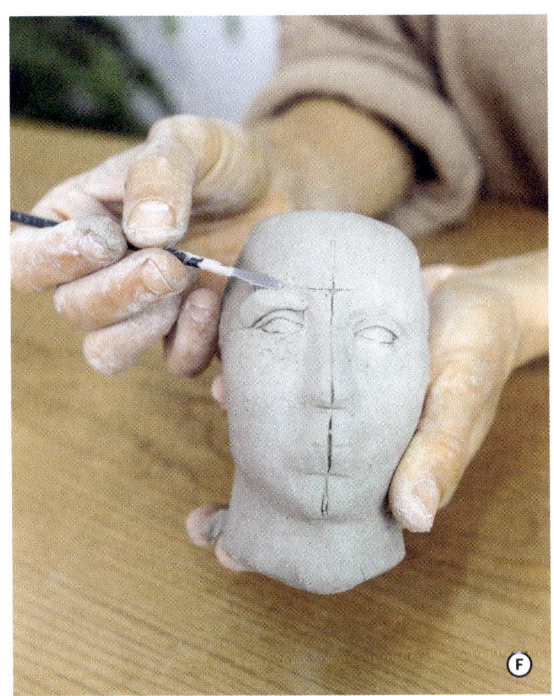

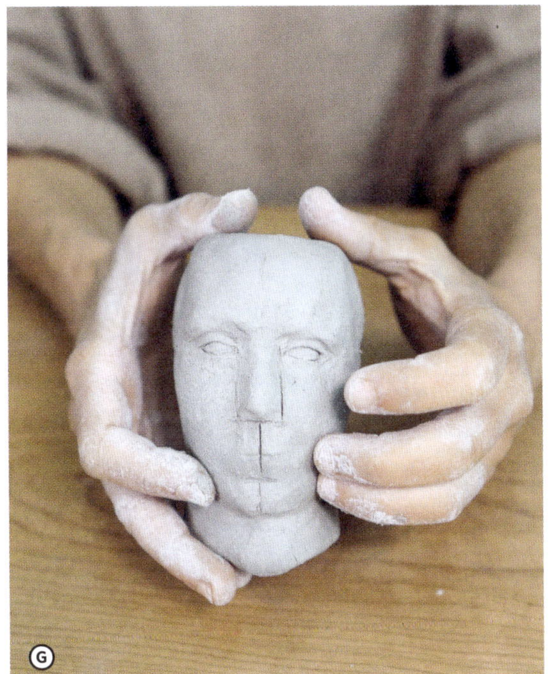

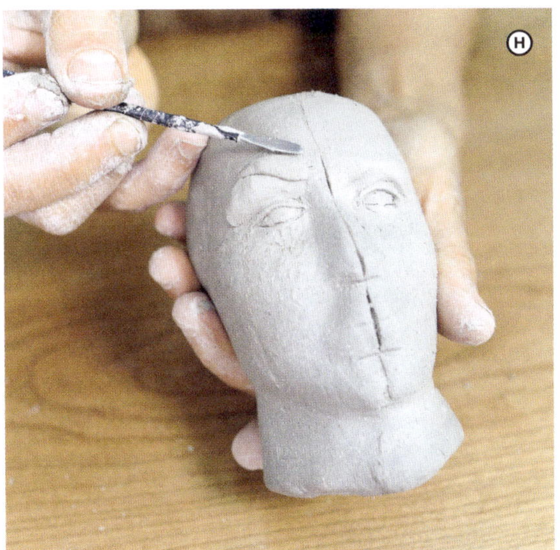

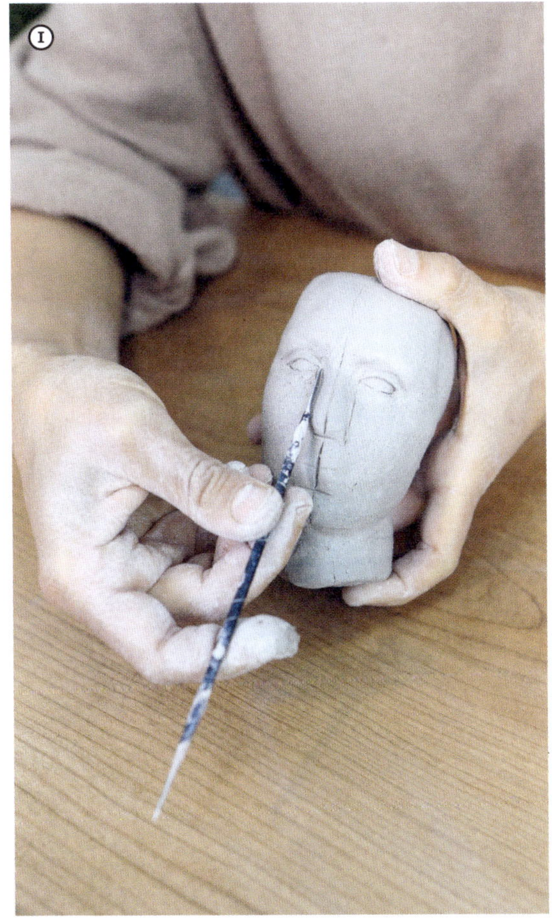

5. Moving into the nasal area, establish
    the width of the nose by extending your
    inner eyelines down to intersect with
    your bottom of the nose line. (I) Lay a
    mass of clay between these two vertical
    lines in the form of an elongated triangle.
    Vertically, your triangle should extend
    from the eyeline to the bottom of the
    nose line.

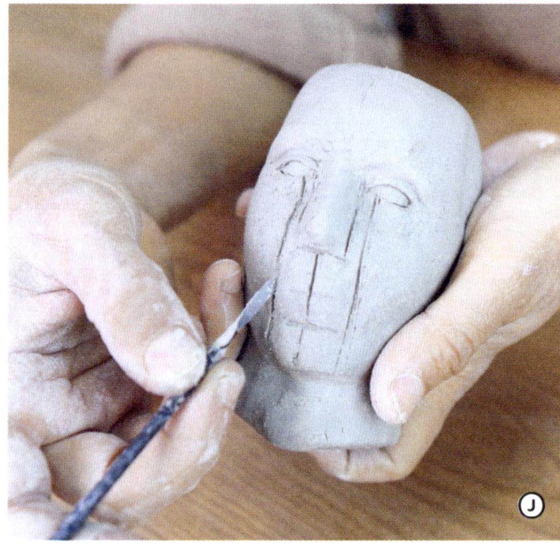

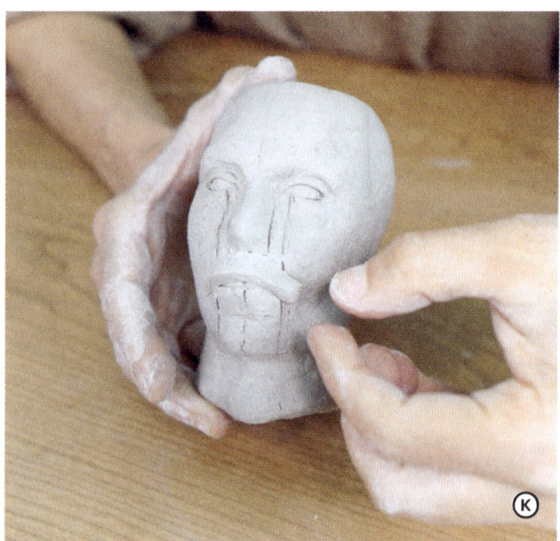

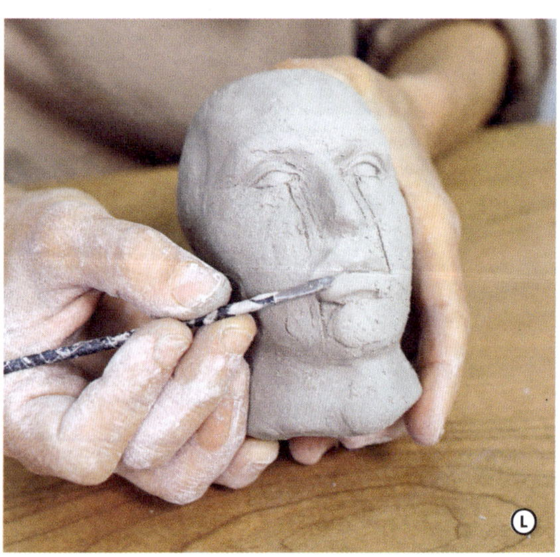

6. Establish the thickness of the mouth by drawing vertical lines from the inside of each eye, where the iris would start, all the way down to intersect the mouth line. Ⓙ Add a coil of clay just under the base of the nose sloping down, laterally and back, in the shape of a mustache. Ⓚ You have attached more material than you will need, so once you have developed the philtrum, upper lip area, and upper lip in the subsequent steps, you can carve or smooth away any excess. Now apply the lower lip material, pressing against the upper lip. This mass will comprise the lower lip as well as the tissue around the lip and the transition to the chin. Ⓛ Ⓜ

7. Add some clay to articulate the chin. Turn your head to the side to adjust the relationship between the forehead, brow, nose, upper and lower lip, and chin. Ⓝ

8. To find the placement of the ears, turn your head to the profile view and find the center points on each side of the cranium, halfway between the front of the brow to the back of the cranium. Draw a vertical line down either side of the head through these midpoints. Looking at the head from the front, find the brow line and the bottom of the nose line. Extend both lines around the side of the head until they intersect with your vertical centerline at a perpendicular angle. Draw an outline of each ear right behind the vertical centerline and in between the two horizontal lines brought from the front of the head. Ⓞ Ⓟ To establish the basic shapes of the ears, add masses of clay on either side to fit within the guides, turning your head to assess them from the front to make sure they have a proper lateral projection, created by the concha, and are not lying flat against the skull. It may help to think about a wedge shape when initially laying down these masses. Ⓠ Ⓡ

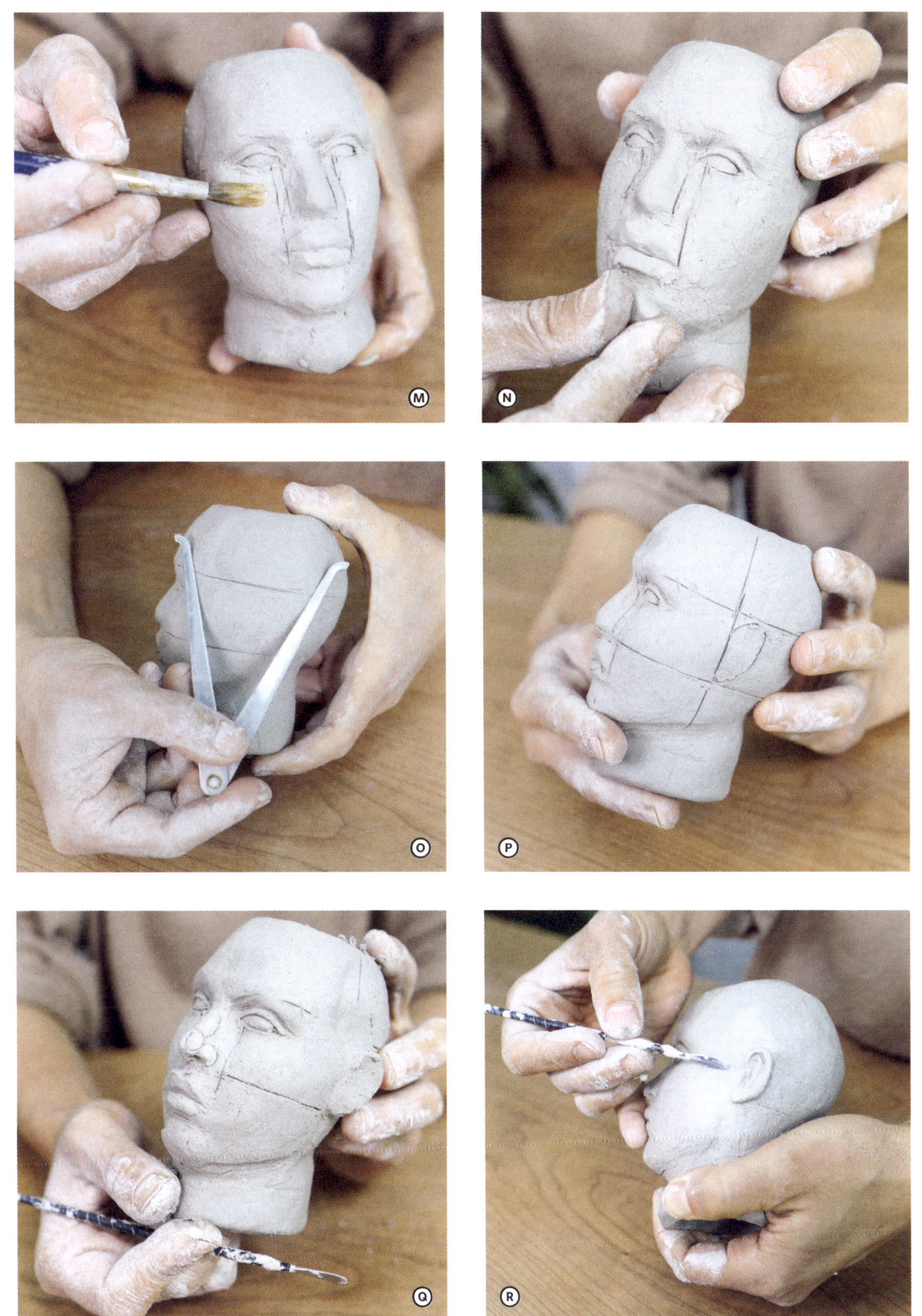

REFINING FEATURES

EYES

Determine the shape of the lids, cutting and resetting the eye opening with an X-acto knife and small stainless tools, if necessary. (See Appendix C, image a.)

NOSE

By carving and adding bits of clay to the generalized nose mass, you are looking to divide the nose into four distinct parts: the bridge, the ball, and two teardrop-shaped wings. (See Appendix C, images d, e, f.) As you develop the nose, turn your head to the side to gauge your adjustments from a profile view. Remember, we see relationally—try to understand how your nose is relating to the other features and where adjustments need to be made to create a coherent alignment between the forms.

LIPS

1. Move to the upper lip area and use your tool to mark the philtrum—the small concavity above the center of the upper lip—just under the nose. The philtral ridges found at either side of the philtrum will be the forward-most points on your upper lip area. Note the curved quality of the form that creates a transition between the nose and the upper lip.

2. From there, adjust the projection of the lips by looking at the head from the side. The standard alignment creates a diagonal between the upper lip to the chin.

3. To begin defining the lips, it is helpful to envision the top and bottom lip as each containing three planes—a frontal plane and two diagonal planes—onto which small bits of clay will be added to further describe the tissue.

4. Start by finding the outer edge of the lip width mark (established by the two verticals coming down from the inner part of the eyes—see proportional breakdown of the head in Appendix C) and move your knife tool from there to the edge of the peak of the lip at a slight diagonal on both sides. As I do this, I turn my edged tool slightly and release pressure as I move towards the front to avoid flattening the projection of the volume. Draw in the planar structure of the lips over your preliminary mouth shape to create one frontal plane and two diagonal planes, and adjust the form to follow the logic of the planes. (See Appendix C, image b.)

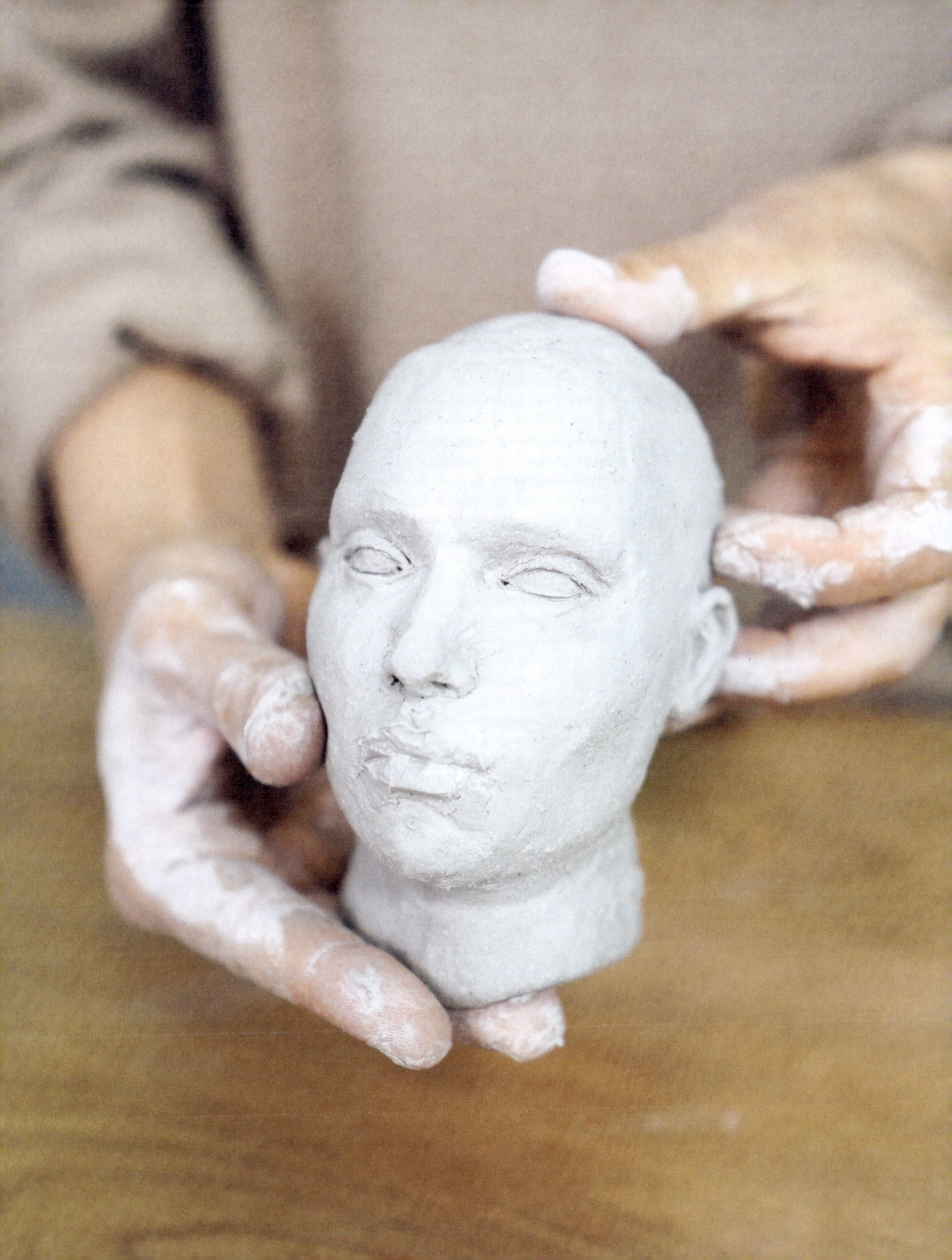

5. Repeat this process for the lower lip, noting slight variations in the distribution of the planes and making sure the lower lip tucks under the upper at the edges.

6. Once the lip edges and planes are established you can add bits of clay to further flesh out this area. (See Appendix C, image c.)

7. As you transition below the lower lip, note the two ovular shapes that rest on top of the chin. Carve at the center, right above the chin and add small amounts of clay at either side to describe this lower segment of the orbicularis oris.

EARS

Once the generalized mass of the ear has slightly firmed, carve away the outer curve of the ear called the helix. Establish the tragus, which is the small projection that meets the skull and partially overlaps the ear hole. Begin carving the inner parts of the ear: the fossa, antihelix, and concha. In tandem with the carving, add bits of material where needed and continue to turn the head to gauge alignments and projections from all vantage points. Study your reference images and use value to gauge the depth of different ear elements.

CHIN

Move down to the chin and add material as needed, informing your assessment by turning the head in profile to check for balance.

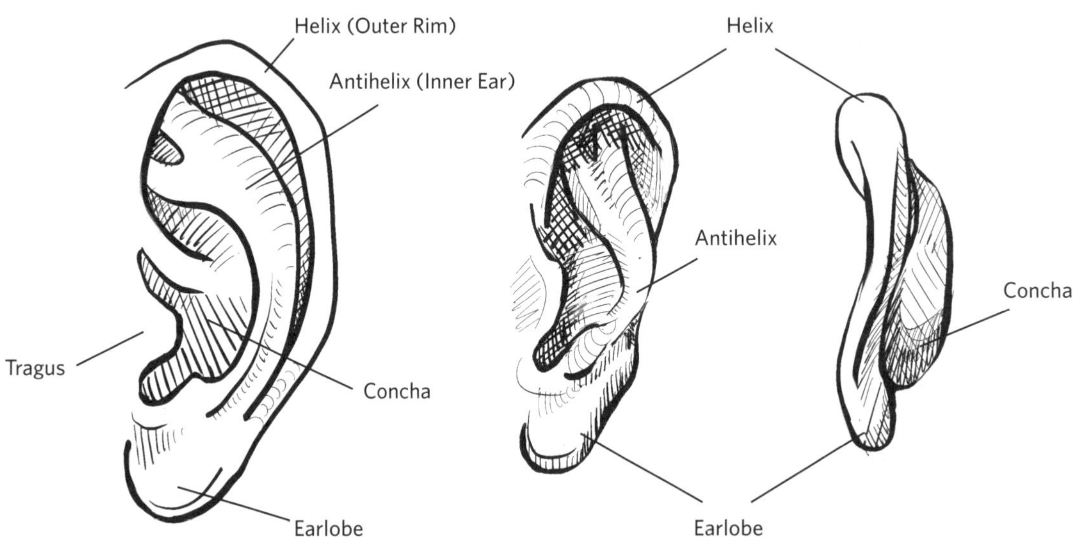

FLESHING: CREATING FLOW AND CONTINUITY

To develop all the features in depth, we have isolated each part of the face and broken it into its basic structural components. Now let's consider the transitional tissues that tie the features together into a coherent whole.

1. Start by locating the area between the bridge of the nose and the cheek. Lay a small coil of clay to create a connection between these two sections. Smooth in with your tool and brush to soften the transition.

2. Locate the area just outside and slightly above the oral commissures or edges of the mouth. Several facial muscles converge at this point, including the orbicularis oris muscle that circles our mouth. This confluence creates a subtle projection, known as the modiolus, that punctuates either side of the mouth. Add little bits of clay here to describe this junction.

3. Under the mouth, at either side of the mentolabial crease, you can add clay to describe the inferior part of the orbicularis oris, creating a transition between the lips and chin area.

4. Continue to scan your composition, adding bits of clay where needed, to enhance volumes and create a smooth correlation between the features.

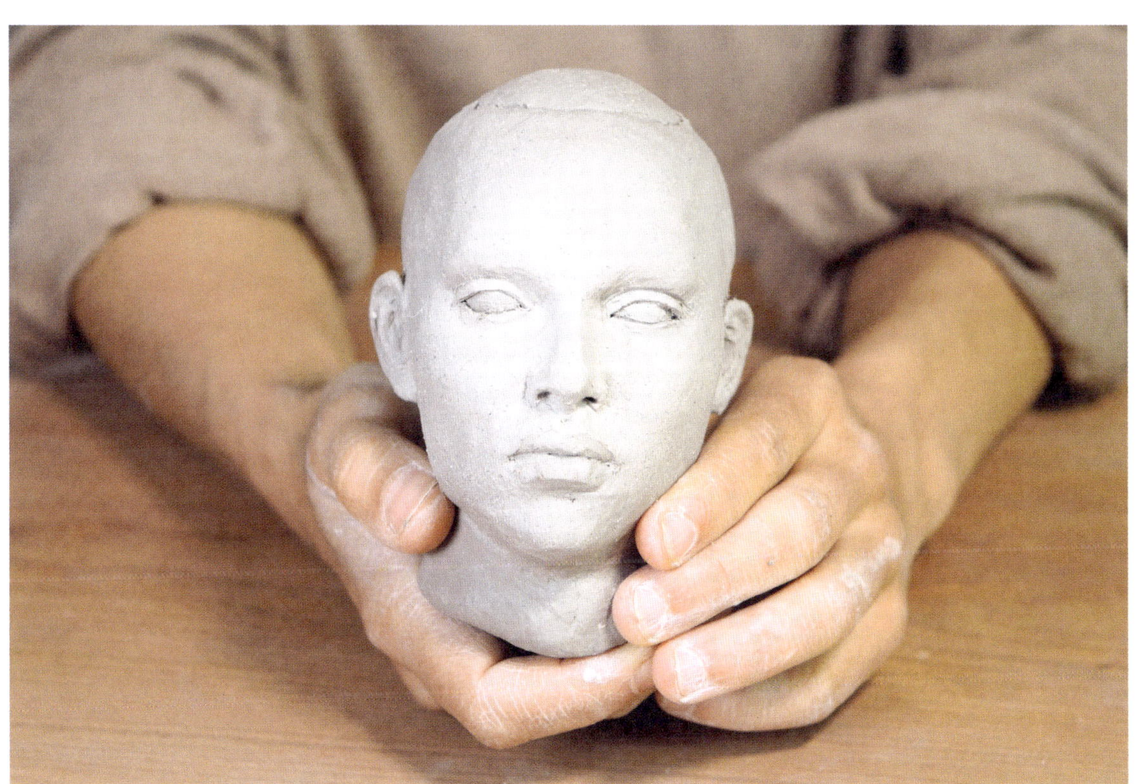

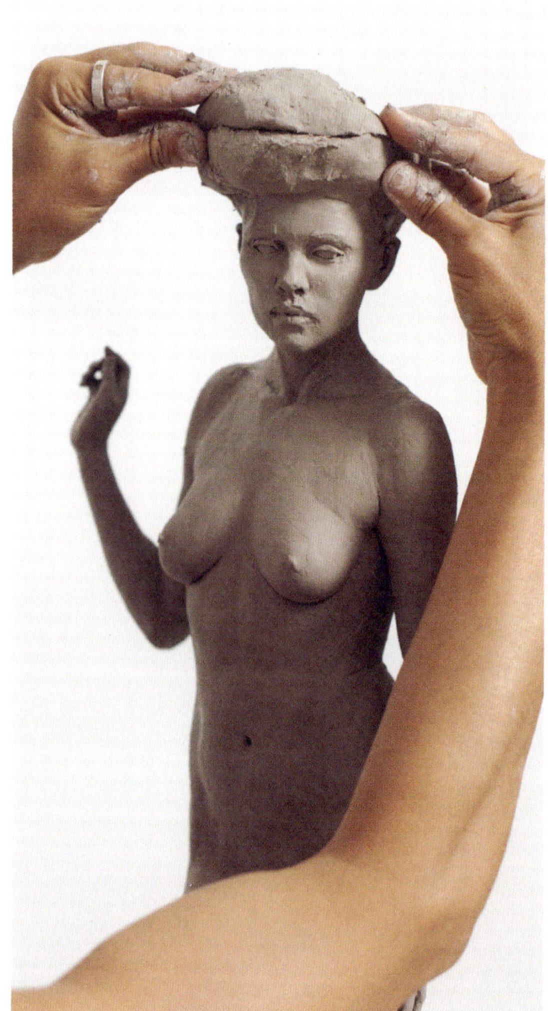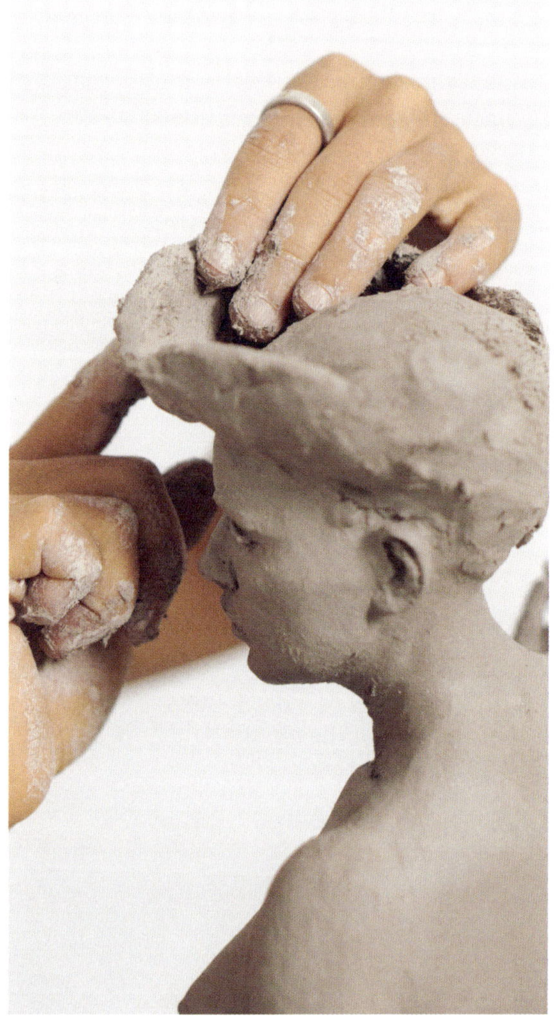

HAIR

Once the head is fully sealed with the cap permanently affixed, slip and score the head to add fresh clay and begin shaping your hair. The hair can be made solid, if not too thick (no thicker than ¾ inch [2 cm]), or as a hollow shape above the head, as shown in these images.

I have a very loose approach to hair and normally add it at the end of the sculptural process when most of the composition is resolved. When developing the hair, there are two considerations that drive my decisions. The first is the silhouette of the hair mass and how it punctuates the dynamics of the rest of the body, in particular the face. The second is the resolution of the strands and how specific or abstract I choose to develop the textual quality of the hair.

ATTACHING HEAD TO NECK

I develop all my heads with extra material under the chin that serves as a handle or stand and is trimmed off when affixing the head to the body. The trim line will be guided by the shape of the cranium and will move from just below the mandible to below the ears and at the level of the bottom of the nose towards the back of the skull. Ⓑ

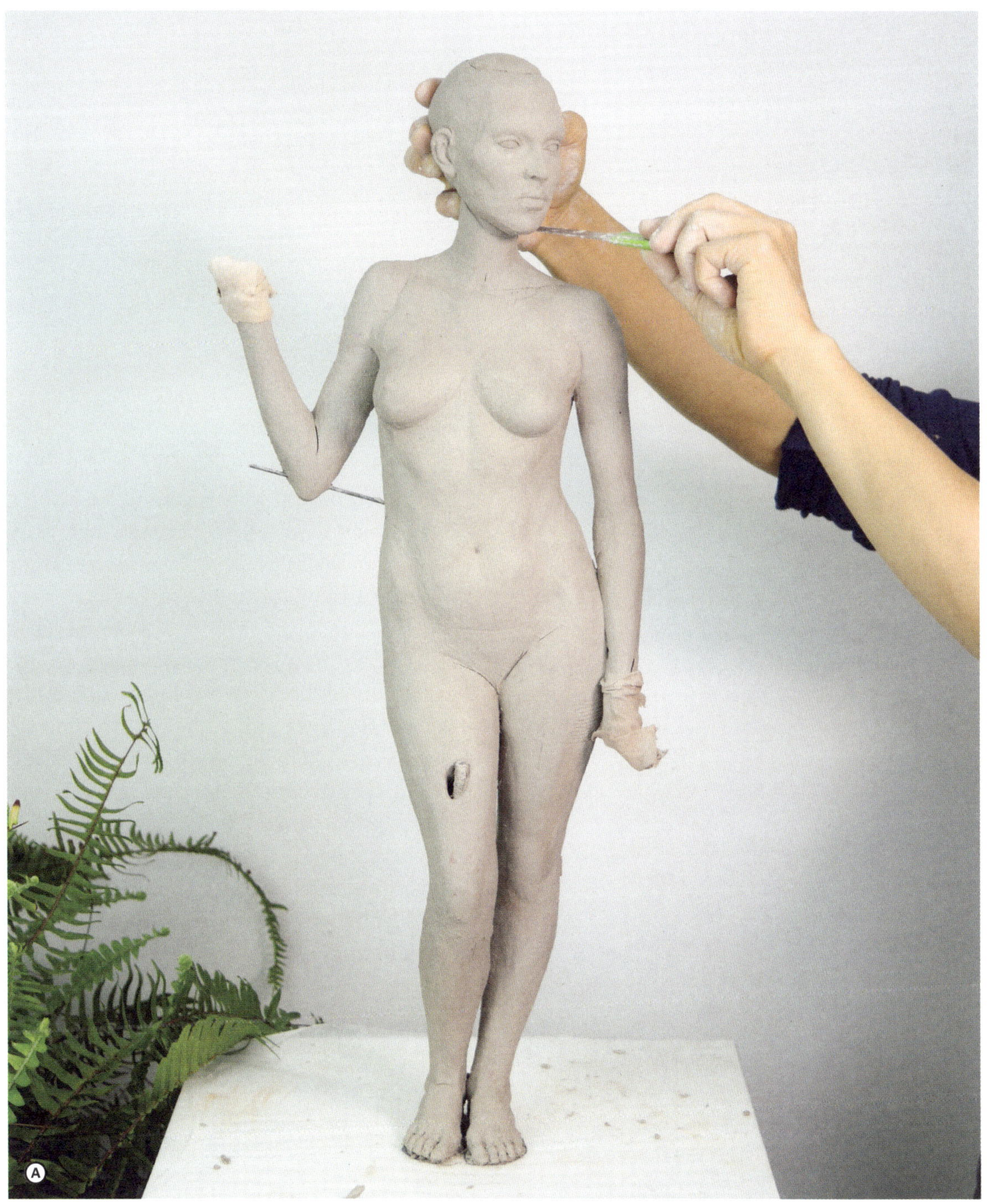

- With the head, as with every other part of the body, we will be moving in waves of refinement, working from the structural core to the outer skin level, waiting for the form to stabilize through drying to gradually bring clarity to the facial composition.

- When sculpting the head, it is important to engage with it from different vantage points to facilitate the alignment of the features and the proper gauging of distances and volumetric projections.

- Photographic references taken in the round or three-dimensional anatomical models can be helpful in guiding the evolution of a head.

- In addition to modeling tools in different shapes and sizes, brushes will serve as important allies in evolving facial details.

- While the head you are developing is still detached from the body, it is important to hold it up to the body and compare it to your photographic references often to make sure it remains in proportional alignment with the rest of the composition. By carving or adding material, it is easy to gradually shift the head into a different scale that will be incongruous with that of the rest of the body.

- If you are exploring building a head at larger scales, you might need to adjust the thickness of your slabs and work in sections by cutting your pattern horizontally to create layers that will stack, as dryness allows, to articulate the full form.

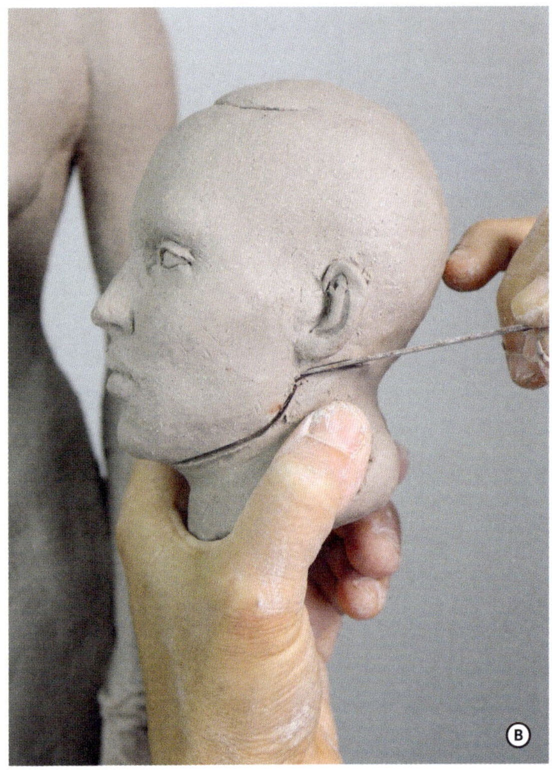

Once you have trimmed your head, bring it to your neck to check proportions, play with gestural possibilities and begin reconciling the head opening to the thickness of the neck in preparation to join. As you slide the head over the neck, you are looking to have enough surface contact between the inner edge of the head and the outer part of the neck to allow for a strong, snug connection. Ⓐ You can accomplish this by trimming or adding fresh clay where needed. When the proper placement of the head has been established, make a horizontal mark under the chin to note the height on the neck and several vertical lines transversing the bottom of the head and the top of the neck that will key the alignment between the two parts. After keying, remove the head and slip and score both sides before attaching. Slip and score around the seam from the outside and compress some fresh clay to ensure a strong joint.

Gallery

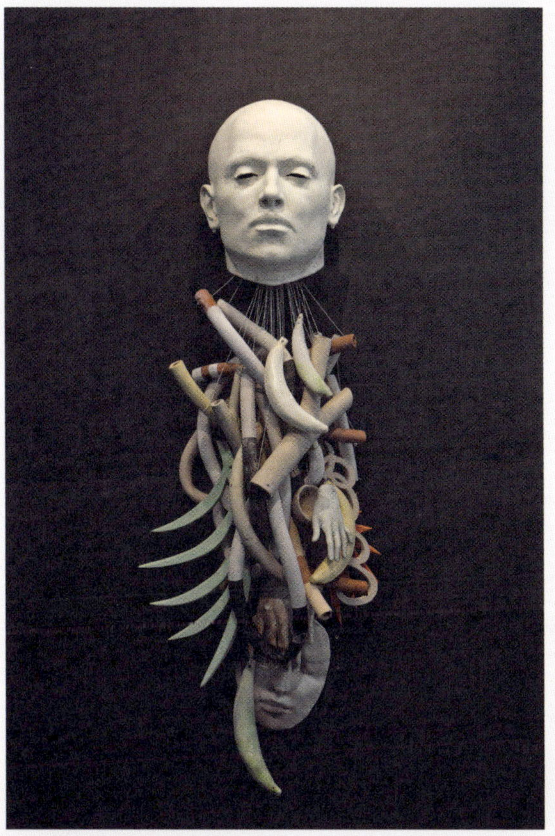

Cristina Córdova, *Recolección*.
Lydia Bittner-Baird, courtesy of Hodges Taylor Gallery.

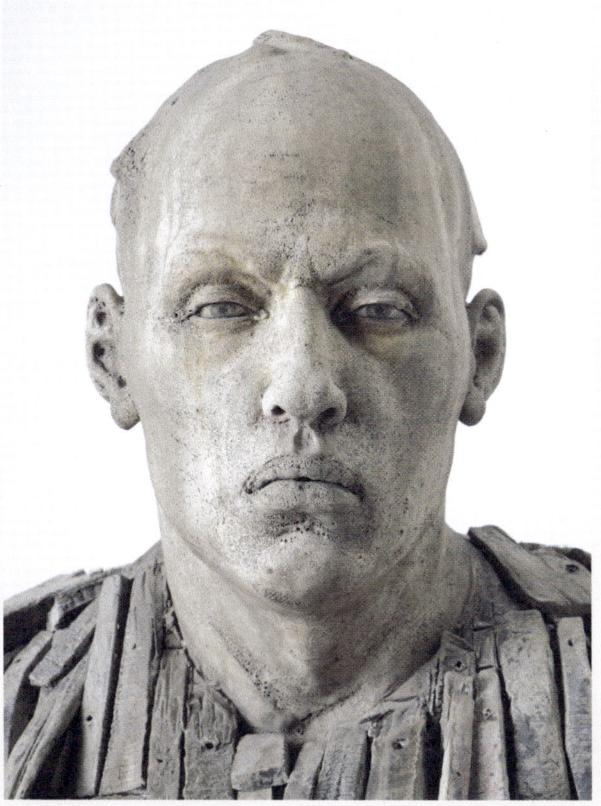

Cristina Córdova, *El rey*. Steve Mann.

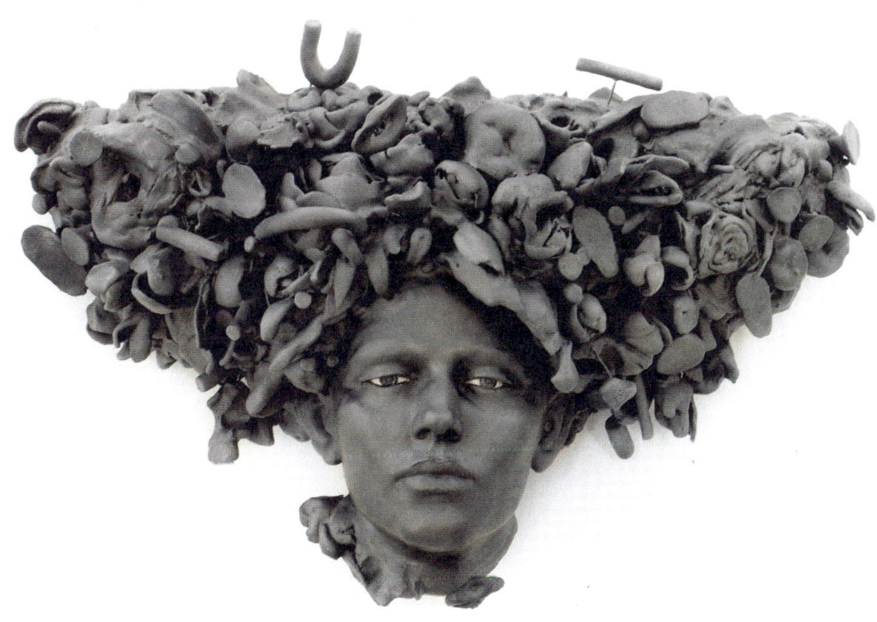

Cristina Córdova, *Cabeza*. Ian Henderson.

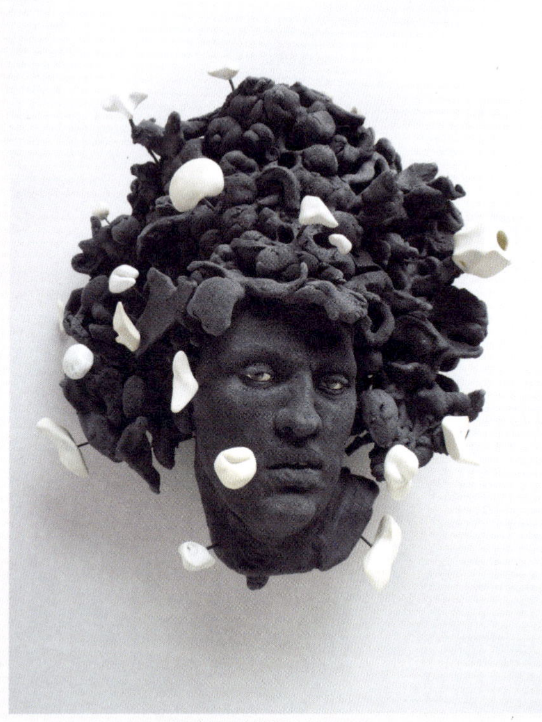

Cristina Córdova, *Vestigios*. Steve Mann.

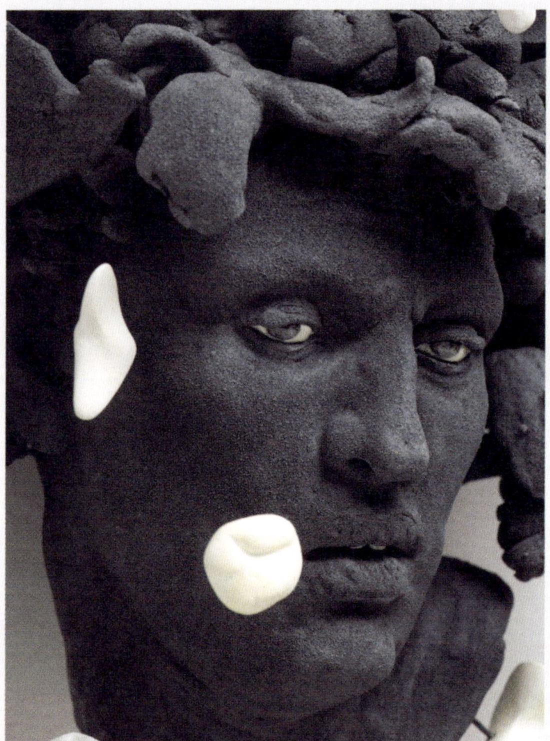

Cristina Córdova, *Vestigios* (detail). Steve Mann.

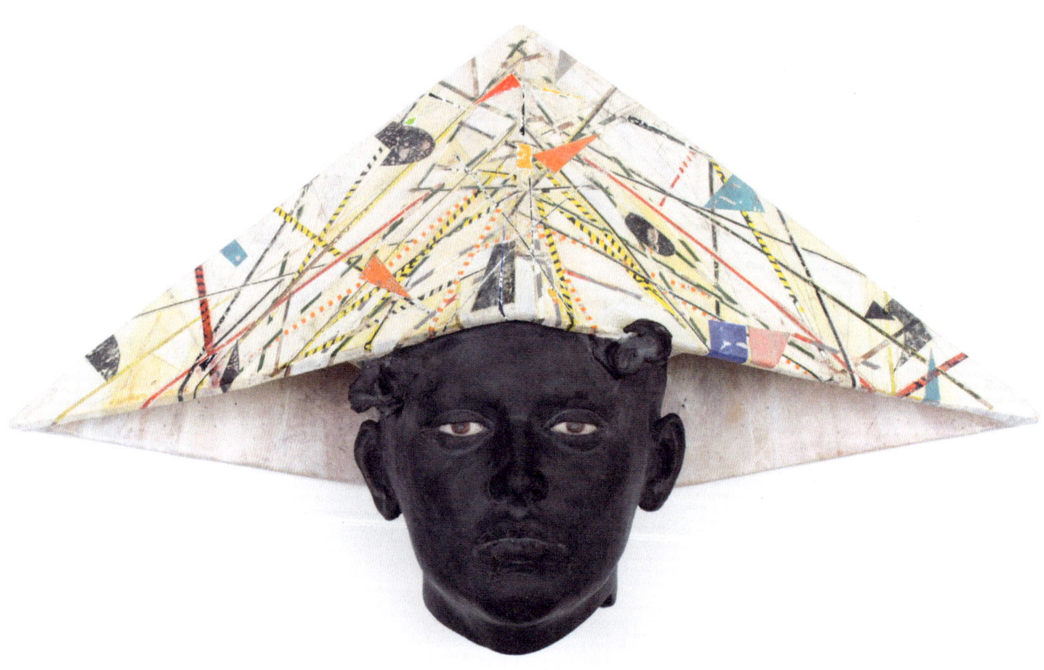

Cristina Córdova, *Cabeza*. Ian Henderson.

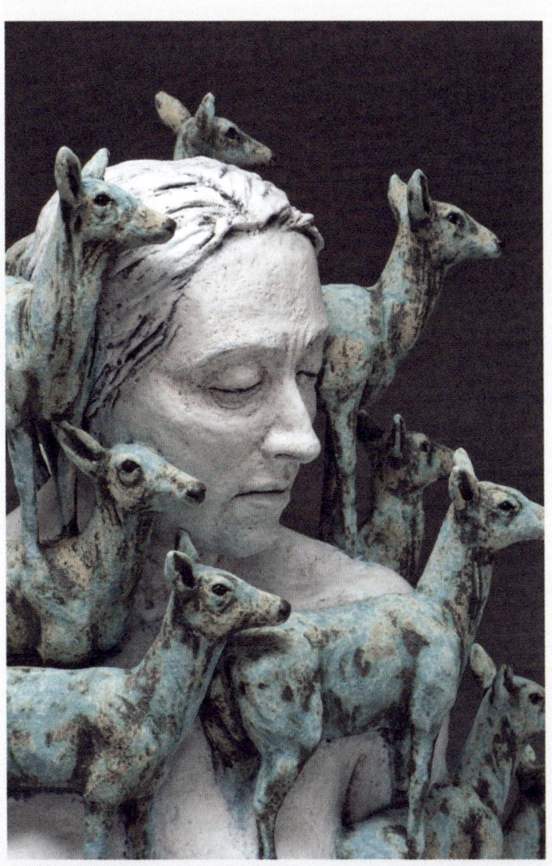

Adrian Arleo, *Heard.* Chris Autio.

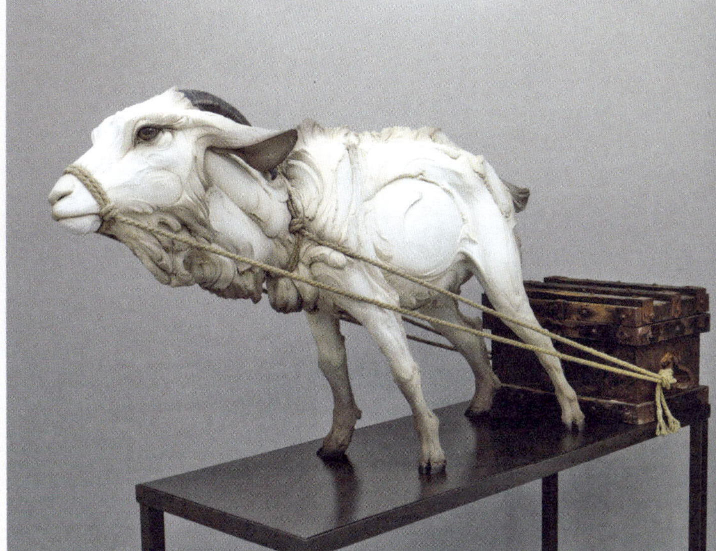

Beth Cavener, *The Secret Keeper.* Courtesy of the artist.

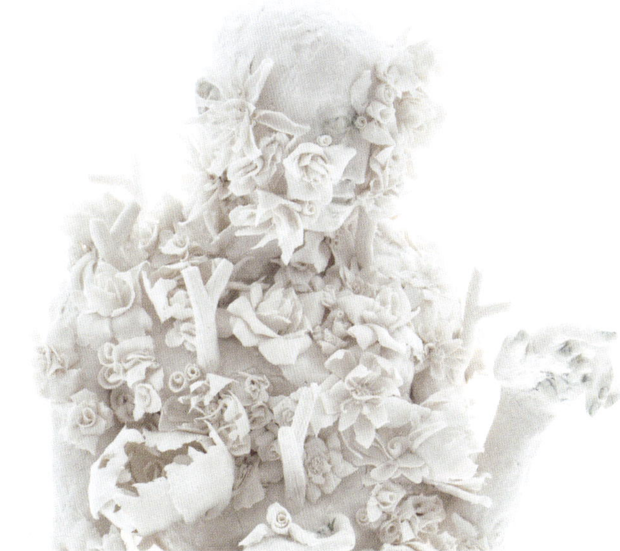

Claire Curneen, *Still Life.* Sylvain Delau.

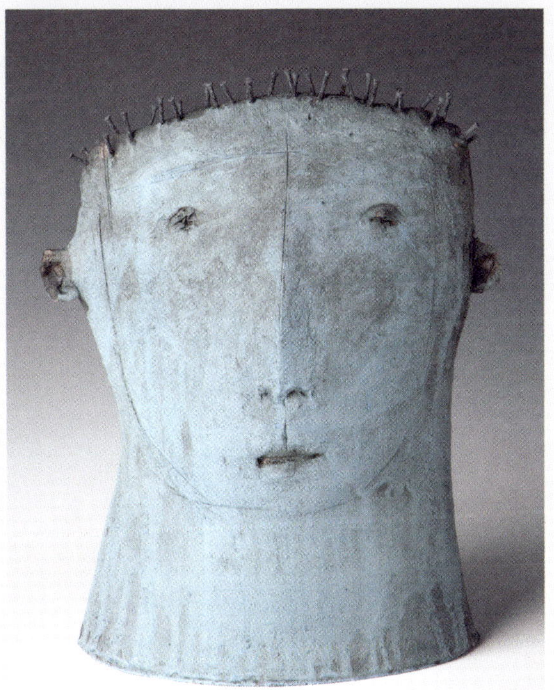

Christy Keeney, *Blue Head.* Fergal Megannety.

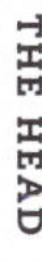

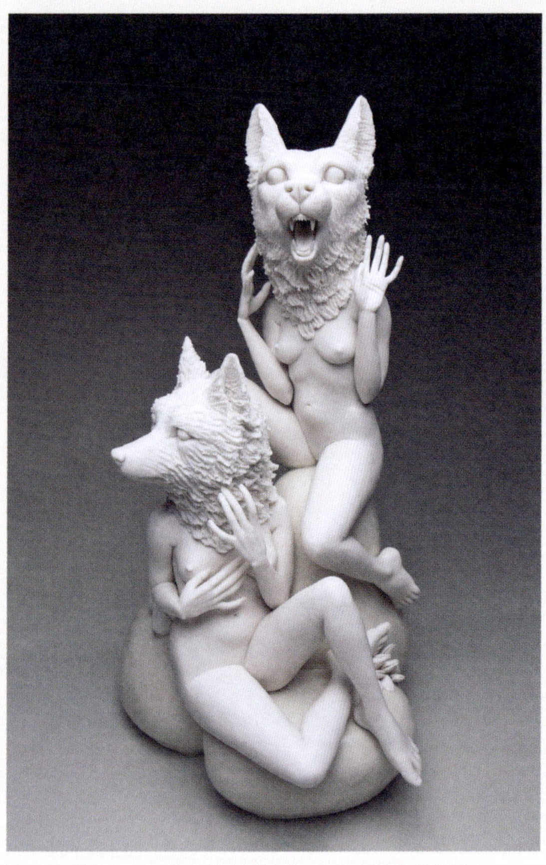

Crystal Morey, *Entangled Wonder*. Courtesy of the artist.

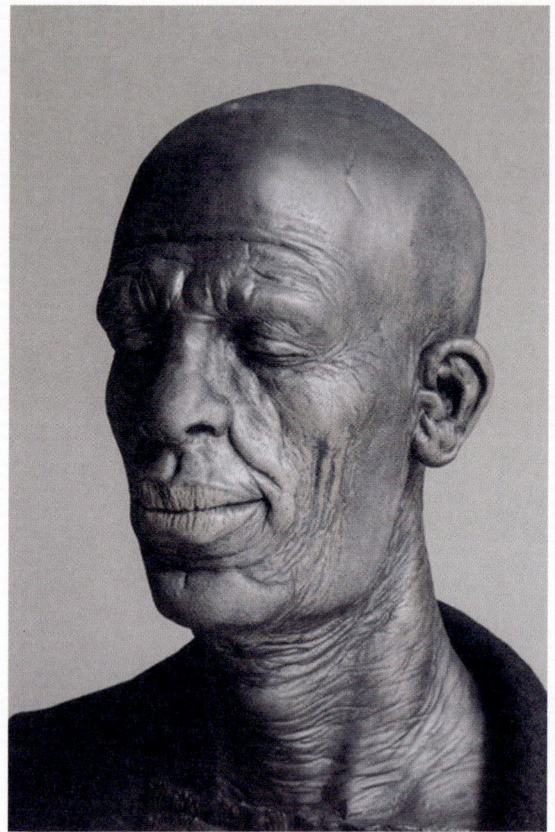

Doug Jeck, *Deacon*. Ben Lernan, courtesy of Traver Gallery.

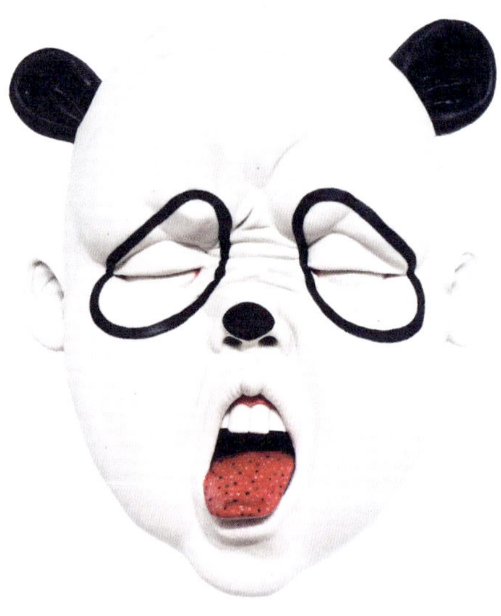

Kyungmin Park, *Be Like a Panda*. Courtesy of the artist.

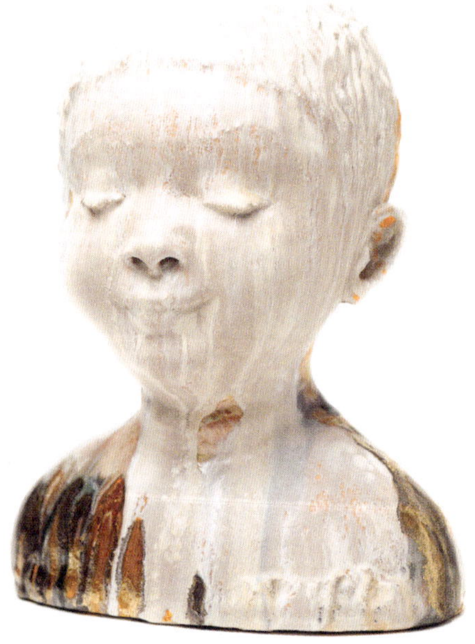

Jacob Foran, *Orange Boy*. Barry Wong.

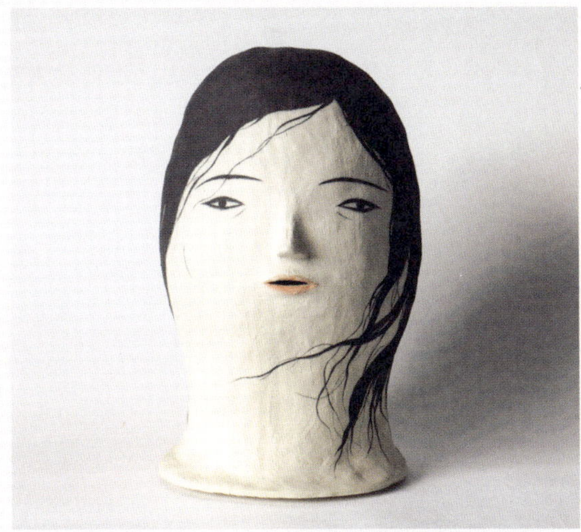

Rami Kim, *Untitled.* Courtesy of the artist. .

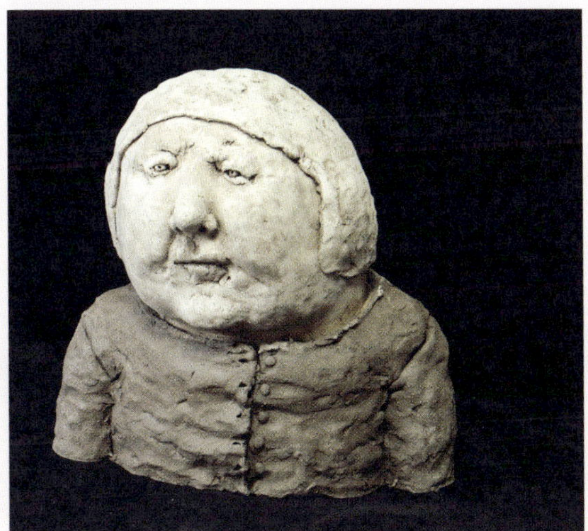

Sophie Favre, *Le Bonnet.* Courtesy of the artist.

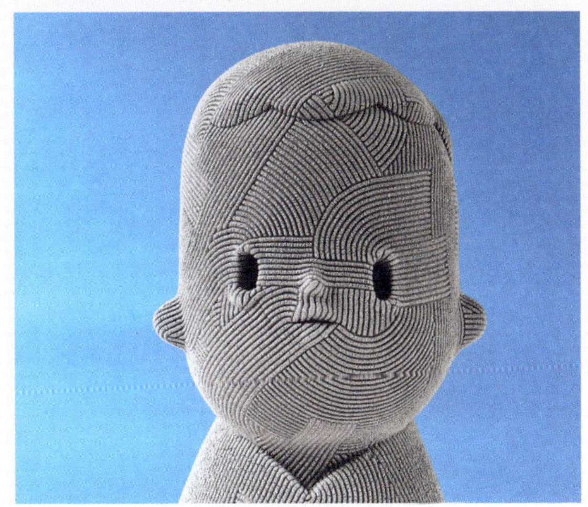

En Iwamura, *NEO-JOMON: HOODIE BOY.*
Courtesy of the artist.

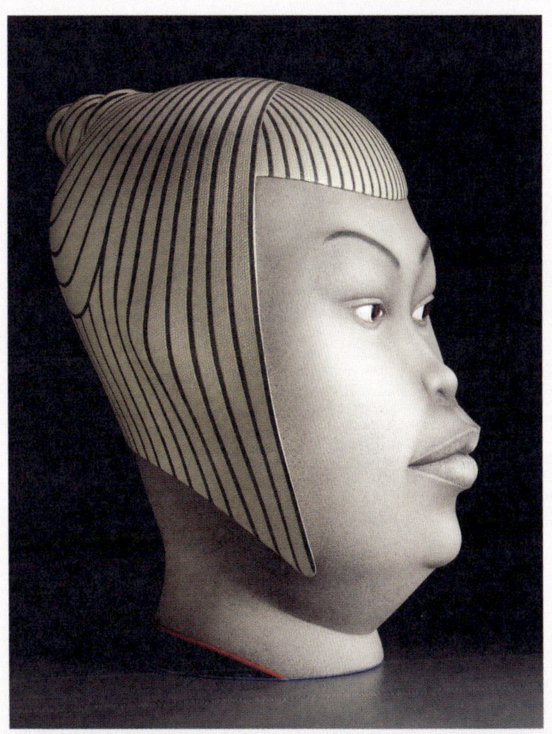

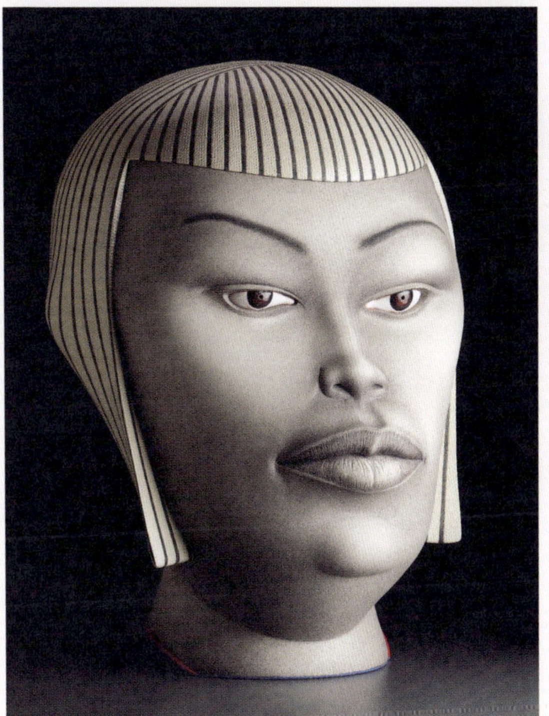

Sergei Isupov, *Chosen One.* John Polak.

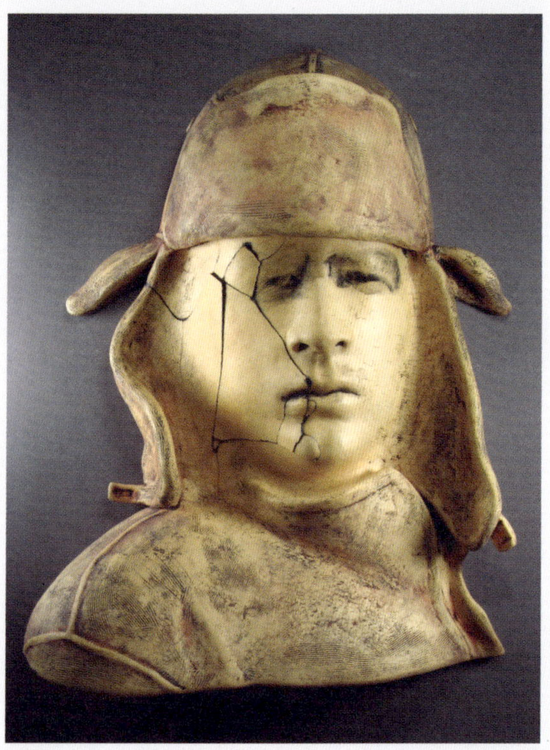

Suzanne Storer, *Alec, My Son.* Courtesy of the artist.

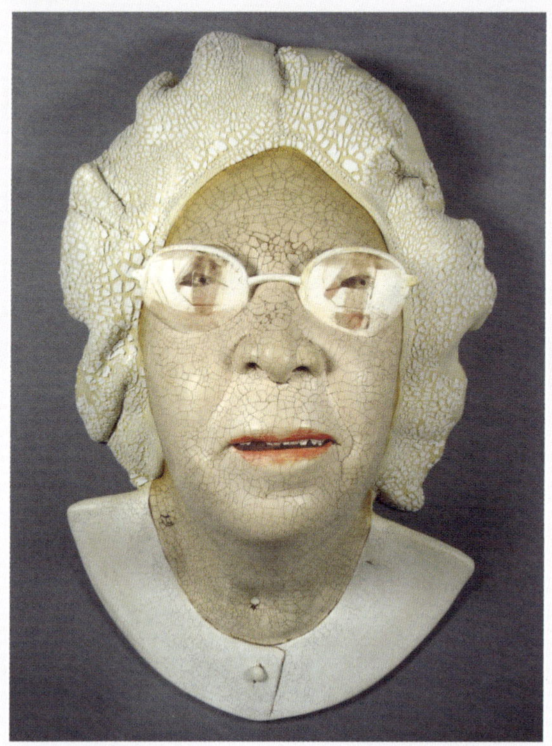

Suzanne Storer, *Lunch Lady.* Courtesy of the artist.

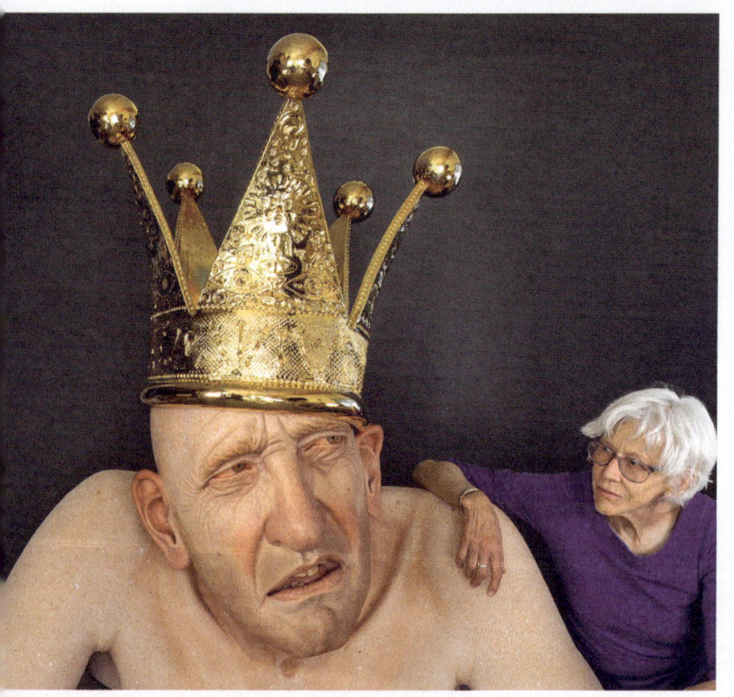

Tip Toland, *Greedy King.* Ann Welch.

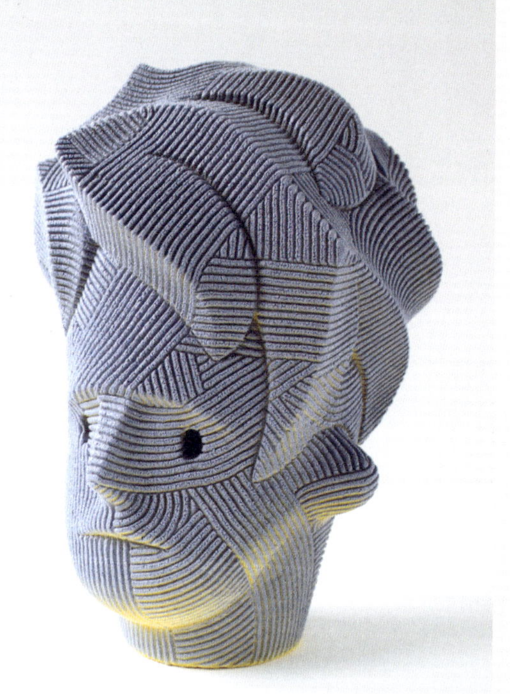

En Iwamura, *NEO-JOMON.* Courtesy of the artist.

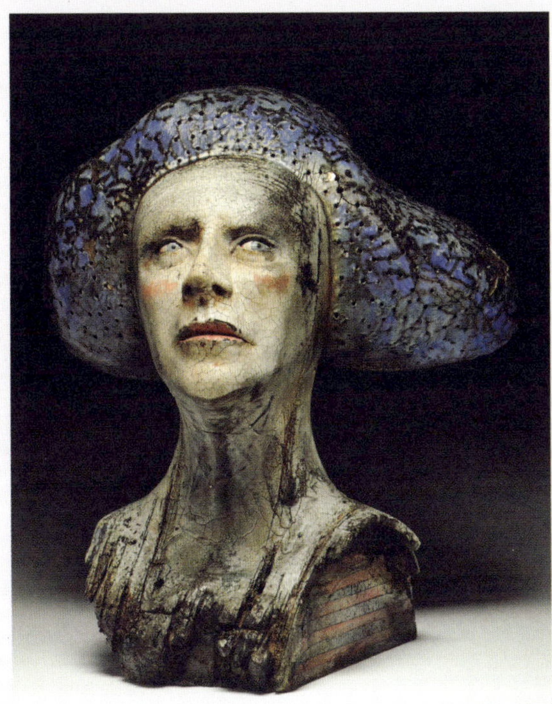

Thaddeus Erdahl, *Flavia.* Charlie Cummings.

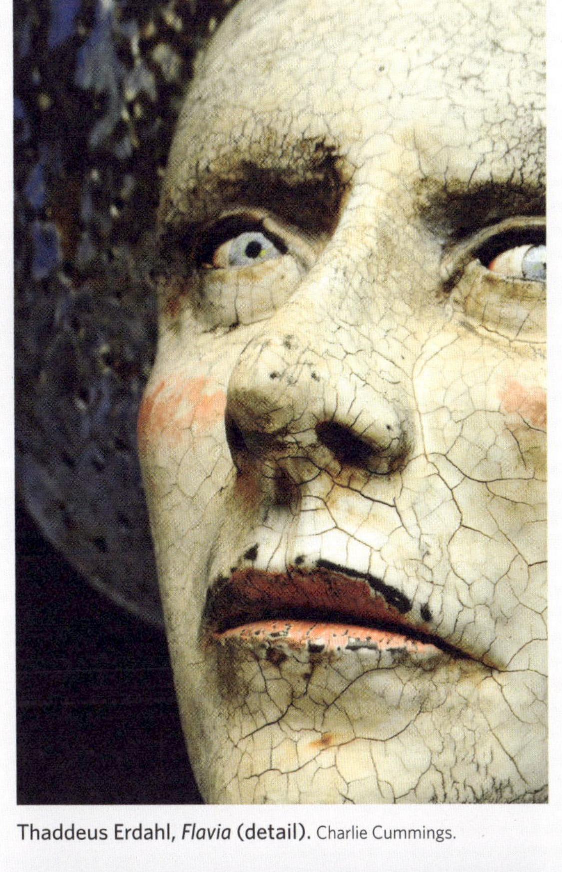

Thaddeus Erdahl, *Flavia* (detail). Charlie Cummings.

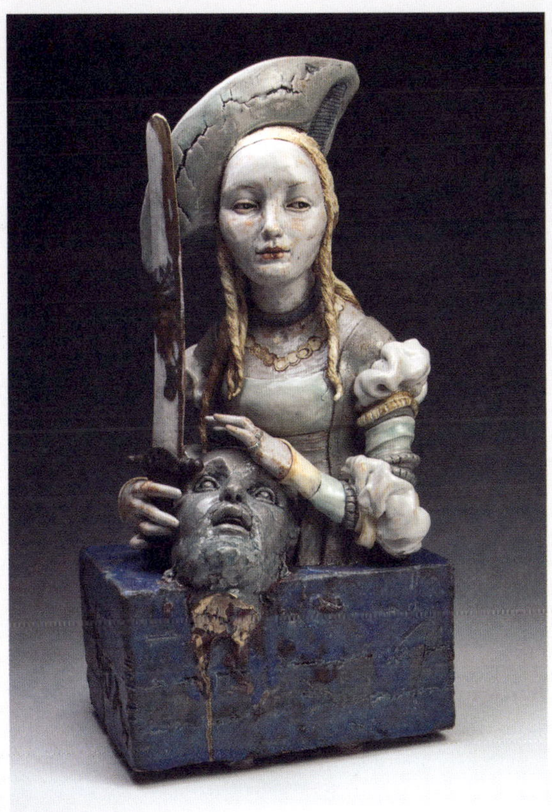

Kelly Rathbone, *Judith.* Ryan LaBar.

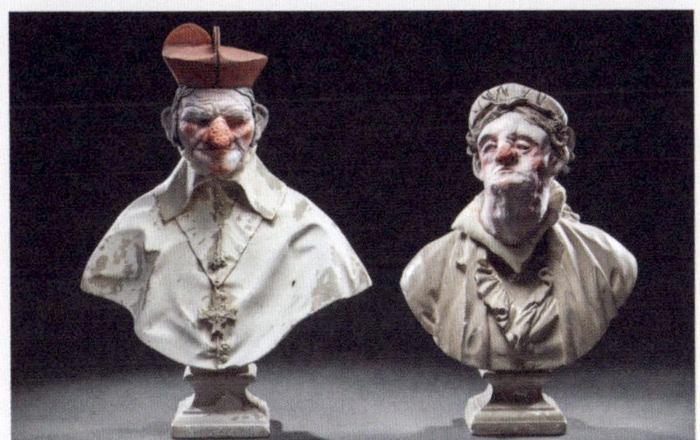

Richard W. James, *Punch and Judy.* Robert Batey.

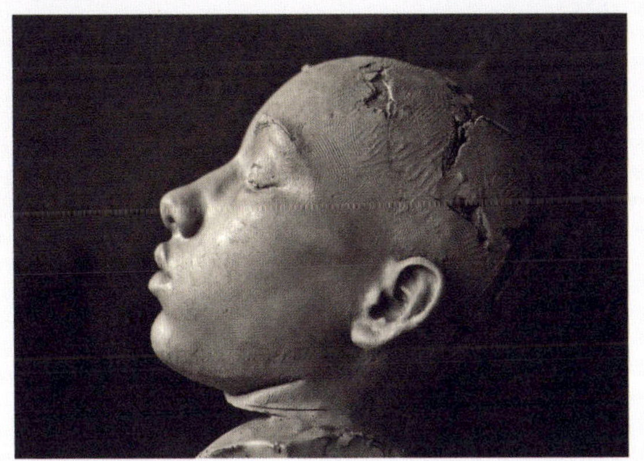

Eudald de Juana, *Dis-connection.* Courtesy of the artist.

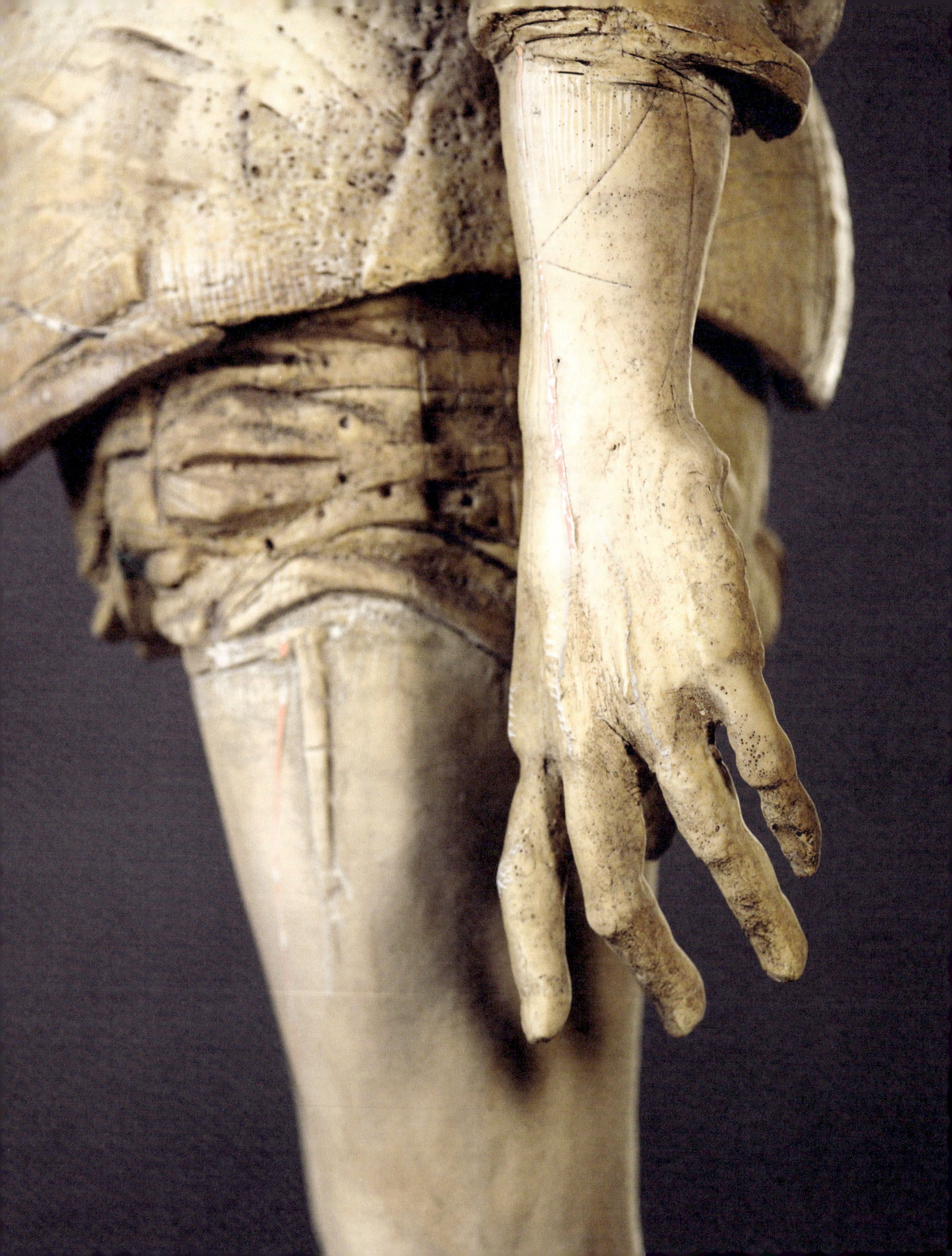

6

HANDS

HUMAN HANDS ARE master storytellers. Second only to the face, the hands have the most expressive potential in our figurative sculptures, capturing a sense of yearning and grasping or serenity and peace with the slightest variations in shape and orientation. Hands can activate the story of a body. Like developing the gaze on a face, positioning the hands can take me quite a long time as I play and explore the myriad possibilities that could actuate the gesture in unique and unexpected ways.

In this chapter, we will start by establishing the structure of the hands. I will offer a set of guidelines to develop a basic hand that can be further adjusted and fine-tuned once it is attached to the body. The gestural energy and positioning of your sculpture's hands will extend the dynamics of your figurative composition, offering an extreme point of attention as the viewer's eye moves throughout the sculpture.

WHAT YOU'LL NEED TO GET STARTED

- Templates (hand)
- Slabs (¼ inch [6 mm]) big enough to cut two 1¼ inch (3.2 cm) palms
- Fresh clay to work over seams
- Joining slip
- Ruler
- Wire brush scoring tool
- Calipers
- Seamstress tape
- Paddle
- Stainless modeling tools

Cristina Córdova, *Isla* (detail), part of the collection of the Asheville Art Museum.

FORMING THE HANDS

The first thing to understand is how big your hands need to be. As a starting place, I envision the hands being roughly the size of the face. There is quite a bit of variability here. Some hands range in size from chin to brow, while others—particularly within the realm of the masculine—extend almost as far as the hairline.

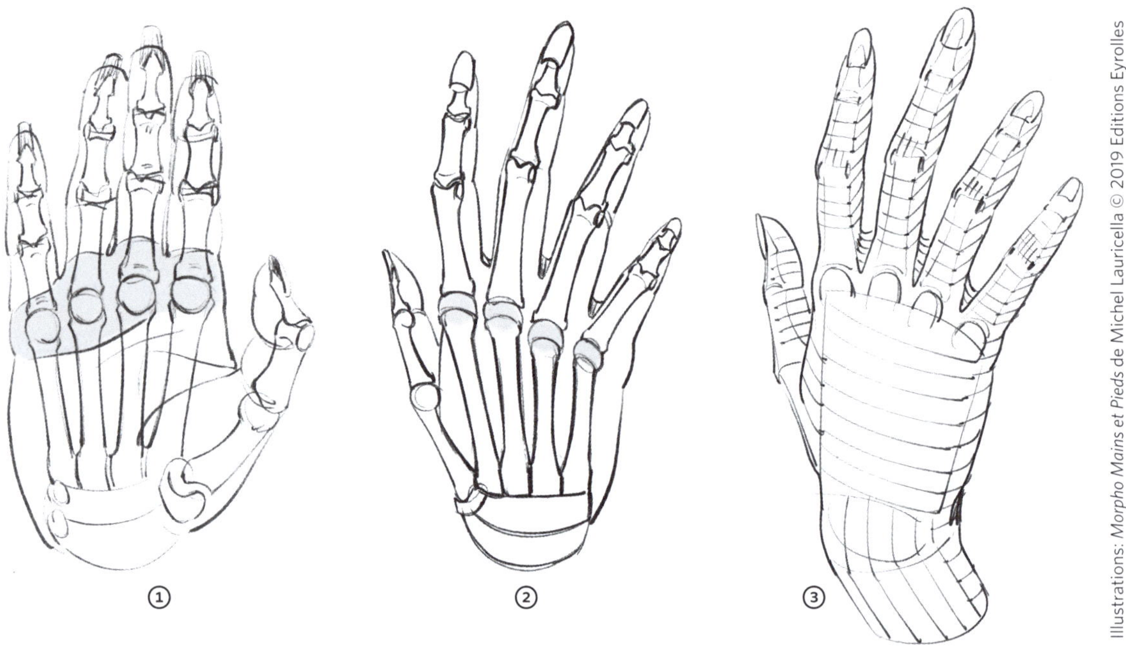

Illustrations: Morpho Mains et Pieds de Michel Lauricella © 2019 Editions Eyrolles

As a starting point, turn to your left-side photographic reference image and use calipers to measure the distance between the wrist and the first knuckle line. Place your calipers over a ruler and note this distance. In this case, we have a measurement of 1¼ inch (3.2 cm). Generic hand proportions dictate that the palm constitutes about half of the overall hand length, so we can deduce that our target size for our hands will be 2½ inches (6.3 cm). Mark this overall measurement onto a piece of paper and find the halfway mark.

This simple guide will ensure that the hands stay in proportion to the overall figure. The palm will fit on the lower half of the guideline, while the fingers will stretch towards the upper part of that mark, with the middle finger reaching full length while the others reach varying shorter lengths.

Looking at your hand diagram in Appendix D, let's make some notes and observations around the structure and alignments in the hand.

- Two planes interact in the hand: we have the plane that holds the four external fingers and a plane that holds the thumb. The interaction between these two planes allows us to grab effectively, yet it also has the power to convey whether the energy running through the figure is tensed or relaxed. ③

- The middle finger is the longest finger, followed by the index and ring fingers slightly lower. Although they rest at comparable heights, the index finger is often a bit higher than the ring finger. ②

- Generic proportions dictate that, when the palm is flat and open, the top of the pinky finger lines up at a slight diagonal with the top knuckle of the ring finger and the top of the thumb lines up with the middle knuckle of the pointing finger. ②③

- Since the top of the palm forms an arch, the fingers extend from the palm in a radial way, not in a perpendicular way along a straight edge. Each finger, comprised of phalanges and a metacarpal, transverses the palm and comes together with the other fingers at a central area where the carpal bones meet the radius and ulna. Together, these bones make up the wrist. ①②

- Finally, in considering the profile view of a finger, notice the curving base of the fingertip in contrast to the flat top of the nail bed.

While holding all these notes present, let's start forming our hand. First, develop the shape of the palm. With your hand facedown on a piece of paper, trace your handprint tight along the perimeter to get a clear sense of the shape you are after. If you want to go the extra mile, you can photograph a female hand in both front and back views, digitally reduce these images to measure 2¾ inches (7 cm) in height from the bottom of the palm to the top of the middle finger, and print them out to use as blueprints. If you are continuing without photographic blueprints, you can use the provided hand diagram in Appendix D or use your traced handprint as a guide to draw a smaller palm shape within the bounding lines you drew onto a piece of paper in the previous step. Next, transfer your small palm shape onto a ¼ inch (6 mm) slab. Ⓐ Cut out your palm shape then flip it over, using it as a template to cut its mirror image for the palm of the opposite hand. Place these palm shapes under plastic while you work on the fingers.

On top of your guidelines, draw in your fingers with the length of the middle finger reaching the top line and the other digits moving down

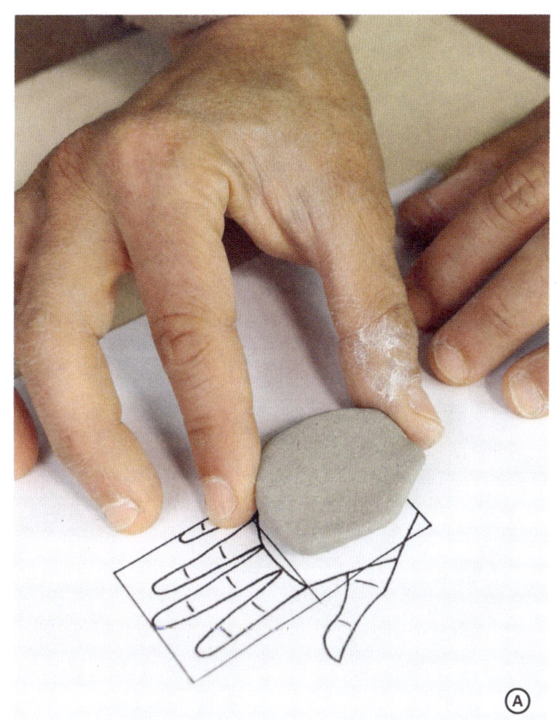

Ⓐ

accordingly based on our previous notes and your own hand observations. Roll eight tapered coils of comparable width in between your palms. Next, make two slightly thicker tapered coils for your thumbs. Leave extra material at the base of each coil, exceeding the respective lengths dictated by your diagram. This extra material will keep the clay hydrated where your fingers will attach to your palm.

Pinch each fingertip to create a finger silhouette that is round on the bottom and flat on top. Next, put some marks onto the coils and develop the knuckle articulations to bring these fingers to life. In your paper diagram, divide each finger into nine equal sections. Each articulation will take a fraction of that overall, nine with the first one from the base out measuring around ⁴⁄₉, the second articulation around ³⁄₉ and the last one around ²⁄₉. Draw these articulations onto your diagram and then place your rolled clay fingers on top of your diagram, registering them with your fingertip marks.

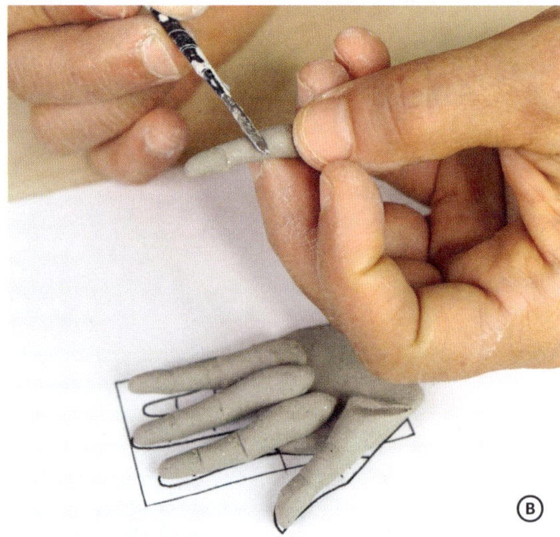

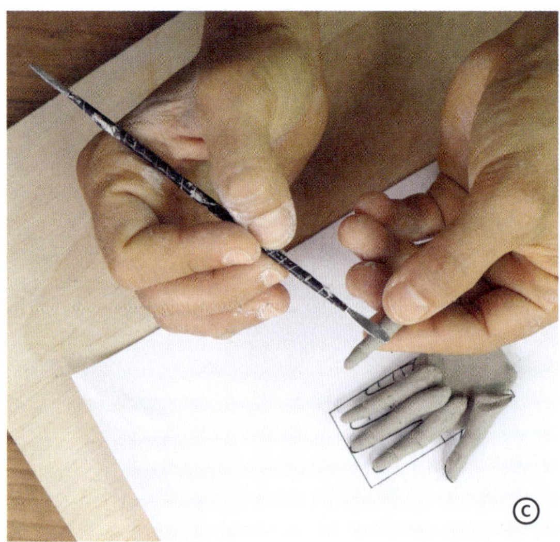

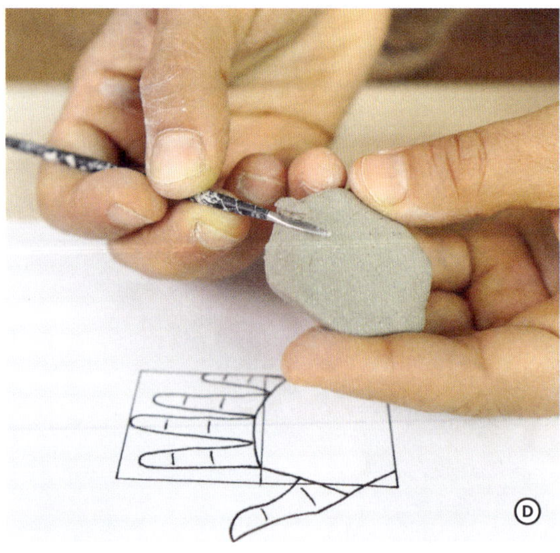

Now transfer the information from the diagram onto the clay, marking where each finger meets the palm as well as the articulations that establish where the fingers will bend. Ⓑ For a simpler path, you can approximate your articulations. Starting at the base of the fingers where they intersect with the palm, the first articulation will fall just under the halfway point of each finger. Ⓒ From there you can eyeball your second articulations. With these articulation marks in place, hold the back side of your knife to each mark and roll the fingers to create soft indentations that encircle your coils.

To attach the fingers to the palm, start by beveling the top edge of the palm-shaped slab before slipping and scoring the underside. Ⓓ Begin attaching the fingers to that beveled underside by aligning each drawn-in base line with the upper edge of the palm. Ⓔ Strive to maintain a sense of radial connection. Take a minute to integrate these fingers with your palm by compressing with your stainless-steel tool, adding bits of clay if necessary, to secure the connection. Ⓕ Ⓖ Using your own hands as models, add bits of clay along the backside of this connection curve to articulate the knuckles. Ⓗ At this scale, small nylon brushes are going to be essential allies. They will help you apply, shape, and smooth these tiny clay additions. Next, add small clay coils tracing the movement of the metacarpal bones across the palm, then smooth these in with your brush. Ⓘ

An easy way to suggest fingernails is by taking a small knife and running it across the tip of each finger in an arch motion. Pressing in at either edge of the nail and releasing pressure at the top will create the effect of the nail bed grabbing the finger tissue.

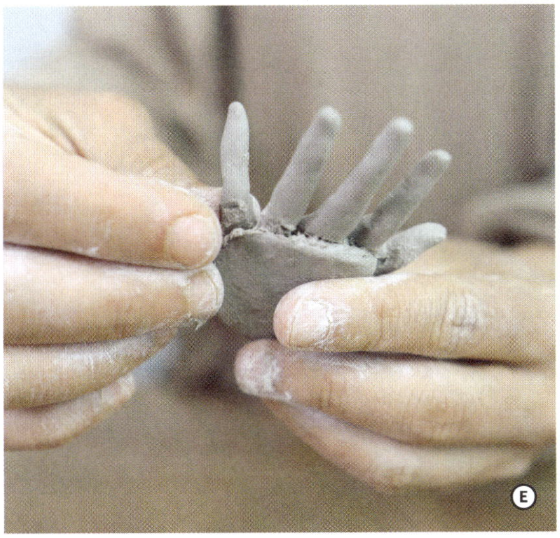

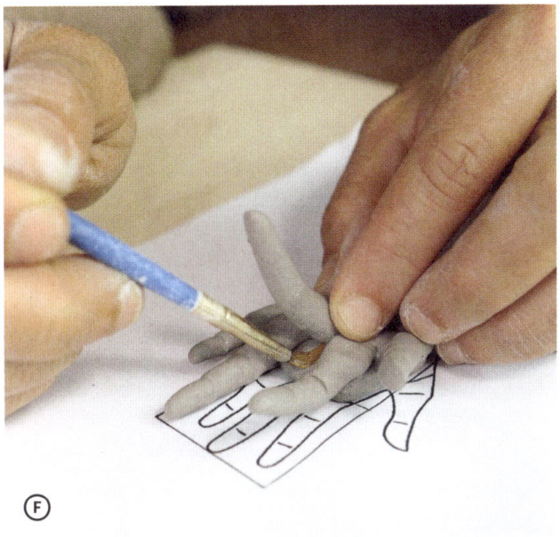

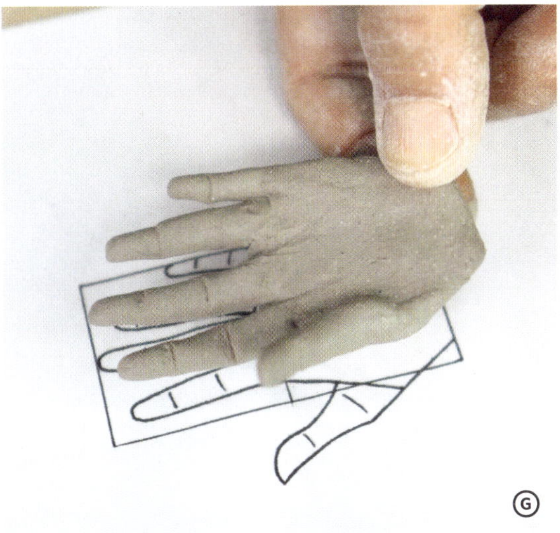

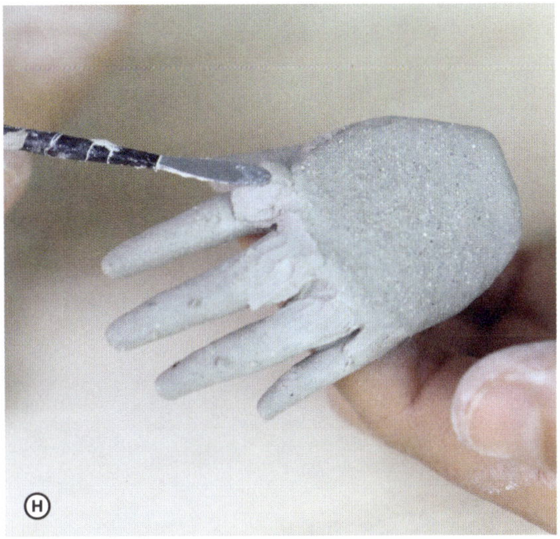

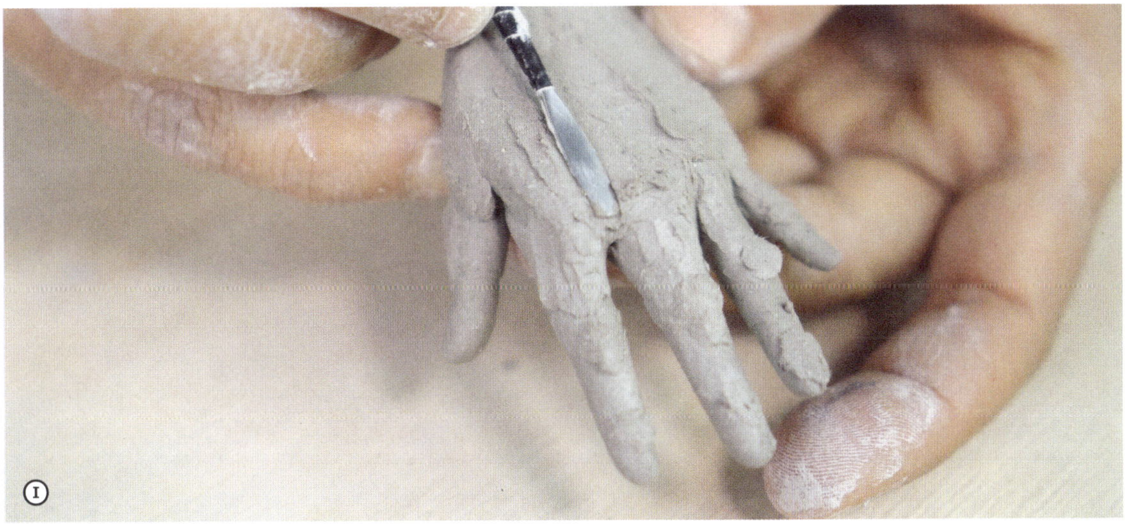

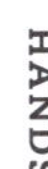

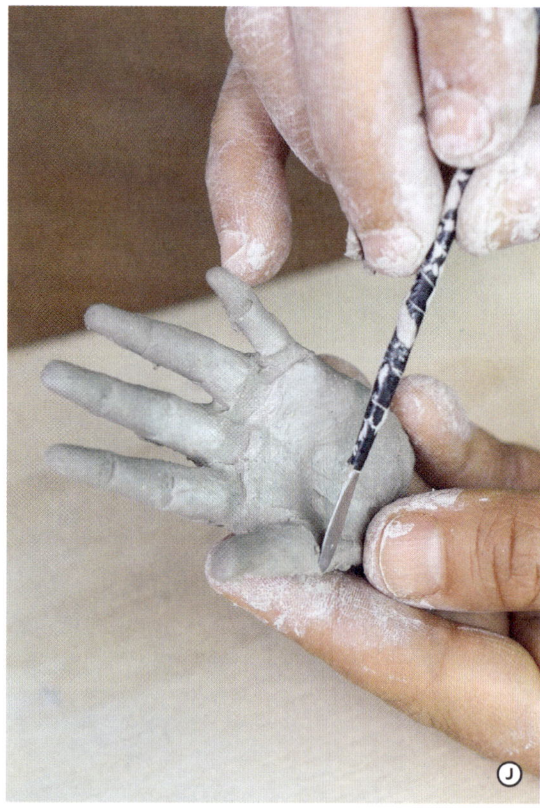

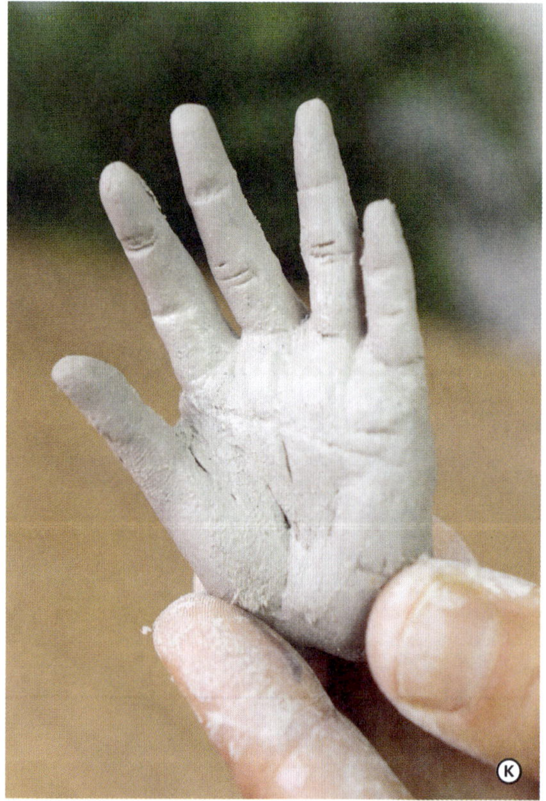

The level of attention that I pay to the inner palms depends on their ultimate visibility within my composition. If they face outwards rather than inward and towards the body, I need to account for them. To develop the inside of the palm, start by carving a groove on the inside of the hand that follows a path just below each of the fingers. Ⓙ Next, make a small, pinched flap about ⅛ inch (3 mm) thick that matches the contour of the palm. Slip and score both the grove and the perimeter of the flap, and then affix the flap over the palm, guiding it into place with your stainless tool and brush. Your palm will resemble a little pillow full of trapped air.

Using the trapped air to your benefit, gently push down to articulate the palmar flexion creases, looking at your own palm from the front and sides and transposing what you see onto the small hand. Ⓚ Your pressure should be firm yet gentle so as to not collapse the volume. Once you are satisfied, take a small needle tool and pierce a vent hole along one of the creases to allow air to flow during the firing. Remember to turn your hands so that you can experience how the volumes are developing from the sides as well as from the front and make adjustments accordingly.

At this stage, place the hands in a safe place to keep them moist and pliable until you attach them to your sculpture.

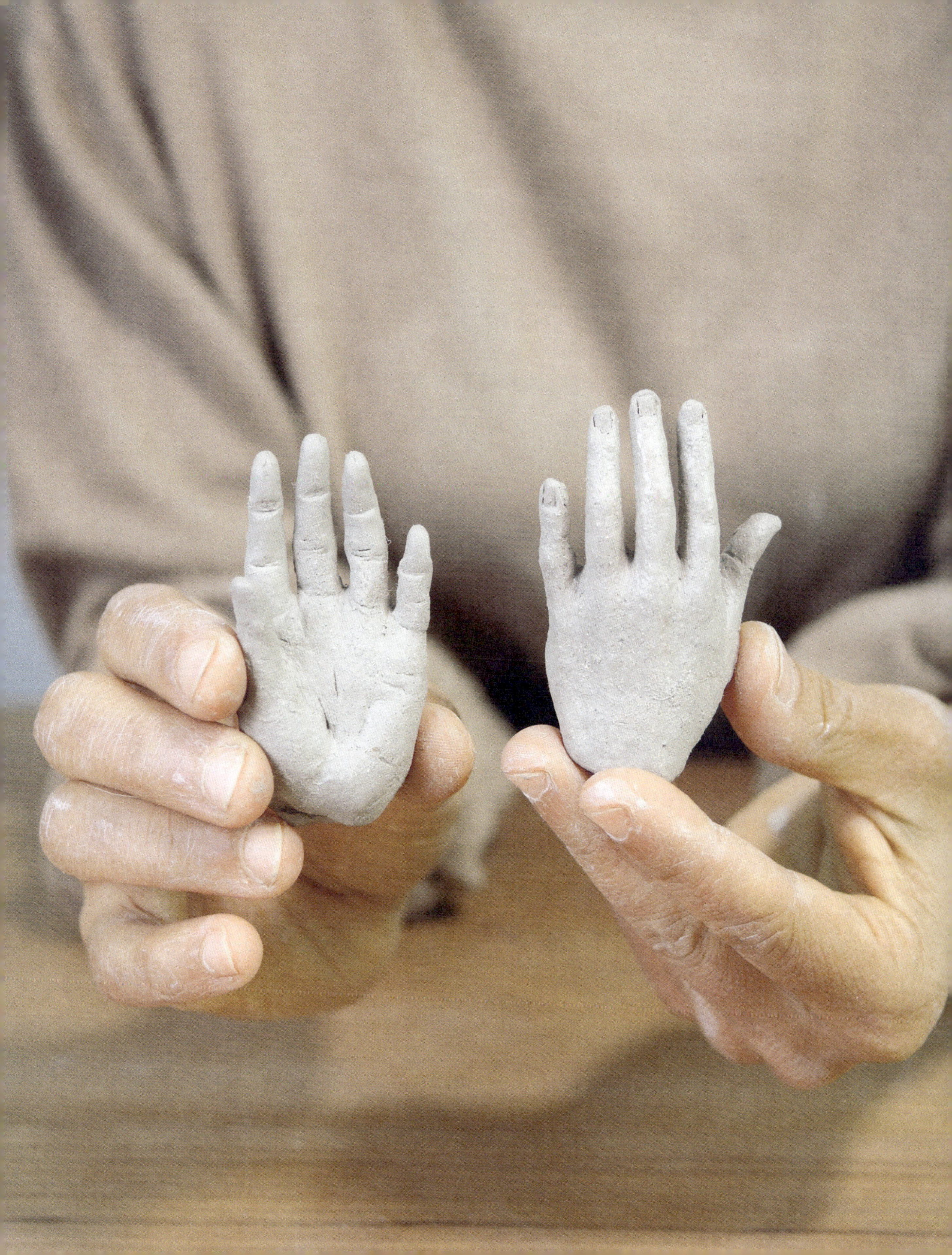

ATTACHING THE HANDS

To attach the hands, establish with your calipers the distance between the elbow and the wrist, right before the palm, and trim accordingly on both sides. Use your calipers, back and forth, to make sure both sides are consistent in length. Take each hand and trim it right below the palm, adjusting the angle of the cut to get the desired position as the hand attaches to the cylinder of the lower arm. Once in place, make gentle adjustments to the fingers, focusing on the individual sections as they bend to create a sense of articulated bone. Look at the positioning from all angles and compare it to the photographic references to replicate the gesture. Once satisfied, make your keys before slipping, scoring, and attaching. Use extra clay to reinforce the connection and articulate the tendons, knuckles, and the bony parts of the wrist. Ⓛ Ⓜ Ⓝ

Once you have attached your hands, explore positioning possibilities. Play around with either echoing your photographic reference or developing variations to convey a specific energy moving through the figure. The expression of your hands can be either in alignment or in slight contrast to what you set in motion with the gesture of the body. This tension can build on the conceptual resonance of a piece. As with every part of this process, the full articulation of the forms will happen in cycles or refinements as dryness allows for more and more detail to accumulate, revealing the interplay between the hands and the whole of the body.

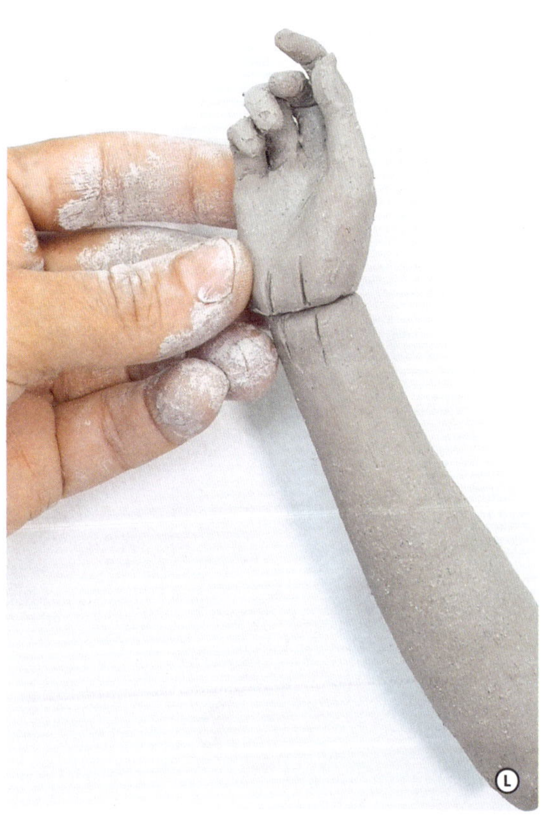

Ⓛ

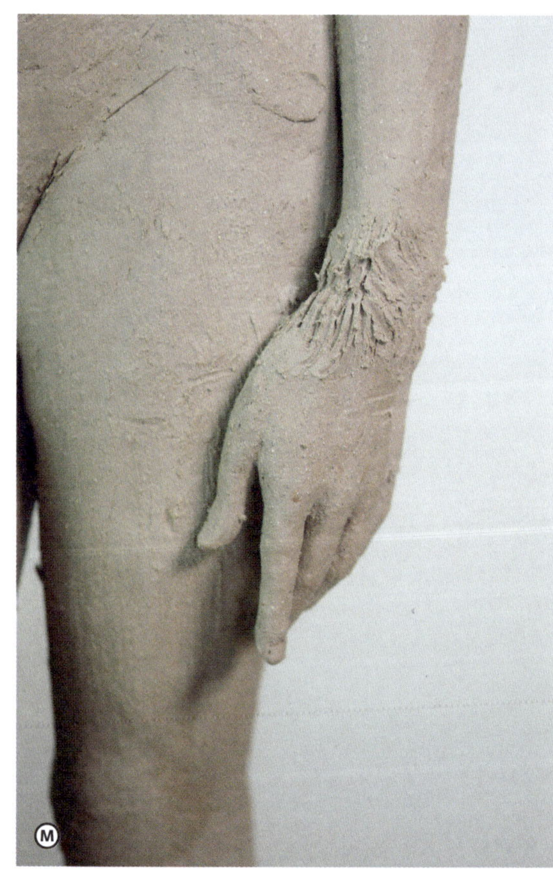

Ⓜ

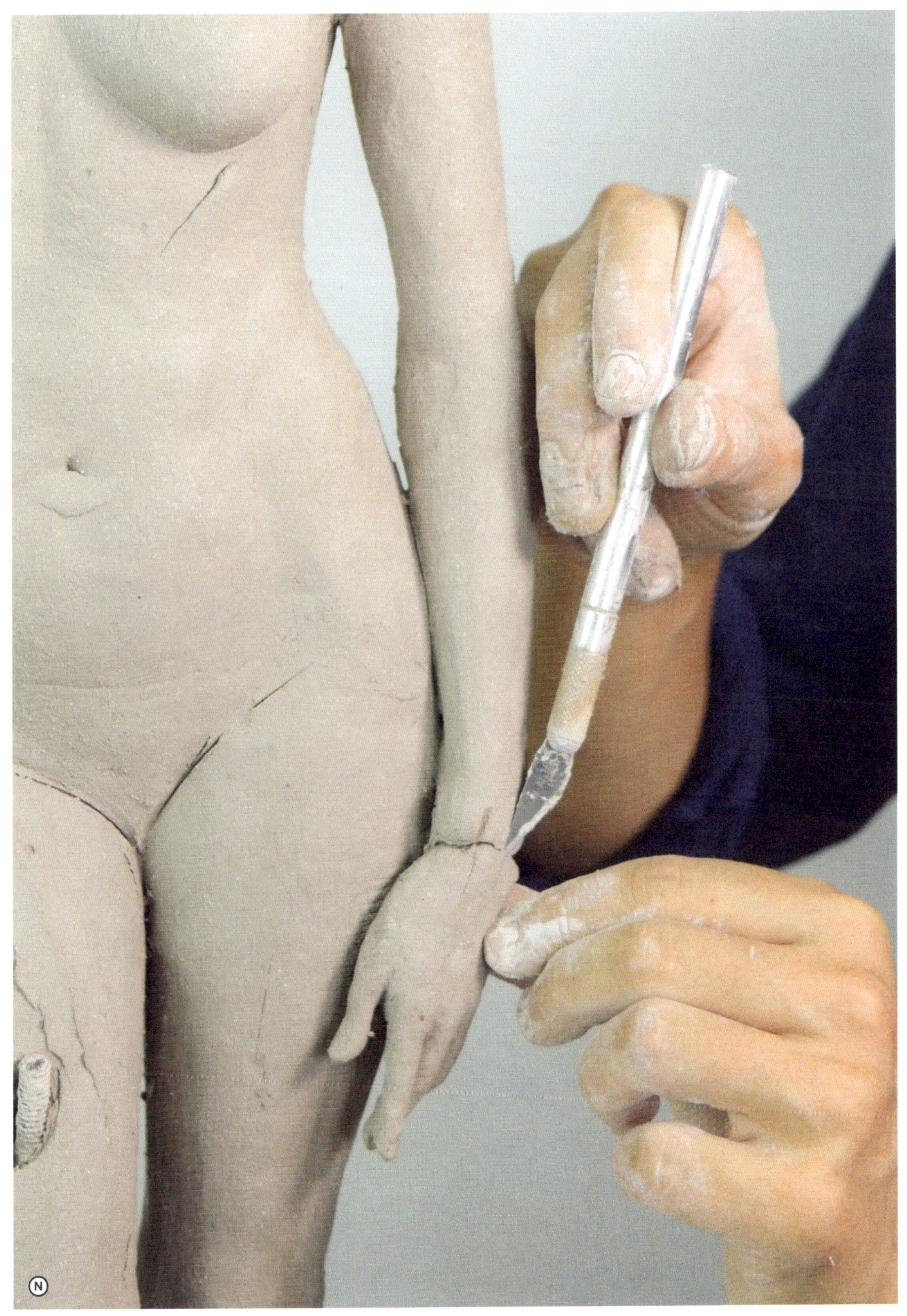

Gallery

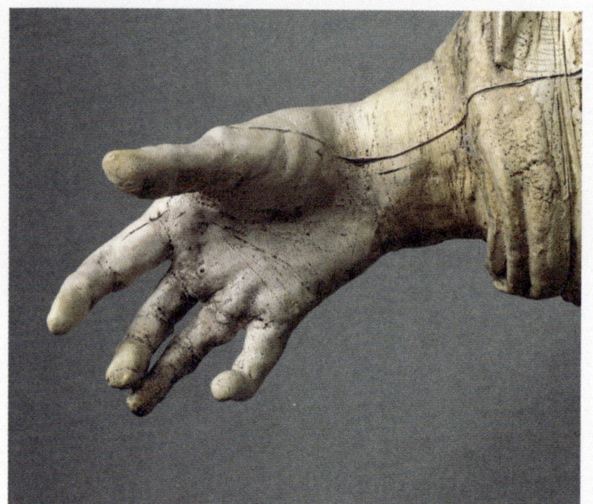

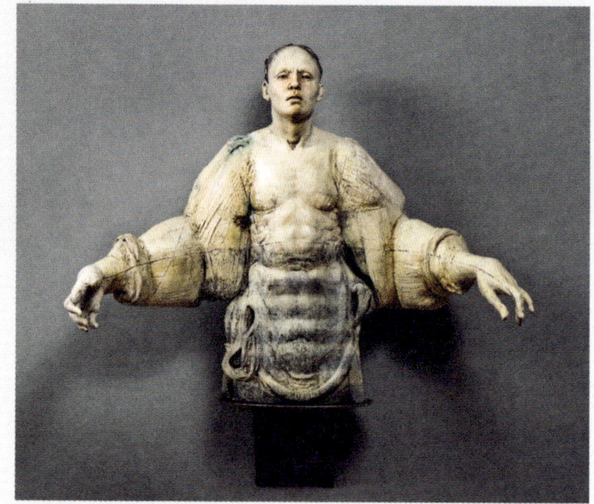

Cristina Córdova, *Abrazo.* Courtesy of the artist.

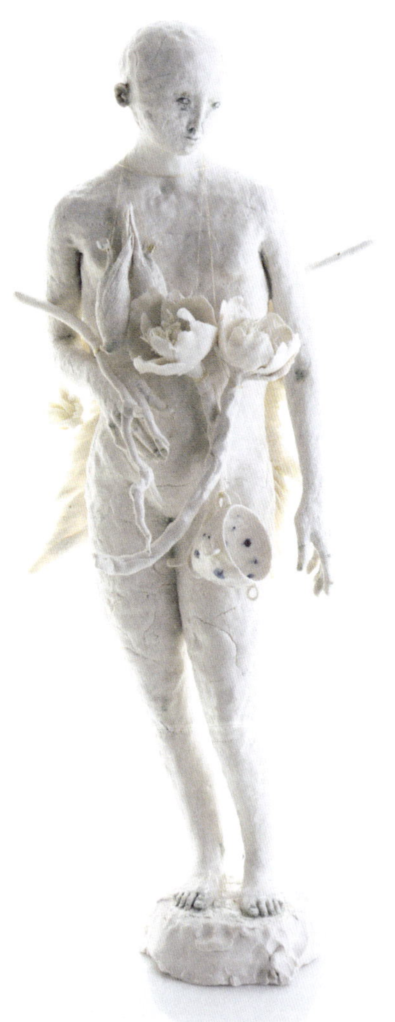

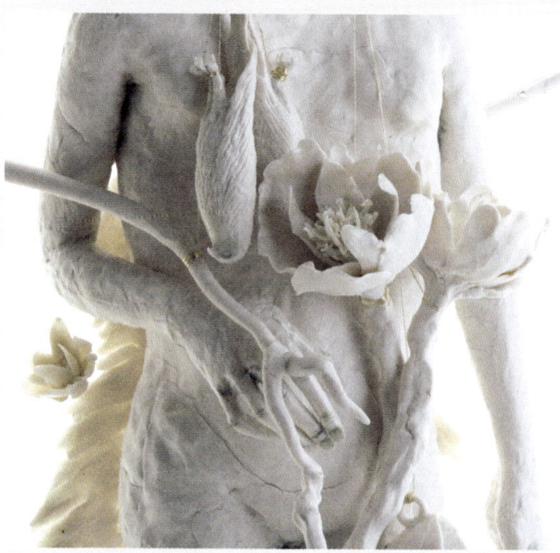

Claire Curneen, *Pilgrim* (left and above). Dewi Tannatt Lloyd.

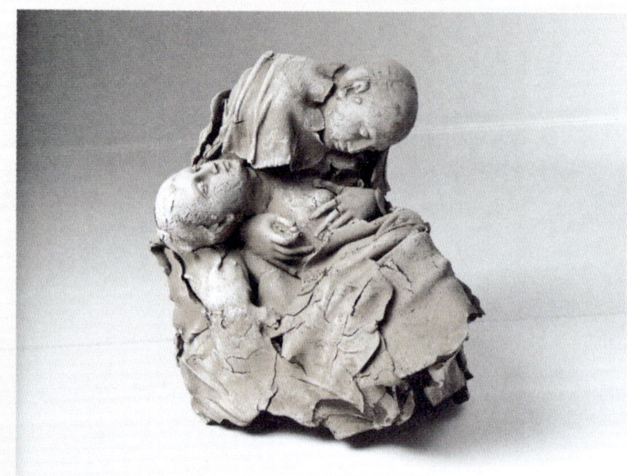

Georges Jeanclos, *Couple.* Denis Durand / Galerie Capazza.

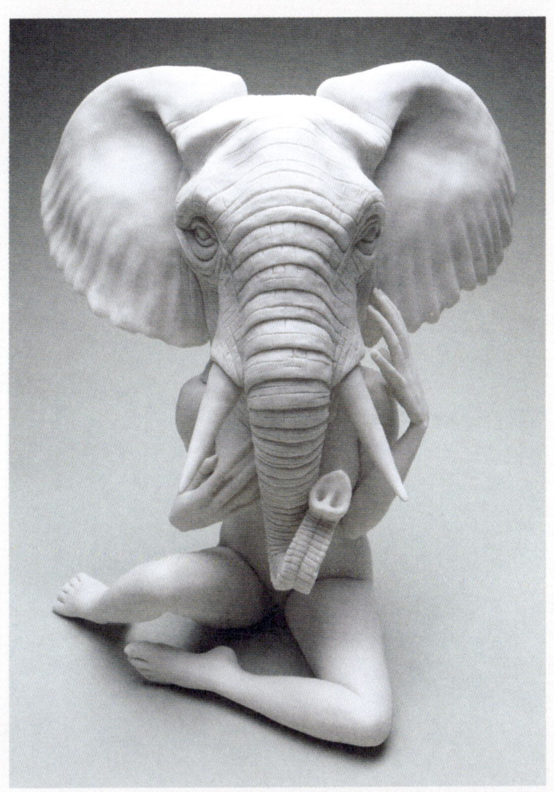

Crystal Morey, *African Bush Elephant.* Courtesy of the artist.

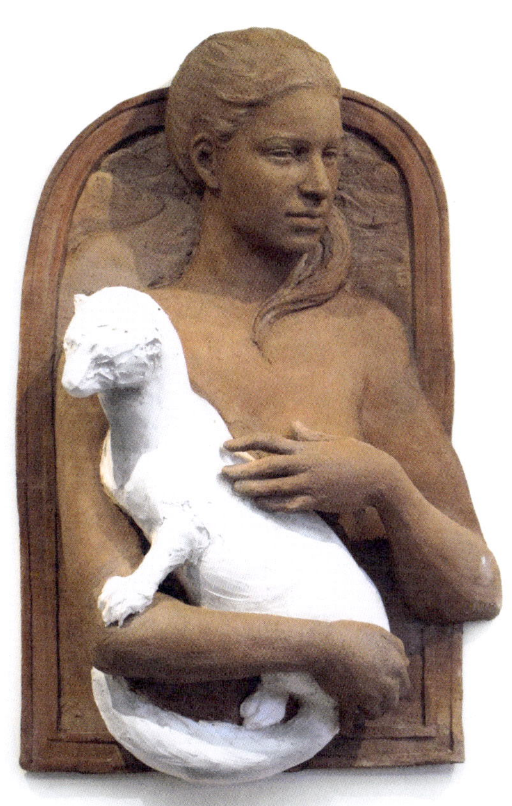

Lisa Reinertson, *Girl with Ermine.* Courtesy of the artist.

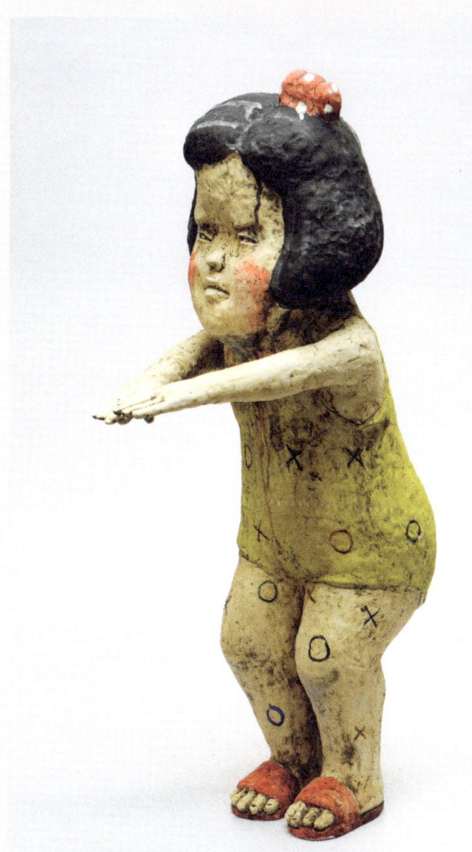

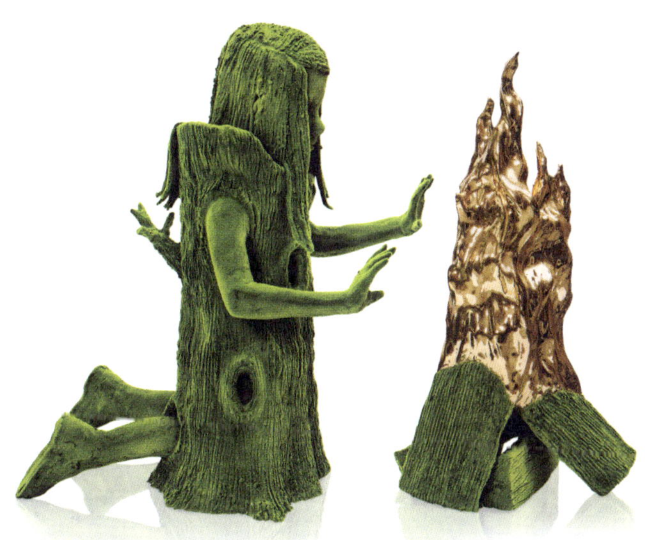

Kim Simonsson, *Girl at Campfire.* Jefunne Gimpel.

135

Kensuke Yamada, *Diver.* Courtesy of the artist.

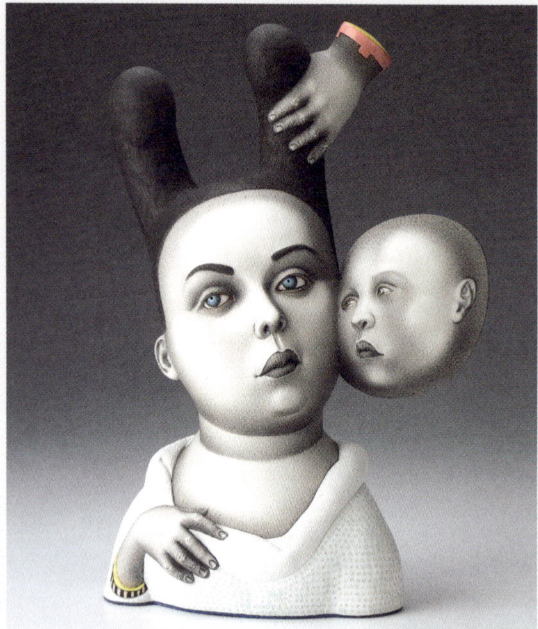

Sergei Isupov, *Influence.* John Polak.

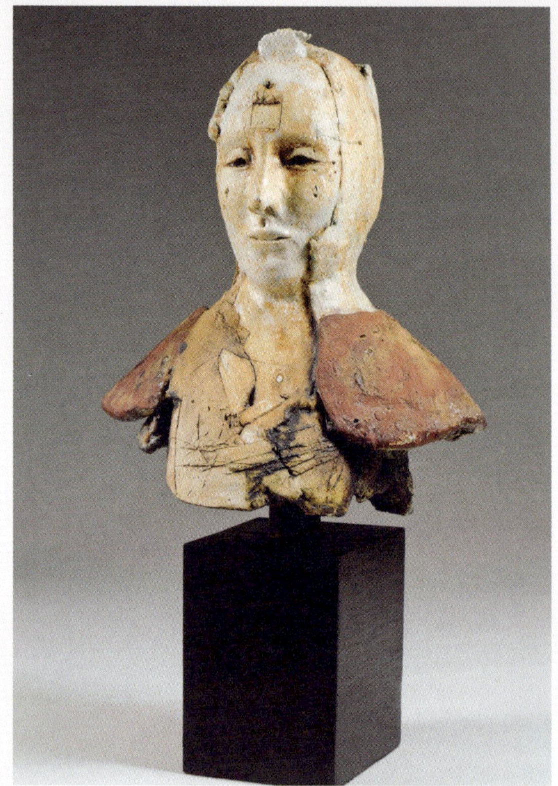

Susana Espinosa, *Un Pasado Real.* Johnny Betancourt.

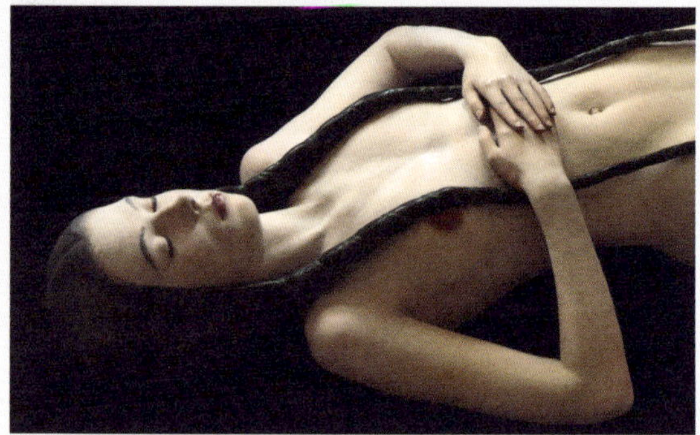

Judy Fox, *Snow White.* Courtesy of the artist.

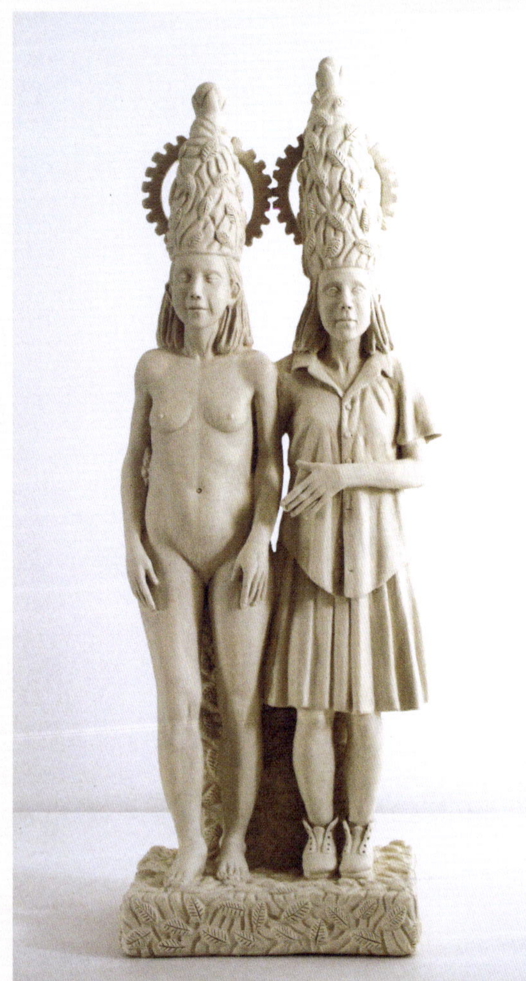

Tricia Cline, *The Witness Stripped Bare.* Courtesy of the artist.

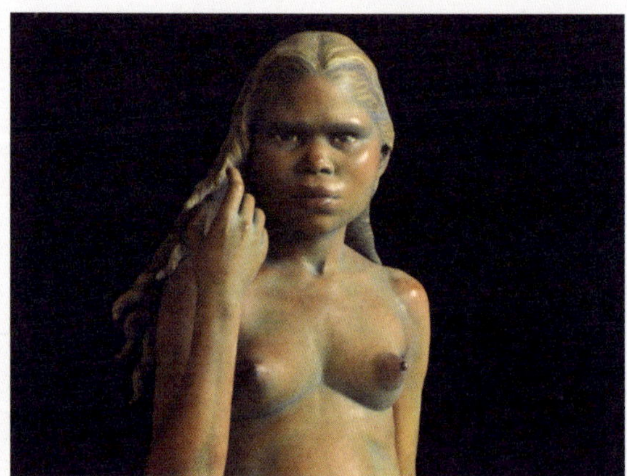

Judy Fox, *Eve.* Courtesy of the artist.

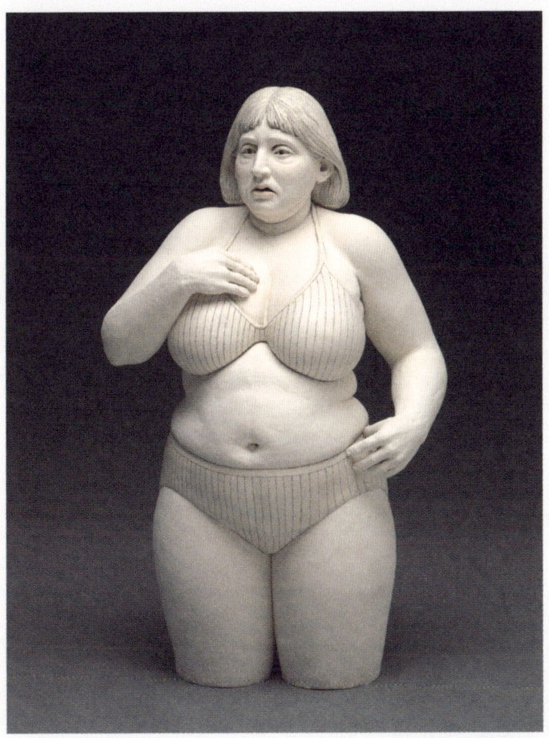

Claudia Olds Goldie, *Beauty.* Will Howcroft.

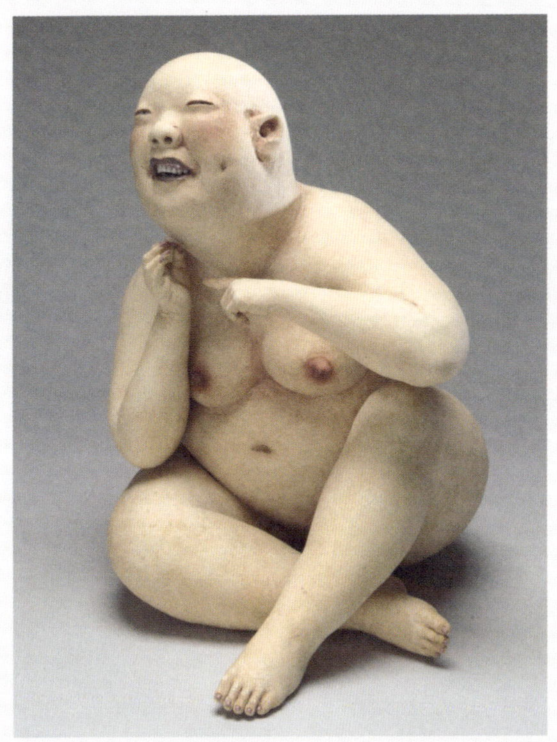

Esther Shimazu, *You Know.*
Paul Kodama, courtesy of the John Natsoulas Gallery.

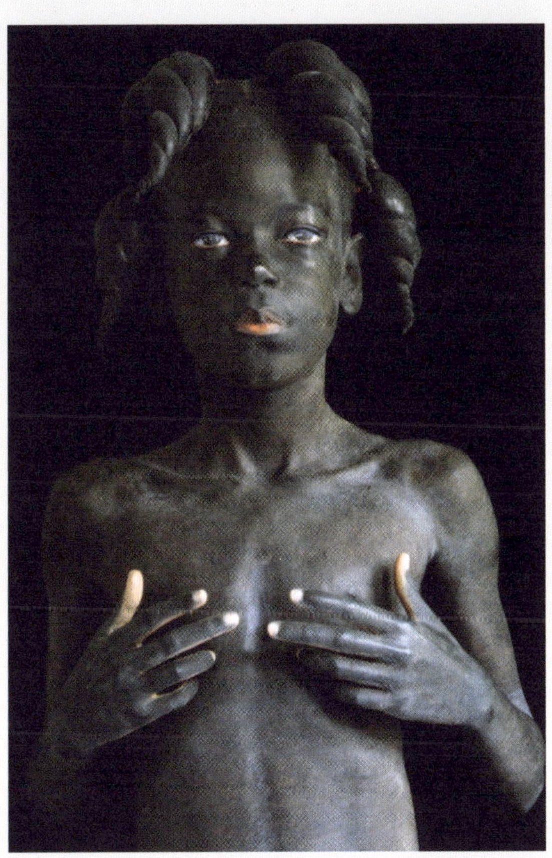

Judy Fox, *Onile.* Courtesy of the artist.

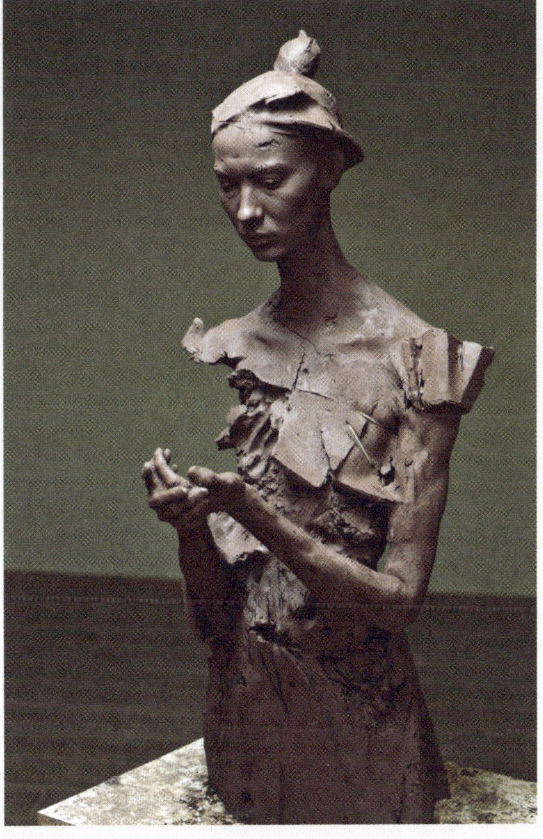

Eudald de Juana, *Hope.* Courtesy of the artist.

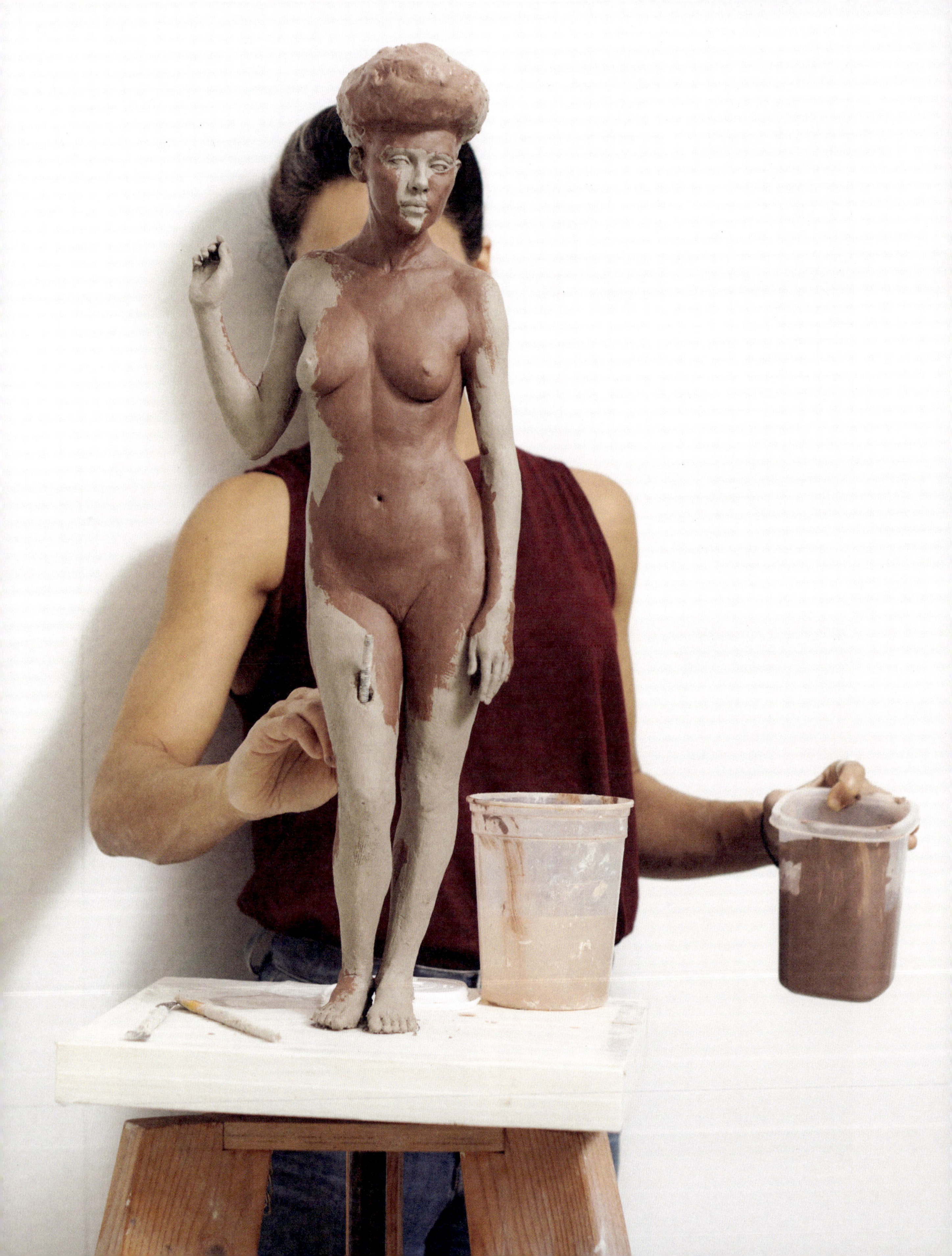

FLESHING OUT CORE FORMS

EACH FORM IN the human body consists of a series of underlying planes. As we make our way into the fleshy layer of our figurative renderings, these planes assume a curvilinear quality. To develop the nuanced variations that activate the volumes on our sculptures, we fall into a rhythm of gradual observation and modification. Starting by reconciling the external contours of our sculpture with those in our four cardinal reference images, we gradually narrow our lens of observational focus, turning to our in-between photographic views and reconciling the information they contain with that of the cardinal views.

During this part of the process, you will make your way around and around your sculpture, diligently turning it into alignment with each reference image before drawing notational insights, adding clay, or removing clay.

As you move from one photograph to the next, you are deciphering the logic of the gesture and allowing insights from one side to carry over to the subsequent view, ensuring that your new adjustments remain congruent with the overall feeling of the work.

**WHAT YOU'LL NEED
TO GET STARTED**

- Fresh clay
- Rakes
- Stainless modeling tools
- Terry cloths
- An assortment of brushes

VENTING

After finishing sculpting a piece, but before the final refinement of the surface, there is a step I take to help ensure a safe firing. This is venting: perforating the clay wall of the sculpture to allow any trapped air and moisture to escape. To do this I use a thin, stiff, steel rod (approx. ¹⁄₁₆ inch [1.6 mm] diameter) and push it all the way through the wall of the sculpture and into the hollow interior space. I concentrate on the thickest areas of the piece, particularly where I have added additional clay to the surface. (For example, in a figure sculpture, clay mass that has been built up for hair or clothing.) I may pierce many holes close together in an area where the clay is especially thick, or just a few in areas of less concern. After venting one area of the sculpture, I cover the small holes in the surface by smoothing them over with a piece of terry cloth and a little clay slip. Because you are covering the holes in the exterior, it is very important to ensure they were pierced all the way to the inner hollow, so that air is not getting trapped inside the clay wall. At the end of this process, you will just need to leave one open vent hole anywhere in the sculpture. After finishing with the venting, you can continue with the surface treatment.

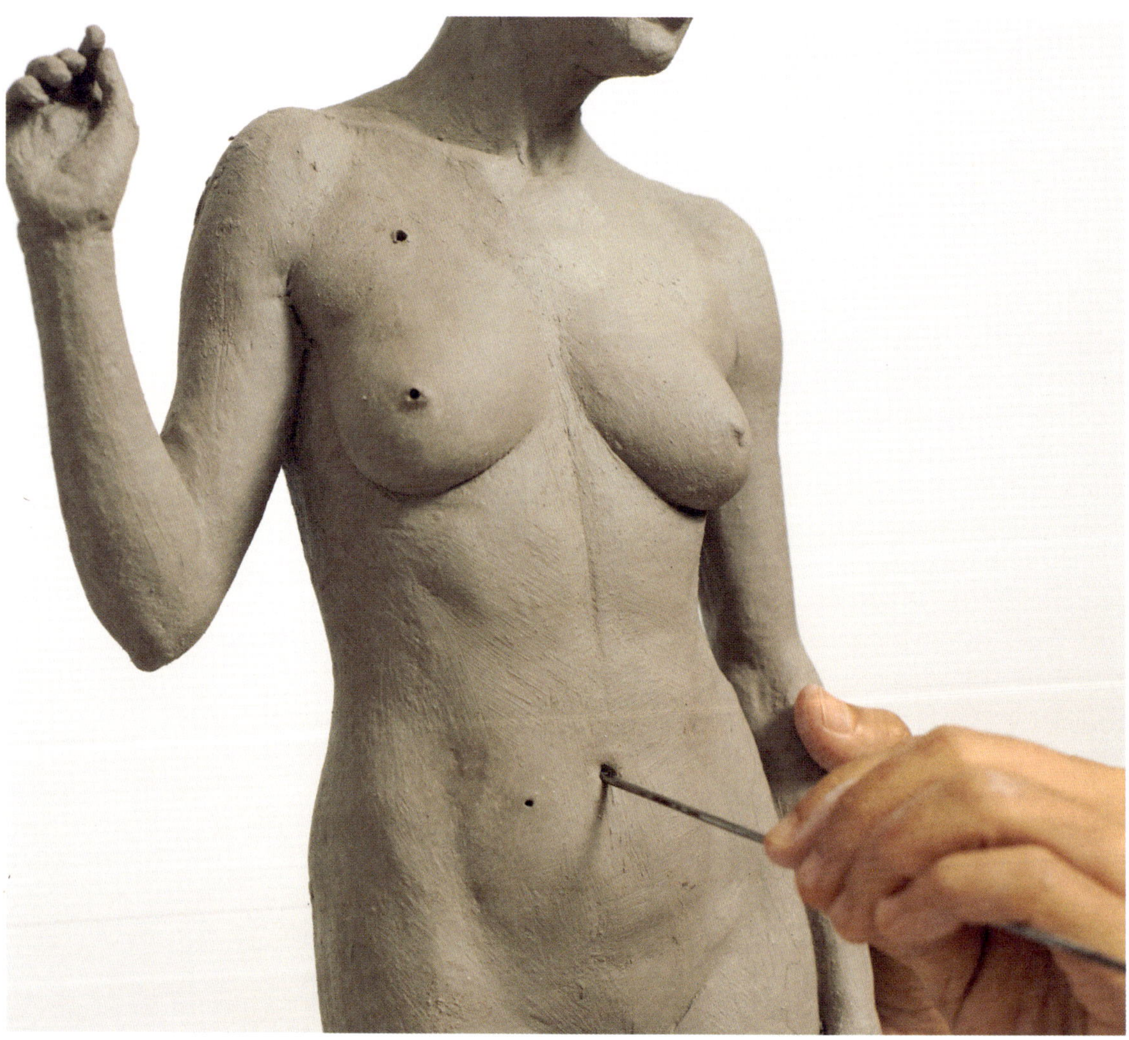

READING CONTOURS WITH ADDITIONAL PHOTOGRAPHIC VIEWS TO ACHIEVE ACCURACY

When studying with artists Robert Bodem and Lotta Blocker at the Florence Academy of Art, I practiced a traditional method of rendering from a live model in the round. I learned to align the perspective of my sculpture with my view of the model and then reconcile those two perspectives by making methodical observations, adding and subtracting clay, and paying close attention to the relationships between clay volumes and negative spaces. I now emulate this process when working from photographic references.

Now that the forms of your sculpture have come together using your scaled blueprints, let's turn to the rest of the photographic views included (see Appendix B). These images offer additional vantage points that fill in the gaps of anatomical information between your four photographic blueprints. Just as a painter moves from initial bold strokes to more detailed brushwork, you should start by rigorously attending to measurements, alignment, and overall gesture, and then move into more nuanced engagement with the interplay of forms throughout the surface of the human figure.

Since you have already established scale by adhering to the measurements in your four cardinal blueprints, you can get away with either printing your transitional views at a smaller scale or referencing them directly off the page (or screen). I usually immerse myself deeply in this layer of modeling once I have most of my composition assembled, but if I need help deciphering part of the gesture earlier in the process, I will pull up these additional images for quick reference. In some seated and reclining poses, looking at a direct top or bird's-eye view image early in your process can provide clarity as you assemble your forms together and hone in on their relative orientations.

For me, this modeling part of the process demands a heightened level of attention comparable to a meditative state: my breath slows down, and I fall into a rhythm, gathering anatomical insights in cycles and then carefully integrating them into my foundational composition until a sense of coherence and interconnection permeates all the parts of the figure. In my work teaching groups, I have enjoyed experiencing the breadth of my students' interpretations, which reveals the immense variety contained within each pose. Your final composition will be a collage of all that your perception has captured through the unique filter of your attention.

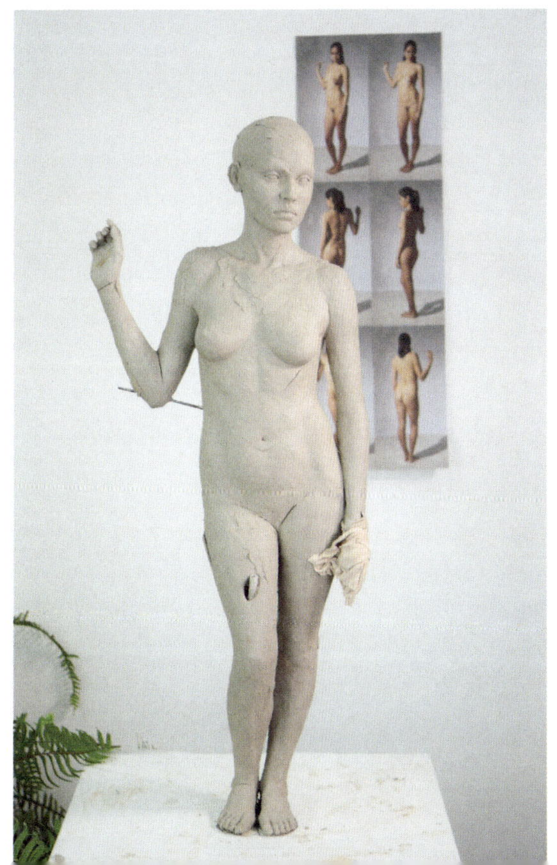

141

THE PROCESS

Unlike other sections of the book, the process of fleshing out core forms is not as linear with regards to there being a specific place to start and finish. With that in mind, I encourage you to read the rest of this chapter (and study the photos), begin the process on your own, and come back to review this information as necessary while you work.

Before you begin working, make sure you have a bag of soft clay ready to engage with this modeling part of the process. To make a bag of soft clay for modeling onto your core forms, separate some fresh clay into an empty clay bag, pour a small amount of water into the bottom of this bag, then twist the bag closed and allow the clay to slowly incorporate the water. After a couple of hours, flip the clay over within the bag to immerse the less saturated top clay into the puddle of water at the base of the bag. Allow some time to pass, then pour out any unincorporated water that is still at the bottom of the bag. Wedging clay at this consistency will only cause the clay to stick to your wedging surface, so knead the softened clay with your hands to integrate the moist clay around the exterior with the firmer clay at the center until you achieve uniform consistency.

You can add small thumb-fulls of moist clay over your core form without needing to score and slip, as the clay's moisture content will aid in adhesion. However, if your core form is rather dry or if you plan to add a significant amount of fresh clay to one area, I do recommend scoring and slipping.

ALIGNING WITH REFERENCE PHOTOS

When turning your sculpture to the same position as a reference image, rely on obvious visual landmarks such as the angles of the feet or the negative space between the legs. Take your time with this process to avoid confusion and unnecessary work.

Negative spaces have a crucial function in your rendering process. Seeing these spaces as *shapes* will help you assemble your composition accurately. For example, perceiving the shape of the negative space between the legs from a particular vantage point not only helps guide you into alignment with your reference image, but also enables you to see and refine the external contours of your sculpture's legs.

GETTING TO WORK

Make your way around the figure, focusing on distinct silhouettes and comparing those with the silhouettes of your sculpture. Revise external angles, distances between set points, and the shapes of negative spaces as you go. From those external contours, make your way inward, articulating forms by first noting the boldest shadows and highlights on your model, followed by the more subtle values.

Note: To orient your eye as it continues to recognize and render anatomical features, draw onto your sculpture to indicate stark shadow lines such as those visible under the breast or at the armpit.

Keep moving! Continue turning your composition and try to engage with a new vantage point every half hour to avoid getting stuck working exclusively from a limited number of perspectives. Each perspective offers an important piece to the figurative puzzle you are deciphering.

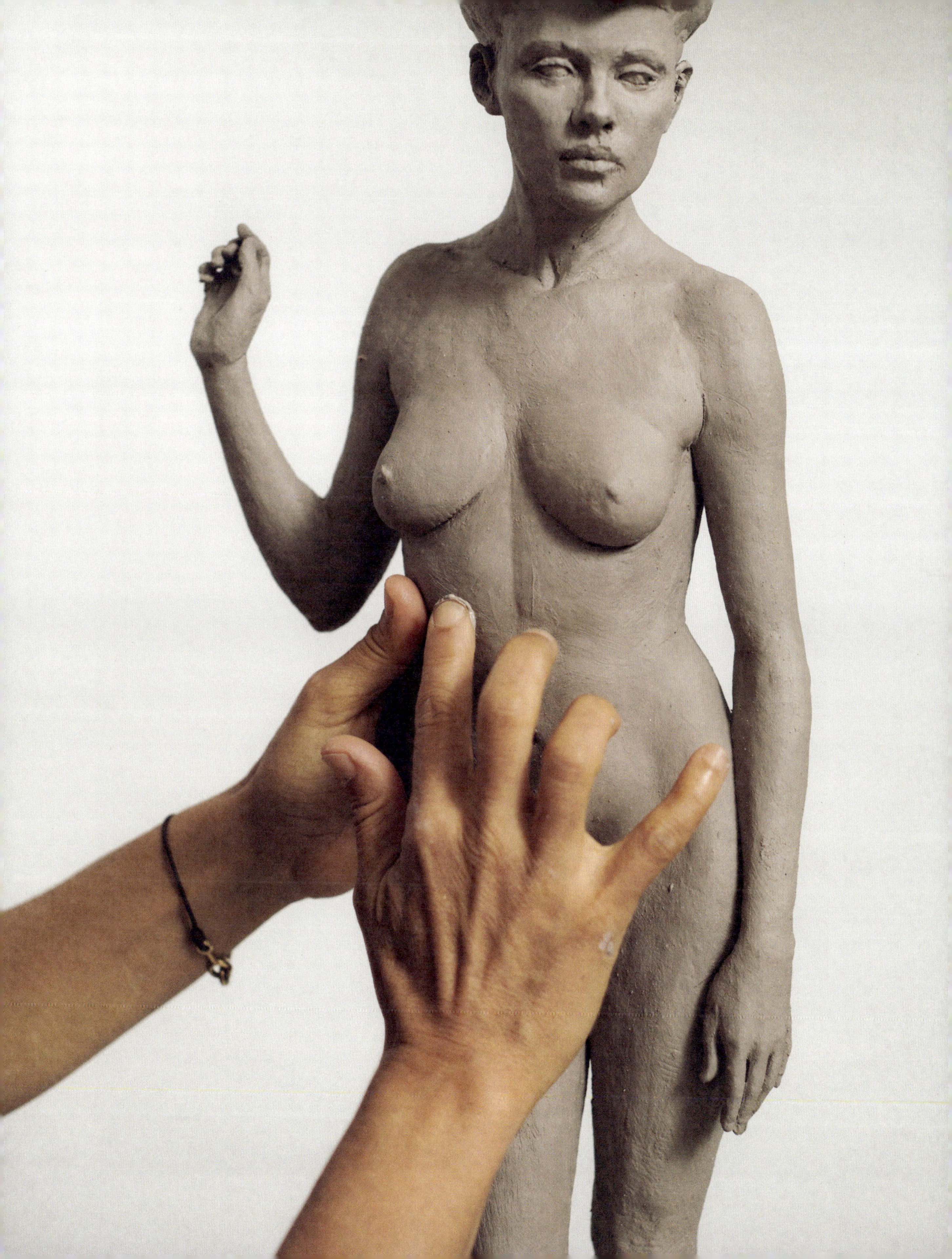

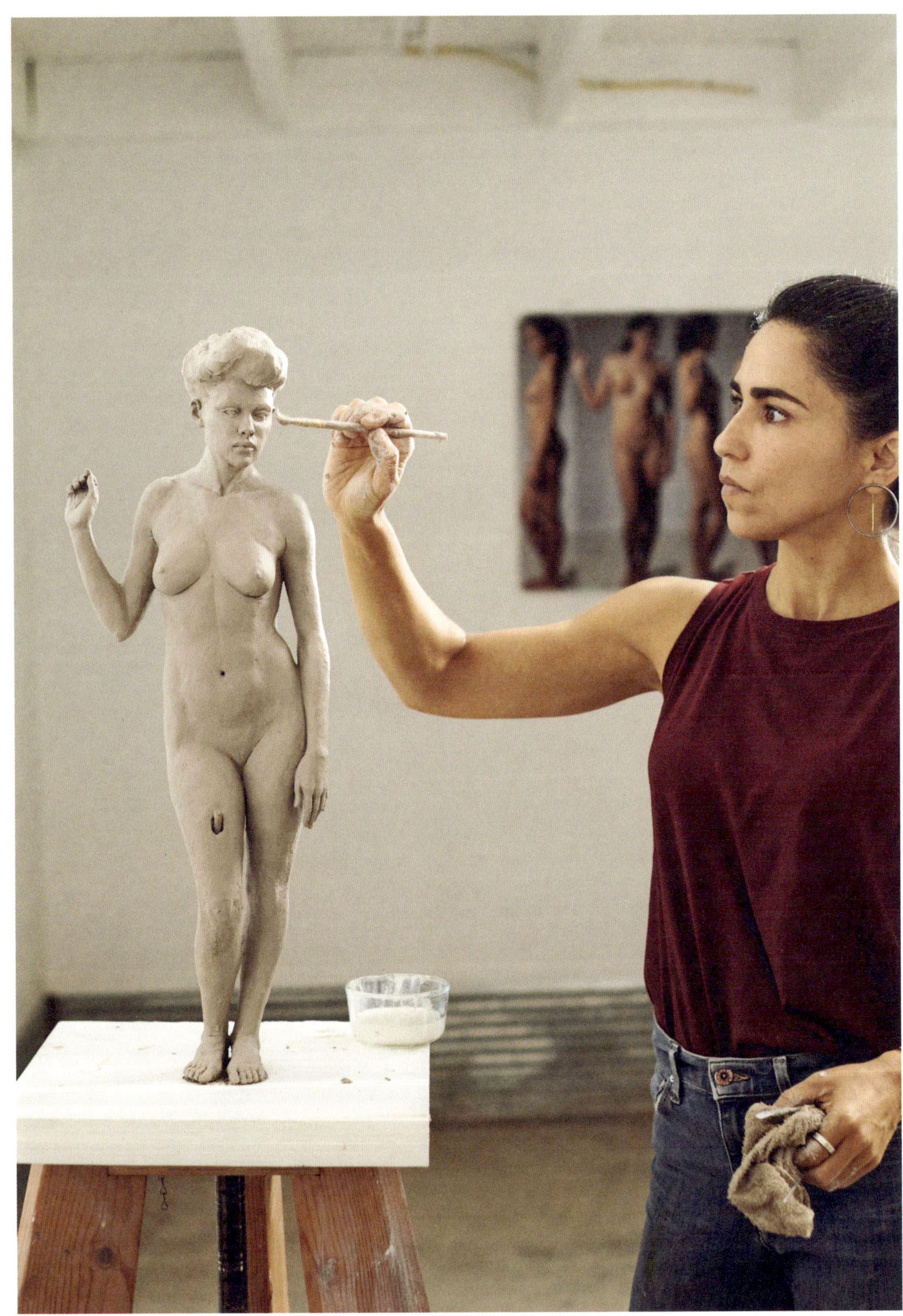

Note: *If you are aiming for a naturalistic rendering, keep looking at your references. It is common to get swept away by the process of articulating volumes and refining the surface from memory, relinquishing the references prematurely.*

While it can be tempting to sculpt from your imagination or assume the unfolding of a volume beyond the image that you are referencing in a given moment, your piece will more closely resemble your references if you train yourself to sculpt only what you can see from each vantage point. It is the information from all the separate images that will collectively induce your piece with a spark of veracity.

As visual information accumulates, take time every so often to integrate new bits of clay and smooth your sculpture's surface with a rake, ribs, terry cloth, and brushes. Cleaning your sculpture's surface in this way will quiet visual noise and allow your eyes to continue building information.

USING SLIP

In the final layer of refinement, I am looking to impart onto the surface a skin-like quality while preserving and enhancing features and volumes. To this end, I use a layer of smooth sieved slip to fill in any surface texture and aid in micro-sculpting details. To do this I take about 1 cup (236 ml) of scoring slip and thin it with about a ¼ cup (59 ml) of water before pushing it through an 60-mesh sieve, extracting some of the grog and paper pulp to end up with a buttery slip, the consistency of Greek yogurt. You will need a rubber spatula to gradually work the material through the mesh, scraping it little by little from the underside of the sieve. Although it is a slow process, a little goes a long way. Every so often, wash out the mesh to open the pores, allowing the sieve to strain properly.

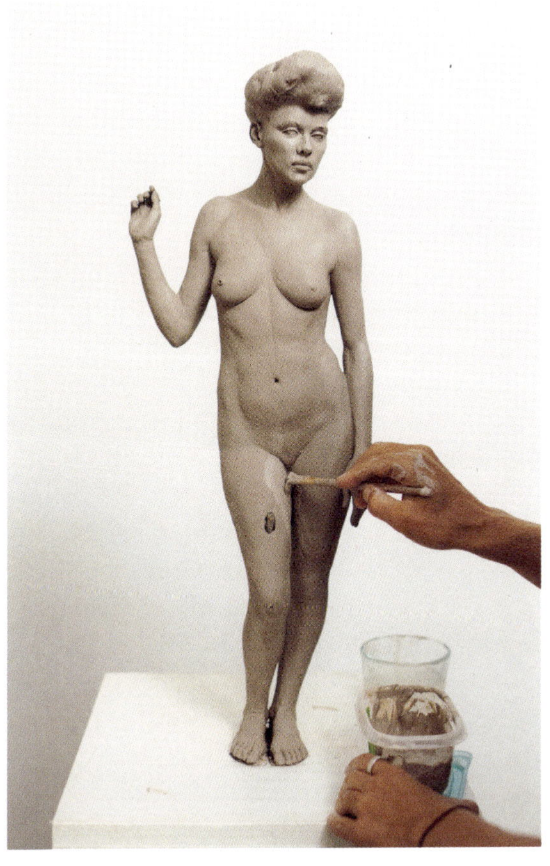

When the slip is ready, it is applied with smooth goat hair brushes of different sizes as well as with small detailing brushes. Using a cross-hatching motion and a discerning eye to regulate the application, work around your sculpture responding to the underlying forms to preserve the subtle information as you gradually smooth and fill the areas that need more refinement. Because the slip is quite thick, it can be built up and used sculpturally to articulate small details or enhance pre-established volumes. Once the initial application of the soft slip has set, use small- to medium-sized soft mop brushes and a little water to erase any slip marks left behind and soften any minute detailing additions such as in the area around the mouth and eyes.

Your sculpture is now complete and ready to be taken off the armature to dry.

ARTISTIC CONSIDERATIONS

The process of fleshing out a figurative composition unfolds at the limits of our perceptive range, drawing us into deeper alignment with those underlying systems that activate the topography of the body. This practice plays on our human predisposition to recognize patterns. It connects us with the realm of the subtle body; through careful scrutiny of the myriad elements of form, we gain access to a new abundance of expression. With each new composition, I am humbled and exhilarated by the ability to immerse myself in this path of discovery. Because my creative goal is not solely naturalism, this exploration assumes different depths depending on what I require from piece to piece. In a sense, each sculptural venture tells a story of insight, time, resilience, and vision. Transcending the specifics dictated by a model, a sculptural rendering reflects the phenomenon of sustained awareness fed by the thread of curiosity that nourishes any impassioned undertaking throughout time.

In my practice, I sometimes borrow terminology from other mediums. Since many of my students have found this slightly more technical information useful over the years, especially in regards to the fleshing and refinement of their sculptures, I am including it on the pages that follow.

Core form: Developing my figurative sculptures in water-based clay through a slab-based method of construction has led me to a unique two-stage process of form development. When I say "core form," I am referring to the first layer of my sculpture. Akin to the skeletal system, but summarized and targeted towards establishing gesture, this layer also includes some muscular elements. The full fleshing of my forms comes in my secondary layer of modeling once my core form has gained sufficient stiffness to be resistant to the pressure of my fingers. Unlike traditional figurative modeling, there is a constant awareness of the nature of the clay medium. At its most basic, the dryness of the piece is always carefully monitored and correlated with the evolution of the construction process to safeguard the piece's stability in relation to gravity as well as proper integration between clay parts and soft clay onto the core. In addition, the thickness of the walls is also carefully monitored to ensure that every part of the piece is properly vented before firing.

Value: In a two-dimensional value drawing, the artist uses black, white, and a series of gray tones to describe light and shadow as it falls onto form. While the artist engaged in drawing practice—the translation of a perceived 3D form into a 2D rendering—uses value to describe form, in the sculpting process we manipulate form to approximate the values we perceive in our photographic blueprints. Through pushing the walls of our sculpture in and out, modeling fresh clay onto the surface of our form, and using a sculpture rake to gradually remove material and integrate forms, we are essentially drawing in space. As previously noted, this is why a bright and diffuse lighting situation works best for sculpture. When you are decoding a two-dimensional reference and using it to construct a three-dimensional rendering, the lightness or darkness of a value in your reference image correlates to forward or backward projection along the z (depth) axis. Dark shadows can also describe the space between two compressing volumes. A shadow indicates that something is receding, or shifting planes, while a highlight signifies either forward projection or a plane shift towards the

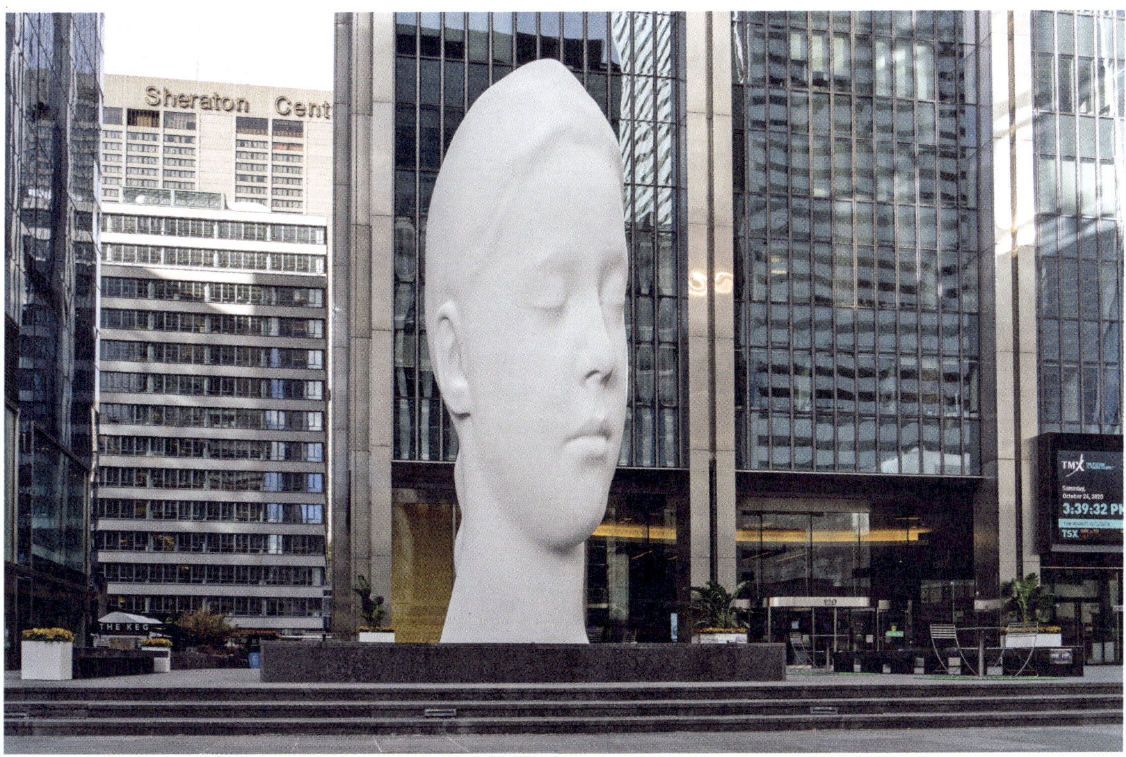

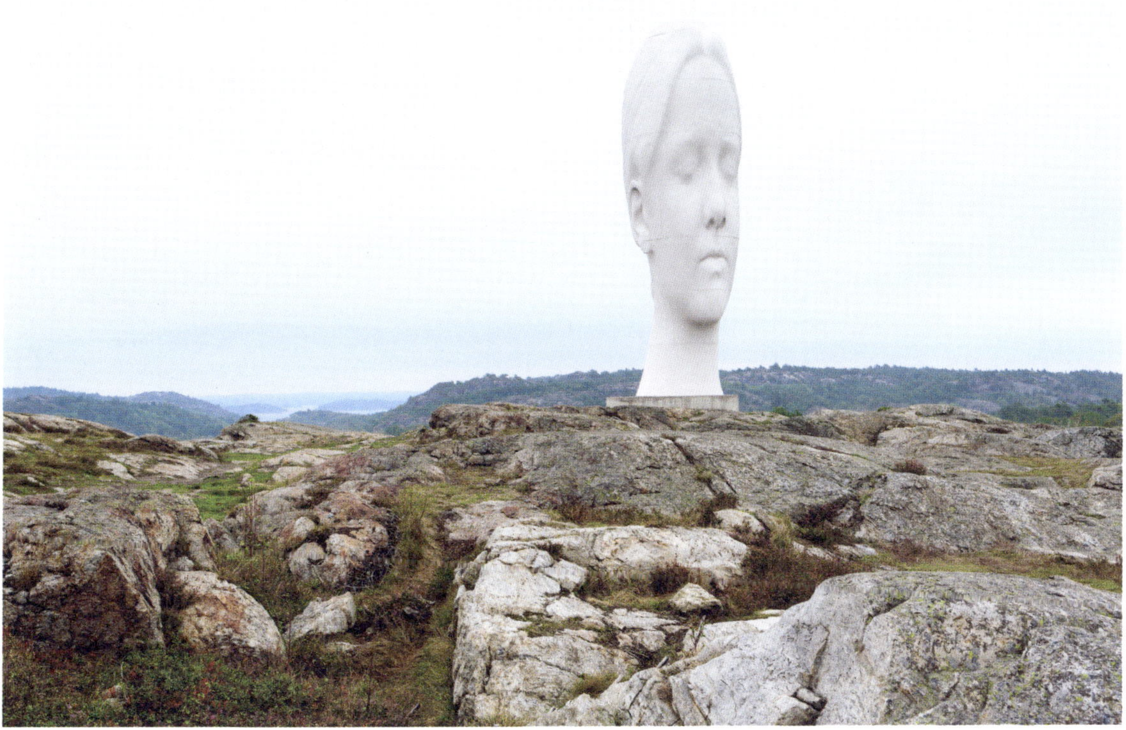

(top) *Dreaming* by Jaume Plensa in Toronto, Canada. *(bottom)* *Anna* by Jaume Plensa in Pilane, Sweden. Jaume Plensa masterfully subdues sculptural values to create softened compositions that come across as dreamlike and evanescent.

light source. Observe the shapes of these shadows and highlights. How dark are they? How diffuse are their edges? How do they inform the logic of the volumes throughout the body?

Shadow lines on the human form: While the majority of the values visible in your reference images transition softly into one another (the effect of light moving over rolling organic form), in some areas of the figure, you will perceive dark, graphic lines. Created by deep recessions, these lines describe edges or folds where two forms meet, such as the intergluteal cleft, the armpit, lines of shadow below the breasts,

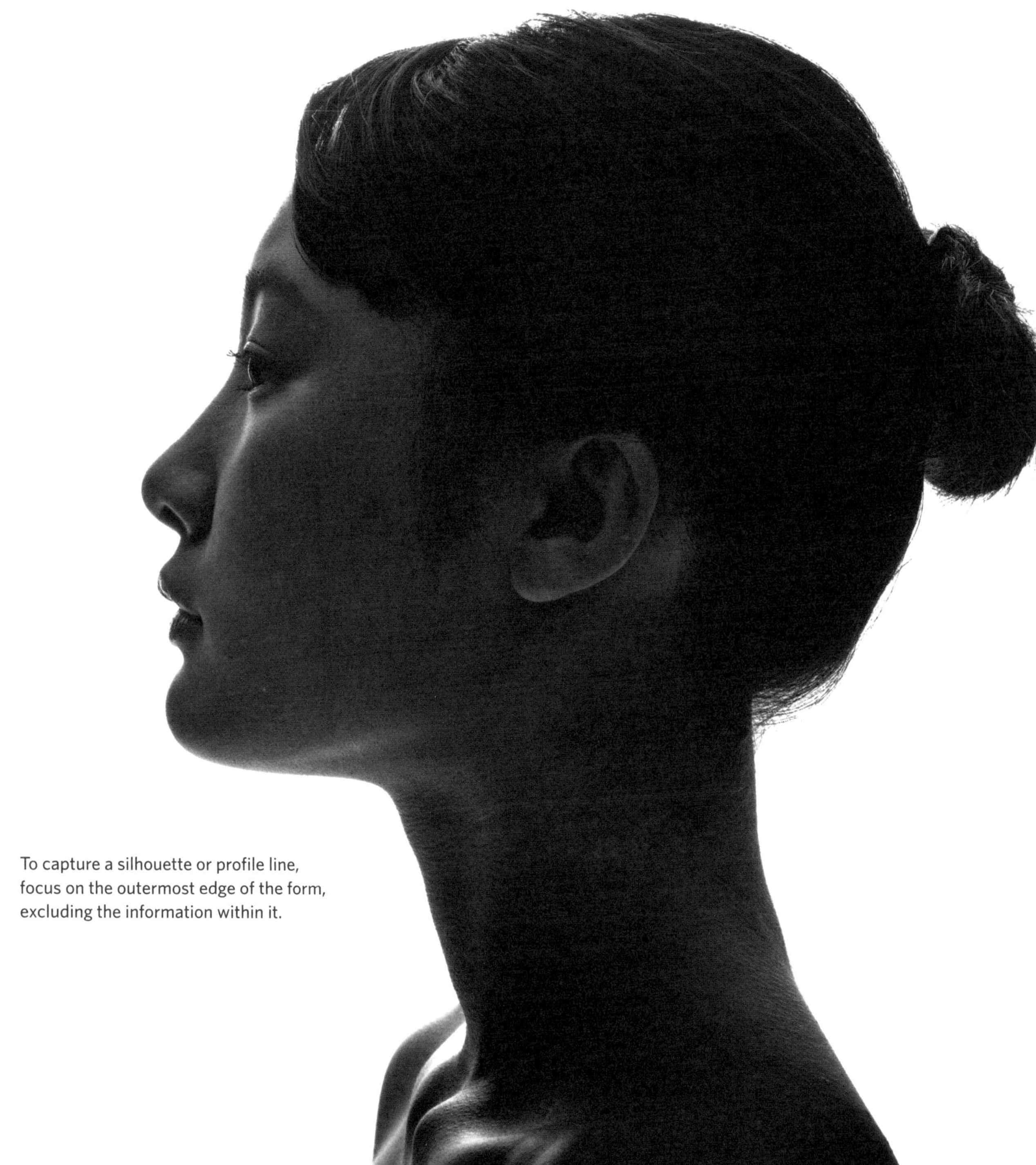

To capture a silhouette or profile line, focus on the outermost edge of the form, excluding the information within it.

etc. I find that using a fettling knife to draw these lines onto the surface of my sculpture helps me map out my forms and gives my eye high-contrast landmarks to use when aligning my figure to my reference images.

Silhouette or external contour lines: It takes time and practice to train your eye to perceive the nuances of light and shadow as they fall onto clay forms because our brains are attuned to contrast; it is much easier for our eyes to grasp and analyze the external contour lines created by the outermost edges of a form, where clay meets air. These contour lines describe organic undulations that are made of interconnected high and low points. Detecting these points and the angles between them enables you to break down form in a preliminary, planar way and establish the basic structure of the composition before introducing curves.

To aid your eye in its analysis, you can emphasize contrast by minimizing the visual noise behind your sculpture. For example, you can work in front of a white or black wall, with the image you are referencing taped off to one side at the same height as your sculpture. With your sculpture on a rolling stand, you can then move it from side to side. When it is in front of the clean wall, stand at a distance and bounce your eyes back and forth from sculpture to reference image, comparing both the silhouettes and the shapes of negative spaces. Next, try rolling your sculpture directly in front of your reference image. Position your body so that your eyes align with both the sculpture and the reference image. Stand back until the edges of your sculpture line up with those on the photograph, note inconsistencies, and reconcile them by either adding or subtracting clay along the edges of your sculpture at this particular viewpoint. Repeat this same process from all four cardinal viewpoints.

Symmetry: In 3D space, we locate form along three axes: the x (horizontal) axis, the y (vertical) axis, and the z (depth) axis. When standing up straight with feet parallel along both x and z axes, the human form is symmetrical across the y axis. Looking at someone in this position from the front view, you can draw a line down the center of their body and see that all components of the body are mirrored across this line of symmetry. Now, visualize that bisecting line projected back into the z axis as a plane. Imagine that you are a bird flying over this person and observe that, even from the top view, y-axis symmetry is preserved.

Often underutilized, the top view of your sculpture can be helpful in reconciling forward projection from left to right sides of the body. It is rare to see a person oriented in such a balanced, static position. Nonetheless, more visually engaging gestures with asymmetry and torque still maintain y-axis symmetry within bony structures such as the head, ribcage, and pelvis, aiding in achieving coherence and balance as you orchestrate your gesture around these fundamental osseous forms.

Planar perception: As you become acquainted with the gesture reflected in your references by reading contours and translating them into a series of intersecting angles, you can use the detection of the high and low points throughout the body, in the round, to establish the primary planes that make up your form. Throughout this stage, your knife and your paddle will aid in articulating generalized planes that respond to your observations. This approach will help you understand the topography of the body in a clear, simple manner by distilling form into its basic geometry. The next step will be to overlay this planar foundation with additional material to articulate the full expression of volumes, evolving them into more complex curvilinear structures.

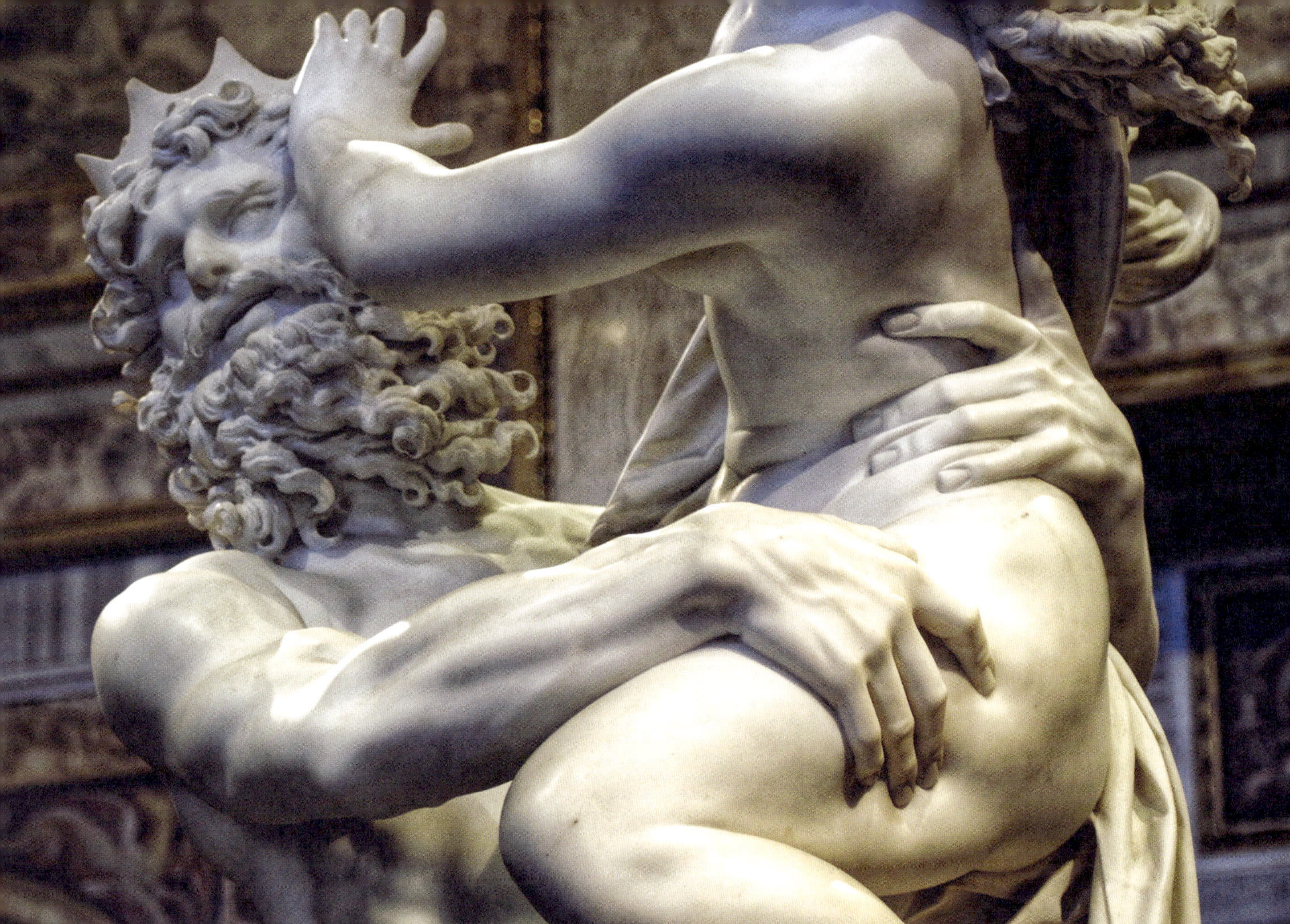

Detail of *Ratto di Proserpina* by Gian Lorenzo Bernini, Galleria Borghese, Rome.

Curvilinear perception: In your process of form development, you will move from large planes into smaller and smaller planes that gradually become unified into curves. While the organic nature of the human form tempts us to bypass planar articulation and move directly into the development of rounded forms, planar perception is essential if you want your figure to appear naturalistic rather than oversimplified or imagined. The angle at which the volume of the cheek slopes back into the ocular cavity is different from the pitch at which it transitions towards the nose. Having these two angles established as planes and then gradually running your sculpture rake over the line where the two planes meet in a cross-hatching motion erodes the geometric-looking quality of a planar sculpture while preserving the anatomical insights you gleaned from your observation and placement of distinct angled planes. This holds true for any given high point on the human form. As I transition from planar perception into curvilinear perception, I add fresh clay that I have softened with water to optimize adherence. In addition to eroding high points with my sculpture rake, I apply thumb-fulls of this soft clay onto the surface of each plane to fully develop my volumes and create the illusion of soft tissue followed by an additional layer of smoothing and fine-tuning involving my terry cloth and brushes in combination with slip. Sometimes the positive curve overlaid onto a plane in fresh clay is *extremely* slight and subtle, while other times it is thicker and more substantial.

Rhythm: At its most basic, rhythm can be defined as a regular, repeated pattern of movement or sound that grounds and activates a composition. In the context of sculpture, this principle of design creates an optical tempo that organizes the way in which our eyes move throughout a three-dimensional composition. The presence of a well-developed rhythmic system is key in creating energetic and compelling gestural renderings.

As you move from planar to curvilinear articulation, stand back occasionally to appreciate the cadence of S curves throughout the body. Look at how S curves move throughout the form and relate to one another, creating a sense of balance from each perspective. From a profile view, the positive curve of a chest is echoed lower down on the back of the form by the gluteal muscles: the upper back curve transverses the pelvic area and creates an S as it meets the curve on the front of the thigh. S curves on the human form are both large and small. For example, an S curve around the ankle gives way to a large S curve that moves throughout the leg. Turn your sculpture gradually and pick up on the different manifestations of S shapes throughout the composition. Let your eye use their cadence and the quality of the curves that comprise the S shapes (shallow/deep, symmetrical/asymmetrical) to develop the series of rhythms that will activate the dynamics of the gesture and propel the eye to actively move across a composition.

Gian Lorenzo Bernini is considered the most important sculptor to emerge from the Baroque period in Rome. Bernini's work epitomizes the power of rhythm to infuse a composition with stirring, dynamic energy created by the masterful interplay of sculpted volumes.

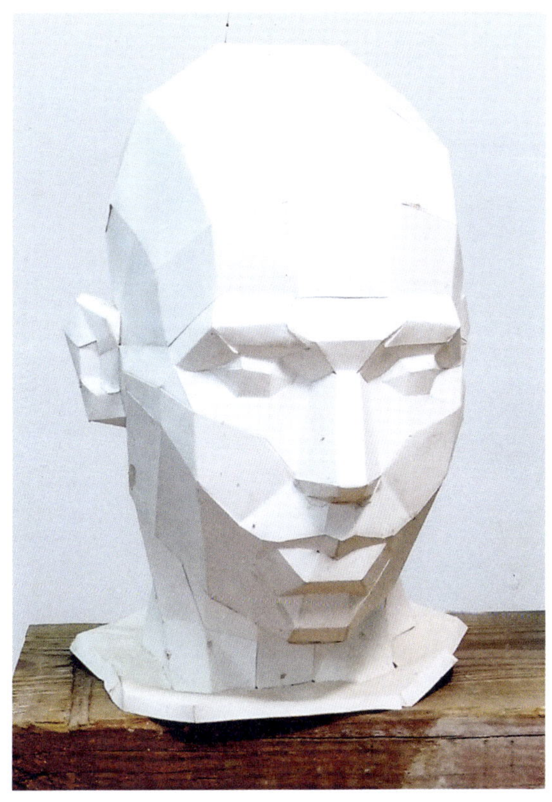

This anatomical model exemplifies the translation of the volumes of the head into planes, facilitating an understanding of the structural relationships below the skin.

Blocking in: In two-dimensional value drawing, it can be useful to block in large shapes of distinct values before adding in smaller-scale details or fluid transitions between values. In the realm of sculpture, blocking relates to the generalized planar breakdown of the primary high and low points that transverse a figure from the four cardinal viewpoints. A focus on big compositional elements at first helps in establishing accurate gesture and proportion— the details come later once structure has been established. As with blocking in the realm of two-dimensional work, this zoomed-out lens of focus limits the quantity of visual information you are taking in and enables you to establish a clear foundation before moving into the realm of tissue.

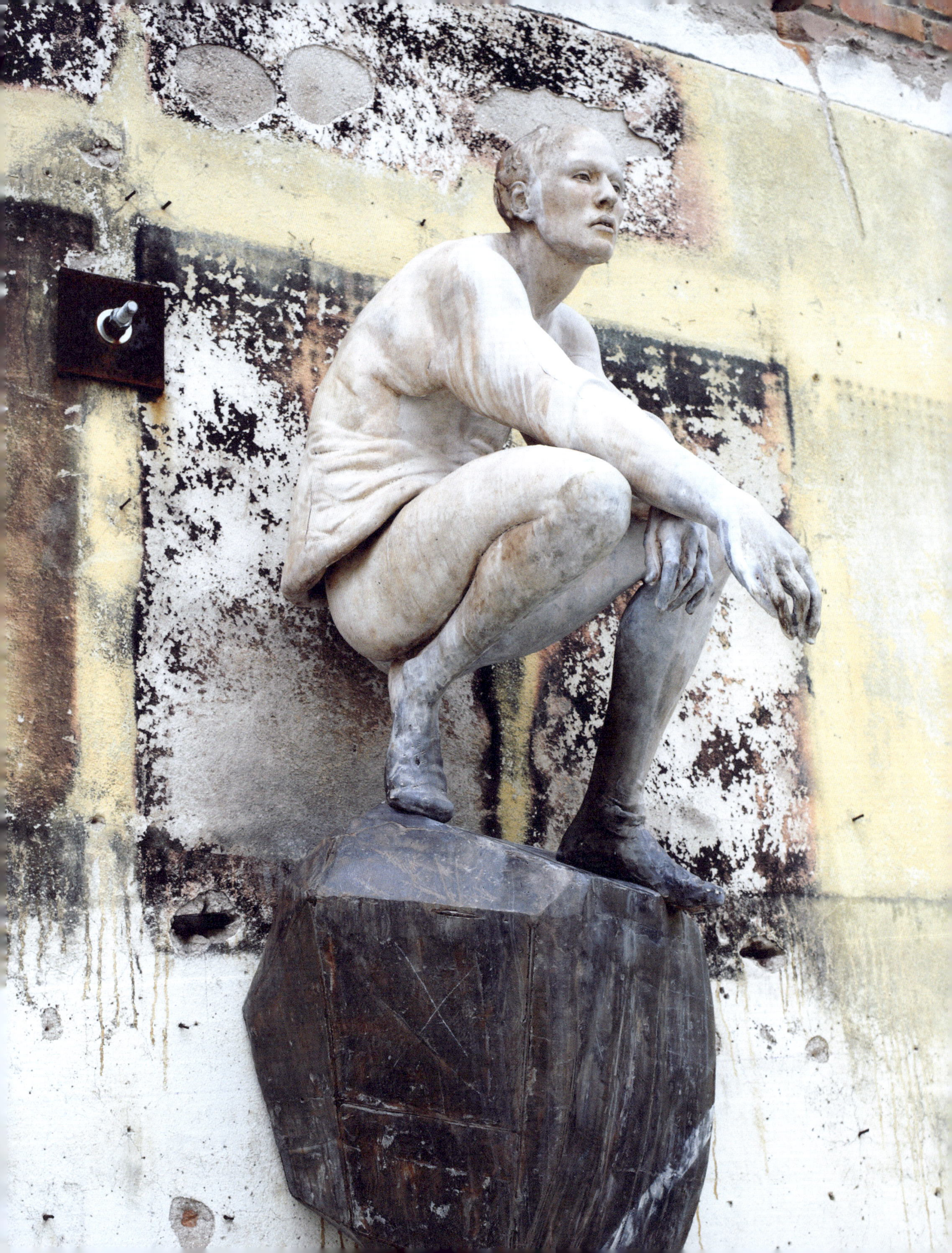

SURFACE DEVELOPMENT, DRYING, AND FIRING

ONE KEY ELEMENT that sets figurative ceramics apart from the overall world of figurative sculpture is its innumerable options for surface treatment. Developing surface treatments has been one of the most challenging aspects of my career in ceramics. I remember spending many hours sculpting a form, only to feel insecure and lost when it came time to transition into the realm of surface development and glazing. It gradually dawned on me that glazing and pigmenting a ceramic surface are essentially re-sculpting through layers of color, texture, and light. Much more than a finishing afterthought, embracing this mindset will help you expand on what is set in motion through our rendered form, helping you complete the overall narrative of a piece. By understanding the possibilities offered by ceramic medium, you can open a limitless range of options to extend the reach of your sculpting and allow the form to coalesce with a surface in ways that amplify its impact.

Cristina Córdova, *Preludios y Partidas,* part of the collection of the Mint Museum of Craft and Design.

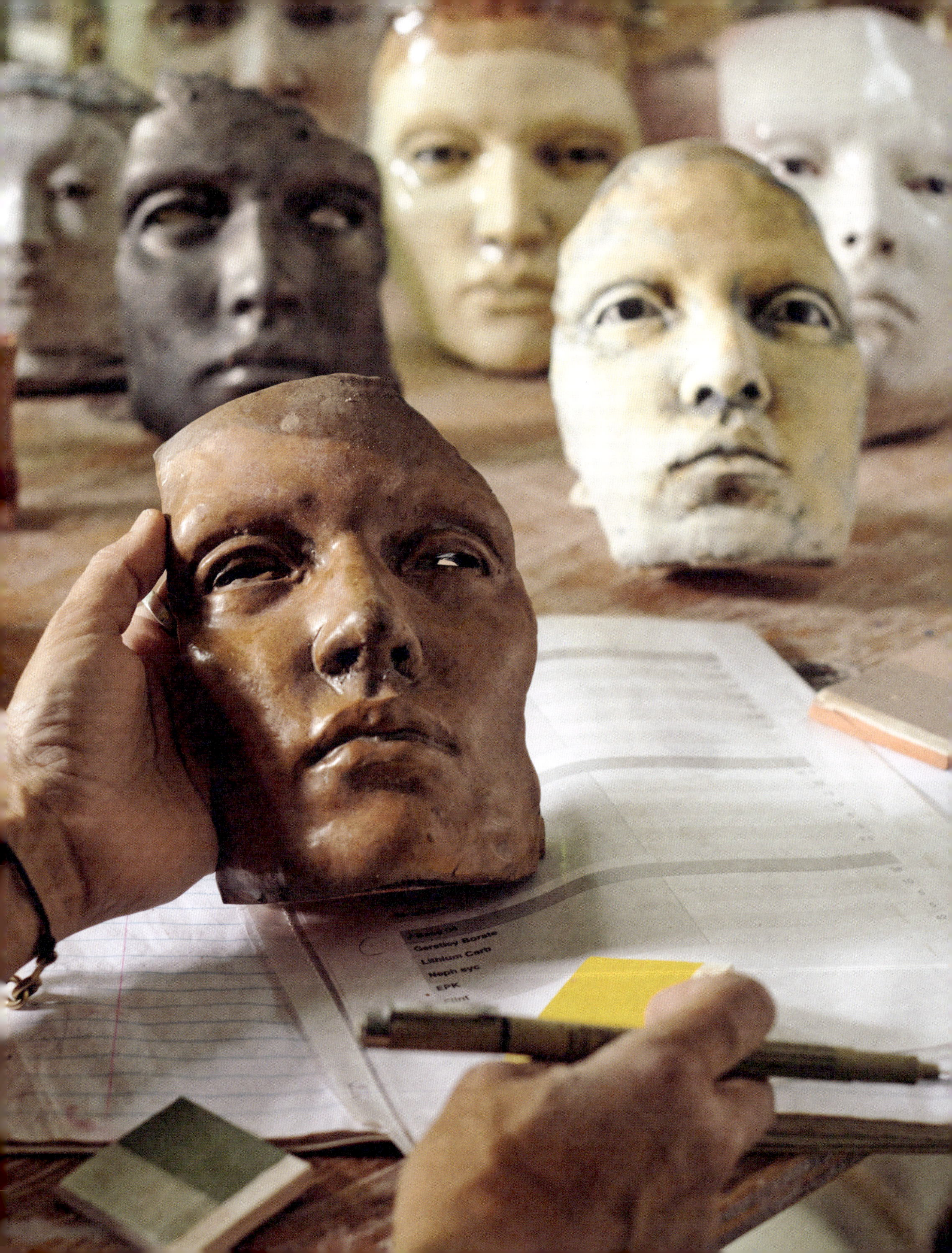
Geratbry Borate
Lithium Carb
Neph syc
EPK
Flint

SURFACE DEVELOPMENT

When thinking about the surface that will overlay the sculpting, I begin to make decisions before I start the form, considering the color of my clay body and the range of temperatures that it will fire to. For example, I have surface combinations that I will develop over red clay, capitalizing on the richness of the surface by covering it with glazes that will be in dialogue with that red, revealing it around the edges and allowing it to warm up the piece. Conversely, I have different options for white or buff-colored clays, which preserve the vibrancy of colors. These combinations also change depending on the temperature I will be firing to. I normally low fire my surfaces between cone 04 (1945°F [1062°C]) and cone 2 (2088°F [1142°C]), occasionally venturing into cone 5 (2167°F [1186°C]).

The key thing to understand is that in the realm of electric-kiln fired ceramics, the kiln environment offers no atmospheric impact other than heat. Therefore, the most interesting surfaces must be researched and staged—and usually involve layering and multiple firings.

In addition, it is important to keep in mind the dialogue with the dynamic figurative forms that comprise our sculpture. You never want the surface treatment to dull, confuse, or mute your form's power. To this end, how you apply your surfaces, be it via brush or sprayed, thick or thin, will have a big impact on the results. These applications strategies may vary within the same piece to respond to the evolving volumes and to protect detail.

This might sound like a lot to figure out and to juggle, but surface development does not have to be intimidating. There are simple, straightforward ways to achieve great results. For example, when I first started working with the figure, I would finish most of my surfaces with oxides (mostly copper and red iron oxide washes), later introducing underglazes. I felt I could control these materials more easily. Eventually I entered fully into the realm of glazing through a process of trial and error that developed alongside my sculptural practice, with plenty of testing.

Testing is a very important part of your ongoing exploration into surface development. Because working with the figure is such a laborious undertaking, when combined with the many variables that could affect how a piece looks after firing, it is key to experiment with lower stakes. I recommend developing a series of tiles that you can use to try different surface combinations, informing how you'll finish your sculptures and improving your chances of success.

When I test surfaces, I do it in several phases. First, I will use tiles that are simple, essentially a textured slab standing upright. Here I just want to get a sense of the color, the reflective quality of the glaze or surface, and how it flows with gravity when fired. After testing a large array of different recipes on these tiles, I will move to the second phase, which involves tiles that are a little bit more articulated, usually formed as an abstracted torso and face or just a face. These are generated through a plaster press mold that helps expedite the creation of multiple tiles. With these figurative tiles, I'm starting to introduce more depth in how I'm staging these surfaces, usually applying washes before layering glazes so that I can really begin to see the dynamics between the layers in the context of the figure. As I accumulate interesting possibilities, I start to discern which combinations will work best for skin and which ones could be used for clothing or other parts of the composition.

Javier Marin

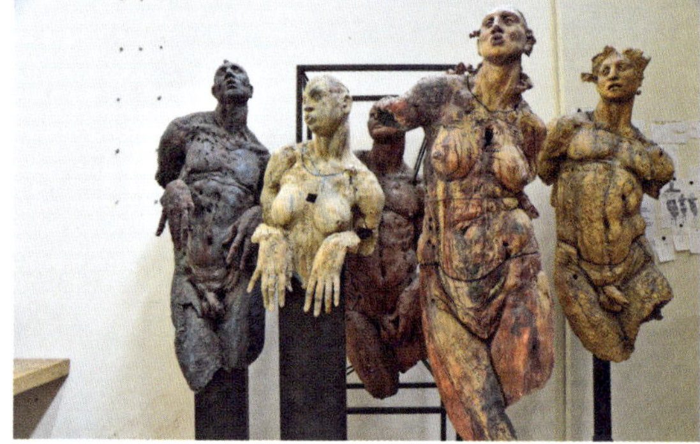

Javier Marín, *Por aqui, por aqui.* Courtesy of the artist.

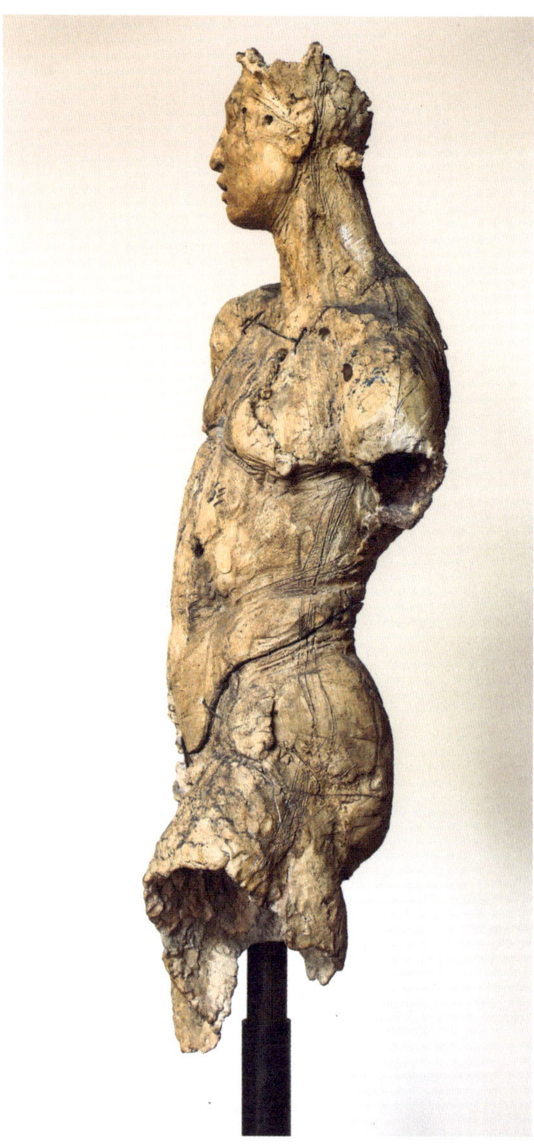

Javier Marín, *Torso hombre.* Courtesy of the artist.

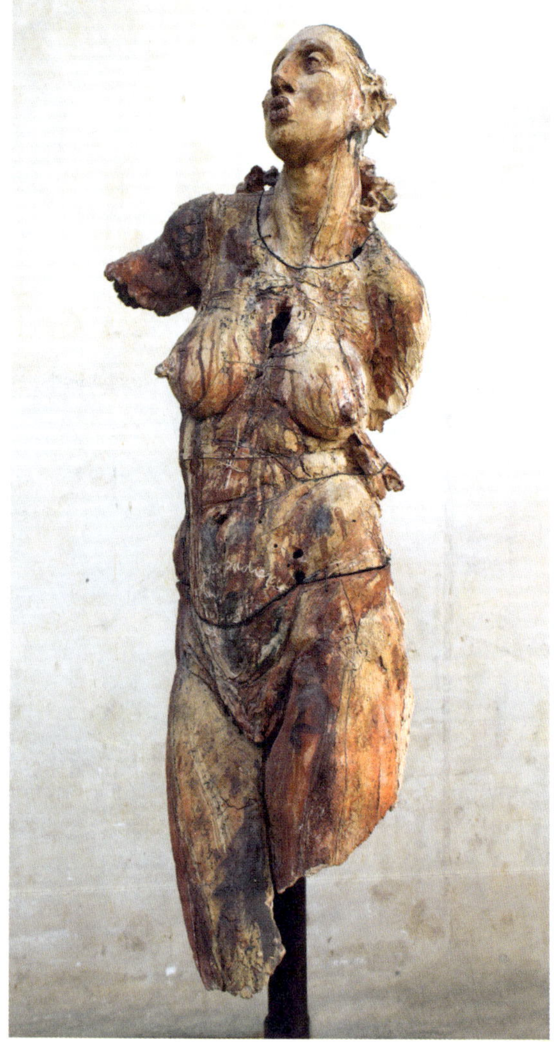

Javier Marín, *Por aqui, por aqui.* Courtesy of the artist.

Expressive, dynamic renderings, the use of various scales, and the orchestration of multiples within a space all play a role in the extraordinary impact of Marín's sculptural interpretations in the world.

Marín's figures speak to the shared reality of being human in bodies that, as vessels, accumulate the incessant marks of life.

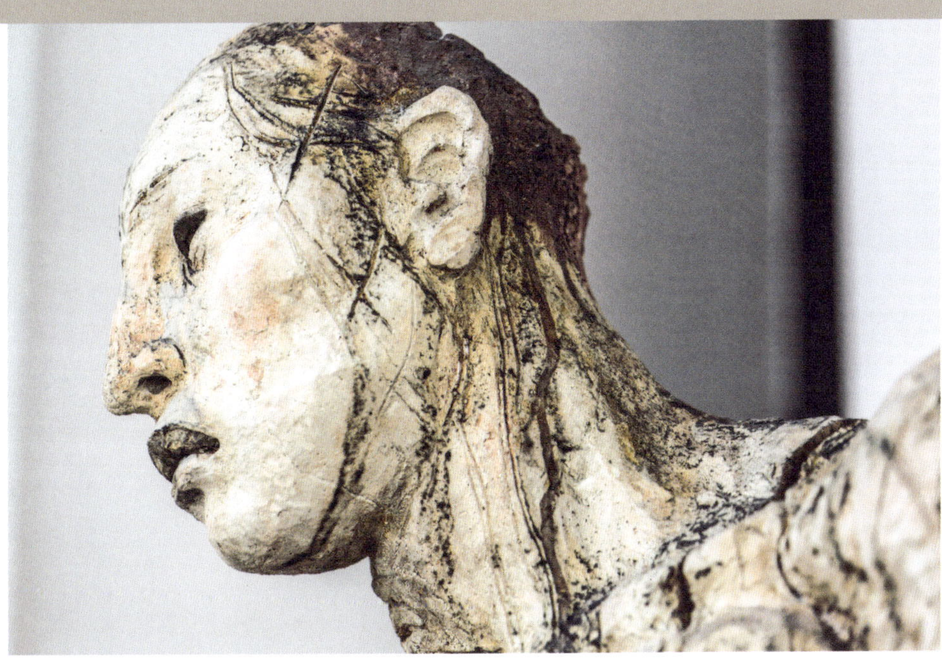

Javier Marín, *Torso de hombre, yo no se.* Courtesy of the artist.

Marín is a master at evoking a sense of pathos and power in his heroic renditions of the body. His potent manipulations of the human figure infuse his compositions with an energy that appears to be perceptive, invoking into the illusion of sentiency.

Cathartic textures add a patina that speaks of time, experience, and embattlement.

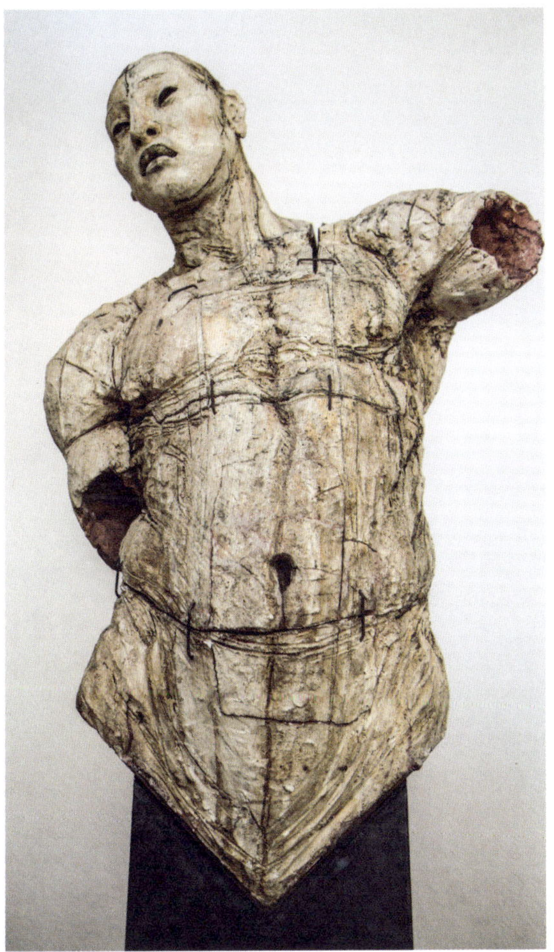

Javier Marín, *Torso hombre.* Bernardo Arcos.

Grzegorz Gwiazda

The artist's profound knowledge of the human form and its potential for expression brings forth a powerful body of work that walks a fine line between the exquisite and disturbing. I consider him one of the most important sculptors of our generation.

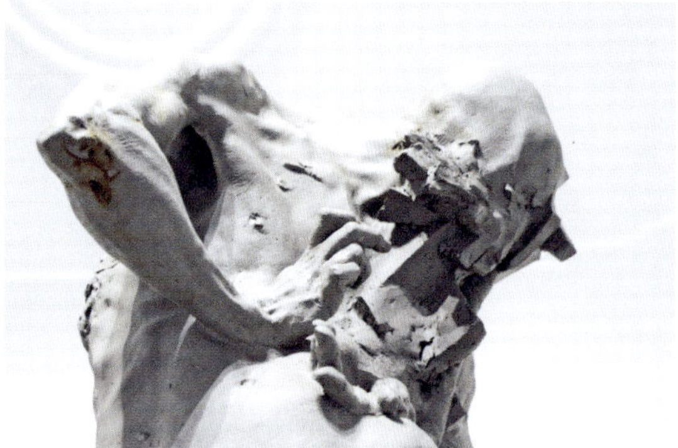

(*above and right*) **Grzegorz Gwiazda**, *Bad Fruit*. Courtesy of the artist.

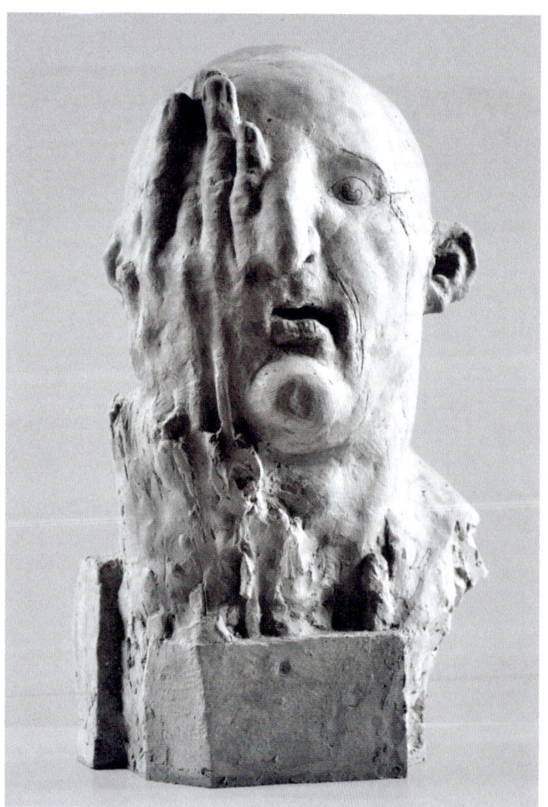

Grzegorz Gwiazda, *Teacher.* Courtesy of the artist.

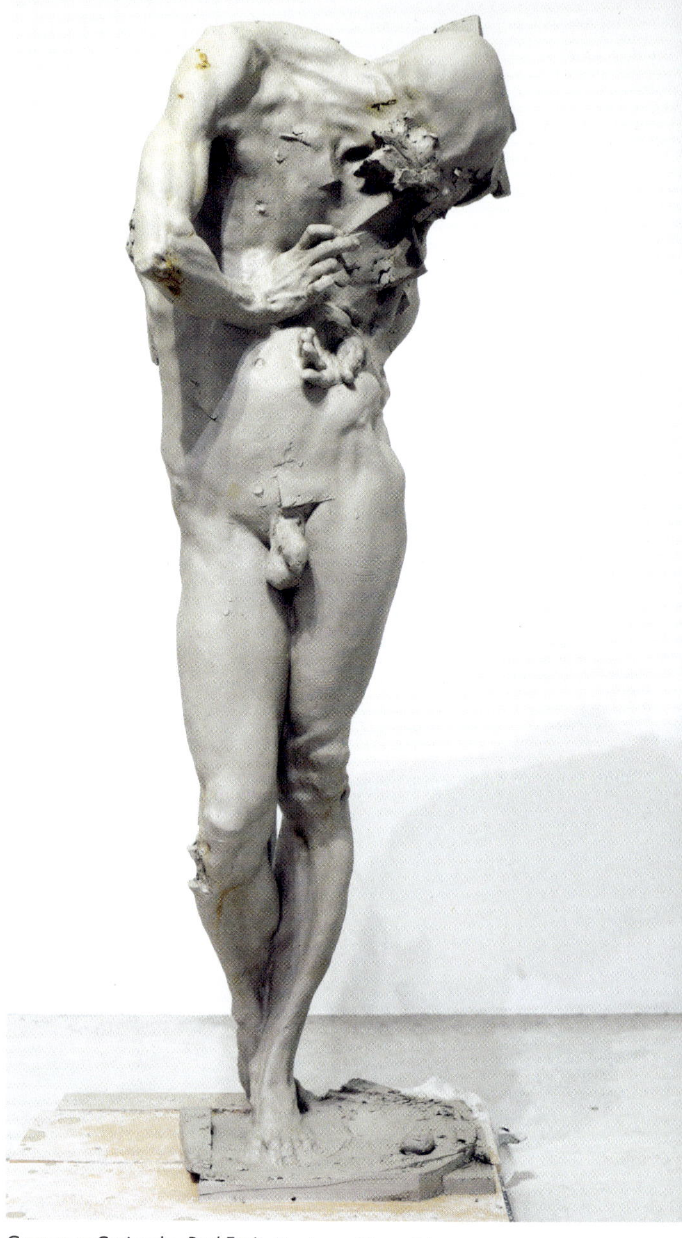

Grzegorz Gwiazda, *Bad Fruit*. Courtesy of the artist.

A master at gestural transmission, Gwiazda's compositions speak across material and conceptual realms, revealing a vivid emotional range achieved through a profound attention to the dynamics of the body, captured and amplified by the clay.

In his work, forms appear and disappear, slipping in and out of focus, at times transgressing the natural logic of the figure and allowing the viewer space to decode the poetics of form.

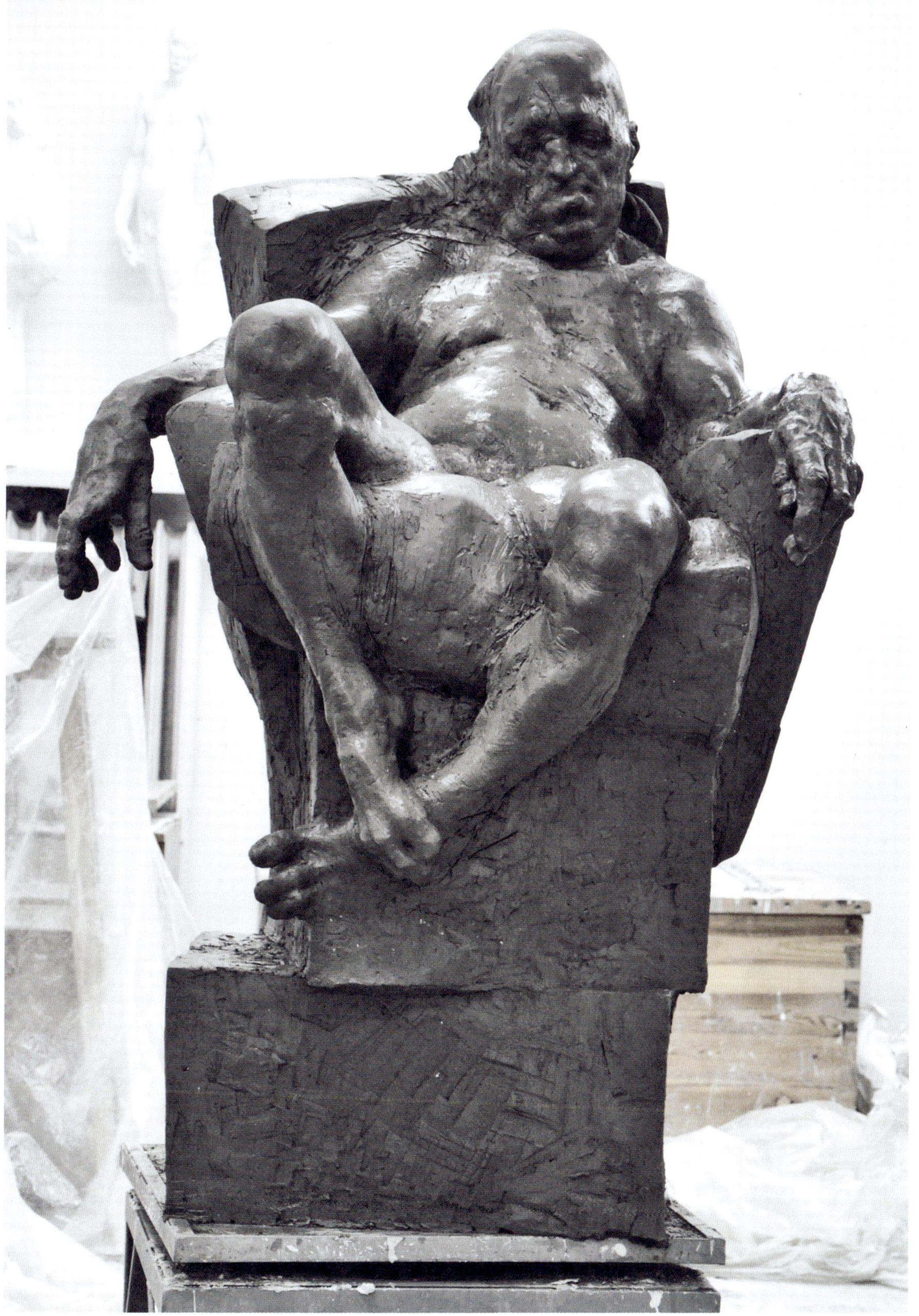

Grzegorz Gwiazda, *Sitting Man.* Courtesy of the artist.

DRYING AND FIRING

SHRINK SLABS

When working large, I build on top of a shrink slab, which is loaded in the kiln with the piece and fired underneath it. A shrink slab is a perforated clay waster slab that will buffer the friction between the bottom of a heavy piece and the kiln shelf to avert cracking and warping. It is made of the same clay body as the sculpture and will shrink at the same rate during the firing. To make one, I roll a slab about ½ inch (1.3 cm) thick and slightly larger than the footprint of my sculpture. Then I pierce or drill holes all over the slab spaced every 1 to 2 inches (2.5 to 5 cm), and let it stiffen some before building on top of it. I also put a layer of sand or grog between the shrink slab and the kiln shelf. This layer of sand is very helpful for sliding a sculpture off of a cart or work board and onto the kiln shelf, and it also helps the shrink slab contract easily during the firing. Silica sand, sold as "play sand" at hardware stores, is good for this purpose.

FIRING SUPPORTS

There are some sculptures that require the help of external supports during firing to prevent sagging or cracking. Primarily, these are pieces that have elements projecting off of the main form, such as a figure with an outstretched arm, or pieces that are carefully balanced with a lot of mass supported on a relatively small base, such as a standing figure. Even a standing figure that is fired laying down may require support, if the head, arm, or leg does not make contact with the kiln shelf. In these situations, the ideal supports are those made from the same clay body as the sculpture, because they will shrink at the exact same rate during the firing. You can use clay slabs to make standing cylinders, perforate them with holes for quick drying, and

place them under cantilevered portions of the sculpture. For taller supports, another option is to stack soft kiln bricks into a tower and top it with a smaller clay support that makes contact with the sculpture. If a figure sculpture is laying down in the kiln and needs just a short support under an appendage, it is often possible to put just a small piece of kiln brick or a pile of sand under it.

Once a sculpture is glazed, it becomes harder to support during firing, since the glaze will stick to anything it touches. In this case, you can use the same kind of supports, but top them with commercially available firing stilts so that only their small metal prongs make contact with the glaze surface. If the piece has already been bisque fired at or above the glaze temperature, it won't continue to shrink, so any kiln furniture can be used for support under the stilts. If the entire surface of a sculpture is glazed, the whole thing can be fired with stilts between it and the kiln shelf. Just remember if the piece is heavy, you may need many stilts spread out to support its weight.

DRYING

Most of my sculptures are loaded into the kiln when they are "leather-hard," before they are completely dry. At this stage, the clay is strong and not yet brittle, so it is an ideal time to move the piece. Drying can continue after the sculpture is safely in the kiln. If you have time, you can allow the sculpture to air-dry completely before starting the kiln by leaving the lid open with a fan blowing across the top to help circulate air. You can also start the kiln immediately on a drying cycle if you need to speed up this process. Even if the clay is totally dry, it is important to use a kiln drying cycle

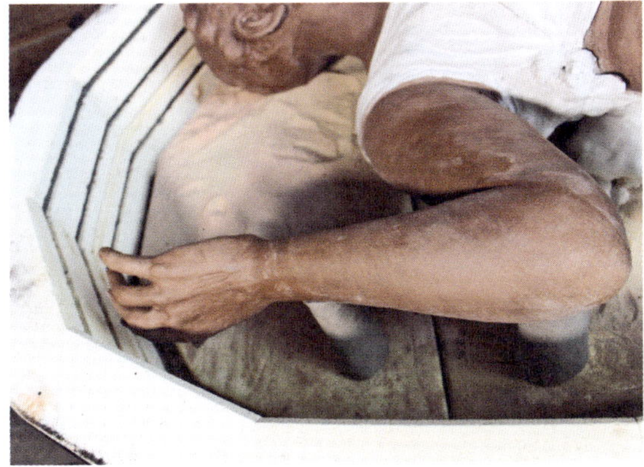

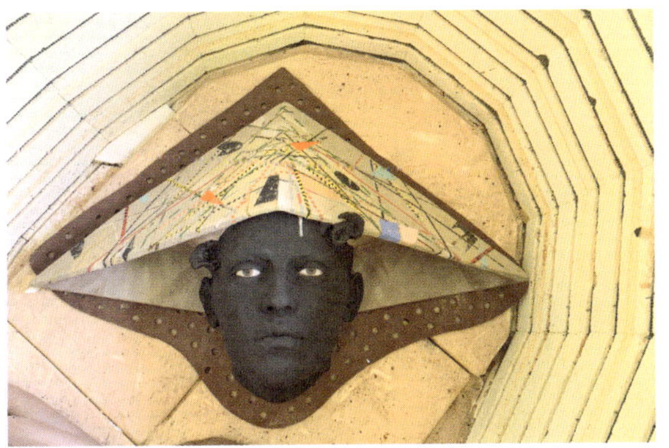

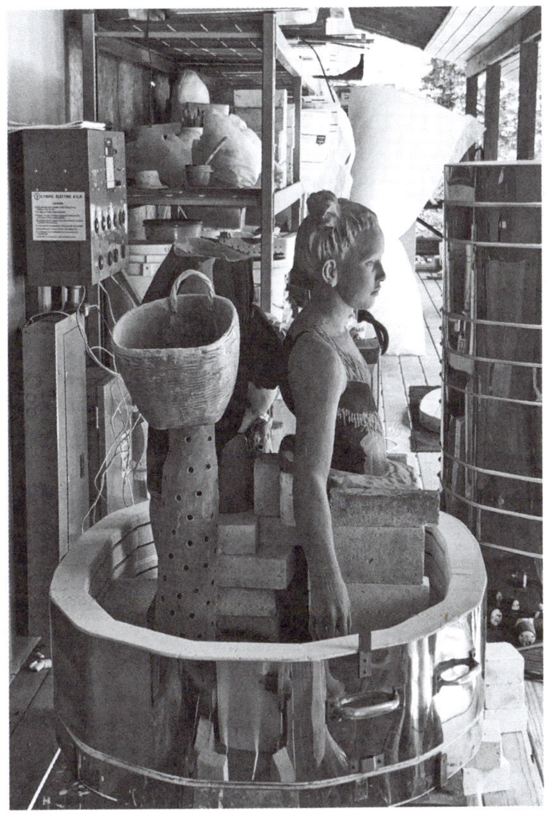

before the true firing begins. The key is to raise the temperature gently and hold it as long as necessary at 180°F to 190°F (82°C to 88°C). This is safely below the 212°F (100°C) boiling point of water, at which point moisture in the clay can turn to steam and cause a crack or explosion as it escapes. How long you hold your sculpture at this temperature depends on how large and thick it is and how dry it is when you start the kiln. For my largest sculptures, if fairly wet to start, I may hold this preheat for up to 60 hours. For small, dry pieces it might be as little as 2 hours. A helpful way to gauge dryness is to hold a mirror or piece of glass to one of the kiln's top peep holes and see if it fogs up with condensation. If it does, there is still moisture in the kiln, and you should probably continue the drying cycle. It never hurts to dry a sculpture too long, but rushing this stage can be disastrous! It pays to err on the side of caution after you have invested so much time in making your artwork.

FIRING

After the drying cycle, you will move into the real firing. If using a digitally controlled electric kiln, the initial drying at 180°F to 190°F (82°C to 88°C) is usually programmed along with the rest of the firing, so the kiln will continue straight into the firing after that period. For smaller sculptures, it can be okay to use a pre-set "Slow" program on most kilns, but for larger pieces, you will need to program a slower, gentler firing to keep your sculpture from cracking during the firing or cooling. The paper clay I use for large-scale sculptures can be fired all the way to cone 10, but I choose to fire only to cone 2, which gives it sufficient strength for a sculpture. Firing below the point of full vitrification (when clay particles fuse to become glass-like) puts less stress on the piece, keeps it from shrinking as much, and reduces the likelihood of cracks and warping. Here are my recommended firing schedules.

(Like the standing figure demonstrated in this book.)

Segment	Ramp (deg/hr)	Temp °F	Hold (hrs)	Notes
1	50	180	6–20	6–8 hours if the piece is fully dry to the touch, up to 20 if your piece is still leather-hard, or extremely thick. This hold is safely below water's boiling temperature.
2	75	250	1–2	Length of hold depends on the thickness of the piece. This hold ensures all the water is forced out of the clay.
3	120	1000		It's okay to climb a little faster here.
4	75	1200		This slow ramp takes place during quartz inversion. In ceramics, this refers to the sudden volume change crystalline quartz particles experience as they pass up and down through 1063°F (573°C). Cracks during firing are often related to this transition.
5	180	2100		It's okay to climb a little faster towards the end. After reaching peak temperature, the kiln will cool naturally.

EXTRA SLOW CONE 2 FIRING FOR VERY LARGE CLAY SCULPTURES

Segment	Ramp (deg/hr)	Temp °F	Hold (hrs)	Notes
1	50	180	20–60	20 hours if the piece is dry to the touch, up to 60 if you are starting while clay is still leather-hard, or if your piece is extremely thick. This hold is safely below water's boiling temperature.
2	75	250	6–8	Length of hold depends on the thickness of the piece. This hold ensures all the water is forced out of the clay.
3	100	1000		It's okay to climb a little faster here.
4	70	1200		This slow ramp is during quartz inversion. In ceramics, this refers to the sudden volume change crystalline quartz particles experience as they pass up and down through 1063°F (573°C). Cracks during firing are often related to this transition.
5	110	2100		It's okay to climb a little faster here.
6	-250	1200		This begins the down-fire cooling period that allows temperatures to equalize in pieces with a lot of thermal mass.
7	-50	300		This final segment takes the clay gently through quartz and cristobalite inversions. Cristobalite is a less stable form of quartz. Cristobalite inversion occurs in cooling clay bodies at around 437°F and causes a sudden volume change. After this segment, the kiln will finish cooling naturally.

Gallery

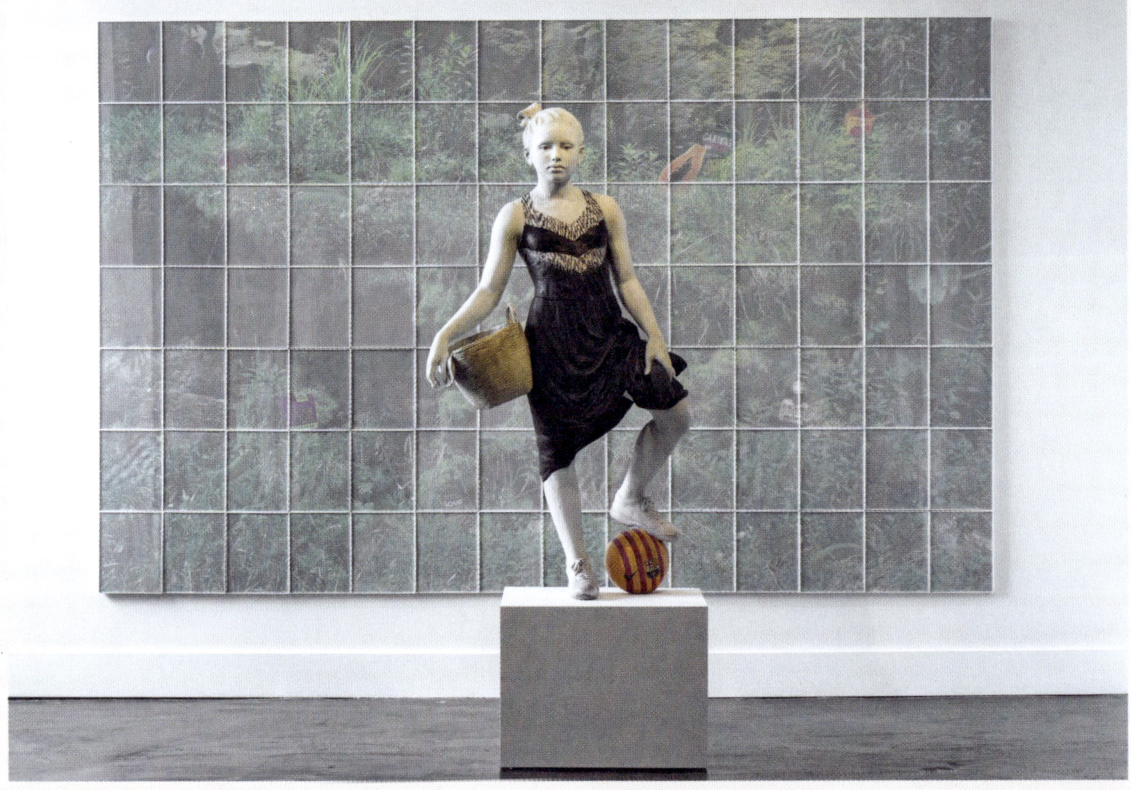

Cristina Córdova, *Busca, recoje.* Lydia Bittner-Baird.

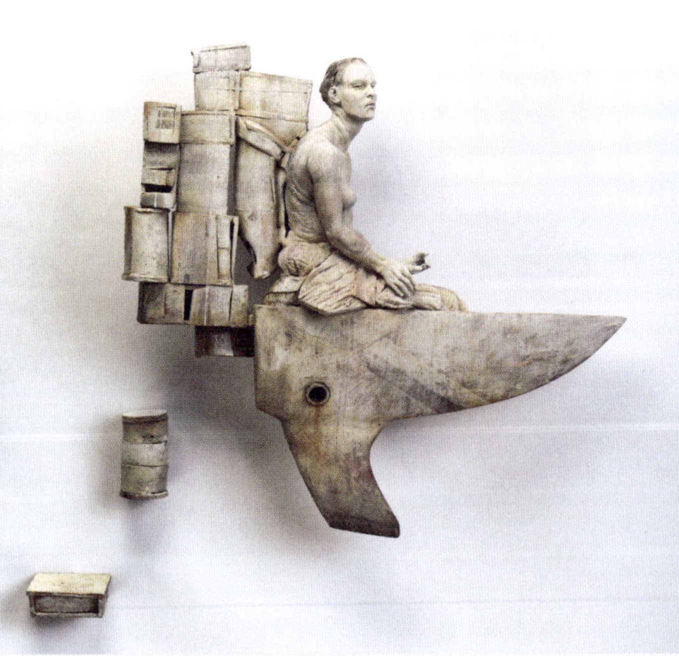

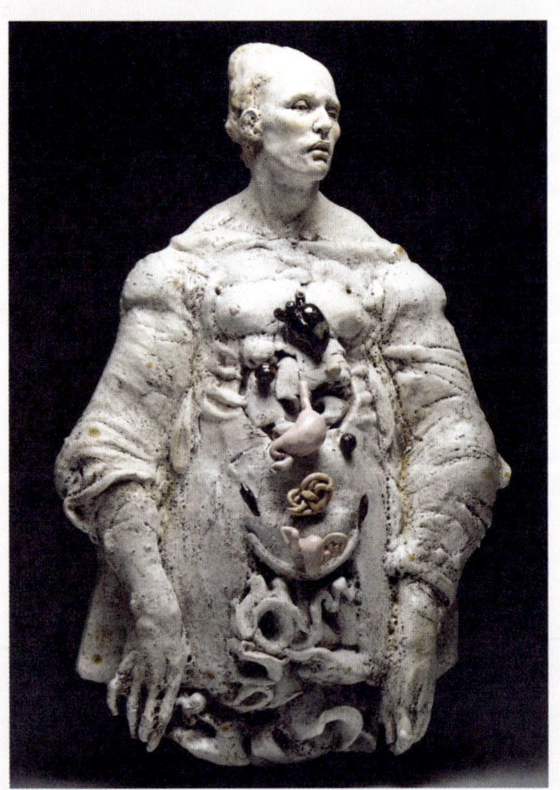

Cristina Córdova, *Nave.* Courtesy of the artist.

(right) Cristina Córdova, *Adentro.* Courtesy of the artist.

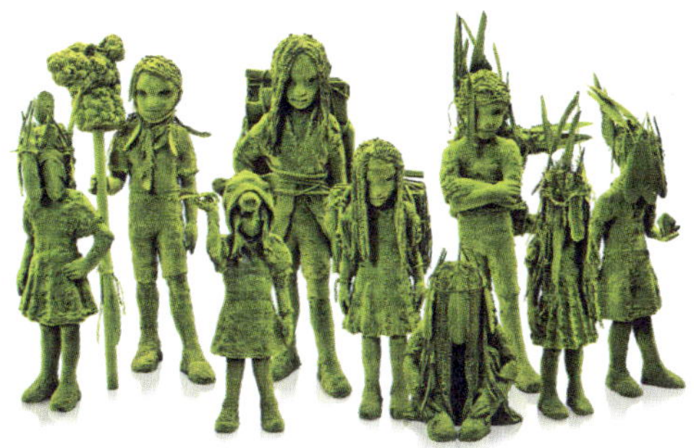

Kim Simonsson, *Group Image of Moss People.* Jefunne Gimpel.

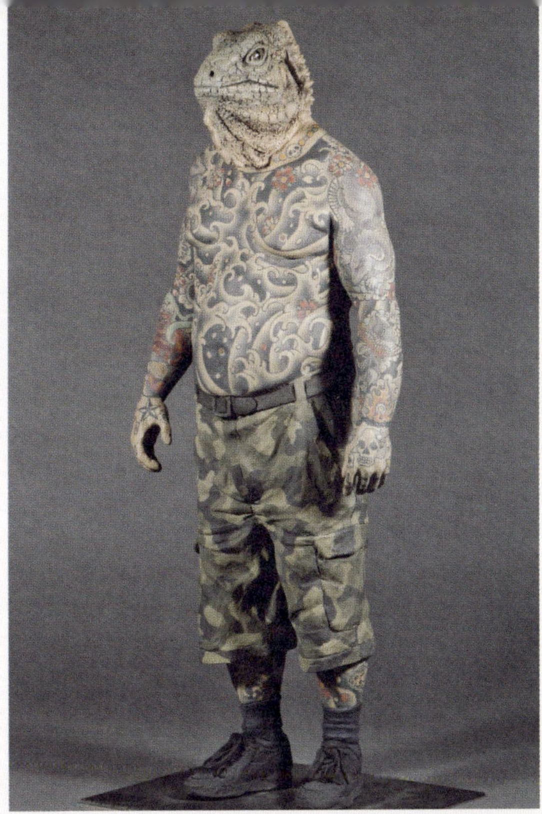

Alessandro Gallo, *Tattoo Iguana.* Courtesy of the artist.

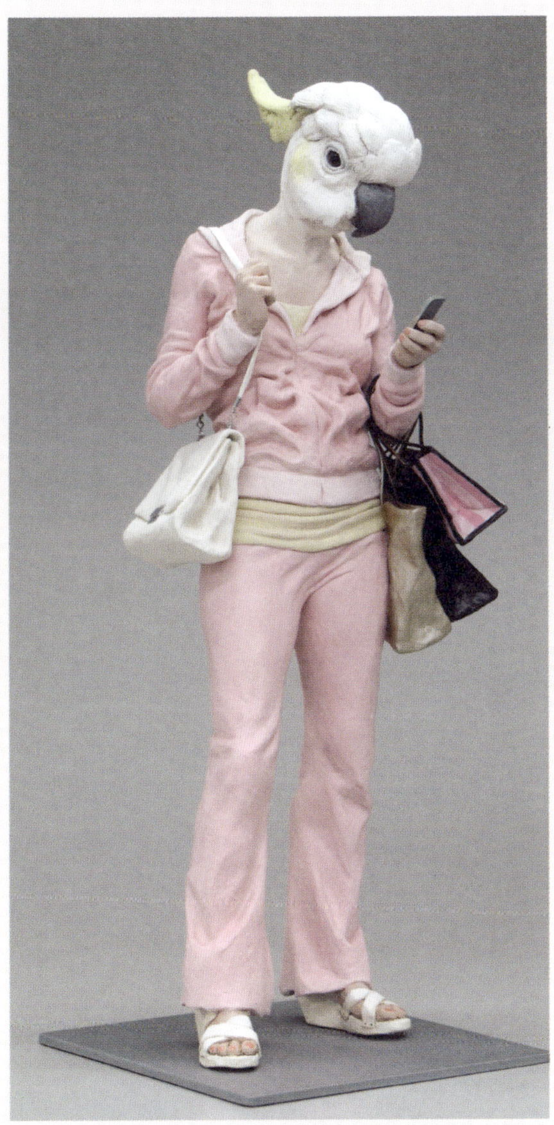

Alessandro Gallo, *Whatever.* Courtesy of the artist.

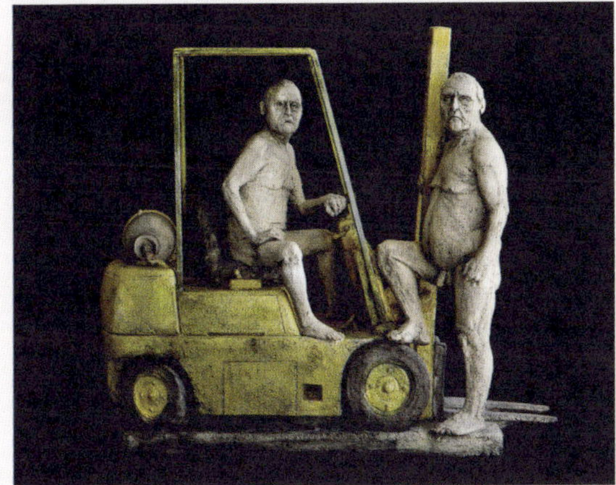

Lars Calmar, *Workers.* Bjarne Stæhr.

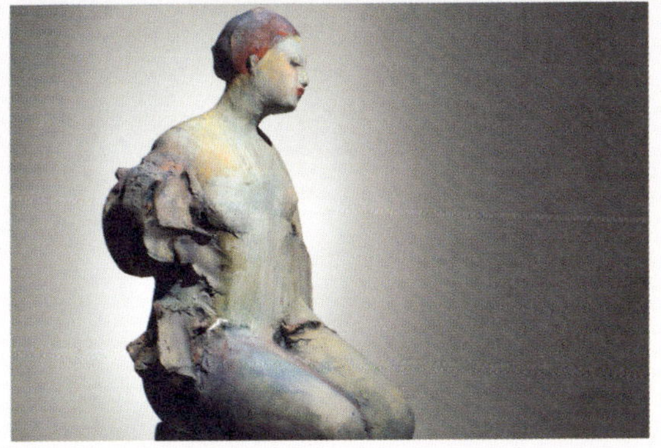

Michelle Gregor, *Gregor Guardian.* J. Wilfred Jones.

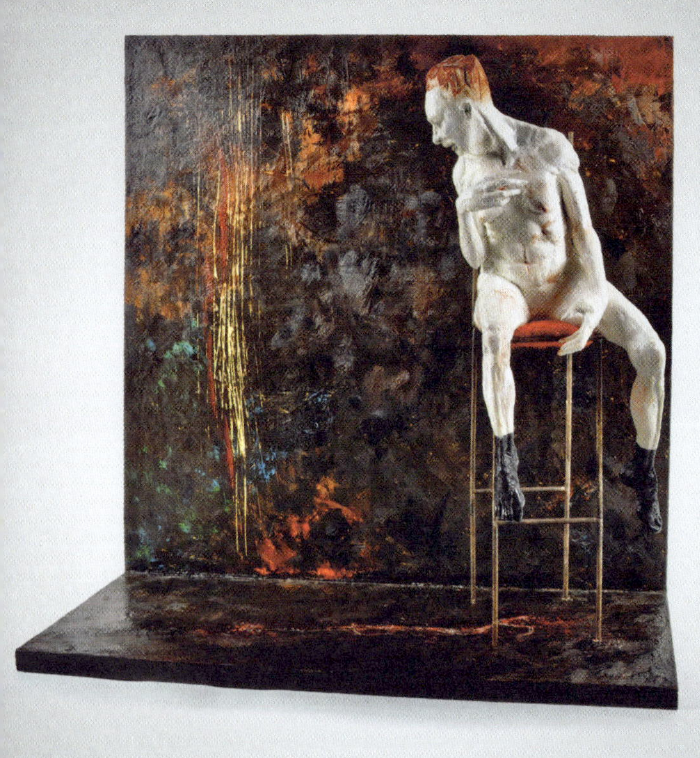

Melisa Cadell, *Realization.* Courtesy of the artist.

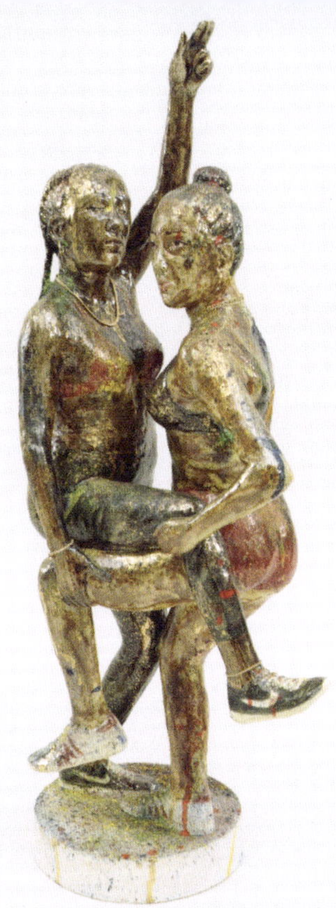

Claire Partington, *Innamorati.* Dan Weill.

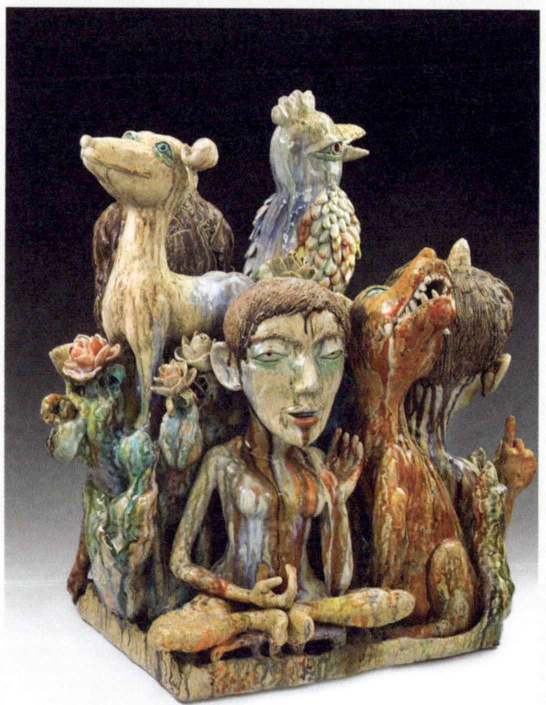

Sunkoo Yuh, *One More Chance.* Kim Chan-soo and Choi Kyu-bok.

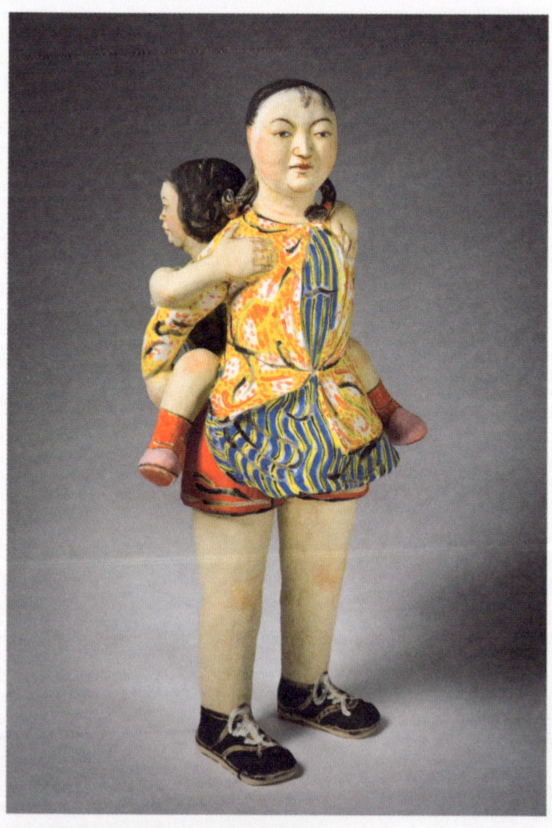

Akio Takamori, *Girl in Yellow Jacket.*
RJ Sánchez | Solstream Studios.

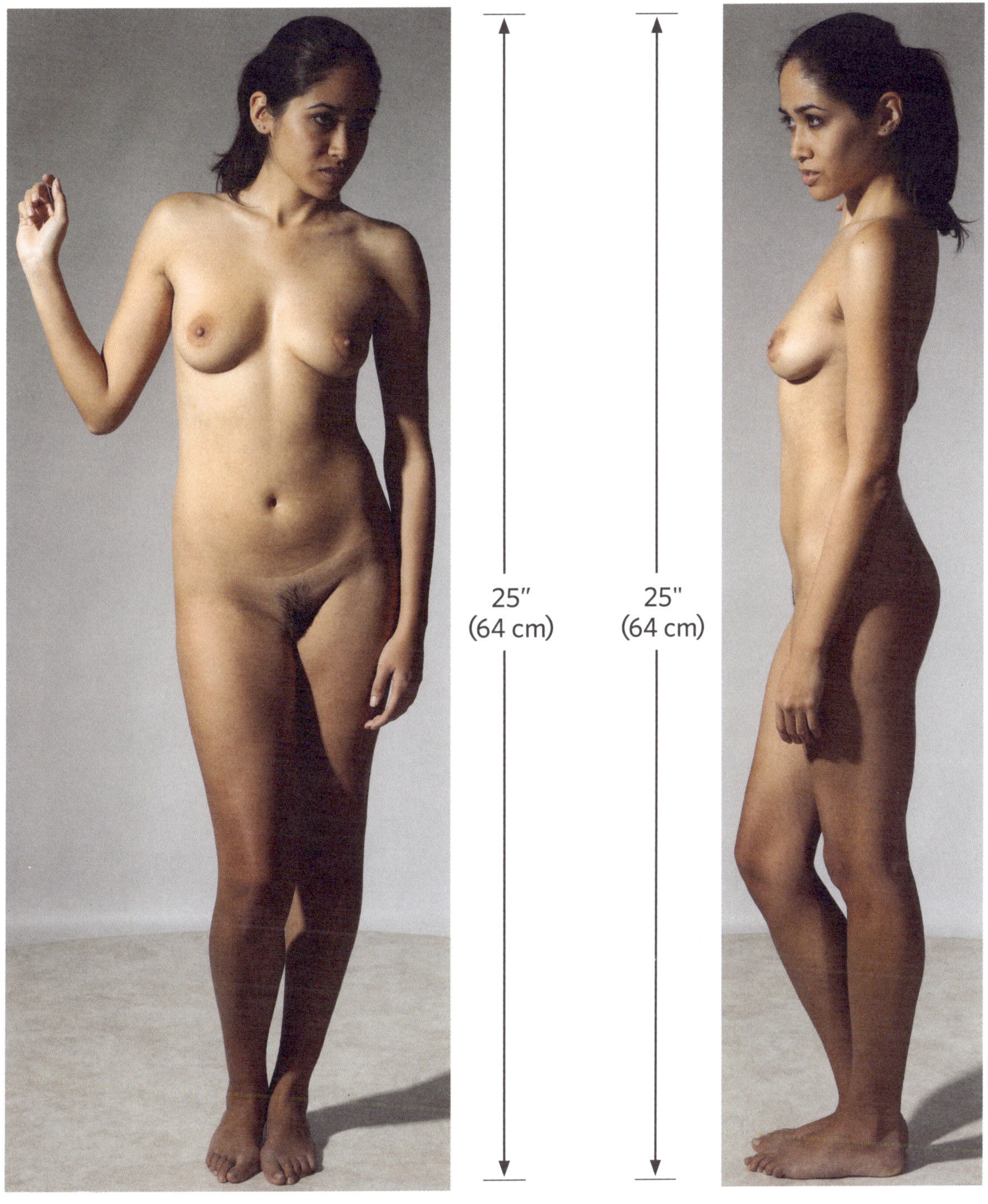

Please scan and resize to 25" (64 cm) before printing.
For more information follow the additional resources link at the end of the book.

All reference photographs are from the photo set titled jenb_407 by Live Model Books LLC/ Douglas Johnson, Publisher found at Posespace.com.

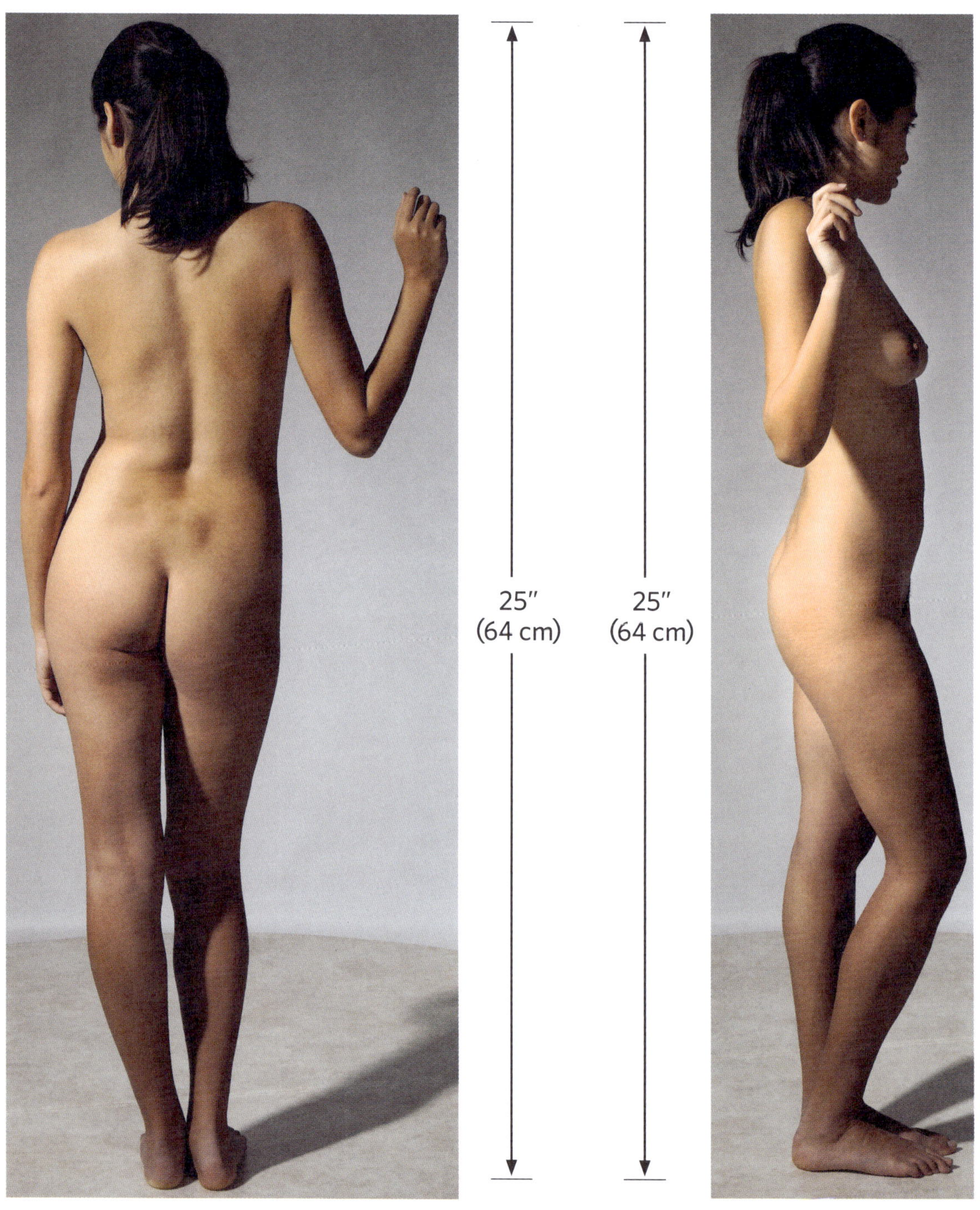

Please scan and resize to 25" (64 cm) before printing.
For more information follow the additional resources link at the end of the book.

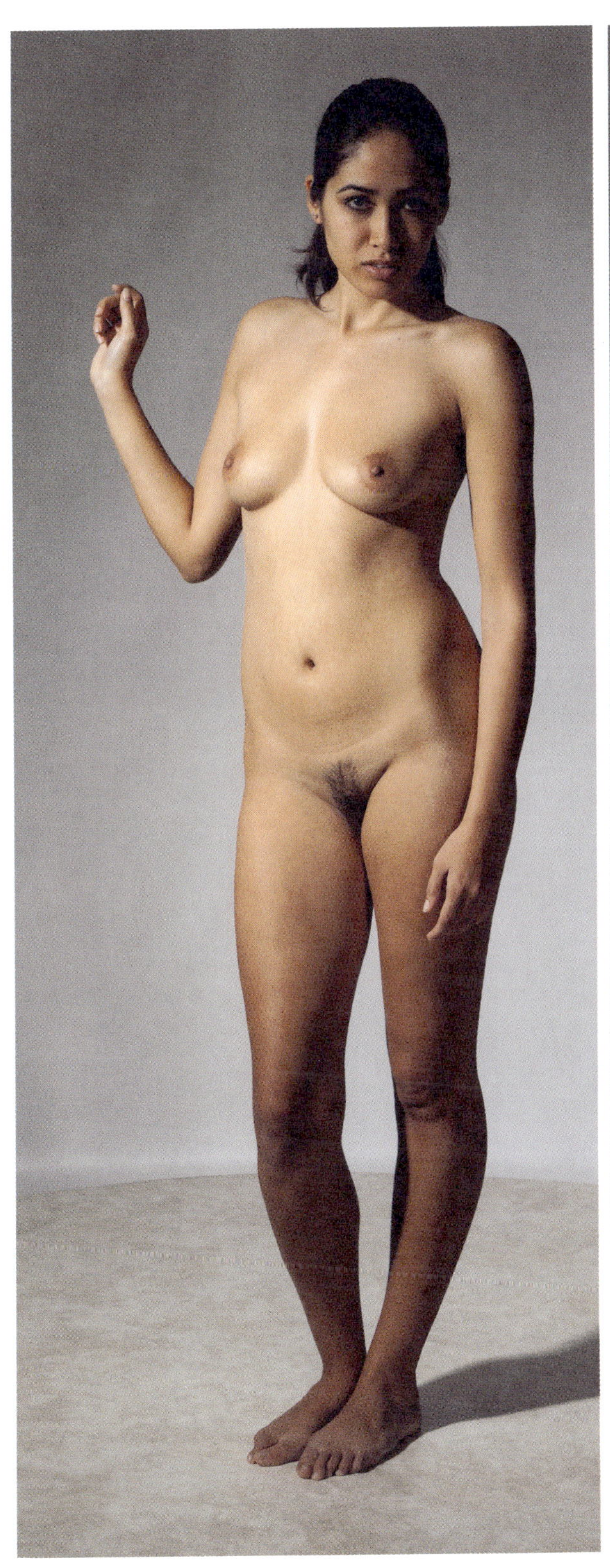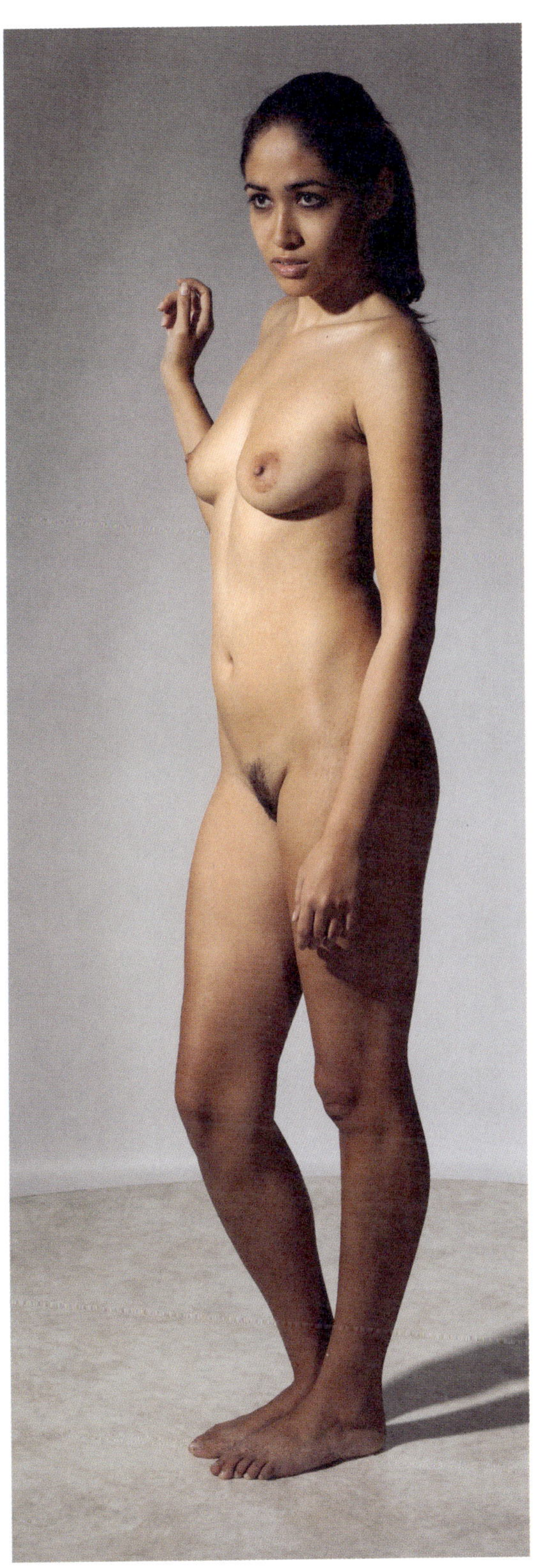

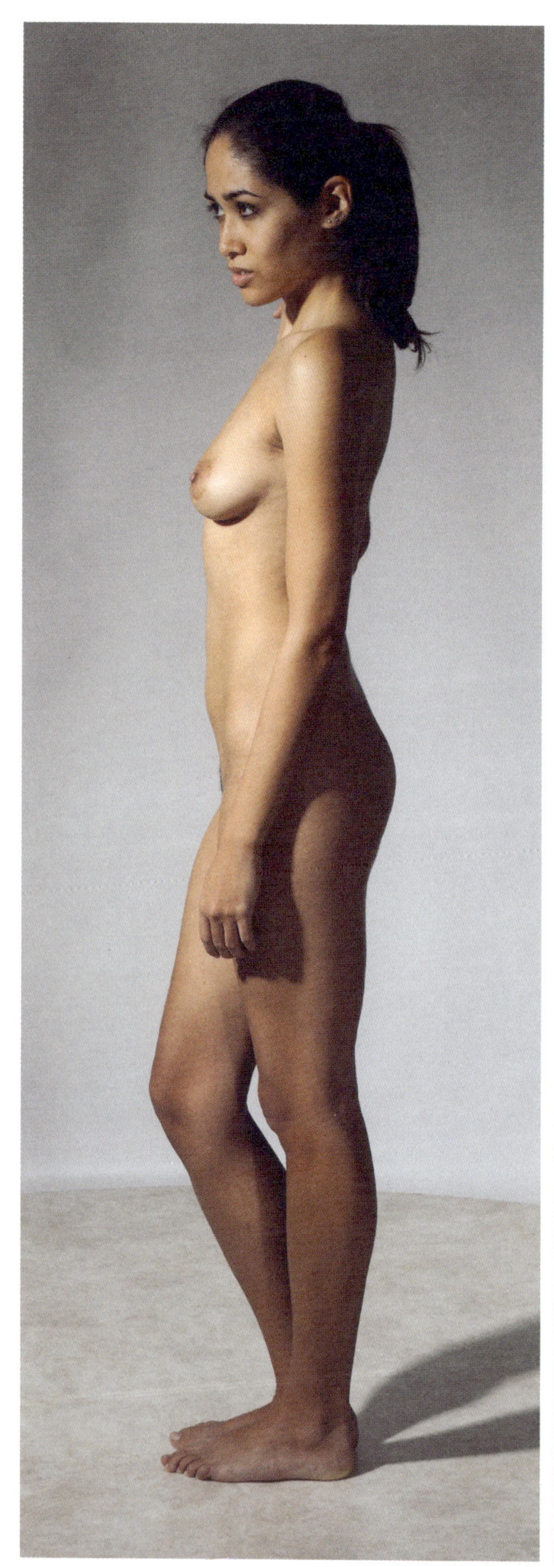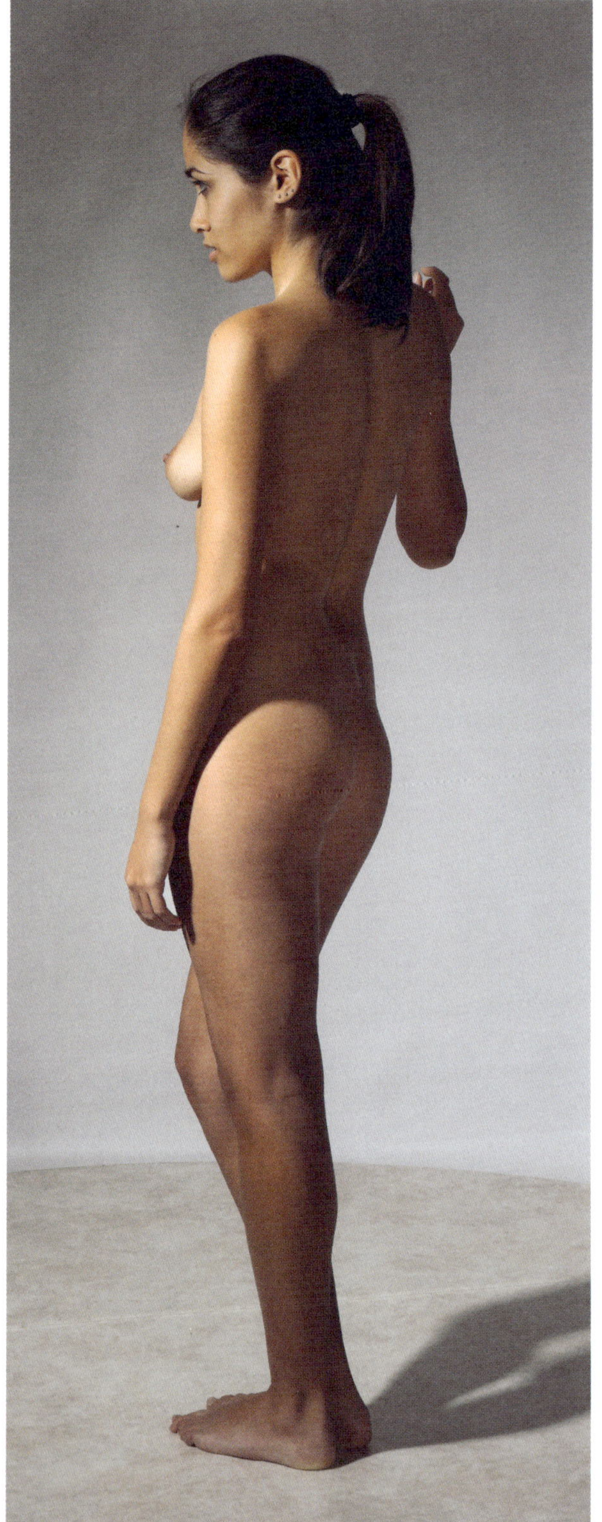

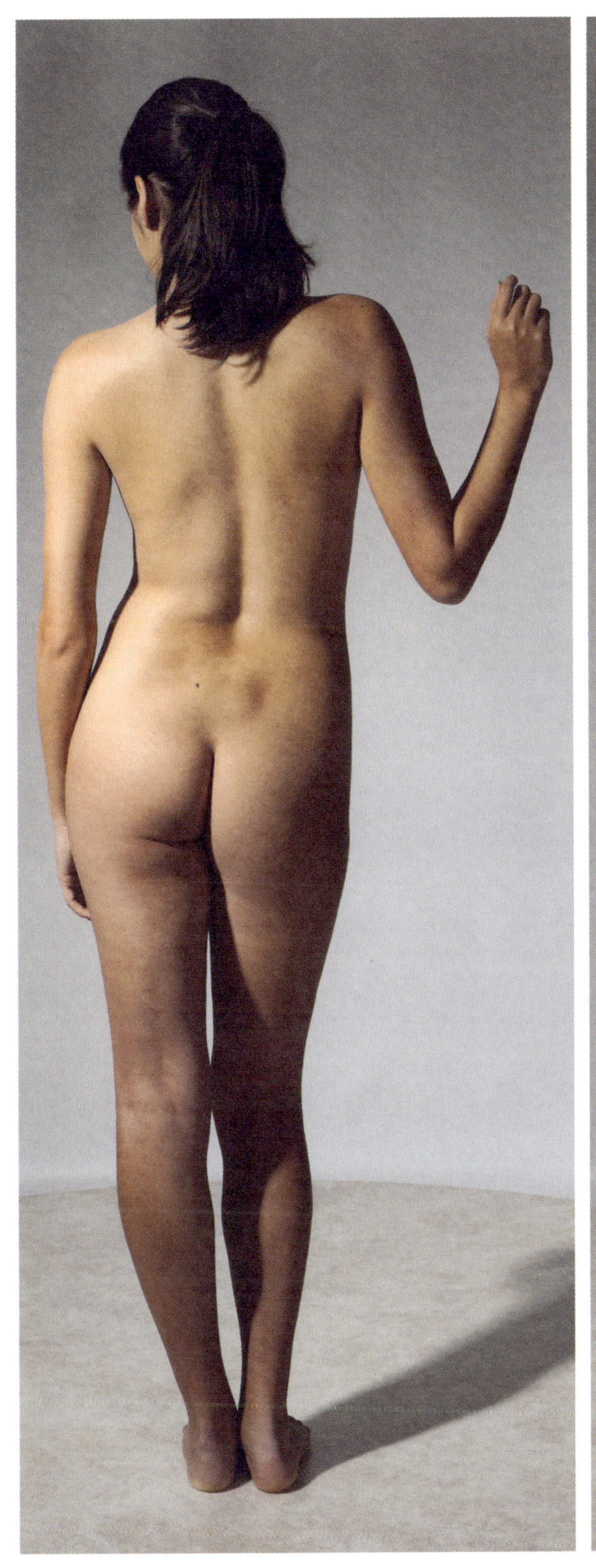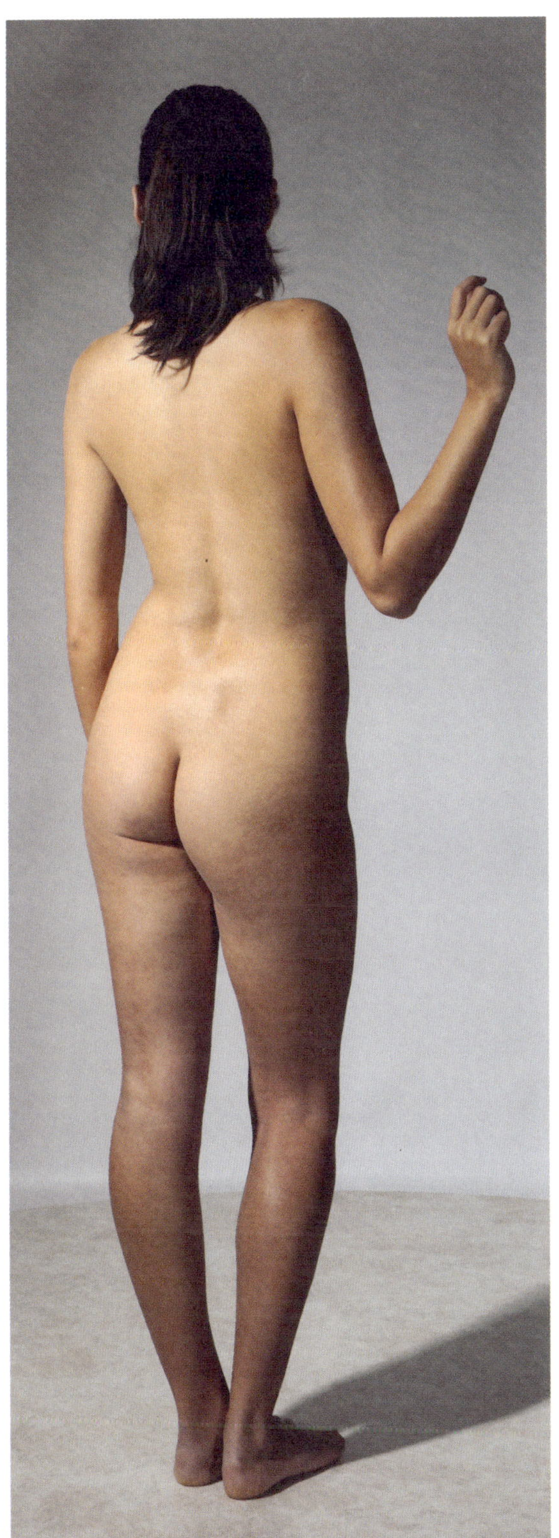

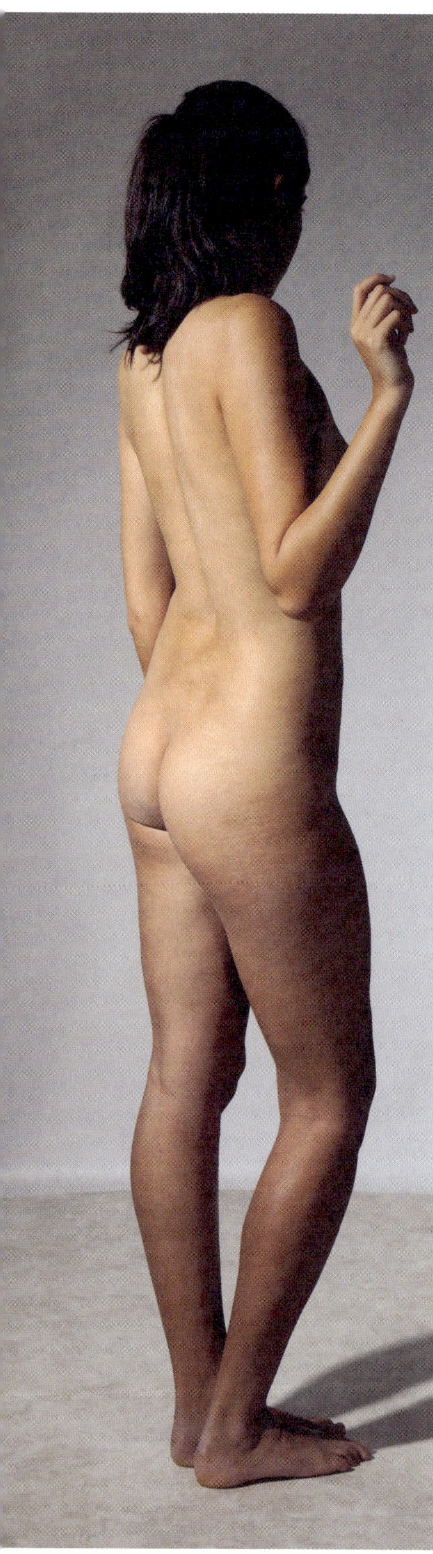
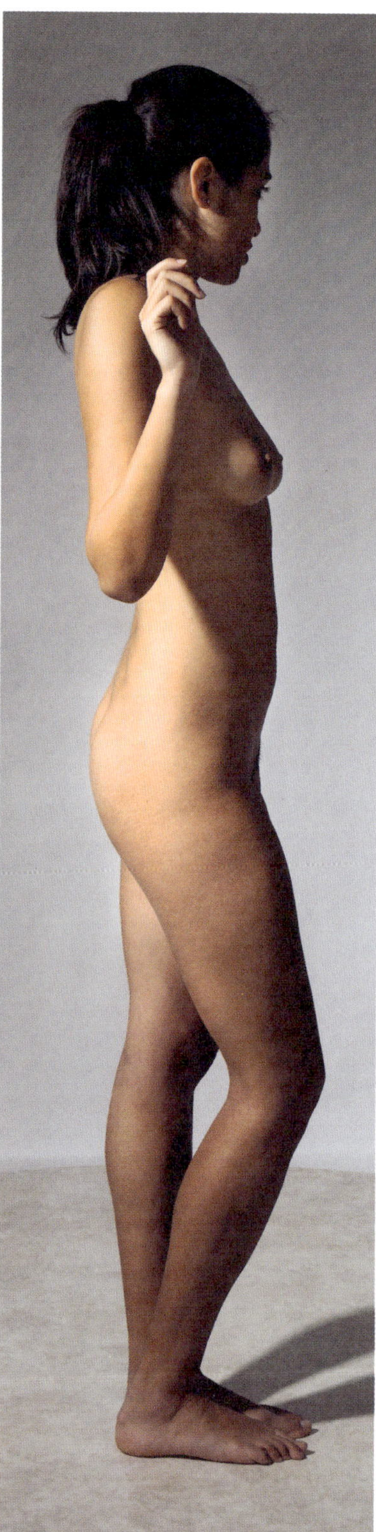
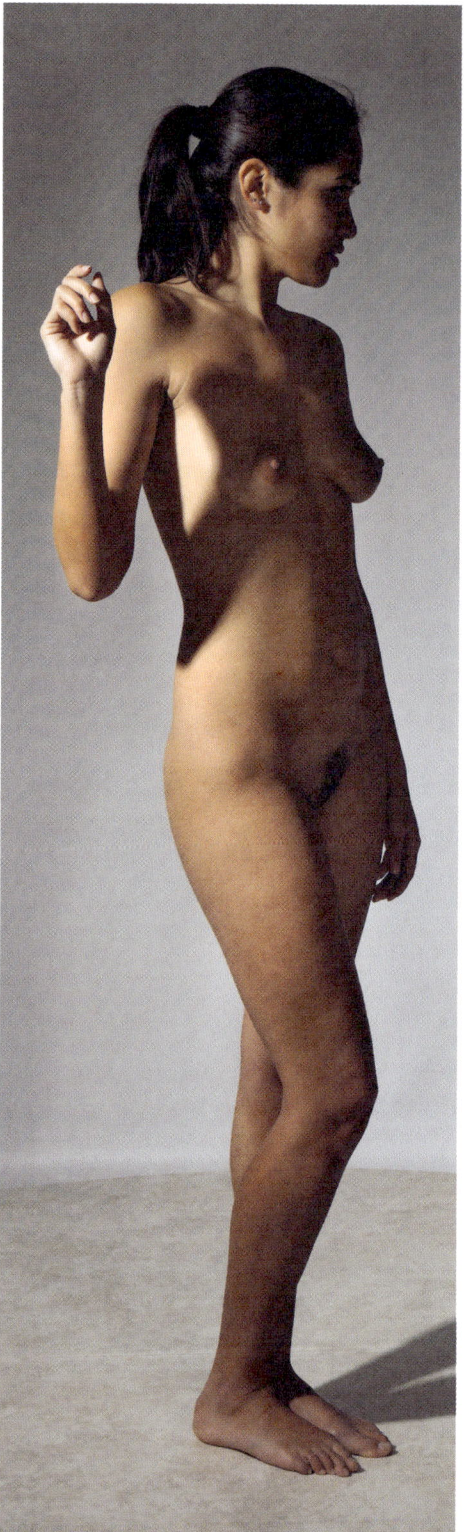

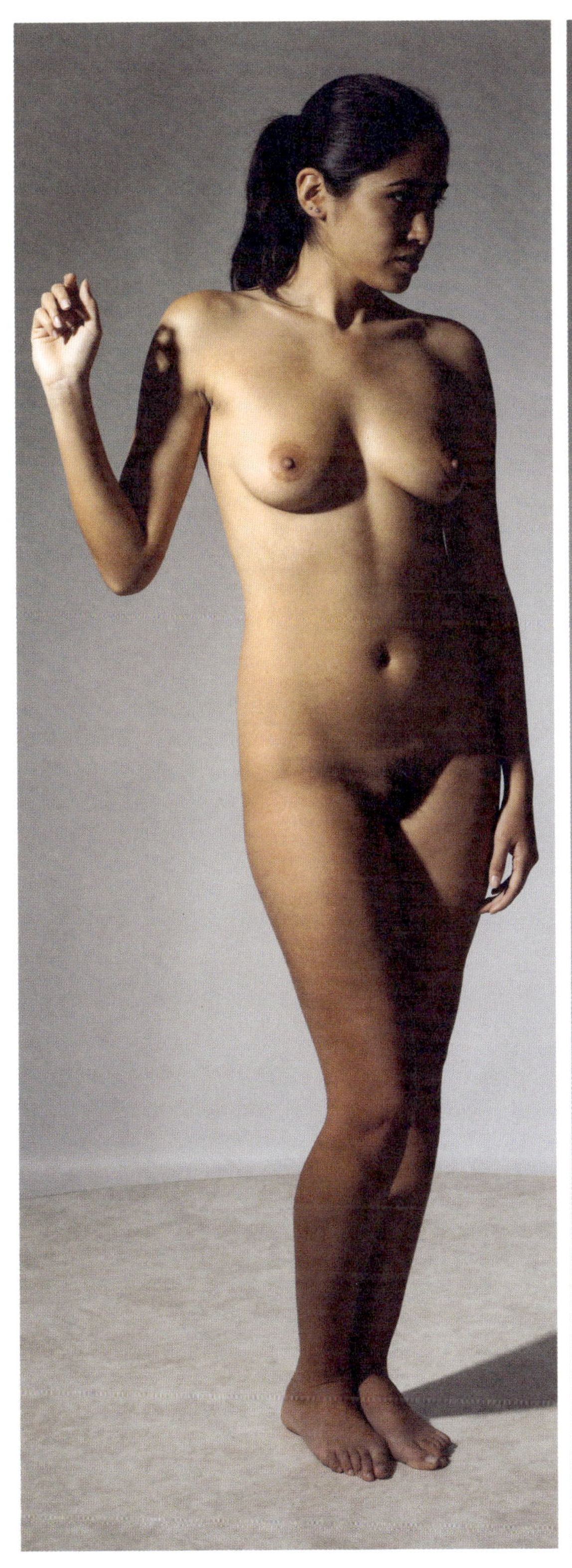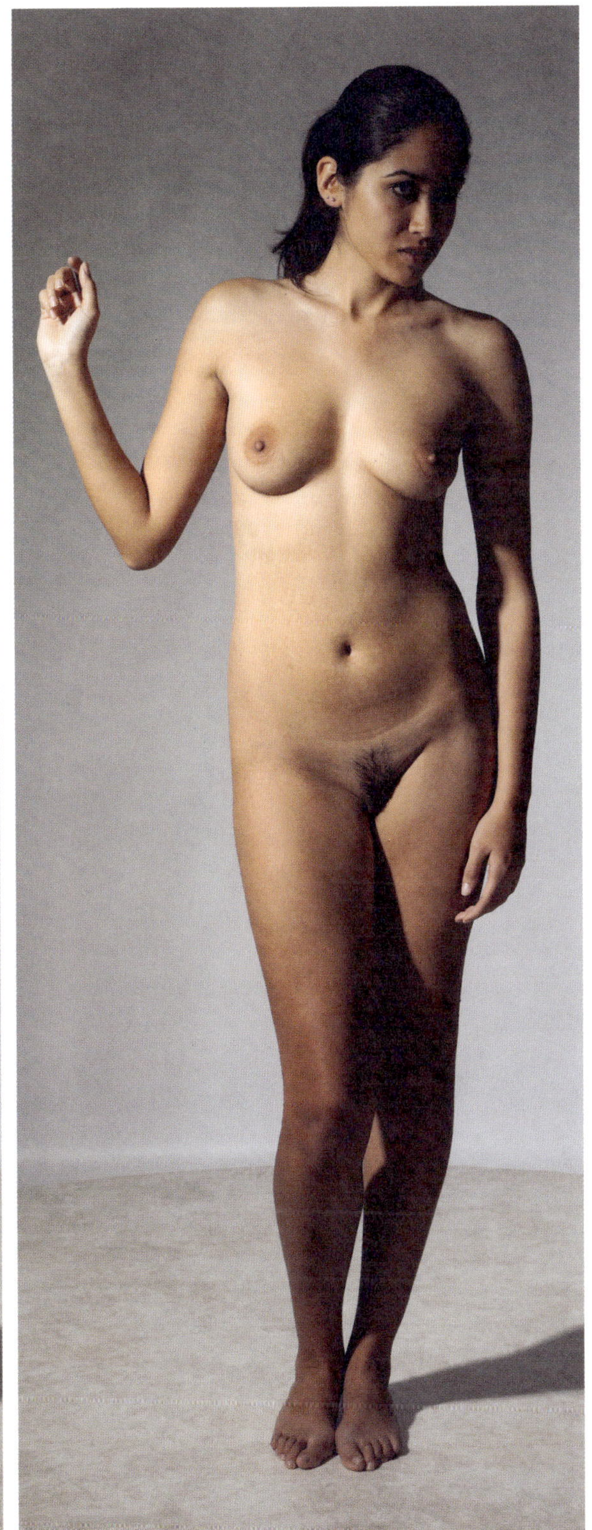

APPENDIX C: ILLUSTRATIVE REFERENCES

In addition to the photographic references that elucidate the dynamics of a specific pose, having a general sense of the proportions of the body as well as an awareness of the underlying musculoskeletal elements that serve as landmarks can be helpful in effectively rendering a figure.

To ensure the anatomical forms remain in balance to each other at any scale, a generic system of measurements called a *canon* can be used to make sure the lengths and widths of the figurative components are proportional and properly positioned. Throughout history there have been varying preferences regarding these proportional systems, giving place to a rich variety in figurative styles across time and throughout cultures. Some of these systems achieved a great level of naturalism, as in the case of the ancient Greeks and Romans, while others gave forth more stylized figurative depictions that spoke to specific ideologies and shared values within a culture, as in the case of Egyptian or Byzantine art.

It was the ancient Greeks who first developed a mathematical system for rendering a figure based on taking one part of the body as a unit of measurement to establish idealized proportions throughout the rest of the body. Rediscovered by artists of the Renaissance, the canon of Polykleitos, a Greek sculptor who proposed one of the first set aesthetic principles to govern proportions, was most likely where the idea of dividing a figure into seven or seven and a half heads in height originated, favoring the creation of balanced, realistic figures. Another popular variation ascribed to Lysippus establishes the height of an average figure as measuring eight heads, creating a more elongated and stylized version of a figure. Together, these are the most prominent systems utilized to establish generic measurements throughout the body.

The importance of the use of a canon in my own practice lies in offering a system to quickly detect inconsistencies throughout a composition and facilitate insights as I am deciphering a three-dimensional gesture. It is particularly helpful when sculpting without a model or photographic references. Using a proportional guide also offers one more layer of support in neutralizing distortions from the camera lens that could manifest throughout the photographic references as well as checking one's own distortion tendencies. As with any generic measurement system, it is important to note that these are always in the service of the unique variability present in human bodies as well as the stylistic dispositions of an artist. Nonetheless, this guide alongside scaled blueprints and photographic references are the next best thing to having a live model to sculpt from (see page 177).

Further into the sculpting process, I utilize a series of bony and fleshy landmarks to help me understand a pose by breaking down the body's information into smaller more digestible parts that interlock one with the other.

In the following images, the model's front and back views have been overlaid with the skeletal system to give you a sense of the structural underpinning of the pose. I pay particular attention to the bones that are most prominent and evident through the skin. This, of course, may vary from pose to pose, but I can usually locate the following bones to ground my understanding of the pose and bring it into focus.

STARTING FROM THE TOP of the torso on the front, you find the clavicles, which have the shape of a handlebar and move laterally and back to connect with the acromion process of the scapula on either side, creating a visible notch that is evident in the tip of the shoulder through the

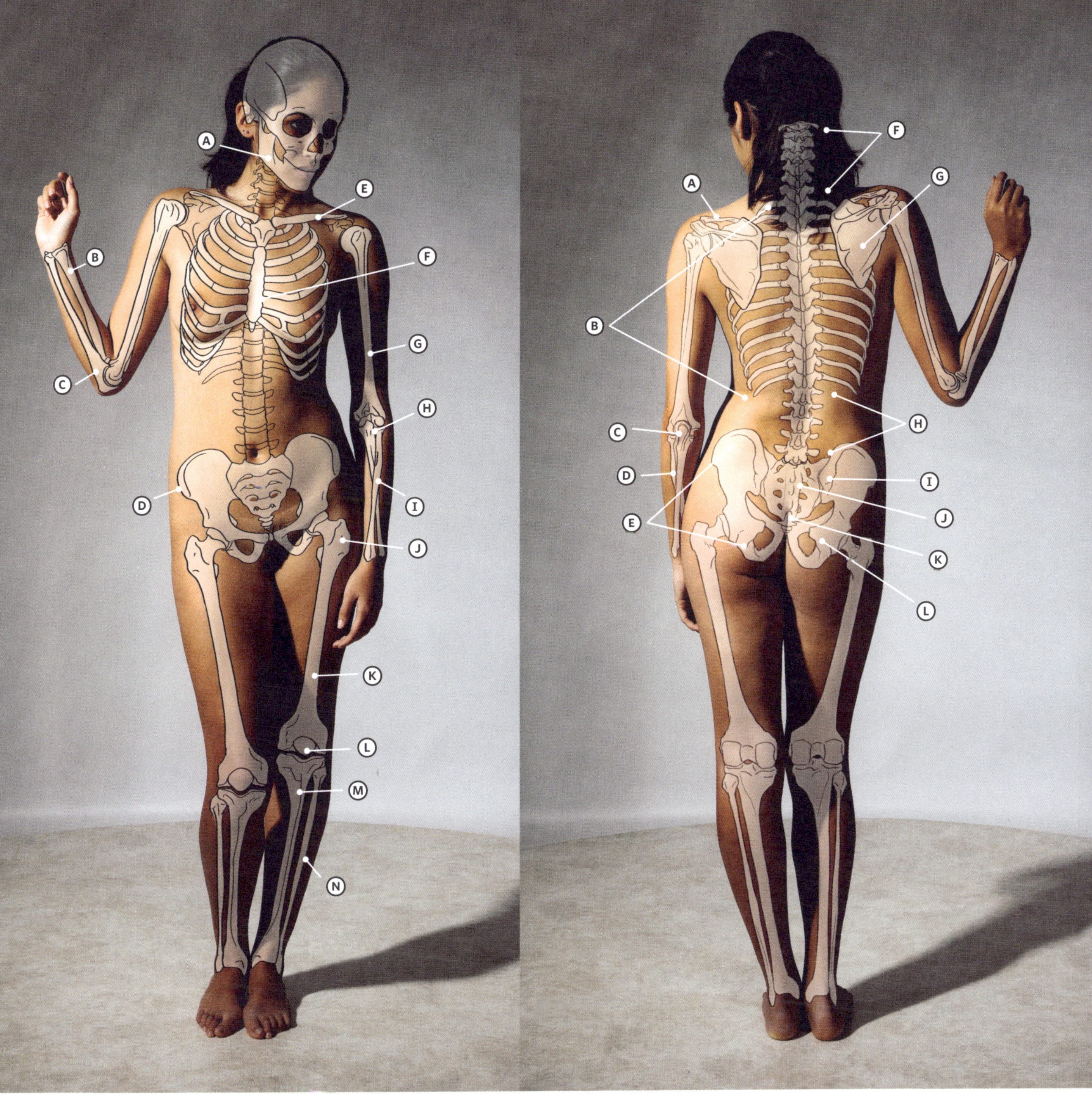

KEY TO THE MAJOR BONES OF THE FEMALE BODY

FRONT VIEW

(A) Mandible
(B) Radius
(C) Ulna
(D) ASIS (Anterior Superior Iliac Spine)
(E) Clavicle
(F) Sternum
(G) Humerus
(H) Ulna
(I) Radius
(J) Greater Trochanter
(K) Femur
(L) Patella
(M) Tibia
(N) Fibula

BACK VIEW

(A) Clavicle
(B) Thoracic Spine
(C) Ulna
(D) Radius
(E) Pelvis
(F) Cervical Spine
(G) Scapula
(H) Lumbar Spine (5)
(I) PSIS (Posterior Superior Iliac Spine)
(J) Sacrum
(K) Coccyx
(L) Ischium

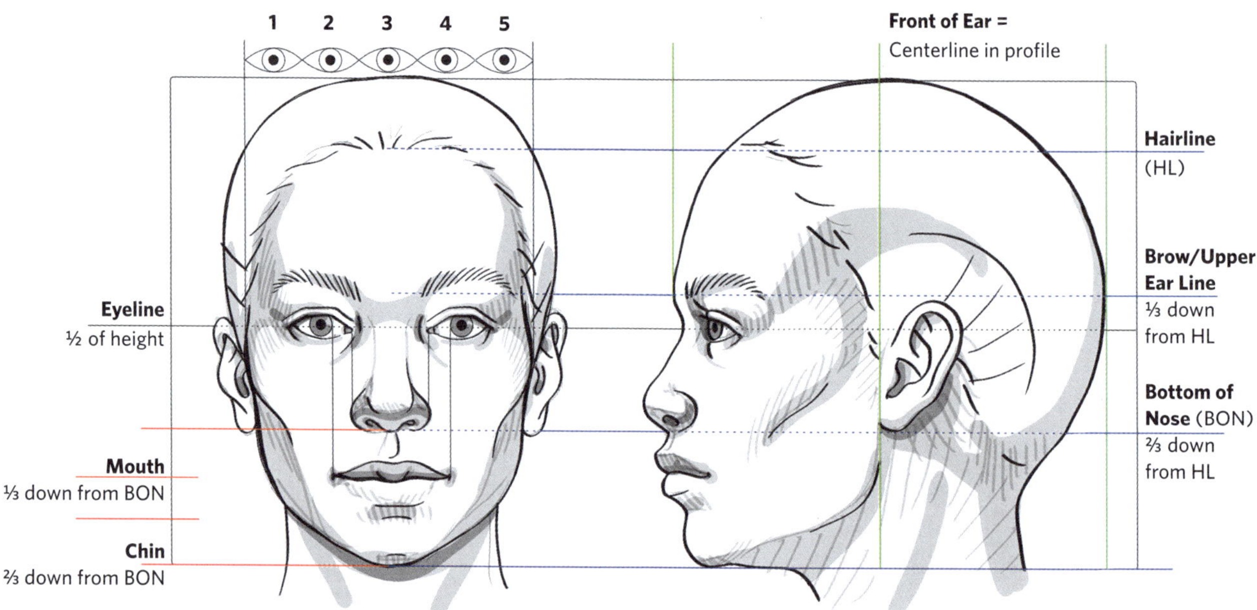

Illustrations by Audrey Bell

skin. On the back, the seventh cervical vertebra is often visible between the trapezius muscles, marking an inward shift in the curve of the spine. I also locate the scapulae, defining their shape and checking their alignment with chest line (nipple line) at the front.

The pit of the neck, or suprasternal notch, also offers a stark landmark.

Moving down from there, I look for a triangular shape at the center of the upper chest, with its base starting right below the clavicles, created by the sternum.

Continuing down the torso, I note where the last rib ends and the lumbar spine begins, creating the cinch of the waistline.

Looking at the arms, the elbow, or olecranon process of the ulna, will align with the waistline. The head of the ulna will create that bony projection on the outer part of the wrist.

At the pelvic level, I look for the iliac spine. Toward the front of that ridge, one finds the ASIS or the anterior superior iliac spine, a part of the pelvic bone that creates a projection that is noticeable through the skin and is particularly helpful in establishing the top two points of the pelvic box. Toward the back of the iliac crest, the PSIS or posterior superior iliac spine also creates two subtle depressions that, when connected to the ASIS, can help trace the path of the iliac crest front to back. The PSIS at either side also mark the two top points that create the sacral triangle.

Continuing below, the widest part of the female body is created by the external head of the femur, referred to as the greater trochanter of the femur. This is also traditionally considered the center (top to bottom) of the body.

Moving to the legs, the bottom of the patella, or kneecap, from the front creates a very clear sense of where that center of the knee is.

The lower ends of the tibia on the inside of the leg and the fibula on the outside lead to the ankle bones, two distinct lateral projections that precede the feet.

PROPORTIONAL GUIDE: 7.5 HEADS

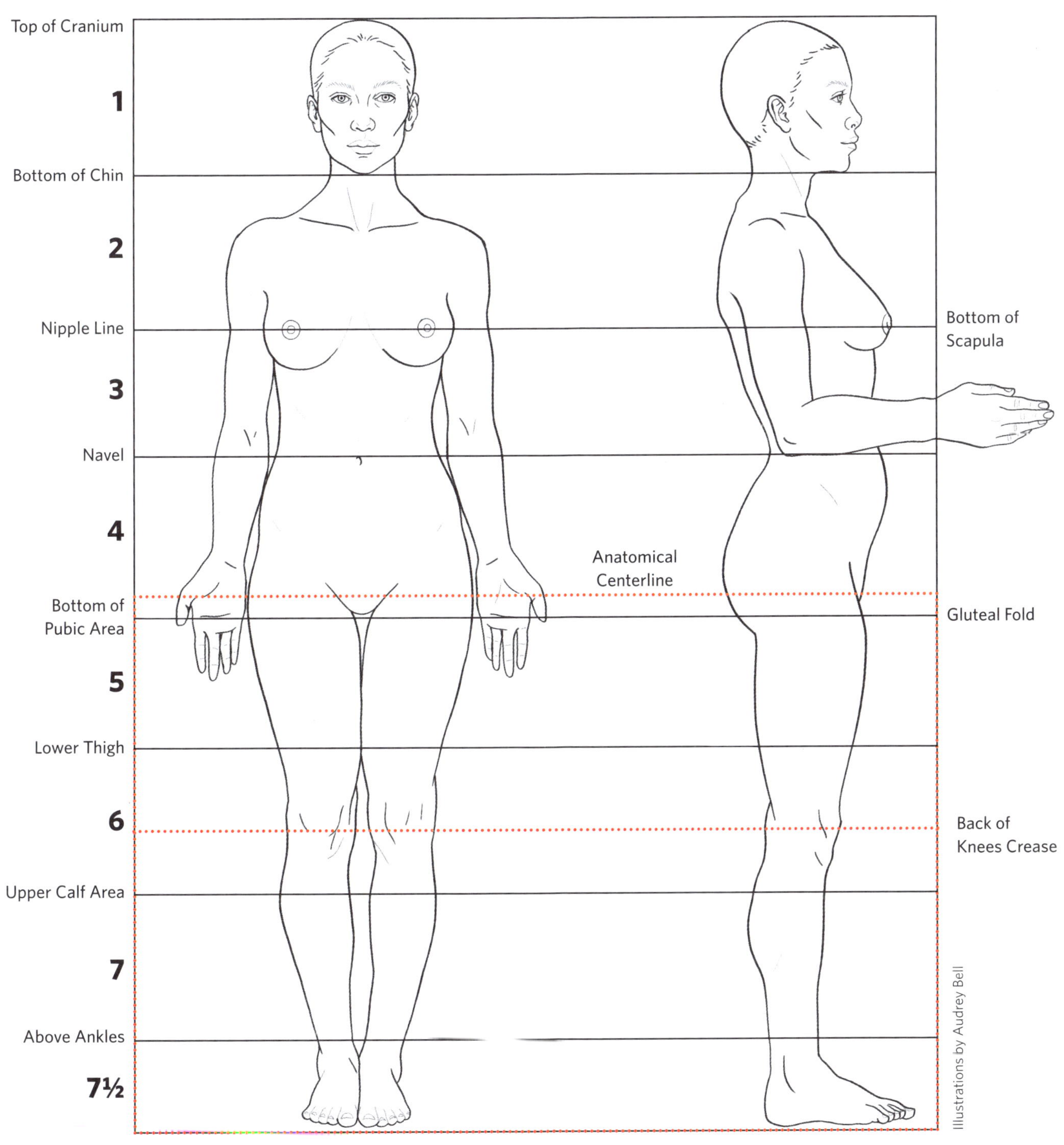

NEXT, I CONSIDER the fleshy landmarks, or those comprised of muscles and connective tissues throughout the body articulated by adding bits of clay to slowly develop the myriad shapes over our core form.

Starting at the neck area, I locate the sternocleidomastoid muscles that connect the lower, back of the skull or mastoid process with the sternum and clavicles as well as the trapezius muscles, which from the front, appear as triangular shapes at either side of the neck in between the sternocleidomastoid muscles and the clavicles. From the back, the trapezius muscles create a distinct spear-like shape that points down and culminates around the center of the spine.

Moving laterally past the clavicle, I find the deltoid muscle, which is called such for the delta shape it creates as it nestles in between the bicep and the triceps.

I then look for the topography in the belly area developed by the obliques and the rectus abdominis punctuated by the belly button. There is a break in between the left and right abdominals as well as in between the rectus abdominis and the external obliques that can be drawn onto the surface of the sculpture to help organize the volumes in relation to a gesture, noting the asymmetrical shifts created by the movement of the pose.

Moving down, I locate the quads and the opposing hamstring muscles. From the side, I begin to note the S curves that form between the front of the leg muscles and the calf muscles (gastrocnemius) toward the back of the lower leg. I continue to find these S shapes in the legs from different angles, using them to detect and articulate the dynamics of the upper and lower leg muscles, side to side and front to back.

From the back, I note the gluteus medius and, below, the gluteus maximus aligning the bottom of the gluteal cleft with the bottom of the pubic area to the front in more grounded poses.

KEY TO THE MAJOR MUSCLES AND CONNECTIVE TISSUES IN THE FEMALE BODY

LEFT SIDE FRONT

- (A) Biceps Brachii
- (B) Flexor Muscles
- (C) Triceps
- (D) Latissimus Dorsi
- (E) Serratus Anterior
- (F) External Oblique
- (G) Rectus Sheath with Rectus Abdominus shown underneath
- (H) Tenor Fasciae Latae
- (I) Sartorius
- (J) Rectus femoris
- (K) Gracilis
- (L) Iliotibial Tract
- (M) Fibularis Longus
- (N) Tibia (Bone)

RIGHT SIDE FRONT

- (O) Sternocleidomastoid
- (P) Trapezius
- (Q) Pectoralis major
- (R) Deltoid
- (S) Biceps brachii
- (T) Flexor M.
- (U) Extensor Muscles
- (V) Extensor Digitorum
- (W) Gastrocnemius
- (X) Soleus

LEFT SIDE BACK

- (A) Lateral Dorsi
- (B) Triceps
- (C) Extensor muscles
- (D) Extensor digitorum
- (E) Flexor muscles

RIGHT SIDE BACK

- (F) Trapezius
- (G) Deltoid
- (H) Triceps
- (I) Extensor muscles
- (J) Extensor digitorum
- (K) Flexor muscles
- (L) External oblique
- (M) Gluteus madius
- (N) Gluteus maximus
- (O) Gracilis
- (P) Biceps femoris
- (Q) Gastrocnemius
- (R) Soleus